Volomin; a Memorial to the Jewish Community of Volomin (Wołomin, Poland)

Translation of
Sefer zikaron kehilat Wolomin

Original Book Edited by: Shimon Kanc

Originally published in Tel Aviv in 1971

JewishGen
מרכז עולמי לגנאלוגיה יהודית
The Global Home for Jewish Genealogy

A Publication of JewishGen, INC
Edmond J. Safra Plaza, 36 Battery Place, New York, NY 10280
646.494.5972 | info@JewishGen.org | www.jewishgen.org

MUSEUM OF
JEWISH HERITAGE
A LIVING MEMORIAL
TO THE HOLOCAUST

Volomin; a Memorial to the Jewish Community of Volomin (Wołomin, Poland)
Translation of *Sefer zikaron kehilat Wolomin*

Editor of Original Yizkor Book: Shimon Kanc
Project Coordinator: Brian Snyder
Layout and Name Indexing: Jonathan Wind
Reproduction of Photographs: Sondra Ettlinger
Cover Design: Rachel Kolokoff Hopper

Printed in the United States of America by Lightning Source, Inc.

Library of Congress Control Number (LCCN): 2022933552

ISBN: 978-1-954176-38-6 (hard cover: 334 pages, alk. paper)

About JewishGen.org

JewishGen, an affiliate of the Museum of Jewish Heritage - A Living Memorial to the Holocaust, serves as the global home for Jewish genealogy.

Featuring unparalleled access to 30+ million records, it offers unique search tools, along with opportunities for researchers to connect with others who share similar interests. Award winning resources such as the Family Finder, Discussion Groups, and ViewMate, are relied upon by thousands each day.

In addition, JewishGen's extensive informational, educational and historical offerings, such as the Jewish Communities Database, Yizkor Book translations, InfoFiles, Family Tree of the Jewish People, and KehilaLinks, provide critical insights, first-hand accounts, and context about Jewish communal and familial life throughout the world.

Offered as a free resource, JewishGen.org has facilitated thousands of family connections and success stories, and is currently engaged in an intensive expansion effort that will bring many more records, tools, and resources to its collections.

Please visit https://www.jewishgen.org/ to learn more.

Executive Director: Avraham Groll

About the JewishGen Yizkor Book Project

Yizkor Books (Memorial Books) were traditionally written to memorialize the names of departed family and martyrs during holiday services in the synagogue (a practice that still exists in many synagogues today).

Over the centuries, as a result of countless persecutions and horrific atrocities committed against the Jews, Yizkor Books (Sefer Zikaron in Hebrew) were expanded to include more historical information, such as biographical sketches of famous personalities and descriptions of daily town life.

Following the Holocaust, the idea of remembrance and learning took on an urgent and crucial importance. Survivors of the Holocaust sought out other surviving residents of their former towns to memorialize and document the names and way of life of those who were ruthlessly murdered by the Nazis. These remembrances were documented in Yizkor Books, hundreds of which were published in the first decades after the Holocaust.

Most of these books were published privately, or through landsmanshaftn (social organizations comprised of members originating from the same European town or region) that still existed, and were often distributed free of charge. Sadly, the languages used to document these crucial histories and links to our past, Yiddish and Hebrew, are no longer commonly understood by a significant percentage of Jews today. As a result, JewishGen has undertaken the sacred responsibility of translating these books into English so that the culture and way of life of these communities will be preserved and transmitted to future generations.

In 1986, a group of farsighted JewishGenners started a project to pool their efforts together in groups based upon their ancestors from each town and donate money to get the Yizkor books of their ancestral towns translated into English. As the translated material became available, it was made accessible for free at www.JewishGen.org/Yizkor. Hardcover copies can be purchased by visiting https://www.jewishgen.org/Yizkor/ybip.html (see below).

It is our hope that the translation of these books into English (and other languages) will assist the countless Jewish family researchers who are so desperately seeking to forge a connection with their heritage.

Director of JewishGen Yizkor Book Project: Lance Ackerfeld

About the JewishGen Press

JewishGen Press (formerly the Yizkor Books-in-Print Project) is the publishing division of JewishGen.org, and provides a venue for the publication of non-fiction books pertaining to Jewish genealogy, history, culture, and heritage.

In addition to the Yizkor Book category, publications in the Other Non-Fiction category include Shoah memoirs and research, genealogical research, collections of genealogical and historical materials, biographies, diaries and letters, studies of Jewish experience and cultural life in the past, academic theses, and other books of interest to the Jewish community.

Please visit https://www.jewishgen.org/Yizkor/ybip.html to learn more.

Director of JewishGen Press: Joel Alpert
Managing Editor - Jessica Feinstein
Publications Manager - Susan Rosin

Notes to the Reader

The images in the original book were reproduced from photographs from the time of the first edition. These reproductions were already of poor quality, being pre-war and at least 30 or more years old. As a result the images in the book are not very good and the best achievable.

A reader can view the original scans of the book on the websites listed below.

The original book can be seen online at the Yiddish Book Center website:

https://www.yiddishbookcenter.org/collections/yizkor-books/yzk-nybc314102/kanc-shimon-sefer-zikaron-kehilat-volomin

or at the New York Public Library Digital Collections website:

https://digitalcollections.nypl.org/items/e6198ff0-28b1-0133-6b29-58d385a7bbd0

To obtain a list of Shoah victims from Volomin (Wołomin, Poland) the reader should access the Yad Vashem web site listed below; one can also search for specific family names using family name option. These lists are continually updated by Yad Vashem, so it is worthwhile to periodically search these lists.

There is more valuable information (including the Pages of Testimony, etc.) available on this website: https://yvng.yadvashem.org/

A list of all books available from JewishGen Press along with prices is available at: https://www.jewishgen.org/Yizkor/ybip.html

Acknowledgements

I owe an enormous debt of gratitude to everyone at Jewishgen.org. Without this organization, I might never have discovered the existence of the Wolomin Yizkor book. In particular, I extend sincere thanks to Lance Ackerfeld. You have been both patient and encouraging. Your guidance and leadership have made this translation possible. I am also grateful to Susan Rosin and her team of volunteers who have been instrumental in the publication of this book in its current form. I know there are many others at JewishGen who work tirelessly in the background. While I may not know your names, I acknowledge your efforts and thank you.

I am immensely grateful to Ted Steinberg for his beautiful translation of the original Yiddish, which captured not only the words but the emotions of the original authors. I would also like to acknowledge and thank Sara Mages and Yocheved Klausner who volunteered their time and effort to translate from the original Hebrew into English. From the bottom of my heart, thank you all.

I would like to thank my mother, Anita Yellen Snyder, who instilled in me a love for my heritage and inspired a desire to understand and make sense of the world that came before me.

While there are no words that could fully acknowledge her contributions to all that I do, I would like to thank my wife, Pamela Recoon Snyder, who has supported and encouraged me through the years as I have peeled the layers leading to this translation.

Brian Snyder
Buffalo, New York
March 2022

Credits and Captions for Book Cover

Front Cover Illustration:
From *A Memorial to the Jewish Community of Volomin*, Page 20 [33]
Front and Back Cover Background Color, Texture and Photograph:
Rachel Kolokoff Hopper

Back Cover Poem:
Remember What Amalek Did to You by Shamay Baum, page 12 [20]
Back Cover Illustration:
Upon the Ruins, page 275 [557]

GeoPolitical Information

Wołomin, Poland is located at 52°21' N 21°15' E 13 miles NE of Warszawa

	Town	District	Province	Country
Before WWI (c. 1900):	Wołomin	Radzymin	Warszawa	Russian Empire
Between the wars (c. 1930):	Wołomin	Radzymin	Warszawa	Poland
After WWII (c. 1950):	Wołomin			Poland
Today (c. 2000):	Wołomin			Poland

Alternate Names for the Town:

Wołomin [Pol], Volomin [Rus, Yid], Wołumin

Nearby Jewish Communities:

Radzymin 5 miles NNW

Marki 5 miles WSW

Okuniew 6 miles SSE

Rembertów 8 miles SSW

Praga 9 miles SW

Tłuszcz 10 miles ENE

Warszawa 13 miles SW

Falenica 13 miles S

Stanisławów 13 miles ESE

Jabłonna 13 miles W

Serock 14 miles NW

Otwock 15 miles S

Mińsk Mazowiecki 18 miles SE

Jadów 18 miles ENE

Dobre 18 miles E

Karczew 18 miles S

Jeziorna Królewska 19 miles SSW

Wyszków 20 miles NNE

Piaseczno 21 miles SSW

Kamieńczyk 21 miles NE

Pruszków 22 miles SW

Kołbiel 22 miles SSE

Nowy Dwór Mazowiecki 23 miles WNW

Siennica 23 miles SE

Brańszczyk 24 miles NE

Łopianka 25 miles NE

Nasielsk 25 miles NW

Góra Kalwaria 25 miles S

Kałuszyn 26 miles ESE

Nadarzyn 26 miles SW

Baczki 26 miles ENE

Pułtusk 26 miles NNW

Zakroczym 27 miles WNW

Osieck 27 miles SSE

Leszno 28 miles WSW

Błonie 29 miles WSW

Sobienie Jeziory 29 miles S

Poręba Średnia 30 miles NE

Poręba-Cocęby 30 miles NE

Liw 30 miles E

Jewish Population: 3,079 (in 1921)

BALTIC SEA   LITHUANIA

RUSSIA   Vilnius ●

GERMANY   POLAND   BELARUS

● Berlin   Poznan ●   Wołomin   Brest ●

                      Lodz ●

                              Lublin ●

          ● Wrocław

      ● Prague

CZECH REPUBLIC   ● Kraków   UKRAINE

              SLOVAKIA

    AUSTRIA

250 miles

250 Km   500 Km

POLAND – CURRENT BORDERS

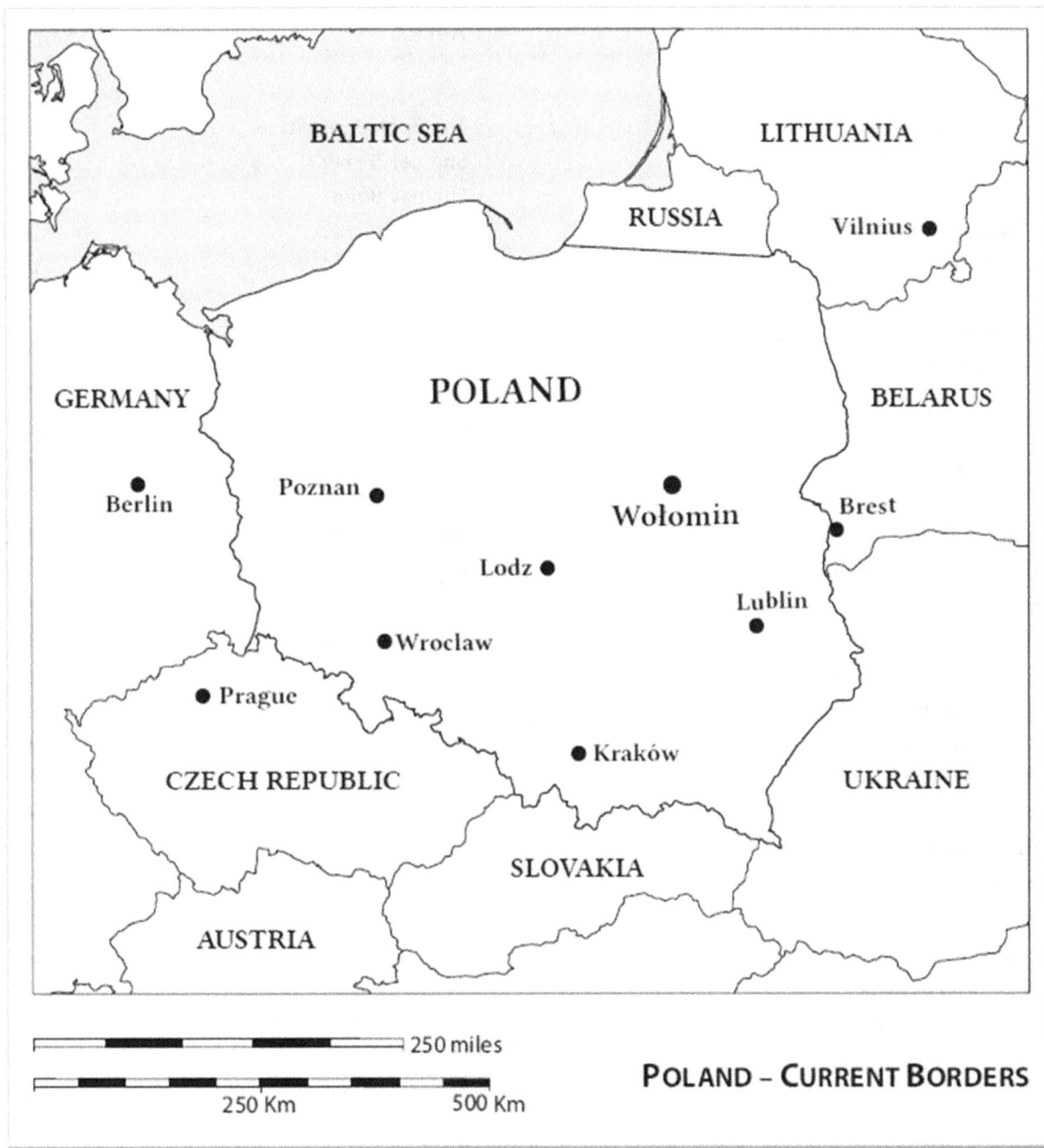

Map of Poland with **Wołomin** indicated

TABLE OF CONTENTS

The Horrors of the Holocaust

Dedication

I dedicate this translation to the memory of the Jews of Wolomin who perished in the Holocaust and for whom there is no one to say Kaddish. And to the survivors who faced the demons of their past with strength and courage and created this Book of Remembrance. It is also dedicated to the memory of my maternal grandparents, born and raised in Wolomin, who lost entire families in the Shoah. The trauma of those losses prevented much discussion, but left me with mysterious photos of their families which inspired a search for my roots and ultimately led to this translation.

Brian Snyder
Buffalo, New York
March 2022

Volomin; a Memorial
to the Jewish Community of Volomin
(Wołomin, Poland)

52°21' / 21°15'

Translation of
Sefer zikaron kehilat Wolomin

Editor: Shimon Kanc

Published in Tel Aviv 1971

Acknowledgments

Project Coordinator:

Brian Snyder

Yiddish Translator:

Theodore Steinberg

This is a translation of: *Sefer zikaron kehilat Wolomin* (Volomin; a memorial to the Jewish community of Volomin), Editor: Shimon Kanc, Wolomin Society, Published: Tel Aviv 1971 (H,Y 600 pages)

Note: The original book can be seen online at the NY Public Library site: Wolomin

---

Please contribute to our translation fund to see the translation of this book completed.

JewishGen's Translation Fund Donation Form provides a secure way to make donations,
either on-line or by mail, to help continue this project. Donations to JewishGen are tax-deductible for U.S. citizens.

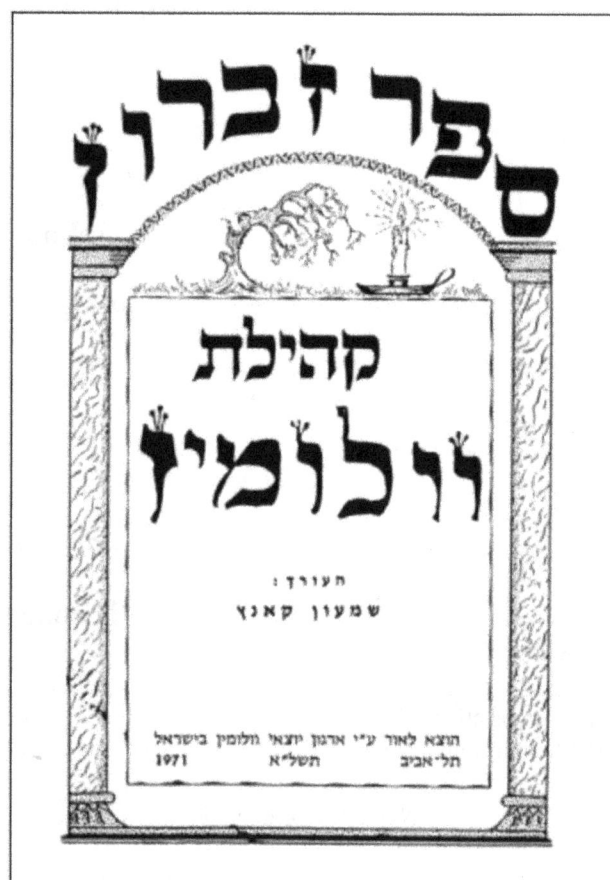

ספר זכרון
לקהילת
וולומין

ספר זכרון

קהילת
וולומין

העורך :
שמעון קאנץ

הוצא לאור ע״י ארגון יוצאי וולומין בישראל
תל־אביב   תשל״א   1971

[Page 5]

"And you shall tell your son"

by the Book Committee

Translated by Sara Mages

It was not easy for us to publish the book, which we present with feelings of satisfaction and reverence for the survivors of Wolomin in Israel and the whole world. Years ago we expressed the idea of publishing a book about our destroyed community, a book that will reflect its history and unfold the full extent of its vibrant life in spirit and deed. However, we encountered countless obstacles, and most importantly - we could not find people who were willing to take on this sacred and responsible work.

Many destroyed communities, large and small, have been commemorated in books of testimony and remembrance, thanks to the efforts of their surviving members. Wolomin lagged behind in this area because our town was small and few are its survivors, but we had a strong desire for a great creation that would commemorate the holy and the pure of our community.

Whenever we talk about our beloved town, Wolomin, which was destroyed in the destruction of Polish Jewry, we are immediately reminded of Jewish Wolomin with its personalities, activists, people, institutions, and Jewish way of life. How precious was this town for us, where we were born and educated, and where we lived our peaceful childhood years.

[Page 6]

Only ruins, dirt and ashes, remained from our community, ashes of the terrible fire and ashes of our tortured martyrs. We only have a past there, without a shred of a future. We do not want to go back and erect our ruined and abandoned homes, we do not want to go back and plant new seedlings of life in the muddy soil that is saturated with the tears and blood of our victims. We left the Diaspora and will never return to it. We learned a lesson and felt the curse resting on that Diaspora, and now we working hard to see a blessing in our work in our homeland. Here, we are willing to accept with love the hardships of labor and the torments involved in building the homeland that has been desolate for many generations. The bridge to the Diaspora is burned and destroyed forever, and there is no way to return to the Diaspora of Poland.

Its holy inhabitants were desecrated by strangers, its spiritual values were lost, its assets plundered and set on fire - and the Jews, the bearers of these values and assets, were destroyed and no longer exist.

And we, the survivors, the few who were left after the Holocaust, what is to us in far away Poland without our brothers and sisters? What do we have in Wolomin? We cannot even visit our ancestors' graves, because we do not know where the graves are, and where are their tombstones.

Our loss is as great as the sea, and we have no consolation.

And yet, after all, we remained attached in our hearts to our town, Wolomin, as it once was, as it lives in our blood and in the depths of our souls.

The heart sighs and trembles with pain as we recall its sights and the picture of Jewish life from days gone by.

Now, this life has been silenced, and deathly silence reigns.

The voice of school children fell silent, the voice of Torah students in Beit HaMidrash fell silent, and the sound of joy and the sigh of mourning in the town's streets and alleys fell silent.

Jewish life ceases on weekdays and on the Sabbath, on holidays and festivals.

And only in our hearts will we be able to keep the precious memories of days gone by.

We, the few remnants of the Holocaust, feared that there would be no certificate of truth left for our community for future generations, and with awe and love we went to place a memorial for it.

We tried to weave chapters from the life of the town, life of toil and creation, material and spiritual, a vibrant life in all its forms and periods.

[Page 7]

Diverse Jewish life has grown in them and deepened their roots - should all this be lost after our death? Is it a decree that all the abundance of pictures and memories will fade and disappear?

Is it not our duty to convey the feelings of our hearts and the sights of our eyes from the days that have passed to our sons after us, to tell orally and in writing, so that they will also know that the history of a Jewish people is multi-generational history, history of efforts and difficulties of building, history of ruins, torments and riots, aspirations and failures - a history of thousands of years, and of two thousand years of exile in the Diaspora, until we returned here, to start anew and build a better future after the past was destroyed.

The next generations will find in this book, as in all memorial books for the victims of the Holocaust, testimony and sights of what was in the European Diaspora before the terrible destruction, and before all trace of Jewish life in Wolomin was erased.

We, the few who were privileged to join the builders of the homeland in the Land of Israel, felt that we had a sacred duty to place a monument to our community. We did not rest or be quiet until we finished the work - the sacred work.

And in this way we will sanctify the memory of our martyrs.

We cannot erect tombstones on their graves, because we do not know where the dust of the dead and the ashes of the burnt are scattered. Therefore, we will commemorate the memory of the lives of our holy ancestors in Wolomin before the Holocaust.

We will keep them in our memory, and pass on our memories to future generations, so that the memory of the dead will be preserved in the pages of this book.

We will light a perpetual candle in memory of the holy and the pure, in memory of the elation and devotion.

The book will be a monument for eternity!

[Page 8]

El Maleh Rachamim

God, full of Mercy
defender of widows and father of orphans
be not be silent or restrained
regarding the blood of the Jews which was split like water
grant proper rest beneath the wings of Your Presence
in the great heights of the holy and the pure
who like the brilliance of the heavens give light
and shine for the souls of the
martyrs of

WOLOMIN

men, women, boys and girls
who were killed, and slaughtered, and burnt,
and suffocated, and buried alive
all of them holy and pure
and He will bind their souls with the bond of life

Earth, do not cover their blood

[Page 9]

We will remember

These I will remember and pour out my soul within me.
For wicked people have swallowed us, like a cake, unturned.

The beginning of piyyut "Asereṯ hāRūgēi Malḵūt" for Yom Kippur

It's impossible to describe in words the destruction of the Jewish people over the years 5700–5705.

It is impossible to find an adequate expression to the magnitude of our grief over the loss of the six million Jews, holy and pure, who were murdered during the terrible destruction of the Jews of Europe.

It is impossible to find anyone who can lament the lamentation of this destruction.

We can do nothing now for these martyrs.

It is not even possible to erect a tombstone on their grave, because the accursed villains, who murdered them, burned their bodies and it is not known where their ashes are.

But we cannot forget them!

Although we cannot erect a stone monument on their graves, we can erect a spiritual monument for them.

This monument – the history of the town and the memories of its people – is a candle in their memory, so that they may live forever.

And we will end with a prayer that is also the end of *piyyut "Asereṯ hāRūgēi Malḵūt"* ["The Ten Royal Martyrs"] for Yom Kippur:

> Gracious One! Look down from Heaven,
> at the spilled blood of the righteous, and their life blood.
> Look from the place of Your holy Presence and remove all stains,
> Almighty, King, Who sits upon a throne of mercy!

[Pages 10-16]

Thus Have We Begun

by Shmuel Zucker

The desire for continuity, for ongoing life and creation, always goes together with a strengthened sense of the beauty and the value of the past, for the history of one's own people, for the soulful and spiritual in its former home, and therefore each person feels the powerful command–

"And you shall tell it to your children!"

This desire to transmit to future generations the living well from which our fathers and grandfathers drank circulated among the Jews of Wolomin wherever they found themselves after the great devastation, in Israel, in both Americas, and in a variety of European countries.

Each of us has been filled with the desire to eternalize the life and environment of our shtetl.

Natives of Wolomin before the Second World War were scattered in different countries and lands, but in their minds they brought with them the heartfelt warmth of their old home, the idealism, the initiative and activity of their youth, which gave them zest and stature in their foreign lands. Volomin Jews participated in community activities wherever they went.

So was it, too, in Israel. We were few, and our activity was always limited, satisfied with moral, and often material, help for new arrivals.

However, we always made an accounting that if we lagged behind other remnants of destroyed Jewish communities in Poland, that we have not repaid our great debt, that we are guilty regarding our martyrs.

That debt weighed heavily in our hearts, but we were too few and too poor to fully repay it.

It must never be thought that we have for even a moment forgotten our obligation to the martyrs. Every year we have held a memorial service, just like our compatriots in America and Argentina.

As witnesses we cite the announcements in the Yiddish newspapers, where Wolomin natives were called on the fourteenth of October, the day to memorialize the dead, the yahrzeit of Wolomin's Jews killed by the German murderers.

In these announcements, people of Wolomin were called on not to forget to kindle a light and give honor to the five thousand Jews who on that day made their last journey from the Sosnovke Woods to the hell of Treblinka.

Truly, the daily worries, needs, and too often the sorrows incline us to forget the great misfortune that befell our people. It happens, too, that we are simply incapable of understanding the mass slaughter that struck our former home.

A day comes, however, when we are reunited with our martyrs. we all,. people of Wolomin, who find ourselves in Israel and in other lands around the world, remember our martyrs, our dearest and most loved, who in the recent past, only several decades ago, lived and hoped to see in the future a better, more peaceful and more beautiful life.

They did not live to see it.

We must remember, therefore, and take care not to forget them, remember and recall all the true Jews of our shtetl, that their lives and their memorials should be preserved.

We must consider that those in Treblinka, where such slaughter was unloosed by the German murderers and their Polish cohorts to solve the "Jewish question" in Wolomin, that there lie in huge communal graves the bones of those whose last wish as they surrendered their holy souls, was that we, the living, wherever we may find ourselves, must preserve their memory, must be united in warning and reminding the world of the most murderous slaughter of people in human history.

We remember with gratitude the activities of the Wolomin Association in America who helped with great devotion in the publication of this Yizkor Book. They helped not only with money but also with moral support, calling on Wolomin survivors to help with materials, with testimonies, documents, and pictures.

Here is one of the last appeals that the committee in America distributed to the Wolomin Association:

Announcement to All People of Wolomin

At the last memorial that was held on October 17, 1969, it was decided to extend until the middle of January, 1970, the deadline for materials in order to accommodate all who have not yet sent them in. But we add, whoever does not contact friend Joshua by that time should know that he alone is responsible for not perpetuating his near and dear, and that will be a sin that cannot be forgiven, and no one can complain about it.

Attention:

1. Sit down soon to write what you think is acceptable. You do not have to be fastidious with your language, because it will be corrected by a specialist.
2. Photos should be labeled with the names of those who are pictured.

Every submitter should send on a separate sheet the names of his departed family members. You can write in any language you choose. The material should be sent to

S. Adelson, 1836–48th Street, Brooklyn, NY

P.S. This is the last announcement

Respectfully,

The Committee

We living have committed ourselves to the sacred obligation of erecting a monument for all those whom we will never forget.

That we will do in the Yizkor Book for our annihilated shtetl Wolomin.

Therefore we have distributed letters, circulars, and announcements to all of our fellow citizens in Israel and around the world.

Here is one such announcement that we sent out three years aago, before the publication of the Yizkor Book:

To All the People of Wolomin in the World!

Dear Brothers and Sisters,

Twenty–four years have now passed since the destruction of our ruined native city Wolomin. It hurts our hearts and there is no consolation.

A horrible slaughter that has no parallel in the history of martyrdom of our people was perpetrated by Hitler's hordes in our shtetl.

Of generations of Jews and Yiddishkeit, only huge common graves remain, without monuments, without the least memorial, which should cry out to the world the awful tragedy that happened there.

We have been searching and trying for years to make amends for our mothers, fathers, brothers, sisters, and all our relatives whose bones are scattered and are still unburied–from Sasnover Woods to Treblinka, Maidenek, and Siberia.

Our nearest and dearest surely murmured in their last minutes, with bloody lips–"Remember us!" Therefore we have undertaken to immortalize their memory in a Yizkor Book, which will make amends for our martyrs and for the coming generations–an eternal. memory.

We must gather everything that ties us to our dear destroyed home, so that we know how to erect a monument.

It is we upon whom lies the obligation to memorialize our slaughtered nearest and dearest.

Let this announcement be before your eyes until this sacred obligation will be fulfilled.

Every landsman is requested to send material about our old home (religious and social life, places and characters) and about the destruction, and also necrologies of the murdered and dead, possibly accompanied by photographs and documents–to the address of the secretary:

Dr. Sarah Mandelberg, 44 Montefiore Street, Tel Aviv, Israel.
Organization of Wolomin Exiles in Israel

*

We have been successful in appointing as editor of this sacred task Shimon Kantz, and it is a pleasure for us to see how he is filled with our enthusiasm, even though we have as yet no materials for the book. Under his organizations directions, we have directed our efforts toward collecting them. Documents and memories, episodes and pictures. Little by little our modest building has grown, the memorial book to the memory of our native shtetl Wolomin.

We seek no professional writers and no historians; only the shocking suffering in the form of horrible mass death opened our dumb lips and made them speak. Each individual note, even if it is written with a gentle smile, is an expression of concentrated sorrow. Therefore every recollection, every line has its place and its value in this book–a monument which will remember our nearest and dearest.

The heart weeps for the tortured, for the lost ones, but heir bright memory draws from us a strong and encouraged heart, so that their deeds should make a repair in our ongoing, illuminating project.

Talking about all these places, our hearts are suffused with love and recognition of each one who was but now exists no longer.

Speaking of them, we see also the faces of our parents, brothers, and sisters–of all those who are a part of our body and soul.

Those of us who merited to be saved from the awful slaughter have standing before our eyes the ancient commandment that is engraved for us in letters of fire and blood:

"Remember what Amalek did to you!"

The Amalek of the twentieth century.

This is truly the function and expression of this book:

Not random memories from the distant and recent past, not simply a memorial light for the pure and holy souls who died all manner of horrible deaths. Writing down our memories, we felt the necessity to bring forth the special brightness of the everyday Jews in our shtetl.

May it give coming generations deep knowledge of the Jewish beauty which has been destroyed.

With bowed heads and folded hands we stand by our modest memorial to our destroyed Jewish community in Wolomin, and we unite it with the holy memory of the murdered martyrs.

Let the outcry from this memorial book not be quieted or unheard for many generations.

They, our fathers and grandfathers, with their whole spiritual lives, in all the wonderful colors of Jewish beauty, gave us the belief in our historic role, the understanding and the great feeling of responsibility about our endeavors.

By the red light of their flowing blood we swear:

We will never forget!

Organization of Wolomin Exiles from in Israel

Let Them Rise for the Blessing

Those who have true, self–sacrificing devotion and determined wills to publish the Wolomin Yizkor Book with the moral and financial aid that helped with collecting materials and encouraging us with words and deeds.

> Yehiel–Yehoshua Adelson
> Shimon Vishnievski America
> Saul Rosenbloom
>
> Shmuel Vinograd
> Eliezer Vagman Argentina
> Shmuel Manne
> Moach Schultz

[Page 17]

זכור את אשר עשה לך עמלק

"Remember what Amalek did to you"

by Shamay Baum,
chairman of the organization of former residents of Wolomin in Israel

Translated by Sara Mages

Jewish Wolomin was and is no more. Together with its Jews it was wiped off the face of the earth without a trace, and there is no possibility of discovering its past.

This is what the enemies, the Amalekites of the twentieth century, intended, and their plot was largely successful. The total destruction that came upon our community, as to other Jewish communities in Poland, ruled out any possibility of gathering material and accessing sources, searching and finding information and documents. Without them, only one source remains, the power of human memory that allows us to reconstruct, to the proper extent, the segments of our recent past.

[Page 18]

The memorial in 1968

…and so we mourn our loved ones, the martyrs of the Holocaust, and commemorate their memory. May every day, every hour in our lives be imbued with the idea of memory.

Therefore, we made an effort to draw from this spring, to weave chapters from the life of the town, life of matter and spirit, in all their forms and periods.

Indeed, the way to achieve them was not at all easy throughout the preparation of the book. Difficulties and restraints filled the whole way: absolute lack of material in the areas of the life of the Jews of Wolomin; searching for information in various forms as a substitute for non existing material, non–response, sometimes even unfortunate and disappointing, on the part of former residents of our town to all our requests for material, information and memories, and even as to the list of names of the deceased and the martyrs from their families.

What has been said will serve as an explanation for the questions that readers of the book may ask about alleged discrimination, omissions versus repetitions, on speech reduction versus speech expansion. Hence, also the explanation for the lack of equal appreciation of personalities, or for the lack of appreciation at all, failure to address the importance, or existence, of an institution, and maybe cases of inaccuracy in names, dates and the like.

On the other hand, there is great satisfaction from the many achievement points in the book.

[Page 19]

Mrs. Chaya Rubinstein lights the candles at the memorial meeting for the martyrs of Wolomin

Future generations will find in this book, as in all books of remembrance for the victims of the Holocaust, testimony and understanding to what was in our town before the great destruction, and before any trace of Jewish life was erased there.

It was clear to us all that in light of the situation regarding the material, its quantity and quality, special dedication is required on the part of the editor, such as searching for material in broader areas, vigorous collection activity, special editing while recognizing the uniqueness of our community, willingness and ability to deal with what we have and lacking, a clear feature of enthusiasm and creativity to complete what is missing, difficulties in dealing with the material submitted, dealing in various ways, mostly known and understood.

We saw, and knew, the dedication of the editor to his work at all stages of the preparation of the book.

We have also found in this work a kind of consolation in our grief, and a preservation of the past that will not be forgotten from the heart of future generations.

May the "Book of Wolomin" be kind of a bridge between the past, which ended with such great cruelly, and the future whose sun rises before our eyes.

May we succeed in discovering the source of beauty and purity, the moral power by which we have been able to withstand for all generations, against every wave of evil that comes to swallow us, and thanks to them they proved, in days of panic and confusion, devotion and courage, and sanctified the name of the Jewish nation.

[Page 20]

May these few lines be like a stone in the monument for our town, Wolomin.

There used to be a Wolomin community and it is no more.

It was cut down from the multi–branch tree of Polish Jewry by German murderers.

Its memory remains in the hearts of dozens of its survivors scattered around the world, most were absorbed in the homeland, in the State of Israel.

May the book be a monument and an eternal memory!

Yitgadal v'yitkadash...

> I will carry with lamentation and wailing
>
> Wolomin my town,
> How I will carry with lamentation and wailing,
> For your Jews because they are gone,
> For their destruction and loss.
>
> I am silent, suffocating a sigh all my life,
> But the shouts of pain were not silenced,
> The pure shouted from generation to generation;
> We will remember them forever.
>
> In their sacred memory,
> We will dedicate our memories,
> We will pray *Kadish*
> And will dedicate our thoughts.

[Pages 21-22]

May God Rememberthe Souls of Our Martyrs

by Shmuel Zucker

Where are our dear Jews?

From year to year the dust of their bones settles in the Wolomin ghetto and in Siberian woods.

Where are the Jews who with sun–, wind–, and frost–browned faces, with beards and with big boots, trudging, fatigued, half–asleep contemplated a chapter of the Psalms, with an occasional glance toward heaven and a hope for a better tomorrow?

Where are Leibush Farber and Ephraim Avry, who used to sit with their pale faces and learn from the huge, tattered Gemaras and argue about the finer points until late in the day?

Where are those who said the morning prayers with their eyes showing worry and trembling over the problems of making a living, clasping their tallis and tefillin like the greatest treasures, attending the early minyan so they would not be late for work, in order to have an income for their wives and children.

Where do the fathers and mothers sit who used to cry out to God to help make a match for their ageing unmarried daughters.

Where are the Roses and Hannahs–the mild dealers who used to get out of bed at dawn in order to carry milk canisters from house to house to earn a bit of bread?

Where are the schoolboys whom Fishele the teacher showed the letters in the book of Exodus with a wooden stick: "A" "A" "B"…

Where are the older students, with their drawn white cheeks who, in the dark early morning stillness used to pour water on their fingers, study by the light of a candle until late in the winter nights until the words "Happy is the man" [Psalm 1] was engraved deep in their hearts?

Where is the young man who used to go behind the green trees in the woods on summer Shabbos afternoons with books of Yiddish and European literature and dreams of the highest ideals?

And where is the young man who filled in the spots of "Gordonia," "Hashamir ha–tzair," "Hechalutz ha'tzair," "Klal tzionim," "Maccabee," "Y.L. Peretz," "Max Nordau," and others which filled the streets with their songs, dances, and debates, and others who were attracted to the Red Banner and other ideals?

May their memory be honored.

[Page 23]

On the threshold

by Shmuel Zucker

Translated by Sara Mages

A

What can be said at the opening of this book, and not said in its pages, which contain the memory of its past and the images of its personalities, its vibrant life, nobility and inspiration, the greatness and the destruction of the community of Wolomin.

Indeed, Jews built and developed it, generations invested their energy and skills, and it became a Jewish town, a hive of activity and creation, delightful life and good virtues, lofty ambitions and love of Zion and Israel.

From between the lines rises in the reader's imagination a storm of life, a pulse of talent, action and diligence, a frequent war for existence, stubbornness and optimism, love of the nation and mankind, a world of righteousness and Torah, Zionism and pioneering, workers' and youth movements - a Jewish nation on a small scale, a warrior and creator nation, proud and brave.

[Page 24]

The short life of the community of Wolomin has been powerful and active in all areas of human effort, in economics and organization, spiritual creation and public leadership, in Torah and good deeds.

The people of Wolomin were active and vigilant, worked and studied, dreamed of redemption and fought for their existence.

Indeed, it was an existence under constraints that was difficult to adapt to, yet, at the same time, it was a life full of intensity, full but subdued, rich and modest.

The Holocaust completely destroyed it, as it erased hundreds of other Jewish communities from the face of the earth. Evidence and documents were destroyed.

The only source available to us, to the proper extent, for our recent past, is the power of human memory. That is why we strived to draw as much as possible from this spring.

Obviously, we are well aware that human memory is deficient and mistaken, but, on the other hand, we also know that this spring will not always flow and the sooner we draw from it - the better for our cause.

B

The sight of grief and joy, of flocks of pigeons working in building their nest is always touching the heart. They come, from time to time, in flight, with a bustling chirp and a lot of noise, and in their mouths a dry leaf, a straw stalk, a grain of dirt, a bit of clay, or any crumb, a contribution of building materials for the construction of their dwelling for the future to come.

I have often followed this vision in nature, and also read a lot about it in the descriptions of writers who are well versed in the way of life of birds, but I do not know if this is truth, and I have not found it written, whether the flock of pigeons carry the building material only with joy or also with lamentation, only with passion or also with tears.

It turns out, that even in tears, because the pigeon's nest is well built - is there a better glue than a tear?

[Page 25]

And it turns out, even in lamentation, if not, what is that sweet-bitter melody that comes out from the chirping of the pigeon while doing its work, to warm and suck the attentive soul that follows every voice by force, a voice of glory, a voice of a song, and a voice in tears?!

The same lament also erupts from the work of the people of Wolomin, the remains of the remains, as they excitedly convey building materials, sparks of memory, dry leaves from the great tree of life, crumbs of impressions, a short story or description, a photo of landscape and face, a song, a moan and a drawing. Every sound and echo from the past - not for the sake of building a nest for the future to come, but the image of the nest in the past, a heavenly nest for the town below, a nest in a dream, a nest inspired by the soul of the destroyed body, a tombstone of feelings of love and longings. Their inside is lined with tears of fire for their town, their birthplace.

C

I was not among those who brought up memories and carried building materials for I am not a son of Wolomin, but circumstances led me to be the conductor of the work, and how surprised I was to see their great love for their town, the intensity of the thirst of each and every one of them who said to the well of memories: "rise!"

I saw the main concern of each member of the Wolomin organization to add in it, to bring up another character and another vision, so that, God forbid, the memory of one soul, of one of the community's dignitaries or one of the poor, one of the richest men in the community or one of the teachers, would be lost.

I saw how the remnants of Wolomin awoke, in Israel and abroad, and immediately sent their contribution, in writing and orally, long and short chapters of memory, and the short was no different from the long, for even the short content was full of great love.

And at the same time, great is the pain, the pain of the sons who left their home and walked happily to the distances to establish their status in the world.

Indeed, there were not many who dared to leave in time and prepare places of refuge, and new focal points, for the existence of the State of Israel in its ancient homeland and in the new world, and in all these new places they left their mark. The bond of emotion between them, and their town, developed and followed them into the distance, until the terrible Holocaust arrived.

[Page 26]

Therefore, it is no wonder that since entering the company of these people I was immediately caught up by their enthusiasm, my imagination opened up and I saw myself as a son of Wolomin for everything, to the same addiction to doing, serious consideration and dedication to collecting, filtering and writing, editing, printing and fundraising, and then I felt what set Wolomin apart from the rest of the holy communities.

D

The reader will be proven, by the detailed descriptions, that all the colors of the rainbow were represented in Wolomin, from the extremist Hasidim to the Communists. There were many craftsmen there: shoemakers and leather workers, tailors and glaziers, blacksmiths, carpenters, bakers, butchers, carters and peddlers, who came out of attics and cellars and engaged in all kinds of crafts that encompassed the needs of life in those days. Their lifestyle of all these was not easy. They worked hard to support themselves, ate bread and blessed God on it. Without any resistance the body accepted the supreme authority of the spirit and voluntarily gave it a status of honor because in the inner life system there was no authority forcing its will by force.

The Jews of Wolomin did not neglect their education and culture even in the most difficult moments. Their main concern was to provide an education to their sons. There were many educational institutions in the town, *cheders* and Talmud Torah, in which Jewish boys studied the Torah from the age of four.

In the early morning hours boys were seen in the streets rushing to their schools, to the *cheders* to study the Torah from the rabbi, and to the elementary schools. Upon graduation from the c*heder,* there were those who turned to the yeshiva which was the highlight of traditional education.

Mentally, and spiritually, the Jew in Wolomin felt himself in a place that allowed life, as much as it was possible on a foreign soil, under the nose of hostile rule. The rule, which was indeed a tyrannical rule, had not yet penetrated all the cells of life, and as far as the Jews could ignore it and forget its reality, they had done so.

[Page 27]

The richest Jew, and the poorest Jew, found their spiritual elation in our square letters and their main pleasure was a page of Gemara, a chapter of Mishnayot, sections from *Ein-Yaakov*, paragraphs in *"Chayei Adam"* ["The Life of Man"], or just the recitation of psalms in public or in privacy, each one according to its rank and the society he belonged to. Each of them integrated into the society that suited him, and came to his satisfaction, not only the satisfaction of the soul, but also the satisfaction of pleasure and enjoyment, literally, the Jews were renewed and refreshed spiritually.

E

In the first generations, as well as in the last generations in Wolomin, they had to fight for air and light, for right and honor, for work and livelihood, but when there was an opening, even the tiniest, for the possibility of comfortable life and action, a wave of initiative, talent and ability to act, arose among the masses and the individuals, and there was no corner in, and around the town, where the constructive hand of the Jews of Wolomin did not work.

And who can recall, without a shudder, the boundless idealisms, the total devotion of the Zionist activists, the flame of courage and the sacrifice of the pioneering youth. And from the pages of the book we hear the singing, or the *hora* dance, around the camp fire in the woods. And indeed, there was hardly a boy or a girl who did not belong to a youth movement in the town, and their activities were tense, full of content, emotion and enthusiasm, for the sake of pioneering fulfillment in Eretz Yisrael.

With love and longing the people of Wolomin recall their movements, tell their experiences, shed light on their concerns, victories and failures, and also on their relationship with each other.

Each review was written by members of the movements and parties. The writers have been given complete freedom to tell the history of their organizations and parties, and the reader will be able to make comparisons and find the unifier, the synthesis in life and the struggle that caused the rise and fall of the Wolomin community, which was destroyed and will no longer arise like the suffering Polish Jewry.

The Jews of Wolomin felt that they were part of the great Jewish nation, which was advancing towards its resurrection and redemption, and was unwilling to buy their equality at the cost of sacrificing its uniqueness and resurrection.

[Page 28]

In this book we present detailed chapters on the way of life. They reflects the daily life of the Jewish public, changes that have taken place in their way of life over time, and also interesting chapters on the activities of public figures, who acted independently, through their parties and the trade unions.

Great value is known for their public vigilance, thirst for knowledge and Torah, willingness to do good deeds, and the provision of social assistance not for the sake of receiving a reward. In this Yizkor Book we bring up the noble figures of wise scholars, community leaders, public activists, and humble, simple and poor people that no one would carry a festive speech in their honor. However, those who saw them in their insult and greatness, well-being and controversy, despair and hope, joy and sorrow, got to know them, their way of life, their thoughts and experiences - and know to tell about them and themselves, describe their wisdom and intelligence, holiness and all their lofty virtues.

In addition, chapters of general and family memories are also presented, and they expand the scope of acquaintance with social and family life in Jewish Wolomin.

F

There is no doubt that if a person, who specializes in Jewish social sciences, received the material presented in this book before it was printed, he could have written a comprehensive and profound work on the history, life, essence, contents, culture and the society of the young community.

However, we did not pretend to utilize to the fullest all the development processes of the community, its struggle and all its inner aspirations. Everything written here is the work of the people, who were not, and do not pretend to be Jewish writers. In this, we see the special value of the book that is characterized by simplicity and directness.

The sole duty of this book is to serve as a living testimony to a community that perished in the horrors of the Holocaust, as described by its sons, builders and survivors in Israel and the Diaspora.

The role the editorial staff was to fulfill this first task. Indeed, this is how the action involved in collecting, filtering, editing, and printing it as a book of remembrance for the Wolomin community was defined.

[Page 29]

In this period of documenting and commemorating Jewish life in tens and hundreds memorial books, the time of the researcher, and the historian, has not yet arrived. The generation, which felt the horrors of the Holocaust that befell our nation, is still alive. No research work today will succeed in encompassing the dimensions of destruction on the one hand, and establishing a perfect and uniform architectural structure that will describe life in all its various shades on the other.

Therefore, the way the editors of the memorial books have taken is reasonable. To provide documentary material, collect documents, impressions, testimonies, articles and stories, which will serve as living testimony to destroyed Jewish communities, and provide a faithful source for scientists and historians when they come to build a scientific and historical building for a third of our people who perished in the Holocaust. This building will be a source of life and inspiration for our generation, and for future generations after us.

The time has not yet come to build the scientific building. Our dead are still standing before our eyes, the pillars of smoke are still rising in our former homeland, and the bloody rivers of Nebusaradan [chief of slaughter] are still boiling and roaring loudly.

This is not the time to write a comprehensive work for our generation that has experienced the Holocaust in all its anger and rage.

G

The specific nature of this book presented the author of these lines with both simple and complicated problem: how to edit?

The nature of the matter requires that this tombstone, which many hands create it and is connected from donations of many hearts, bustling and cuddling, and by many mouths shouting aloud, "it is a pity for those who are gone," will not be made of one piece and will not reach the heights of a temple whose angels are sculpted. It was easy to write all the materials in a uniform style, in the style of the editor, and the printed book will appear in explicit, elegant, beautiful and meticulous language.

However, this was not the goal that stood before us when we approached the work of writing and editing, the collection of articles, notes and memoirs of the residents of Wolomin, a simple and bustling Jewish town. We wanted that the memories and descriptions will describe the life of the and the individual, the special and the unifying, the equal and the unequal side, not to see a face of a person and a town, but the face of a resident of Wolomin, a town near Warsaw the capital of Poland.

[Page 30]

We wanted them to deliver in their words, and in their notes, faithful echoes of the way of speaking and writing as preserved in their memory, the way of life, a fine riddle and a juicy joke, as heard in streets and the houses of Wolomin.

Therefore, there was great value in accurate editing that does not detract from the initial juiciness of the written words, and even if they are written in weakness, but are honest and modest, they work on us not only in their renewal, but also in that they are above all old and new - in the vibration of the soul.

These are the principles that confronted the editor: the escape from effect and aesthetics, so to speak, to the pursuit of truth and its responsible meaning; examining the sources and accumulation of precise details. However, in contrast to the manner of dry scientists, and poetic writers, I was mostly inclined to the authentic expression and left the articles as they were written. Then, I edited it twice until we put out a proper thing under the right conditions And yet there is no lack of personal depth which expresses, in the symbol of the word, the essence of the soul, and leads to the hidden corners of the soul, and even if the word is weak, it is full with yearnings.

Such is the magic in the stories and the articles in the book of Wolomin: the grace of popular simplicity that emerges from the writings by the survivors of the intelligentsia, the community and party activists, those enthusiastic young people, dreamers and warriors, whose heads have turned gray over time; each with a chapter from his memoirs. Everyone and his own world, style and ways of expression, but to our eyes they seem to fill and complete one great world, to which we return with a new awakening and enthusiasm, for when we return to them we become acquainted with ourselves and return to our source.

H

In the following pages the readers, those who grew and educated in the town and its memory is etched in their hearts, and those who only know its name but the sentimental affinity, or emotions, will motivate them to flip through the book dedicated to their parents' roots, will find a picture of a rich and diverse town and a gallery of different characters and personalities.

[Page 31]

And they will become one earpiece, of heart and ear, and listen to whispers of prayers and whispers of love, to the abundance of echoes of riddles of life and secrets of man, and they will be able to breathe the air of the world that sunk, been destroyed and knows no peace.

And if anyone will ask about the small town, about the light hidden within it, the magic and the glow that has disappeared, if it still has a name and memory in the hearts of its sons, the preacher will tell him: on the contrary, open this book and read it, as you go through broken hearts, you go through the pages of this book, in which beating hearts embrace generations of our ancestors and the vision of the landscapes. Read and see that the charm of the town is like a seal in the hearts of its sons. Weren't these simple words of the people of Wolomin torn from the mourning heart of a bound and slaughtered nation? Could it be that a tone of ancient prayers of lamentation, which were murmured by the martyrs in their last moments, did not quiver in them!?

These writers who experienced the horrors, and the sights of the massacre sank into the depths of their souls, and the reader, will find here a horrific account of what happened in the Wolomin community and chapters of horror, suffering and desperate struggle of individuals, who suffered and went through terrible agony until they were privileged to see the fall of the Nazi beast. Therefore, the heart will sigh for the resurrection of its sights and their salvation from the flame of annihilation, for their preservation in the treasure of memories.

The book contains human documents that shock the reader to the core, and testimonies of crimes and murders that a person cannot deal with. In a silent outpouring the survivors present their pain, the pain of the tortured, and a cry of protest is heard in it, the cry of all those who have been slaughtered, whose blood was shed like water. This prayer is full of rage and bitterness, shock and horror that have sunk into the depths of their souls and become part of their being. Chapter after chapter they bring up the changes in the town and in people's hearts, the horrors and terror, the sufferings and heroism in its various forms in those terrible days.

I

And great is the measure of gratitude and blessing that the editor owes to those who helped him in obtaining all this material.

I would like to express my gratitude to the members of the Book Committee, the workers and activists, each according to his ability, for their constant vigilance and consistent interest in all matters concerning the book.

[Page 32]

The secretary of the Wolomin organization, Dr. Sarah Mandelberg, who contributed a lot to the success of the enterprise and in her lists gave a faithful expression to the life of the community in Wolomin, is entitled to a special appreciation.

In appreciation and respect I will mention the dedicated work of Mr. Shamay Baum, Chairman of the Book Committee, for his daily activity of preparing and publishing the book.

My deepest appreciate to the Deputy Chairman of the Book Committee, Mr. Shmuel Zucker, who devoted his energy and talent to collecting and editing the material.

My thanks are given to the members of the committee: Tzipora Bondy-Einderstein, Malka Grinszpan -Tamari, Yisrael Levitau, Yosef Eisenberg, Malka Greenberg-Yelin and Alter Carmeli.

[Page 33]

The Town and its History

Translated by Sara Mages

[Page 34]

Wolomin, a town near Warsaw, the big city left its impression on it, in a blend of a Jewish town with all its simplicity and diversity. Hasidim and men of good deeds lived in the same place with *Mitnagdim* [opponents] and modern intellectuals, merchants with working men, learners with craftsmen, and so life flowed slowly in the town for decades. When people tell the life story of the community of Wolomin and about its innocent and honest Jews, simple and humble folks, wise with deep thought, immersed within the confines of *Halacha* and live in the atmosphere of the world to come; about people of education and science, broad-minded and visionary; about young Yeshiva students and young people who sacrifice themselves for the ideas of *Tikkun olam*, repairing humanity; about men of passion and revolution, rebellion and aspiration; about all those who have walked through the streets of this town, situated in rigid mode of life, customs and habits, which cast their rule on Jewish life and determined the behavior of the Jew, every day, morning to evening. And when we talk about the town, it is impossible to skip the Hassidim and the God-fearing, who drew from the ancient springs of the nation and conducted pure family life; Torah scholars who spent all their time in the study of the Gemara and their most favorite song was: "Purify our Hearts to Serve You in Truth."

Shimon Kantz

[Page 35]

The beginning of the town

Told by Dr. Sara Mandelberg,
Mrs. Chava Rubinstein and Mr. Kopel Berman

Translated by Sara Mages

The town of Wolomin is 19 kilometers northeast of Warsaw, in Radzymin District. In 1939, it numbered about 3,000 Jews, and in 1921 - 3079 out of a total population of 6248 people.

It was a young community. In the 1880s Wolomin was still just a rural point with a little more than a hundred residents, amongst them a few Jews. The completion of the construction of the railroad line Warsaw-Petersburg (1861), that Wolomin was its first stop after Warsaw, created the conditions for the development of the settlement, first as a resort for summer vacationers from Warsaw and, in the course of time, an industrial center that included metal plants (agricultural machinery, iron beds), glass, tanneries and flour mills. Until the First World War there was also a cane industry for the Russian market.

It seems that, from the outset, Jewish initiative played an important role in the development of the place. At the end of the last century there was already a Jewish community in Wolomin with two rabbis who competed for the rabbinate there.

Around 1900, Beit Midrash was established. Around 1900, a cemetery was dedicated.

Rabbi Ze'v-Wolf Bergazin (appointed 1904) played an important role in the development of the community.

The Admor, R' Efraim Taub of Kuzmir, lived in Wolomin until the First World War, then he moved to Warsaw.

Economy

The livelihood of the Jews of Wolomin was mostly in commerce and crafts, but they also had a share in industry (the factories owned by Jews: a glass factory, two bed factories, a leather factory and a foundry).

There was also a considerable source of work in the place. Several branches of labor were all Jewish, such as porterage, painting, baking, etc.

About 300 Jews worked in the factories, most of them in administrative and service positions, but also in professional jobs.

The Cooperative Bank played an important role in the economic life of Wolomin's Jews. It was affiliated with the Cooperative Center in Warsaw and *Kupat Gemilut Hasadim* (founded in 1935).

[Page 36]

At the head of the community stood an elected committee of eight members and its party composition was as follows: a Zionist chairman, four *Agudah* members and three unaffiliated. The community's personnel included: a rabbi, three ritual slaughterers (one of them a cantor), *shamash* [synagogue beadle] and a secretary.

In the municipal government the Jews were represented by eight council members (out of twenty four), and one, out of three, in the management ("Magistrate").

Only one Jewish woman worked as a clerk in the town's administration.

Community institutions

In addition to Beit HaMidrash and the cemetery, the community had a bathhouse, a synagogue and Talmud Torah (with a special building). In 1935, the community budget has reached the total of 38,000 zloty.

Public institutions

Houses of Worship: the houses of the Hasidim of Gur, Amshinov, Aleksander, Wyskow and Wolomin, and also the "*Minyan*" of the Zionist Organization, Schools: 5-6 "*Hadarim*," "*Heder Metukan*" (established in 1934 with Hebrew as the language of instruction), "*Beit Yakov*" with four classes (established in 1930).

In addition, the children studied general studies in accordance with the education law of the Polish State School for Jews.

Parties and organizations

The Zionist Organization, Mizrachi, Agudah, Organization of Craftsmen. The labor circles were mostly under the influence of Poalei Zion and the Bund whose open activity was mainly in the cultural area and centered at Peretz Library. There was a drama club and a sports group named Maccabi.

A parallel cultural activity concentrated in the Zionist club with evening classes for Hebrew and a sports group "Maccabi."

The Jewish Wolomin community also included about 100 people who were scattered the nearby villages: Czarna, Lipny, Lesniakowizna, Reczaje, Poswietna, Kobylka, and Duczki.

In the 1930s, with the rise of anti-Semitism, these Jews left the villages and moved to the town.

[Pages 37-51]

The History of the Shtetl

by Shimon Kantz

Translated by Theodore Steinberg

The Jewish community in Wolomin is one of the youngest communities in Poland. Trying now to provide a historical overview of the annihilated Jewish settlement in Wolomin, we must start with regrets, since the condition of sources is such that it requires giving a pragmatic and by no means exhaustive historical picture of the past of the Wolomin settlement. The historian's job is in large part like the work of a mosaicist, who has to put together bits and pieces to create a full picture.

We lack sources that could establish when the Jewish community in Wolomin was founded and when it developed. From its name we could argue that it was a village in earlier times, in an area of fertile fields where oxen grazed, surrounding which were thick forests, in which were found many wolves, so that the grazing was accompanied by great dangers. The name Wol-amin signifies in Poland a warning to avoid this place and to beware of the dangers that threatened man and beast.

It is true that in very, very old times there was a tiny settlement, and in the surrounding woods the kings, dukes, and similar rulers went around hunting. However, in those days, hunting often had political overtones, with entanglements of court intrigues and power politics. The beginnings or ends of secret agreements. For the most part, the story of Wolomin is quite poor. There were episodes that were reflected in Warsaw and were tied to Wolomin by political rumors, and from time to time entwined with them are Jewish people or events of varying character.

First Contact Between Jews and Wolomin

Over ninety years ago appeared "The Story of Mazovia" by the Polish historian Vitshak Dzitski. He writes about the decree that in the eighteenth century freed the Jews in the Duchy of Warsaw from active military service and forbade the "blood duty" on paper money. Five months later the French emperor Napoleon Bonaparte crossed the Niemen River. That started the second Polish war with Russia.

From the standpoint of historical development, a French invasion of Russia was progressive, in proportion to how much Napoleon's Codex compares to the Russian "Svad Zakonov." Of course, the Polish orientation was based on this foundation. The Jews thus found themselves in a difficult situation. Jewish politics in 1812 had as its highest goal to declaim and maneuver in order to avoid the traps of both sides.

In Warsaw, the atmosphere was decidedly anti-Russian. Three days after Napoleon crossed his fatal Rubicon, the river Niemen, in Poland a general confederation of Poland was declared, with the aim of restoring the Polish Republic on its historical basis. This confederation was actually nothing more than a decorative agreement with Napoleon's war.

War fever seized Warsaw. Volunteers swarmed to the army. Among them were Jews. Although the decree of January 29, 1812, had exempted the Jews and forbidden exemption payments, many Jews remained in the army. A number of volunteers were raised to officer ranks, a number disappeared with the hundred thousand others in the waters of the Berezina, frozen to death on the broad and cold Russian fields.

The evidence of these sacrifices was lost in those stormy times, just as the Jewish individual soldier was diluted in the regiments and divisions.

It was almost impossible for the community heads in Warsaw to define this political orientation. Individual Jews belonged to separate camps. From the east, huge armies marched through the city, representing many peoples and languages. The soldiers, mostly foreigners, treated Warsaw like every other territory. Particularly the Westphalian soldiers [that is, Germans] excelled. They served Napoleon's brother Jerome, the king of the little kingdom of Westphalia. Their anger at having to serve under a foreign leader moved them to compensate by plundering both Jews and non-Jews, raping women, and even killing for booty.

Jewish musicians, who used to entertain the soldiers with songs and music in the soldiers' taverns, were found in the streets, murdered and robbed.

Then we find the only trace from that time of contact between Jews and the village of Wolomin.

In the memoirs of the German Baron of Lehsiten, *In the Court of King Jerome*, which was published in Berlin in 1905, he tells of two Jewish musicians who were found murdered in the village of Wolomin. Through this fact, the Baron wants to show that the peasants of this village were pro-Russian and that they therefore killed the Jewish musicians who entertained the Westphalian soldiers with songs and music.

In all truth, the musicians were sacrifices of the soldiers who took out their hard feelings on them and released their murderous instincts.

This truth is confirmed in the writing of the German historian A. Kleinschmidt in his *History of the Kingdom of Westphalia*, which was published in 1893. He discusses there the alarm that engulfed the Jewish population, the Jewish merchants, over the German-speaking soldiers. Also the Polish writer Antony Megera in his book *The Image of Warsaw at the End of the Eighteenth Century* describes the comic scenes when Jewish merchants try to understand the German-speaking soldiers, intending to do business with them but instead receiving blows.

This historical fact tells us that the Warsaw Jews knew of the existence of the village of Wolomin and perhaps that there were other contacts with the village that were later obliterated because of the hatred of the village folk for the pro-French element, among whom they also reckoned the Jews.

Trade and Murder

Napoleon came to Warsaw after his defeat in Russia, on December 10, 1812 and then left the city after several days, people knew the war was over and that an end had come to the duchy of Warsaw.

On 18 February 1813, a deputation from the city greeted the triumphant entry of the Russian general Baron von Karf. Most of the Jews looked with trepidation to their future. The bitter facts of life did not give them much hope.

In the appendix to the constitution, promulgated at the end of 1815, it was said that whoever is not a citizen of the land cannot enjoy political rights. Since Jews were not citizens, they had none of the rights of citizens. This decree overturned the daily life of the Jews in Warsaw, forced them from their jobs, and forced them seek other means of earning a livelihood. It seems that Jews sought contact with the village, came to the peasants with their merchandise, and thereby also became victims.

It is worth mentioning again the village of Wolomin as remembered by the Polish writer Kajetan Kasimian, who blamed the obnoxious behavior of the Polish village on the Jewish merchants. As an example, he cites the fact that someone had found in the woods near Wolomin, ten kilometers from Warsaw a murdered Jewish merchant, and that had encouraged other Jews to seek out other villages in that area.

During the years 1815-1830, Congress Poland became truly powerful. People had that to thank for opening a demand for goods in the Russian Empire. In 1819 they removed the trade barriers between Russia and Poland. Three years later they were restored because people suspected that Poland did not produce all the merchandise but only finished up merchandise imported from Prussia. When people decided this was not proper, in 1822 they reestablished trade barriers.

Polish industry immediately found a route to the east. The cotton industry had begun to develop in the country, but Jews did not play a large part in it. On the contrary, it was important that Jews entered the business with raw materials. Also in the grain business, which in those years accounted for twenty-seven percent of total exports, the entrance of the Jews was significant.

In the vicinity of Warsaw, Jews participated in the manufacturing of cloth. In 1820, the government opened a cloth factory at the corner of Smatcha and Gencha, which had, in 1822, fifty-four looms and one hundred eighty workers. In 1824, the banker Samuel Leopold Frankel and two Germans bought the factory. The factory later employed six hundred workers, among whom were scores of Jews.

It was therefore a good time for working class Jews in Warsaw. There were also many Jewish merchants, who could not have succeeded without the village. The village population also began to have somewhat better lives, some of them coming into the town to buy goods, which enriched their economy.

The village of Wolomin, it appears, was among the poorest, because it is hardly mentioned in the various publications about the development of the economy at that time. Only once the Polish historian Wladisloaw Richmanski mentions the suit that a Jewish merchant brought against a landowner, Sachtchanski of Wolomin, for not paying a bill for cloth.

That was in 1827. In that year the Jews played a large role in Warsaw business. There were larger and smaller Jewish businesses. Also a union of Jewish trade workers, which over time developed into a large union that lasted until 1939.

The German traveler H. Haring, who visited Warsaw in 1830, describes Franciskaner Street with Jewish businesses on both sides that were full of good things. "In the Jewish businesses, people find whatever their hearts desire, the finest and the best. Shopping there are military men and rich property owners who encourage the Jews to come to their villages. The Jews, however, do not show a lot of enthusiasm because of the hatred of the servile peasants who see the Jews as offspring of the devil and are full of superstitions."

In the same book we find a description of the mood that in 1830 suffused Poland. It tells of a hard winter with heavy frosts, but it felt the "heat" of the revolt against Russia which lasted some days, not because of the achievements of the Polish rebels but because Petersburg did not hurry to do anything. It was thought that Czar Nicholas I waited for the revolt to burn out on its own, like piles of straw. Then the czar's troops would put an end to the activity and restore order.

In Petersburg they knew that the Polish ringleaders were deeply divided. The older generation, especially the landowners who worried particularly about their own privileges, were drawn into the revolt against their wills, but they did not want to go too far. To the bitter end also belonged Jewish youth who swore to serve in the ranks of the rebels and even walk into fire…

This description is supplemented in Alexander Nowitzki's "Pictures of Polish Villages, 1830-1931" There we read about the "fervent and abject pleas of Stanislaw Vernish," a student in the rabbinical seminary in Warsaw, to the commander General Chaptizki, that they should finally recognize Jewish patriotism, that Jewish patriots would gladly sacrifice their lives for Poland. Stanislaw Vernish was the son of a Jewish merchant on Franciskaner Street. When his father heard the news that the Polish freedom fighters had attacked and robbed Jewish merchants, he fled from the revolt to the village of Zotczenki, about five kilometers north of Wolomin, where he took refuge in the home of the wealthy Kunaczarski, who had lived in Warsaw and who opened his house to the Jewish merchant. The village peasants attacked the Jew one evening as he took a walk and killed him.

This, however, did not deter his son from writing fiery patriotic songs and the above-mentioned letter to the Polish general.

The Jewish Legion

From that comes the claim that Wolomin, just like the other villages around Warsaw, had not at that time admitted any Jews nor tolerated them, greeting with hatred any Jew who wanted to approach. In that tense atmosphere, Jews made an effort to mobilize a Jewish legion. In January of 1839, Jews started to enroll in the National Guard, provided that they appeared European and were shaved. Only a small number of Jews dared to accept this condition, and the leadership of the Jewish community in Warsaw adopted the idea of a Jewish Guard, in which were religious Jews who excelled in the camps with their bravado.

In 1831, the Russian commander Ivan Paskovitch came to Warsaw and some of the militant Jewish youth left the city…General Ostrovsky, the commander of the National Guard in Warsaw, later wrote that he met in the woods near Wolomin with groups of Jewish youth who had fled Warsaw but had no place to settle and who "made a pitiful sight."

History does not tell us what happened to those Jews. Whether they returned to Warsaw, whether they were captured and sent to Siberia, or whether they remained scattered in various villages. The fact is that in later years there were reports from Russian and Polish officers about Jewish young men in the woods around Warsaw and other places. We can cite Wolomin as well as Zanszczenki and Chlarniki, villages that later disappeared from the map, having become urban settlements or having merged with Warsaw suburbs. The Russian traveler Venstrov mentions in his 1835 travel book a Jewish farmer between Zanszczenki and Wolomin.

The Conversion Plague

In Poland in those years a conversion plague raged. Not only among the wealthy, enlightened, assimilated folk but also among the simpler people. Missionaries from England worked among the poor to capture Jewish souls, handing out money, food, and clothing and promising good fortune. The rich converts intended through conversion to make their careers and sought to become high officials. There were also simple Jewish youth, some journeymen, some apprentices, who lacked employment or who loved Christian women.

In the Responsa of the Kaldiner rabbi, R. Shmuel-Leib Epsteyn, the "Olat Shmuel," with the Warsaw community rabbi R. Shlomo-Zalmen Lifshitz, author of "Khemdas Shlomo," we read about the great grief caused by the conversion plague which, God help us, engulfed many Jewish youth, "kneeling before the cross, holding on to a piece of wood, which had less substance than straw."

The question of what prompted the correspondence between the two rabbis concerned a young man who settled, after his conversion, in Wolomin, where he married a village girl, lived with her for some months, and then returned to Warsaw, approaching the rabbi with the request that he be allowed to return to Judaism. This involved the question of divorcing his Christian wife, but from that arose a great tragedy for the young man's family. His father, an everyday worker, a carpenter, could not stand the disgrace and died of heartache. His mother remained along and her converted son was her only source of income.

The Warsaw rabbi sought a way to be lenient with the young man and reabsorb him in the Jewish community after he divorced his Christian wife, who stayed in Wolomin.

Jewish Amusements Around Wolomin

The chief rabbi of in Warsaw, R. Shlomoo-Leib Lifshitz, was a great scholar. He was born in Pozen, and together with R. Akiva Eiger and R. Yakov of Lissa, author of "Chos Da'as," he represented the great trio of rabbinical authorities in Poland. After becoming the rabbi in Nasielsk (1804), in 1819 he came to Praga and from there to Warsaw.

In his classic work "Khemdas Shlomo," he spoke with pain about the plague of dance-and-frivolity that had spread among the Jewish youth in Warsaw. He even went to the municipal authorities seeking help. The rabbi complained that the Jewish youth were desecrating Shabbos and Festivals. They waste their time "with empty things, like dance and frivolity, parks and pubs, and we seldom see them on Shabbos in the shuls and minyans. One who thus transgresses the laws of his faith cannot be a true citizen. Therefore the civil authorities must help the rabbinate stop this lawlessness."

The magistrate agreed, and until the outbreak of the revolution n 1830, people in Warsaw saw police raids on Jewish young people who went to the parks to dance on Shabbos and Festivals.

Be assured that this action did nothing to discourage the young people The Jewish boys and girls simply had to go further afield, outside of the city–in summer, to the woods near the city–in the direction of Atvask and also toward Wolomin. The "Khemdas Shlomo" laments a particular case, the complaint of parents whose son was disobedient and came to the woods near Wolomin. Others, he said, sailed on the Vistula. He says that Satan has his people who make a pretense of liking Jews in order to get them to become Christians. Truly their intention is to demoralize Jewish youth and lead them to apostasy.

As evidence he cites the old Polish author Julian Ursyn Niemcewicz, who in his novel "Leib and Sarah," the first novel with a Haskalah theme in Polish literature, calls on Jews to interact socially with Poles. But ten years earlier, the same author had composed an anti-Semitic utopia about how Warsaw would appear in 3333. The city would be called Moszkopolitz and the Moska dynasty would rule Poland.

From these snapshots we can see that the village of Wolomin was known to the Jewish inhabitants of Warsaw even at the beginning of the nineteenth century, though the Jews had no access to the city, except for a few.

But these are not the only facts. Actually we can find more facts in other sources, which confirm that there was no Jewish life there. It is characteristic of Poland that regardless of their proximity to Warsaw, villagers regarded the Jews as a specter, a devil, an enemy of Christ.

Consequently they accepted a converted Jew with open arms. Missionary propaganda at that time was devious, not only toward Jews but also among Poles, in the city and in the village, that they should accept converted Jews. The Polish aristocracy in Warsaw was not stingy with money for gifts for the new converts, who were even deemed worthy to have godfathers from the Polish nobility. Polish landowners invited Jewish merchants into their palaces, in hopes of converting them.

The same thing was true among the simple peasants. As soon as a Jew converted, people treated him like a brother. Mixed marriages, however, took place mainly among the wealthy and less seldom among everyday people. Consequently, we find fewer Jewish converts in the villages. Wolomin was no exception. Even the occasional convert did not stay there long.

Jewish Peasants in Wolomin

Event followed event–mutinies, rebellions, upheavals. These events and shocks in France, Prussia, and Austria resounded far and wide and spread to Russia and Poland. Mainly the Jews watched and hoped that things would get easier. Jews in Warsaw began to play a larger role in the economic development of the city. Industry grew, especially sugar, paper, and agricultural machinery. "Advanced" Jews played a pioneering role in this environment. Slowly a Jewish bourgeoisie developed from the rich Warsaw Jews. A few Jews received permits to buy goods and houses.

At that time the Warsaw leader Eizik Goldshteyn bought scores of dunams [1 dunam=900 square meters] of land from the Wolomin landowner Wladislaw Kaczytzki, but nothing came of it because the government had attached a provision that a Jewish landholder had to settle on his estate twenty-five Jewish families, in order to move Jews so that they would undertake agricultural work. This was not a simple thing, since Jews who had gladly decided to work the land did not know how to handle the vexations of their Christian surroundings and therefore often failed because of their neighbors. They therefore did not last long even on land that Jews had paid for.

Jewish Rebels in Wolomin

The years 1861-62 are called "the moral overturning," because they brought a "peace" between the Jews and the Poles in Warsaw. People overlooked the tragic events of 1859 and the battle between the conservative Poles and the assimilated Jewish youth. Jews took part in street demonstrations and in assorted political activities.

It was now 1863. In schools and beis-medrashes in Warsaw, people read in Yiddish and in Hebrew the announcements that the underground Polish region had distributed to Jews. Many Jewish young people snuck away from their homes and in naively enthusiastic letters explained to their parents why they would sacrifice themselves for Poland. Lawrence Oliphant, who was then a correspondent for an English newspaper in Warsaw, wrote about the Jew's great sympathy for the rebellion. He also told how the Russian police had seized in Wolomin an arms cache that was guarded by a group of young Jewish rebels. Three of them escaped. Two were badly wounded in a battle with the Russian militia and later were hanged on Muranow Street in Warsaw.

At the end of 1864 the revolt was completely subdued. The destruction among Warsaw's Jews was devastating. The Jewish historian Dr. Y Shatzky estimates that in Warsaw alone over a thousand Jews took part in the revolt. He goes on to say that scores of Jews around Warsaw were active in the fighting, though he does not give the names of the Jewish settlements. But the Polish rebel Gustav Warinski, who was sent to Siberia, writes about his acquaintanceship with Jewish exiles from Warsaw and other shtetls, among which he cites Wolomin.

This is the only historical evidence that already by that time Jews lived in Wolomin and that the settlement was more like a city.

What the Jew's professions were and how many Jews there were is now hard to determine. It is not impossible that more information exists in Warsaw's archives, but our inquiries have never been answered.

It is symbolic that the same Gustav Warinski writes about his return from Siberia to Warsaw in 1881, on a day when a pogrom took place in Warsaw. After all he had been through, the battles side by side with Jewish rebels and later his friendships in Siberia, he saw everywhere "the bestiality of his people toward the Jews, for whom he had brought warm greetings from their brothers and sons, who languished far away in Siberia."

It is a fact that the years 1861-63 had a great effect on the growth of the Jewish community in Warsaw. There were profound changes in the Polish-Jewish relationship. This was a result f the new orientation that began with the destruction of the romantic world outlook and gave new attention to political reality. Thus began the movement of "Polish positivism," in which the Jews played a large role.

Consequently Jews from other cities and from Russia began to come to Warsaw. The local and central authorities began to fear that Warsaw would become a Jewish city. Efforts were actually made that the official Jewish quarter should not be dissolved and in the "non-Jewish streets" some Jews were permitted to live, those who were already "Europeanized"; but the Jewish movement toward Warsaw was strong and the government sought to confine the Jews to the villages and shtetls around Warsaw.

Jews Start to Build Houses in Wolomin

Jan Rabski in his book "The Evolution of Warsaw" says that the city's management wanted to order the elimination of the "long kaftan" on Warsaw streets, but the central Russian authority did not agree, as he took the side of Polish patriots, who after the revolution had remained in their offices in great numbers. The Polish historian of the city of Warsaw regrets that the decree was not carried out, and he shows that the Jews took it as a given and started settling in neighboring areas not far from Warsaw. Among these areas was Wolomin, Asalitze, Wodowlina, and others, and in a poisonous tone he adds: "Their long kaftans will surely not help to dry up the mud puddles, but such places are more appropriate for them than our beautiful Warsaw streets."

This makes it clear that at that time there were already Jews in Wolomin, indeed religious Jews, who, despite their influx into Wolomin, did not want to toss away their long kaftans and Europeanize.

One has to say that those Jews in Wolomin displayed their energy and initiative no less than those who had chosen to stay in Warsaw. They busied themselves not only with agriculture and other trades but also with business and building houses.

Already to Dr. Y. Slatzki the tempo of Jewish movement was so quick that there was no possibility for the "Polish patriots" to organize anti-Jewish groups. From year to year the number of houses built by Jews increased. The Polish landlords did not want to sell their establishments, because their incomes were large. Thus it was not only in Warsaw but in the surrounding area, and of course in Wolomin, where there were no affordable apartments and the incoming Jews were forced to build their own.

The great changes that were occurring in the whole country also had a great influence on the development of the Jewish community in Warsaw. It was the time of Ludwig Nathanson's control in the community, which lasted for twenty-five years. From a small provincial community it developed into an institution of great stature. It was responsible for creating a variety of religious, economic, and cultural organizations; it introduced the community tax, though not every Jew could pay it, which was another reason for a poor Jew to seek a dwelling outside of Warsaw, where expenses were somewhat less than in the big city.

In 1870, the winds of Jew-hatred again began to blow in Poland. Polish journalists began to accuse economic liberalism of being a Jewish movement. They no longer saw the end to the Jewish question coming through assimilation and they began to write that Jews had "set their hands" on Polish culture. The well-known Polish anti-Semite Jan Jelenski began a propaganda campaign to expel Jews from business and industry and put them into Polish hands. In 1881, pogroms broke out in Warsaw. They lasted three days and covered more than fifty streets, from the poorest to the wealthiest. Many Jews were killed or injured. Property damage was later estimated at a million rubles.

Many of the victimized Jews had to leave Warsaw and find a roof over their heads nearby. They found them in, among other places, Wolomin, where the Jews with long kaftans welcomed them with brotherly warmth.

Nathanson, the head of the Warsaw community, issued a declaration that the only cure for the plague of anti-Semitism was to seek rapprochement with the Polish neighbors, to stop speaking Yiddish, and to discard Jewish clothing, "all the external signs of difference between Jew and non-Jew." Immediately the Jew realized that this cure was false. "Polish patriots" were afraid of Jewish assimilation so "they could defend Polish culture." Rather they thought it better to provoke the Jews with the long kaftans who lived in isolated groups. Many were drawn to the small Jewish settlements near Warsaw, among which Wolomin had begun to play a prominent role.

First Active Zionists

In the 1890's, the radical nationalists began to turn their attention to the peasants, getting closer to the people, countering the propaganda of the Russian regime, which accused the Poles of being exploitative lords, barons, and arrogant nobles, who treated the peasants like slaves. The Polish nationalists in their propaganda used anti-Semitism to turn the peasants against Jewish merchants. Again this affected the Jews in Wolomin, who had begun to show initiative for developing the town. The mistrust that the Polish nationalists cultivated in the villages hampered the development of the town.

Traditional anti-Semitism, as formulated by Stanislaw Stashitz and Jan Jelenski, took on a sharper edge in later years. In 1909, Roman Dmowski, the leader of the Polish National Democracy, asserted that the Jews would impose their ideas and goals on Polish society and that there was no alternative except to assimilate the Jews among the Poles. In the Jewish streets, the ideas of the Zionists and of the Bund gained strength. By the side of the older world, a new generation began to emerge with a vision of a new world that would promote new opportunities.

This was mirrored in the Jewish shtetls, but Wolomin appears in hindsight to have stood still. There, traditional Jewish life proceeded until the outbreak of the First World War, when the first active Zionists were seen, and they undertook the development of the first phase of this worldwide movement

[Pages 52-93]

My Life in Wolomin

by Yakov Sigalov

When I came to Wolomin for the first time, in 1915, I found there a small, poor Jewish settlement to which I immediately felt an attraction, like the attraction to friendly Jews. In Warsaw I dwelled in an assimilated society, partly among good Polish people, but deep in my heart I felt a desire for authentic Jews. My grandfather's spirit lived within me. He was a gabbai for R' Dudl Talner, and in me lived the melodies that I used to hear from my father at home. In our shtetl of Galavanyevsk, near Uman, people really knew how to sing. People sang zemiros at melaveh–malkes and at the third Shabbos meal, only Talner Chasidim sang with more zest, with more fire, with joy, and with pleasure.

There were also melodies filled with longing. My grandfather said, "The soul desires to return to its roots." Although I was still a child, these words and the melodies engraved themselves in my memory and my spirit, and when I arrived in Wolomin and encountered true Jewish souls, the longing in my father's Talner and Chabad melodies was revived in me, even though they differed from those of the Polish Chasidim.

Among the first Jews with whom I interacted in Wolomin was R' Nehamiah Mandelberg, whose appearance and bearing called for immediate respect. It was a pleasure to speak with him. Among the prominent householders were Brandes, Shtrawboym, and Goldstein, and among the Chasidim I was close with Moyshe Grodzhitzky and Yankel Margolis, and Boym (whose son lives in Tel Aviv). All were fine people with Jewish ways, merchants with open minds and everyday wisdom.

All day I was occupied with my affairs, with the foundry that I started, and I had to deal with workers, with suppliers. In the evenings I traveled back to Warsaw. But sometimes in the evening I would walk by a school where the teacher taught Torah to children. Also the windows of the beis hamedrash were open and I heard people chanting the Gemara. Young men were sitting around tables, deep in study, chanting, some softly, some in full voice. I stood there for a time as if I had been chained and could not move from the spot. I felt pulled toward the beis hamedrash as though my roots were there, from which I had been torn away.

Memories of my birthplace came to me, as did various stories that people told about the shul land the beis hamedrash, about the souls of holy tzaddikim who came there in the nights, carrying a flaming sefer–Torah. Angels and seraphim would gather. The tzaddikim would pray, the angels would praise God, and the seraphim would say, "Holy, holy…"

The Spiritual Environment

Wolomin, that little shtetl that then had no more than two streets, Warsaw Street and Koshchelne Street, showed itself to be holy with Torah and good deeds. The air was full of music. Even the birds accompanied the Gemara melodies of the devoted young men.

In those minutes I regretted that I was not one of those devoted young men who dwelt with their whole being in the higher realms, in the beautiful world of song and elevated morality.

The whistle of the train that every evening took me back to Warsaw, where I had my permanent apartment in a very different milieu, assimilated and Polish, aroused me from these thoughts. People there had different attitudes toward life. People there persuaded themselves that they were miles from the shtetl, that they attained a higher culture, and that they had a better understanding of great ideas.

In that milieu people spoke only Polish. They wondered how I, a Russian Jew, knew such good Polish. I ran into the same question as I became acquainted with the Polish intelligentsia in Wolomin. The former general Markovsky, Dr. Tshaplitzki's father–in–law, who liked to sit and talk with me, described his heroic deeds and worked to demonstrate his aristocratic distinctiveness and Polish honor in the Polish language. From my frequent encounters with the Polish intelligentsia in Warsaw, my ability in the language was enriched, which sent the general into ecstasy. I noted on his lips a melancholy smile. "Ah so," he said, "you give the Polish language a certain richness, and your accent is nothing like a Jew's."

In truth, he was not only impressed by my Polish. More than my language, he wondered at the national pride that I openly demonstrated. In our talks I often had occasion to discuss the beauty of the authentic Jewish environment in the shtetl. Regardless that Wolomin was so close to Warsaw, the shtetl had a full and unique sense of itself, and it presented a special ability to fashion a human personality. Despite the constant hustle and bustle to earn an income, it had a spiritual Jewish air. The influence of Jewish Wolomin spread to the surrounding shtetls, places where there were only single or a few families.

The Jewish Home

The Jewish home in Wolomin was an organized cultural–kingdom: thus should be people behave, this should people do, or not do. The children and infants were not philosophers or theologians, did no speculating, but they were far from being spoiled or neglected. The father's authority was tremendous. Young and old all felt the obligations of Judaism. The same fate bound them together and tied them to the same yoke.

The Poles did not always want to encourage us. They wanted to show that the cheder was a medieval educational institution. But it sufficed to show them the people who had grown up in the cheder to silence them. Despite all his prejudices, the Pole had great respect for such Jews as Nehemiah Mandelberg, Dovid Goldshteyn, and others, whom he saw as excellent people with sharp minds and a good deal of wisdom.

In Wolomin the Jews spoke primarily Yiddish. Was this not because they were proud? This was an internalized pride, for which they could give no accounting. It was difficult at first to explain to that same Polish general: how could Yiddish be spoken with pride? But gradually he began to pay attention to my words. In flowery Polish I explained to him that in my home we, too, had spoken Yiddish. Children to whom people speak in a foreign tongue grow up with a poor language, even if the language that people speak to them is rich and beautiful and has created a rich culture. Such children are destined to be emotionally bereft.

I have long known the poetry of Miczkiewicz and Slovotzki, and I showed him what a fine appreciation Yiddish–speaking children can have for poetry, for the beauty of language, and for art and culture in general.

This and similar conversations I had also with other Polish intelligentsia in the shtetl, with the structural engineer Tchaikovsky, with Dr. Czaplitzki, with Cafiovitsch, the head of the merchants' organization, who was later one of the major organizers of the anti–Jewish boycott under the motto "Sva do svega," but who himself bought all his merchandise from the Jewish merchant Yechiel–Mayer Tchachnavyetzki and then sold them to other Polish merchants.

But in those early years no Pole thought about a boycott, although the anti–Semitism that came from Warsaw also affected the Poles of Wolomin. The poison of the Jew–hater Szwientachovski and from Dmovski made its way among the different layers of the Polish population. There were some who had a Russian orientation. In the manifesto of Nikolai Nikolaievitch, the czar's uncle, the high commander of the Russian military, they saw their triumph. The manifesto called the Polish people to help in the war against Germany, the historical enemy of the Slavic people. The manifesto declared that the Polish people should remember the times of Grunwald and strike the German enemy. Then victory would bring the realization of the striving of the Polish people for a national rebirth, with the condition that the rights of the minorities should not be changed.

The Polish National–Democrats interpreted this as an invitation to unify divided Poland. They held that the paragraph about minorities referred to White Russians and Ukrainians. The newspaper "Dva Grasha" came out with an article that argued that the manifesto did not refer to the Jews, who relied only on the good will of the Poles. The news that came from cities where the Russians had triumphed told of pogroms, killings, and destruction. In Congress–Poland stories began to spread about Jewish treason, that Jews were spying on behalf of the Germans, giving them signals and information through secret telephones. Every wire was thought to be a secret telephone. Higher society in Warsaw took these stories and magnified them. These were the same people who before the war incited the Poles with the information that the Jews supported the Russians. Now they screamed that the Jews helped the Germans. Jews, they said, hated the Poles and joined up with all the enemies of Poland.

The Jews of Wolomin Take in Refugees

Over the Jews flowed waves of severe persecutions, expulsions, arrests, hangings, and confinements. Warsaw was full of refugees who fled either from the Russians or from the Germans. This stream of refugees laid a heavy burden on the Warsaw community. Many of the refugees fled to surrounding shtetls, and some came to Wolomin.

The Jews of Wolomin received the refugees with the warmth of merciful people. People arranged housing for them with Jewish families and organized all kinds of help for them.

The Polish Central Committee in Warsaw declined to help Jews, but in Wolomin we were successful in receiving the support of progressive Poles, who understood that the anti–Semitic propaganda the Russians, who eagerly accepted the stories of Jewish espionage and who avenged their defeats on the battlefields.

The secret Zionist committee that had formed in Warsaw, undertook an energetic information project to counter the false rumors. Special envoys were sent to the Russian and Polish progressive intelligence forces to demonstrate how false were the paths on which the Poles had wandered.

With my whole youthful fire, I took part in this activity in my section of Wolomin, helping the refugees and showing the Poles how foolish it was to associate the Jews with espionage. This was no simple thing, because the Polish nationalists believed all the latest rumors. Later they raised alarms that the Jews in Russia damaged the interests of Poland because they believed that Poland was imbued with anti–Semitism. Therefore they said that the Jews would darken Poland's reputation in the eyes of the Left. I sought aid from the followers of Pilsudski, but they were silent. It did not matter that they had fought the Polish nationalists and their Russian orientation. They saw that the rumors of Jews and espionage were successful and turned their attention from the Russians and declared that they were not interested in the activities of Pilsudski's legions, which had been organized in the occupied areas.

When the Germans took Warsaw, the underground organizations emerged and took the rudder, began to openly propagandize their German–Austrian orientation. At first the Jews welcomed the German military, hoping that life would improve. The German language sounded familiar, but soon the Poles accused the Jews of having sympathy for Russia…The German conquerors, however, took no note of the rumors. They were victorious. Officers and generals were quartered in rich Jewish homes. Also subordinate officers also gladly lived with Jews, because they could more easily communicate with the Jews.

After a period of vacillation, the German civil government gave up the thought of turning the Polish Jews into an instrument of Germanization and of political influence for Germany. At the same time, they came to the conclusion that they should fashion a Polish government that should be connected with the part of Europe that was led by Germany. But the Jews had to benefit from favorable conditions for their cultural development and for their activities in the cause of social safety. Thus began the process of handing over power into the hands of the official Polish agents. The first step in this direction was the establishment of self–government in the cities, which was based on the agreement of all the citizens in the country.

As soon as this elective process began, the need for a united front of Poles and Jews was proclaimed. The Jews remembered well the fourth Russian Duma and feared anti–Semitic unrest if they went to the polls alone. They feared the loss of the power that they had gained in various districts. The Zionist organization was for a united front and Jews in many places therefore had to resign from their offices.

So it appeared in Warsaw and also in Wolomin, where I agreed to the urging of the rabbi to run for office and was elected to the Wolomin city council.

The First Jews in the Foundry

The compromises into which the Jews entered did not stop the Poles from their anti–Semitic agitation against Jewish businesses. We therefore often had to be on guard to protect the interests of the Jewish merchants, shopkeepers, and craftsmen.

Also, in the factory I had to fight a battle against the Polish workers, who did not want to allow Jewish workers in the foundry. They acted against six Jews, whom I had put to work and who encountered stubborn opposition from the Poles.

I quickly called a meeting of all the workers. Some of the them were really nervy and repeated the words of the anti–Semitic agitators about the danger that confronted Poland as a result of the large number of Jews who control country's economy and displace the Poles from their positions. But there were some who supported my appearance. I wholeheartedly rejected every indication of discrimination, pointed out the senselessness of the anti–Semitic words and rumors that were used by malevolent politicians. I made them understand as clearly as possible that I stood with the clever and progressive workers who understood how awful such malevolent anti–Semitism was and who will fight with all their strength for the rights of Jewish laborers.

It often happened that when the police arrested a Jew, who was caught smuggling meat to Warsaw or doing some other crime, the police would take further action and lead a home inspection. Too often there were false arrests and I was called on to intervene. Usually I succeeded in convincing the powers that be of the arrested one's innocence.

It was not easy dealing with the Poles all the times I worked with them. "The Jews are working with the Germans," Markovski wanted to convince me. "They dealt with them. They have good relations with the Germans. They don't fight for a free Poland." But he had to be silent and roll his eyes when I showed him the woods that Polish workers had cut down for the German and helped them load the wood onto the cars of long trains. The wood was going to the front for German military use, for the German rear. Thousands of Polish workers were thereby employed and no one objected.

The success of the Russian Revolution, the overthrow of the Romanovs and the declaration of the temporary Russian government that it recognized Polish self–government hastened the process of turning over power in the country to the Poles. They formed a Polish government with Jan Kochoszewski [?] at its head. His hatred of Jews dated from the times when thanks to Jewish voices he lost the election to the Fourth Duma. He quickly announced that a solution had to be found to the Jewish problem. But he avoided clarifying how the search for a solution should be conducted. But we felt sure that the solution would not be to the good of the Jews.

Meanwhile the American Expeditionary Army came to France, and Germany, after a hard struggle, surrendered. The new German government freed Pilsudski from the Magdeburg Prison and he returned to Warsaw. Soon the signal was given for a decisive action. In Lublin was proclaimed the establishment of a Polish government as the culmination of a temporary regime that was made up of socialists and workers. In Warsaw, Pilsudski assumed power and mobilized the members of the secret military organization P.A.V. and disarmed the German soldiers. They did not resist and voluntarily gave their arms to Pilsudski's followers. There were cases when individual German soldiers surrendered their weapons in the streets of Warsaw to young men that they encountered by chance, even minors, who made fun of them. But already in the early days of the Polish liberation, Poles began beating Jews in the streets of Warsaw, and this activity spread even to Wolomin.

"Beat the Jews!"

The organizers of the anti–Jewish excesses wanted to show the Jews that they were in their hands and they could no longer count on any strength to protect them. The Jews in Wolomin, just like the Jews in Warsaw, were not prepared for this development and had not organized any self–defense, and the Polish youth simply ran wild, openly grabbing Jewish pedestrians and beating them. Their motto was, "Long live Pilsudski, beat the Jews.!"

Among the representatives of the new power in Wolomin were followers of Pilsudski and the Endecja [the National Democratic Party, a rightist, anti–Semitic party], and there was the danger that both sides would compete in oppressing the Jews. The mood was strained. The Endecja screamed that Bolshevism was led by Jews. The Poles who had been repatriated from Russia, told frightening tales about the Jewish Bolsheviks, and these stories further poisoned the air in the Jewish cities and shtetls. People felt this particularly sharply in Wolomin, where the Endecja had special strength.

The Jews in Wolomin felt oppressed, discriminated against, and unsure about the future. Markowski, the rightist leader in the national council, although he and I had coexisted well personally, did everything he could politically to further the aims of his party. He gave a clear accounting that in the air was the distinct possibility of a civil war between Pilsudski's socialist followers and the Endecja, who had mobilized all their strength, called mass gatherings, and in their propaganda stressed the Jewish moment. The conquering powers supported Paderewski and Dmowski because they feared that Pilsudski might follow the path of the Russian Revolution.

Finally this convinced the Pilsudski camp to enter a compromise with Paerewski, Dmowski, and Korfanty. Maratshewski's government resigned and in its place came Paderewski, who had gained the confidence of the Americans and they had promised him help. The socialists and the radical peasants had pulled back. A few of Pilsudski's followers remained in the government.

This compromise also had an effect on the attitude toward the Jews. I then intended that the Polish councilors of various parties, like others in the Polish intelligentsia who had influence over the populace, should receive information that was not published in the Polish newspapers, though one could read it between the lines. I directed much attention to gathering reports from the foreign delegations from the conquering countries who sought to help Poland both economically and militarily. Among them were influential Jews, and they raised the questions of equal rights for the Jewish minority. This restrained the anti–Semitic tendencies in the government and in the Polish parliament.

The Endecja in Wolomin, who in the beginning had spoken openly about suppressing the rights of the Jews, came to understand that in these new conditions their slogan was out–of–date.

Battle for Jewish Rights

From the first days of my work in the Wolomin national–council I therefore fought for Jewish rights. I missed no opportunity to speak out about any decree that was directed against the Jewish inhabitants to weaken their status and to eject them from their already poor economic position.

There were, however, moments when I was helpless, especially when the decrees came from above, from the government in Warsaw, which feared that the shtetls, where Jews were in the majority, would cause power in the national council to fall into Jewish hands. The government therefore spread the idea of giving more to the little villages that were totally Polish. The Endecja in Wolomin took up this idea so that the Jews would have less representation in the national council. From a half, it became a third.

There arose a problem of the "LItvaks." This is what people called the Jews from the Pale of Settlement in Russia that the Tsarist government had "imposed on" Poland, joining them together. The Endecja created this myth about a hundred thousand such Jews in Poland. Later they began to believe in it and they infected all the other parties with it.

Also in Wolomin Markowitsch's and Wojciechowski's people began to badger the Jews who came from Russia and sought the right to become citizens. Among the most active was Wojciechowski, former postmaster general in Wolomin.

Several times I had to intervene in such these matters. The problem also existed in Warsaw and other cities. It resonated as well outside the country, and thanks to the help of influential Jews pressure was put on Poland to accept the supplementary treaty along with the peace treaty. This treaty established as a principle that the Jews, who were citizens of the parts of the kingdoms that Poland had taken over, had the right to become Polish citizens.

When I met with representatives of the Polish parties, the Endecja and the socialists, they tried to take out their anger on me. They often repeated the accusations of the Polish side that the Jews had besmirched the name of Poland to foreigners. The Jews were guilty of making people regard Poland as a backward nation, without European culture, without a national tradition:

a land that did not know how to treat properly its minorities. They accused me of being one of those who promoted stories of anti–Semitism and pogroms.

Dr. Tschoplitzki often said to me: "Poles are a magnanimous people, and you Jews accuse us of things that we don't do. You make a problem out of every incident and raise a cry throughout the world. You live here in Wolomin as if in the Garden of Eden. Who bothers you?"

My policy in discussions with the Polish community leaders was not to allow them to make me lose my poise or become angry. Fully under control and with a hint of a smile I answered him: "I hold you to your word, Doctor. You will soon have the opportunity to show your magnanimity in relation to the Jews."

The supplementary treaty, which Poland was forced to accept, was not published in the legal code, so that it should not have internal legal power and could not be used as a foundation for the equal rights of the Jews. The majority of the Sejm [the Polish parliament] twisted the idea and made a formal ruling: whereas the "Litvaks," as they called the naÃ¯ve Polish Jews, had settled in Poland at the time of the Russian occupation, for them Poland was a foreign land, occupied, and therefore they had to register in special evidence–books in order to demonstrate that they acknowledged the distinctiveness of Poland. If they did not do so, they thereby declared their foreignness in the country and therefore could not become citizens. The current minister of the interior, Wojciechowski, from the peasant leaders in Congress Poland, wanted to create a stratum of Jews who were not citizens but residents who had all the duties but none of the rights of citizens.

Also people tried to create difficulties for me because I was a Russian citizen and therefore they wanted to close my factory in Wolomin, regardless of the fact that the place, together with the factory building, belonged to my father, who named it after his son–in–law, Wolf Krafman. When the war broke out, my brother–in–law moved the machinery to Ekaterinoslav, which is today called Dnieptopetrovsk. On this basis, when I came of age I took over the factory and established the iron foundry.

The Disputed Franchise

After the Poles took power, the Wolomin village leader Orlovsky did not want to give me the franchise for the foundry. One should note that in general Orlovsky, along with his assistant Fiatrovsky, was tolerant toward the Jews.

For a long time I suffered with this problem of the law, for anyone who was occupied with community activities for three years automatically became a Polish citizen, with all the rights of a citizen. So my many years of activity in Wolomin came to my aid, as did another consideration, that I had chaired a special commission. I was awarded the franchise.

The Jewish deputies in the Sjem led a spirited campaign against this law, but they won nothing except a little relief. In Wolomin the Endecja several times tried to raise this problem in the national assembly. But to my aid came Dr. Tschoplitski, from whom I had asked for the Polish magnanimity of which he had boasted.

The question of citizenship was left for later, after the peace treaty with Soviet Russia, according to which Poland took parts of the Pale of Settlement, in the north and south of Congress Poland. The same Tschoplitski said to me, half–proudly, half–sarcastically, "You see, six hundred thousand â€˜Litvaks" have become Polish citizens…Will the Jews appreciate the generosity of the Polish people?"

The terror against the Jews, which began with the awakening of Poland, actually never stopped. The Halertshikes [?] would attack Jews and shave or pull out their beards and side–curls, often along with pieces of flesh. All signs pointed to a "hidden hand" that organized such happenings. The police took no action and did not defend the Jews. The higher powers also took no strong measures. They denied that these were organized attacks. They called them "pranks" by soldiers

Such things happened also in the streets of Wolomin, in the depot, and in the trains. There were days when it was dangerous for a Jew with a beard and side–curls to appear in the street.

When the war with the Red army began, the affliction became worse. Anti–Semitic agitation in the military was rampant and had as its purpose to portray the Russian Bolshevist as a Jew or as someone sent and supported by the Jews. Trotsky became the symbol of Russian communism. The Polish soldiers who passed through Wolomin distributed caricatures of Trotsky as a

Mephisto sitting on a pile of heads and smiling sarcastically and self–satisfied. In Wolomin, as in many other towns, there were reverberations from the shooting of the Plotzk rabbi as a spy.

False Accusations

Once again stories against the Jews began to circulate among Wolomin's Polish population, stories connecting them to the enemy through underground telephones for transmitting military secrets. Again people concocted rumors about Jewish traitors and about the joy with which Jews greeted the knowledge that the Red army would take all of Poland and would come to Wolomin. The Polish councilmen still tried to be considerate and in my presence did not repeat the accusations. Still, I felt the pogrom–feeling. It created a mob psychology, which affected everyone: to rob, to burn, to murder. They knew that people did so in other towns.

In those days I gave an accounting of the great danger. There were some people who begged me that I should not get too involved, that I should stay for a few weeks in Warsaw. In the big city, they thought, there would be less danger. But I felt that my presence in Wolomin was necessary and I tried to engage more with the Polish community leaders and direct our conversations toward the situation of the Jewish population. At first it was difficult for them to say openly to me what they thought about the Jews, but gradually they opened their mouths and spoke about settling accounts. I listened attentively to the different variations of the collective slanders and malice. From contempt and derision they turned to anger and threats.

Their response was no surprise to me and I never lost my poise, but calmly and in a dignified way I showed them that typifying a people as traitors and only secondarily as moral is arbitrary, and also that even good people give little thought to how much they offend with such awkward generalizations. When I began to list the names of Wolomin Jews whom everyone knew to be excellent and moral people, some brought up Bialystok, among other cities in White Russia, where Jews shot at Polish soldiers or poured hot water from the roofs onto passing soldiers.

Collective slander and collective malice were a curse at that time. Collective malice requires a collective enemy. The whole Jewish people was considered responsible for the defeats of the Polish military. Hatred is hooliganism moralized, and hooliganism is in the first rank of tools to be used against better people, against a weaker community. If a people form a cult of hooliganism, they initiate their own downfall, no matter how large and strong their country may be.

All of these thoughts I expressed in my conversations with the Poles, among whom were stubborn members of the Endecja, and they lowered their heads. One of them tried to use the usual anti–Semitic trope "If all Jews were like you…" I told them how hateful it is to hear such words from educated people who see with their own eyes the lives of their Jewish neighbors, who would take part, with all their strength, in the struggle against a common enemy. In Warsaw, young Jewish students would willingly have joined the Polish army, but the regiments declared that they would not fight alongside the Jews, whom they considered as communists and enemies of Poland.

Discrimination

The state of Jewish security in the first years of the new Poland was quite bad. In the Sejm the Jewish representatives, led by Yitzchak Grinboym, conducted an unceasing struggle against the anti–Semitic policies of the government. After the victory over the Red army, the anti–Semitism was a bit weakened; the terror inflicted by the army and by mobs declined. But it did not end completely. The anti–Semites redoubled their efforts to expel Jews from their economic positions.

This was all reflected, in a smaller way, in Wolomin. Such high taxes were imposed on Jewish merchants that they could barely pay them. Such discrimination was overt. Jewish merchants and shopkeepers were audited, suffered confiscations, and were placed in the highest bracket for paying taxes.

Polish officials did all of this under the guise of alleged legality. Seeing what kind of catastrophes this behavior could cause, I devoted myself intensively to studying the laws and administrative writings so that I could fight against every violation of the laws by the officials in the various government and municipal offices. In a number of cases I was successful. If I had not known how to conduct this business considerately, to give attention to the pitiful state of the Jewish merchant, I would have demanded that the officials stick strictly to the laws and by–laws, which often contained paragraphs devoted to the welfare of the Jews, ordering that Jews be treated no worse than Christian merchants.

In the course of my work in the Wolomin city council, I stood by the principles and aims that I had set forth: to fight against discrimination against the Jewish residents, to oppose unjust taxes, to look after the needs of the Jewish populace, to support Jewish institutions in the same proportion as the Polish. From the beginning I did not want to allow my work to become mere intercession. In the name of what was right, of what the constitution had guaranteed to minorities, I fought against every individual injustice and against injustice in general.

The Sejm and the Polish government were forced to include in the constitution paragraphs that had been imposed by the peace treaty. But as soon as they had done so, their practical interpretations turned those paragraphs into empty words. So it was with the election laws, which had not limited the rights of the Jews, but the election districts were divided in such a way that the Jews could have no more than four or five representatives in the Sejm. If the Jews formed a bloc with the other minorities in order to ensure a larger representation in proportion to their population in the country, they would have provoked the anger and hatred of the people of Wolomin. "You have shown again that you are our enemies"–Markovski said to me when the press published the treaty. Even more bitter was the anger when in the first election for the Polish president the bloc united the parties on the left. As a result, Narutowicz, who was later murdered, was elected.

Jewish Life–A Thorn in the Eyes of Jew Haters

In those days, when I appeared in the national council, the Endecja councilmen greeted me with anger and complaints, yelling that it was unacceptable that a minority, supported by Jews, should rule in Poland. This was an assault on the higher interests of the Polish people.

"You are blind with hatred," I answered them, "and you do not recognize how the hatred harms yourselves and the interests of the country." I illustrated my arguments with facts both from my town and from other cities in Poland where Jews helped to build the country, the industry, the whole economy.

However, in those circumstances anti–Semitism was the deciding factor in all issues that related to Jews. Actually, the higher authorities were aware of the great harm that anti–Semitism caused in both the political and economic development of the country. There was even a moment when they sought a way to bring about a modus Vivendi with the Jews and they began to hold negotiations with the Jewish representatives in the Sejm, but they were incapable of upholding the small assurances that they had given. This took place in the later years. In the meantime, anti–Semitism flourished in all its forms and embittered the lives of the Jews. Even more than in the big cities, it was felt by the Jews in the little shtetls, where Jewish life was a thorn in the eye of the enemies of Israel.

Together with learning the laws and administrative writings I also learned the story of the Polish economy, and in my presentations I often had occasion to cite examples from this history. I used every opportunity to enlighten the Polish intelligentsia in Wolomin about how much Poland should take an interest in the abilities of its Jewish citizens. In the eighteenth century Poland was the most backward country in Europe. An exception was the Balkan countries that were under Turkish rule. Poland was backward even in comparison to Russia, which was further from central Europe. By the end of the eighteenth century, Russia had its own industry and a class of industrial bourgeoisie and rich merchants. The great merchant class had extended its activities into the southern regions that Russia had taken from Turkey. At the same time, Poland was mired in internal political conflicts, suffering a moral and cultural decline, and weakened militarily, the rebellions of the Ukrainians had continued without cease since the Chmielnitzki rebellion in the mid–seventeenth century. Over eighty–five percent of the population of Poland was engaged in agricultural work. Not more than five percent was engaged in industry, business, and production. The remaining ten percent were in the military, the civil service, or the clergy, along with loafers, prisoners, and beggars. In economic terms, the most backward part of Poland was the Warsaw area. The greatest economic area there was alcohol production.

In that era, Wolomin was still a village. Since over thirty–six percent of the Jewish population in the duchy of Warsaw lived in villages, occupied with business, with buildings and workshops, teachers and clergy were not more than two percent of the employed. The situation of the peasants in the village and of the workers in the city was miserable. A feudal lifestyle ruled the land. However, rather than freeing themselves from the feudal regime, freeing up the creative strengths of the country, using Jewish energy, Jewish dynamism, their talents and connections with Western Europe, the Poles went to war with…the Jews.

"Are not the Jews, then, the most appropriate target for a joint war for Poland's economic development?" I asked the Wolomin Endecja councilmen and showed them the great usefulness that Jews brought in the era of industrialization of Poland and the rapid development of commerce in the nineteenth century. The economy at that time was almost separate from politics, and although the Jews at that time were not citizens with full rights, that did not prevent them from taking a leading role in industrial and financial developments, which played a central role in the economic development of all of Congress Poland. The Jews were the first to bring the initiative, the talent, and also international connections that helped mobilize the necessary capital for developing the country's economy.

"See what the Jews have made of Warsaw," I shouted in a discussion with the Endecjas. "From the most backward city in Europe it has become one of the most beautiful. Anyone who knows Polish history knows how great a role the Jews have played in the development of Poland."

They knew that this was the truth. They saw it, too, in Wolomin, but jealousy and hate were stronger than logic. After the war, Poland had become weak and poor and subject to great dangers. And it really needed Jewish initiative.

A Home in Bleak Fields

At that time Jewish refugees began to stream to Poland from the Ukraine and central Russia. The greatest stream flowed toward Warsaw, but the city was closed to them. The city council feared the influx of Jewish refugees, even though they were only in transit, with the intention of continuing their flight, mostly to America and South America.

The leaders of the Jewish community in Warsaw felt responsible for the exile of these Jewish refugees, but despite all their efforts, they could not break through the wall of hatred. In regard to the smaller towns, too, the Endecja members in the national assembly stood opposed to the admission of Jewish refugees from Russia.

In an attempt to counter this attitude in the Wolomin council, the community leaders in Warsaw asked me to undertake a project to allow the refugees entrance into Wolomin.

I quickly began to deal with the Endecja councilmen, expecting that the greatest opposition would come from them. Markowski, whom I approached first because I knew he had the greatest influence, at first angrily opposed my proposal. His first words were, "What? We don't already have enough Zhid–commies?"

It seemed like I was confronting an iron wall of Endecja hatred for Jews and Bolsheviks, a wall that could not be broken through. At that moment I felt like I wanted to leave him and seek understanding from other councilmen and to form with them a majority voice in the national assembly, where I intended to place the matter on the agenda. But our conversation went on. I spoke of the exile of the eternal wanderers who could find no friendly welcome on Polish soil. Despite the fact that they were fleeing from Communist oppression, people called them communists, not understanding that they were united in the battle against the communist camp and they wanted no more that a place to rest as they fled from the Ukrainian murderers, to regain their strength, to take care of formalities and then continue wandering, seeking a coast where they could anchor and build a home in bleak fields.

Suddenly I noticed a muscle move on his military countenance. But he remained silent. I decided to appeal to his practical sense. At that time in Wolomin several Christian businesses had opened dealing in food and other commodities. They benefited from a variety of privileges, sponsored by the Endecja, in an attempt to supplant the Jewish merchants and shopkeepers. This attempt did not succeed because the Christian merchants could not compete with the Jews and the Polish customers preferred to buy at the lower prices offered by Jews. I depicted for him the revival that such a mass of refugees would bring to commerce. They would come not to settle, not to open their own businesses, but while they were here they would buy from the local merchants and would be a gold mine for the local economy.

After a longer discussion, I finally got his agreement, but when the matter was discussed in the city council, to my great surprise, opposition came from the side of the socialist councilmen of the PPS. Their opposition to admitting refugees was motivated by the fear of shortages that would be caused by the influx of so many people.

They were, however, in the minority, while a majority of voices agreed to allow the Jewish refugees to come to Wolomin.

Jewish Refugees Bring New Life

Several thousand refugees thus came to Wolomin, and the Jews welcomed them with the greatest warmth. Many lived in houses that had been abandoned during the World War. The people of Wolomin welcomed others into their own apartments and shared their homes with them, doing whatever they could to help the newcomers find a temporary rest.

It became clear that that rest would not last a few weeks or months. Everyone estimated that it would last for years, until they received papers that would allow them to move on. We, the leaders of the Jewish community in Wolomin, did everything we could to fashion a favorable environment.

Among the refugees who came to Wolomin were many interesting people who had a long history of communal work. Among them were some who had fought for Jewish rights in Czarist Russia and, later, among the Bolsheviks, sacrificing themselves to their work.

During those years when these Jews were in Wolomin, they brought life to the shtetl. Their experience was instructive for the Jewish leaders in Wolomin. From them we learned everyday wisdom, tact, and enthusiasm to revive the economy of our shtetl.

I can't remember everyone's name, but even now I remember many conversations, descriptions and tales about their experiences and about their community work. I, like the other community leaders in Wolomin, learned much from them. One of the leading Zionists from Russia described for me a scene that played out at a conference of Jewish community leaders soon after the February Revolution in 1917: the first democratic government had just rescinded all the restrictions and decrees against the Jews. It seemed that a peaceful time of independence was beginning for the Jewish population. In this context, one of the participants in the conference declared, "Now our work is done!" But immediately one of the Russian Zionist called out from his seat with full determination, "For us the work is only now beginning!"

The community leaders of Wolomin knew how right that Zionist activist was. The Zionists were the first victims of the ongoing stormy developments. At first the Bolsheviks were preoccupied by their own problems, and it seemed that they gave no thought to the Zionists, but almost immediately there began a war against the Jewish counter–revolution, and attacks commenced against Zionists throughout Russia, everywhere that Jews lived. The greatest fury was directed against the Jews in Moscow and Kiev. The Commissariat for Nationalistic Questions, which was then under the leadership of Stalin, distributed a circular in which Hebrew was declared a counter–revolutionary language. It was forbidden for children and young people to learn Hebrew. Systematic accusations against the Zionists as "counter–revolutionaries" and as spies for England began to appear. House searches and arrests were carried out. All Zionist organizations in the Kiev district were shut down. Zionist leaders were sentenced to long prison terms, even without trials.

Committee Leaders

One of the refugees who settled here in Wolomin was Greenberg, who, in the time of Kerensky's government, was the head of the community in Kiev. When I think about him, I picture a man who had powerfully and for many years immersed himself in Jewish tradition and community activities.. He was full of Jewish wisdom and Jewish folklore. He was completely suited to lead the Jewish refugee committee that we had organized in Wolomin. However, since he lacked Polish citizenship, he could not serve as the leader of any organization. It was therefore necessary that I serve as the official chairman of the committee, but in fact he was the soul of the whole committee. His brother was, on his wife's side, a relative of the banker Shereshevski, and he remained in Wolomin for his whole life. His daughter was the famous singer Vera Green.

Working together with Greenberg was for me a university education. His mind was always awake and active and he was a total Jew, a total mentsch, with a thousand examples of how our ancestors survived troubles, persecutions, and evil decrees, how they lived and thought. He quickly recognized our Polish neighbors, particularly the ways in which they lurked around Jews like vicious wolves in the night. He had a fighting spirit, which seemed to hide under the comforting Jewish folk sayings that fell from his lips. He reacted to everything and had no fear for his life. Through all his days he struggled heroically with life, with the historic hatred for the Jewish people, with the difficult conditions of the bloody revolution, with the Bolshevik hatred for Judaism and with the anti–Semitism that flourished among the Polish people.

Among the leading figures on the committee was also Gorenshteyn, the former community head in Proskurov, a Jewish with a quick mind, cautious but trusting, with a warm Jewish heart.

There were also among the refugees yet other dear Jews with a developing flair for community work. Unfortunately I cannot remember their names, but the memory of their self–sacrificing generosity still lives in my memory. Even more than I recall the hearts, the thoughts, and the deeds of these people, I know that I bound myself to them; and this binding gave wings to my work and my struggle that I undertook to arrange their affairs and to shape the proper atmosphere for their life in the shtetl.

Soon after the first weeks of the refugees' arrival, one of the parties in the city council demanded that the refugees be expelled. They were motivated by the scarcities of goods, which really existed. The influx of thousands of people resulted in scarcities of products and of articles of daily use. The merchants consequently raised prices, which first affected the workers. There was a first hint that there would be unrest in the shtetl.

And it is also true that among the Jewish poor murmuring and complaints began because of the scarcities. But soon after the first conversations with them, everyone quickly came to an understanding and the complaints ceased.

The First Cooperative

We therefore had to come up with a plan to fight those scarcities. At a meeting of the refugee committee, Greenberg proposed a plan to found a cooperative that would take smaller profits and in this way dictate the prices at the markets, not allowing the prices to be raised on necessities. As a proponent of cooperation, I found Greenberg's proposal close to my heart.

Gifted with both initiative and energy, Greenberg undertook to make his thought a reality, and in a short time the cooperative was established.

The shtetl soon revived. Money regained its value. The murmuring and complaining of the Polish workers and the poor came to a halt. On the other hand, the Polish owners of the food shops went around with bowed heads, though a little while earlier they had made a profit by raising prices. Now they had to lower the prices because of the cooperative. Now the cooperative dealt in excellent products, which brought in customers.

In the shtetl people quickly recognized the excellent quality of the products, the outstanding merchandise. The cooperative grew, and the bigger the turnover, the easier it became to lower prices.

The effect of the cooperative was that life in Wolomin became easier, as it was in the nearby city of Warsaw..

Warsaw at that time was not only a center for small industry and workshops, in which many Jews worked. At the same time, Warsaw had become the center through which nearly half of the business of Congress Poland was conducted. The large Jewish merchants used Jewish employees, who, like the Jewish workers, were badly paid and were a lot less expensive than Polish workers.

It seemed different in Wolomin, where Jews worked in all the factories and were treated just like the Polish workers. Morally they profited from the full confidence of the factory owners.

In Warsaw I was often required to negotiate with the owners, who did not willingly take on Jewish workers and who often dismissed workers from their positions in order to take on Polish workers. They thought the Jewish worker was too smart and calculated the profits of the factory, seeking to lighten the labor and increase the wages at the expense of the boss, while showing no humility. The Christian workers showed respect for the boss not only in the factory where they worked but also when they met in the street, bowing and stepping aside, while the Jew offered not even a "Good morning."

More than once I became irritated when I heard such words about Jews. From my experiences in Wolomin I knew the Jews to be industrious workers. The Jewish factory owners in Wolomin did not expect humility from either their Jewish or their Polish workers, but they received respect and gratitude. The Wolomin Jews understood how to estimate the earnings of the Jewish factory owners in terms of reviving industry in the shtetl and helping to create the impression of growth and construction.

Things grew worse with the Polish workers and overseers, who often showed their anti–Semitism, their ill will toward their Jewish colleagues. The overseers did not want to teach skills to the Jewish workers. We did not know how to force the overseers, because they often became threatening due to the shortage of specialists.

A special problem was working on Shabbos. But in my time there was not a in Wolomin a single Jew who had to work in the factory on Shabbos. The boss of the factory created no difficulties. It hit him in his pocketbook, because he was left with no more than five workers.

Certainly the stream of refugees, whom the Polish populace had so feared, brought with them a revival. Small businesses and workshops developed, which strengthened our ties with Warsaw.

Restored Houses and New Houses

In Wolomin at that time there were many ruined buildings that were abandoned by the Germans and the Russians. People renovated and restored them, and there were also many new houses which were constructed by Jewish contractors. The Jewish entrepreneurial spirit was aroused. Wolomin excelled also in an awakening business life. There were a variety of associations and institutions to help those in need.

There were also a few Zionists, but at first they lacked organized activities. They existed as if in the era of "shivas Tzion," the first form of the modern Zionist movement, which the "Litvaks" brought to Warsaw. A few Jews in Wolomin read the "Hazefirah," which Nahum Sokolov edited. In the beis–hamedrish there was even a conflict between the Chasidim and a few young men who were taken with Zionism.

At that time I often met with Yitzchak Grinboym, with Hartman, with Dr. Levita and we spoke about organizing Zionist activities in Wolomin. Their words are engraved in my memory: that the struggle of Polish Jewry is in fact a struggle against retreat, which had no prospect of winning, and the highest priority is not to allow ourselves to be crushed by Polish anti–Semitism. The war of Polish Jewry is a Zionist war. If we wanted to create a sovereign fatherland in Eretz Yisroel, we had to lead the struggle of Polish Jewry, which was the largest Jewish settlement in Europe, and therefore we had to fight for the national goals of the Polish Jew, not allowing him to be overcome by Polish anti–Semitism.

Consequently I proceeded to lead in organizing and cementing the Zionistically inclined Jews in Wolomin, both old and young. The organization went by the name of "Tarbus."

The First Community Election

In 1925, when the order went out that Jews should conduct elections for the community, I received official instructions from Yitzchak Grinboym to organize the election activities in Wolomin with the goal of strengthening the Zionist influence in the community.

Like a disciplined member, I undertook the task with my whole youthful energy and idealism. At a time when Zionism was already strong in Warsaw, lively and vital, our organization in Wolomin was poor enough. Most of the Jewish population were sympathetic to the Chasidim, to the religious Jews, and the Bund. For them, Zionism was a movement that had rebelled against the reality in which they felt anchored. Truly, there were some who showed courtesy and even respect to our call for redemption, for great deeds. But they did not perceive in us the strength to realize those deeds, and they therefore clung to the old ways of life.

In Wolomin, that way of life was orthodox. The whole administration was in the hands of the rabbi and a group of leading citizens who helped him keep the books. No one controlled them and no one was interested in how the municipal administration was conducted.

Being occupied with the merchants' association that I had formed, I took almost no interest in the municipal administration. Chasidic Jews also belonged to the merchants' association. On the managing committee were outstanding leading citizens, like Shpiegelman, the owner of a tannery, Itshe–Meyer Markusfeld, a wood–merchant, and others from the Ger and Alexander Chasidim who belonged to the Agudas Yisroel. From the misnagdim and the unaffiliated, the most notable was R' Nehamiah

Mandelberg, an excellent man to whose words people paid close attention. The Ger Chasidim had the most influence in town, who were led by R' Moyshe Grodzhitzki. From the Alexander Chasidim there was Mattes Teyblus.

When the election activities began, they were thoroughly discussed in our merchants' association. We had to make clear that it was essential to elect people with a worldly education who would be capable of representing us externally, so that the community could present a disciplined strength, which would reflect the Jewish settlement in the town.

I began to enlist active Zionists in community affairs, but meanwhile I was notified that in the beis–hamedrash certain leading citizens intended to nominate me as a candidate for the community administration. At first they met much opposition from the congregation, whose opposition was motivated by the fact that I was not religious, that I violated Shabbos.

My supporters, however, did not give up and demanded that the opposition bring proof that I violated Shabbos. No one could bring such proof. No one had ever seen me violate Shabbos in public. From my earliest years, I had been careful not to offend religious feelings.

This struggle went on behind my back. No one approached me officially. Only later did I learn the course of the roiling action that my backers conducted without my knowledge. A delegation travelled to consult with Rabbi R' Itshe–Meyer Levin, who was involved with the politics of the Ger Chasidim. The Ger Chasidim consulted with him about whether they should nominate me as a member of the council despite my being a Zionist.

R' Yitzchak–Meyer Levin, I was given to understand, could not decide on a clear response. On one side the Chasidim urged the usefulness of choosing me for the Jewish populace and for the Jewish merchants. But on the other side it was difficult for him to give a clear approval to select a Zionist in the community. He therefore hinted, "See what the other Jews do and do the same thing."

This was a hint that on the part of the rabbi there was no objection to choosing me as representative on the Wolomin Jewish council.

Thus came the first election for the Jewish community, the first organized community in Wolomin. For the first time, the Wolomin Jews were able to choose their own representatives, four representatives and a chairman, , who would guide the economic and community life. The representatives, with the approval of the rabbi, chose me as chairman.

Of the ten thousand Jews who lived in Wolomin, about three thousand could vote in the election. All who took part in the Jewish life of Poland found a warm welcome in Wolomin, and then came the influx of Russian Jews, most of whom were energetic, motivated, and good exemplars and gave the shtetl color and dynamism.

Around Wolomin were many villages that constituted a large population who, during the war, lacked clothing and shoes, as well as other necessities. Wolomin's Jews became the suppliers for the peasant population and also the buyers of their agricultural products.

The First Zionist Organization

The first Zionist organization, the Tarbus, worked hard to create a real community among the Jews of Wolomin. It undertook cultural activities. Young people held spirited debates about problems in literature and culture and over national questions. Speakers came from Warsaw and delivered lectures that interested the Jewish young people. They organized evenings when there were lectures from members of the Keren Hayisod or from other Zionist organizations. Mr. Einshteyn from Keren Hayisod in Warsaw also came.

Initiating these activities in the community was not easy. We established a meeting house on Mikveh Street and gradually began to integrate all segments of the Jewish community.

The work appeared to be more difficult and complicated than we had thought. I had the idea of creating an ad hoc group of ten members who were recommended by the council members. Although they had no public voice, they gave a greater sense of cooperation. These ad hoc representatives demonstrated community responsibility. At their head were Moyshe Grodzhitzki, Mattes Teyblum, Shpiegelman, and Nehamiah Mandelberg.

The new community managing committee paid special attention to matters of hygiene. Its first focus was the mikveh, which we undertook to reconstruct and beautify.

The Talmud Torah

Another focal point was the Talmud Torah, which was led by Goldvasser. He was one of the five teachers at that time. Like one of the ten ad hoc committee members, Goldvasser understood how to consider the special problems that confronted the Talmud Torah, and he always met the committee with open ears and willingness to help them understand. Goldvasser's daughter lives in Israel.

This willingness to clarify the problems of Jewish life in the shtetl was also felt in other areas. It also created a working relationship with the clergy. Monthly payments were established for the rabbi and the slaughterers. The rabbi, R' Volf Bergazen, often took part in our meetings and showed interest in our work of determining the variety of problems.

Linas Hatzedek and Bikur Cholim

Like all Jewish shtetls, Wolomin had a whole array of helping organizations that displayed a characteristic warmth. At the head of such organizations was Amchal–Yidn, who showed such warmth in their work. So, too, was the group "Linas ha–tzedek." The members of this group went nightly to visit the ill and care for their needs, from prescriptions to the need for a bed. One should not forget that many people in Wolomin lived in wretched apartments. Members of the group went to those apartments to bring aid to the ill.

Other touching help activities were conducted by the groups "Bikur cholim," "Hachnesses kallah," and "Hachnesses–orchim." Their organizers and members were simple people with warm Jewish hearts. They often came to the community seeking help for others, and although the community's budget could not support every item, I did all I could to support the poor. I promoted in the council subsidies for institutions and support for poor individuals.

In principle, every Jewish inhabitant was supposed to pay a special tax for the community. So, too, did those who did not live in Wolomin but had real property. Those people actually did pay. At the same time, we exempted from paying those who were known to work for a living.

In Wolomin, people used to give a great deal of charity to Jewish causes and donate to Jewish societies. Writers would arrive or rabbis with their treatises, and no one ever went away empty handed.

Factories and Glassworks

In Wolomin there were factories and glassworks that belonged to Jewish owners, and we would levy heavy taxes on them. For the most part, they showed understanding of our needs and paid regularly. But there were also cases of opposition, when some refused to meet the obligations that the community had laid on them. Then I had to intervene personally, to speak to their consciences, to show them the responsibilities of the community for those who had arrived in need. I cannot remember a single time when my words fell on deaf ears.

There was in a Wolomin a glasswork factory that was co–owned by Flanzreich and Ringlevski, whose name was really Ringleblum. During the war he had worked as my agent. Later on he met a Polish governess. There was mutual love. He abandoned Judaism and married her. And it paid off for him. Her father was the director of the state monopoly and gave his son–in–law the concession for making bottles for the monopoly.

For this business of collecting bottles, Ringleblum–Ringlevski took on as his partner Yishayahu Flalnzreich. The business went well. They made a lot of money and eventually bought the glassworks that had been standing empty. Other glassworks followed.

In collecting the community tax from Flanzreich, we encountered a big problem. His annual tax amounted to three thousand zlotys, which he claimed was too much. His partner in the glassworks was the apostate Ringlevski, who did not belong to the Jewish community, and therefore the entire amount fell to him.

Flanzreich was the director and owner of the huge factory. He, a native of Vilna, brought up in Moscow, had organized in Wolomin a huge factory before the First World War. When the war broke out, they moved back to Moscow. Later they returned, and as a result of our discussions, he showed great understanding of business matters. That understanding was strengthened when we began to undertake Zionist activities.

Zalkin was then the owner of the tannery, Shpiegelman and Lifshitz of the brickyard, and there were others whom I taxed heavily, having explained to them how great was their duty to bear this yoke for the needy in the Jewish community.

Understand that this did not come easily to me. At first I encountered opposition because this was such a big demand as an addition to the taxes from the city, from the government. Their opposition came as no surprise, but I explained to them how vital it was to complete the building of the Talmud Torah, which needed several thousand zlotys.

I devoted a lot of attention to Flanzreich. I succeeded in having a talk with him, because I had known his father, had done business with them when they had dealt in scrap iron and cast iron that they sold to the factories that had been established in 1916. They helped their father with his business.

They were the most respectable merchants of cast iron. And surely that respectability helped him advance, until he was quite rich and built up his partnership with Ringlevski.

I remember that we once met on the train to Warsaw. He sat down in the car next to me and began to complain that it was not fair for the community organization to tax him so heavily. He appealed to my sense of justice and asked me to put myself in his place, since his apostate partner would not contribute to the Jewish community.

I let him talk and then gave him to understand the difficult economic situation of the Jewish community in Wolomin, where there was such great Jewish poverty. The sharp, hard expression on his face began slowly to relax. A good–natured light appeared in his eyes. I saw clearly how his Jewish feelings flickered and aroused his curiosity about the workings of the Jewish community in the shtetl. He asked me questions, and I answered, clarified, and explained to him the work of the special segments of community life, the battle against rising anti–Semitism, and the struggle for physical and spiritual survival.

The conversation lasted until we descended from the train, left the station, and walked in the streets of Warsaw. It seemed as if the Jew, who all his days had devoted himself to business and to working, had suddenly opened his eyes and seen before him another world, a world of spirituality, a higher sphere that held the power of Jewish existence.

He no longer complained about the high taxes. When I said that with his money he helped establish the Talmud Torah and in one of the classrooms there would be a plaque inscribed with his name, his eyes lit up and I saw the change that overcame him. His promise to help sounded sincere.

He kept to that promise. We often discussed with rich Jews the dreams of the Hibat Tzion and Jewish national feelings. There were some who held those to be dangerous dreams for the Jews of Poland. In the early days of Poland's rebirth, many thought that democracy and tolerance would flourish. Those for whom things went well became rich and all doors were open for them.

Flanzreich's case was not unique, and he showed the conditions under which we came to build the Talmud Torah. The law was that every member of the Jewish community must pay the community tax. But I figured that in Wolomin there were many Jews who could not pay. Clearly I could not take upon myself to be in charge of the taxes, and therefore I called together the whole council, among whom were representatives of every stratum so that they knew every inhabitant and could assess the ability of each individual, small sums and large, so that we could put together a budget like a real community.

The collecting of the taxes I suggested we turn over to the government official Yakubian, who collected both the national and the city taxes. My suggestion was accepted, but the official was not eager to come collecting from the Jews after collecting all the other taxes. Many of Wolomin's Jews did not know that paying the community taxes was a governmental law and at first they laughed at the community's documents. Yakubian had no sense, and if someone did not pay, he seized that person's Shabbos candlesticks or other items that he found in their home. Understandably, the first reaction of the Jews was to come running to me in my factory with moans and groans: "What gives? Why did they take my Shabbos candlesticks?"

I immediately understood that tragedies could be brewing, so I quickly ordered the government official to return the confiscated items. I began to acquaint him with the situations of certain Jewish inhabitants and showed him that there truly were some who could not pay even the smallest taxes. A middle–aged woman asked me, "Pan Sigalov, what should I do, buy shoes for my children who go barefoot or pay the taxes?" I answered, "Buy shoes for the children."

Shortly thereafter I assembled the council, presented them with the problem and explained that we had not correctly calculated the ability of the taxpayers. Voices were heard saying that my estimate was wrong, that the people who came complaining to me actually had the ability to pay the minimal taxes.

Reforms in the Community Administration

As time passed, I saw the necessity for reforming the structure of the community administration. The bookkeeper for the community, Krasutski, was a partner in a mill, and I maintained that in his place should be someone who was unemployed, like Sapershtein, a good bookkeeper. Krasutski was understanding and gave up his place for Sapershtein.

Such cases occurred often in the shtetl and thanks to cooperative efforts the Jews of Wolomin showed real understanding for the administrative demands of the Jewish community.

These demands led me to change the structure of community revenues. We succeeded in carrying out the principle of oversight for ritual slaughtering, which brought in enough revenue to cover the expenses of the clergy. This increased the revenue of the community.

I also had to settle conflicts, most of all with the butchers. There was even a lawsuit over a butcher who assaulted me. They gave him a huge fine, but in response I declared that I forgave the assault. This caused great joy. People threw a huge Kiddush and there was peace between the community and the butchers; and consequently a larger percentage of Jewish inhabitants were freed from paying the community taxes without harming the budget.

A question arose about hiring an official rabbi. In truth, at first I was against it. I feared it would not fit into our budget. We could hardly afford to subsidize various cultural activities led by Zionist organizations, as well as by the Bund, and they had become a real support for the community.

Jews in Wolomin, as in other towns in Poland, had great hopes he spoke for the victory of Pilsudski's military coup d'etat, which had ended the power of the Endecja and their allies on the right. But after the victory, events began to develop in another direction. Pilsudski himself did not want to become president on the basis of the constitution. The Sejm was not dissolved. Professor Moscicki was elected president. Professor Bartel became prime minister. In his speech describing his program, he talked about a change in attitudes toward minorities, assuring that the regime would not employ any anti–Semitic methods in the economy, because they would be harmful to the whole country. Many Jews saw here the announcement of a new era for the Jewish population.

Mild winds for the Jews blew in the ministries and offices, which were quickly felt in daily life. Still, there were some who did not want to hear about Zionism. They had no love for Eretz Yisroel. What kind of Jew has no love for Zion? But even in hard times they thought more about America and other lands. The most fervent love for Eretz Yisroel was shown by the youth.

The good times in Poland did not last long. The anti–Semitism that had never really disappeared, again showed its face, grew strong in the high schools and burst forth in the towns and shtetls, and it did not bypass Wolomin.

At that time I often met with Yitzchak Grinboym, who used to speak out in the Sejm with sharp words. In private conversation, he predicted harder times. He encouraged me to lead an array of Zionist activities in Wolomin. He saw this as the only way to rescue the Jewish people.

The fact that Wolomin was so close to Warsaw, tied to the big city both economically and socially, had both positive and negative aspects. Wolomin's Jews were not small–town people, having in their thoughts and actions something of the zest of the big city, but at the same time people in Wolomin felt every political shift and the steps that were taken in the economic war against the Jews, which later received the open approval of the prime minister, General Sklodkovski, with his well–known slogan: "Economic war against the Jews–by all means."

January, 1943, marked the understanding between Poland and Hitler's Germany. After Pilsudski's death in 1935, the attachment to Hitler's Germany became even stronger. It was not long before Jews felt the effects. Anti–Semitic agitation increased, and the Jews in Wolomin became the victims of an economic boycott. The Jews became impoverished, and the resources of the Jewish community shrunk from day to day. In the air it seemed like dark clouds were gathering in the Polish skies.

The Onset of Zionist Activities

Quite soon we began fundraising campaigns for Keren Hayisod, and although we were a small group of Zionists, we collected large sums. Keren Hayisod was one of the most important campaigns in Wolomin.

Finally we took steps to build the Tarbus building, for which we eventually organized a minyan for prayers, with a cantor who had a good voice, a real performer, so that the finest Jews of the shtetl came to pray, among them Dimant, Zalkin from Odessa, and other big shots who loved to hear the cantor pray and sing. On holidays, these big shots promised large donations for the Zionist causes.

On holidays we were also joined for prayers by the factory owners who lived in Warsaw but had villas in Wolomin. There were also progressive Jews, men who shaved their beards, and those who had not prayed for an endless number of Shabboses and week days.

In the thirties, a training program for young pioneers to Israel, both male and female, was formed, thanks to my allowing them to work in my foundry. Some of them also worked elsewhere. This program also influenced the beis–hamedrash boys, who began to think about undertaking more physical labor so that they would be prepared to make aliyah to Eretz Yisroel.

Members of the Agudah came to me complaining that I was ruining the Chasidic young men. Thanks to my understanding of religious Jews, it was difficult for me to accept these complaints. I answered one of them, "Remember, there will come a time when you will recall the hard work that is being done for Eretz Yisroel."

So it happened when in a short time people in Wolomin took up communist activities, which also drew the young Chasidim. Opposition to the communist slogans was led by those who had been involved in Zionist activities. A large number of them, consequently, remained alive because they fulfilled their goal of making aliyah to Eretz Yisroel.

There was in Wolomin a rich Jew, , who had a large business. When we would ask him for a donation for Keren Hayisod, he complained, "Will the goyim take me to Eretz Yisroel?"

The upshot was that his son ran away from home, joined the pioneer program, and made aliyah to Eretz Yisroel, where he did the hardest labors, building highways, carting manure. Today in Tel Aviv and in Jerusalem there are synagogues, Shaarei–Tzedek and others, that were built from Asman's contributions to Eretz Yisroel and Keren Kayemes.

In Yisroel there are pioneers from the metal industry who learned their trade in my foundry in Wolomin. When my foundry burned down and I became director of Dimant's metal factory, I also initiated Jewish young men in the work of the factory. I later met them in Tel Aviv and in Haifa, some as workers in a factory and others as owners of their own metalworks.

Not many are left alive from the beautiful Jewish community of Wolomin. Most of them live in Yisroel. They are employed in various sectors of business and labor, and it gives me great satisfaction to meet them and to feel the uniqueness of the Wolomin Jew that reminds us of the holy martyrs.

Today, years later, as we dwell in our fatherland, putting roots into our new reality, we turn to our memories with sorrow and moaning, but with tremendous love for the old places, for the past, as bitter as it may have been. The bitter memories are as holy for us as those that are beautiful and exalted.

R' Haim Levita, ofer Setam [scribe]
Wrote Torah scrolls for synagogues in Wolomin and the area and for Yeshivat Chachmei Lublin

[Page 93]

Jewish Education

by Shimon Kantz

Translated by Sara Mages

[Page 94]

Childhood is homeland! and there is no difference where we saw it, it is the nucleus of the great space and the hub of our world. It is therefore no wonder that we all carry in our hearts the city of our childhood, in which the *cheder* occupied a central place and from which our first journey began. Like the tabernacle in the days of Moses, which was able to accompany the Jews in all their journeys and encampments, the *cheder* was also able to wander and to adjust to the living conditions of the nation in the Diaspora, to its wandering from place to place. It has a long history, from the days of the writers and the *Tannaim* [Rabbinic sages], to the last generations in the Jewish Diaspora. Due to its simple form and limited curriculum, it was able to adapt to any Jewish community, wherever they arrived and settled, in every city and the smallest town. In this way the *cheder* was aimed at the nature of their lives. If a talented man was found to educate their sons, the parents immediately hired him and the *cheder* was established. Sometimes, the parents also came to him to ask for advice, since he was the closest scholar to the common people, and they tended to his advice. The *cheder* was in the *melamed*'s home, in his private apartment. To cut back on expenses he, and the cooks, crowded together in his apartment, a matter that caused many difficulties: the small apartment, the lack of air, the smell of cooking and the school equipment. In the *cheder* there was a table and benches without a backrest. Study time in the *cheder* - all day long. The purpose of the *cheder*: to teach the Torah to Jewish boys, life was Torah and Torah was life. The knowledge of the Torah is the knowledge of life, and the purpose of the study in the *cheder* was to give the boys the information that made them Jews. The community life helped the *cheder* to fulfill its functions, which were the public functions. The studying of the Torah and the teaching of Torah, should be the legacy of every Jew, has always been the aspiration of our nation.

And that was the desire of every Jew in Wolomin.

[Page 95]

The *Melamdim*, the *Cheder* and *Beit HaMidrash*

by K. Shimoni
Translated by Sara Mages

Jewish education is not the same as secular education, even though this education does not exclude itself from the moral concepts of tradition and not from its sources. The secular school also taught Torah and Nevi'im [prophets] but, in them, today as then, the concepts of tradition are only presented in borrowed meaning, not in the perception of those who first said them as a divine command, but as a general human obligation, the obligation of the individual towards the public or just a beautiful and fair measure.

In most cases the *cheder* was not a public asset, it was privately owned. The *melamdim* [teachers] were the owners and the *cheder* was run at their own expense, they provided all its needs, rent and all other necessities that, indeed, were few. At the lower level of the *cheder*, where the *melamed* needed assistants, he financed them and paid their wages, he was, therefore, sort of a contractor.

This was also the case in Wolomin until they built the institution called "Talmud Torah." The community's revenue allowed its foundation. The *cheder* then became a public institution. At first it was used mostly for the children of the poor and supported them with books and other teaching aids. There were always those who refused to send their children to it, they preferred the private *chedarim* to the public institution because they hoped for better results.

The *melamdim*, as a special class in the community, have a very long history. They played great roles in the history of the Jewish spirit. Among the *melamdim* in Wolomin were men of action who knew how to counsel. The *melamed* also dealt with *mitzvot* when a poor man needed his help in time of distress. Even though his situation was not good, he did not prevent himself from dealing with such a *mitzvah*, a charity act, and the boys saw their rabbi dealing with *mitzvot*.

The *melamed* in Wolomin was not excluded from the society he was part of it and fulfilled a role within it.

The *melamed* in the town was a family friend. He participated in their joy and grief, took part in all family events, in the joy of marriage and circumcision, in "*Shalom Zachar*" [welcoming the male] and "*Leil Shimurim*," in "*Pidyon Haben*" [redemption of the first born son] and Bar Mitzvah, and in a simple home he was the most noted among the guests, a scholar within them.

[Page 96]

He entered the parents' home many times a year. The test on the Sabbath required him to come often.

He also visited the house at scheduled times: on Purim, Chanukah, Sukkot, Passover and Shavuot, and each time he was received graciously. He entered the conversation and emphasized his words with a verse or a proverb, and his student felt a mixed feeling of closeness and respect, of the air in the *cheder* and the freedom of home. He stood next to his rabbi and enjoyed himself.

Of all these, "honoring the Shabbat and Yom Tov" will receive a different form, even though it was a kind of obligation.

Sometimes, an old *melamed* also knew how to cast a spell on the "evil eye" and was proficient in remedies, as a friend of the family he did not prevent himself from using his knowledge.

In the Wolomin's *cheder* the boys sat in one row, not in two rows, one before the other, as in the big cities. The advantage of this order is that the *melamed*, and the boys, were not far apart and sat at one table.

The benches were without support and the boy leaned against the table in front of him. It is possible that this caused a habit of movement during the study, which was customary among the Jews from ancient time and was not fully understood.

The study in the *cheder* was calculated in "periods." It was customary to register the boys to the *cheder* for one "period," and so was the hiring of the *melamed*. A "period" is a continuation of six months, from the holiday of Sukkot to Passover, and from there to Rosh Hashanah.

Between the periods there was about a month of vacation. The summer period ended on Rosh Hashanah and the winter period began after the holiday. The studies ended about a week before Passover eve.

During these times the teachers were busy arranging the *cheder* for the coming days.

Indeed, there was not a full vacation even between the periods. They studied matters that time has caused.

Study time in the *cheder* - all day long since was it clearly written: " Who sits all day and a little of the night, in order to teach them day and night."

The boys arrived early in morning and returned late in the evening. The regular hours of study were: in the summer after *Shacharit* prayer to the time of *Mincha* prayer, and in the winter - two to three hours in the evening.

Sometimes, they also studied the Gemara early in the morning before the prayer.

The study in the evening began at the beginning of winter and continued all the time. The departure from the *cheder* at night was joy for the boys.

When winter came, the children made lanterns of paper or glass and every night left the *cheder* in a group, each boy with a lantern in his hand. Sometimes, the assistant accompanied the boys armed with a stick and the boys talked about demons and spirits.

[Page 97]

The *cheder* in Wolomin was a day school, meaning, for the whole day. There were those in which the children did not go home for lunch. Life demanded this regulation. Their mothers were busy in their shops and at work, and it was good for them that the children did not interfere with their work.

The boys brought breakfast with them, the afternoon meal was brought by the assistant in his big basket, and sometimes he brought bread at dusk.

In this order they studied every day except for Friday afternoon. Thursday and Friday were review days.

Saturdays and holidays were, of course, free of study, and yet, on Saturday afternoon they studied a Shabbat lesson for an hour or two, since the parents also studied a lesson at the same time.

The *cheder* was part of the Jewish life in the town, a branch of Beit HaMidrash where the adults studied.

The *melamed* was a simple man and almost a member of the family.

The children were members of the community.

The community life helped the *cheder* to fulfill its duties which were public duties.

All the studies were taught in a melody: a special melody for the Chumash, which is different from the melody of the reading of the Torah: rendition for Nevi'im, special rendition for Tehillim and each of the five scrolls.

There were *melamdim* who used the individual teaching method. The *melamed* did not teach the class, except for once or twice a week at the time of a lecture. He had always taught one boy who read to him, and taught another boy when his turn came. The other boys had to listen but, for lack of supervision, they rested or read on their own. The hour of review replaced the recess and called the students to seek out thoughts and devote themselves to self-diligence.

Of course, it was impossible to teach an entire class, a matter that caused the severity of the discipline that weighed on the boys, especially in good *chedarim*.

However, on the other hand, the *melamed* knew the nature of each boy and adjusted his explanation to each of them, but he did not consciously and willingly grasp the nature of the student. For an excellent teacher, and for a fine student, there was no better method than that.

This method of teaching caused the small number of boys in the class. In its days, the Talmud determined twenty-five boys to whom it should not be added. The Gemara classes in the Wolomin's *cheder* never reached that number, the usual number was about ten or twelve students.

[Page 98]

Sometimes, a celebration, a festive day for the family, preceded the beginning of the *Chumash* in the infant-*cheder,* and its great value was in the symbolic act of accepting the yoke of Torah and the obligation of Judaism.

They began in *Chumash Vayikra* [Leviticus].

Not that they really started and continue in doing so, but an old custom to begin the study took place here.

On the Sabbath, that the celebration took place, invited guests, relatives and neighbors, arrived. The *cheder* boys gathered to see their friend's honor. The latter was decorated in a new garment in honor of the day. On that day the little guests received a good reception. The adults gave them space and served them sweets.

And indeed, on this Shabbat the boy began the first Torah portion in *Vayikra*, but, on the next day, he began the weekly Torah portion and engaged in the study of the *Chumash* in the first class.

After that: the *Chumash* with Rashi's commentary, as well as Rashi's small and odd letters.

Because of the age gap it was customary to study in groups, the "older" groups, the "younger" etc.

There were *melamedim* for whom the most active incentive was the strap and somehow the students progressed in their studies, some more and some less.

Equipped with these basic studies, the students moved to *melamedim* of higher levels. At R' Baruch they studied the Torah and also a chapter in the Talmud. At R' Zusha, a sharp Torah scholar, they studied complex issues with *Tosafot* [additional annotations to the Talmud], Maharam, Maharsha [Shmuel Eidels] and other commentators.

The *melamed*, R' Yehusua, was the one who stood at the head of this learning pyramid. He was very strict and demanded a lot from his few students because only those with outstanding talents were accepted to study with him.

R' Benyamin also engaged his students in special subjects of study in the Talmud and introduced them to the opinions of *posekim* and commentators.

I described the *cheder* from its objective side and in very general terms, so as not to expand the scope of this article. I purposely ignored the subjective side, from the atmosphere that prevailed within the walls of the *cheder*, the personal experiences of the students, the relationship between them and the *melamed*'s family. All that I left for the rest of the members of Wolomin, who would expend the talk about our experiences on hot summer days and long winter evenings, when we returned with various lanterns, with all the phenomena of ups and downs, of standing and falling, of dreams and hopes.

Despite all the disappointments we are in awe at this institution called *cheder* and to our teachers, because we have come out of these religious schools whole in our mind and equipped with basic knowledge that gave us the training, and the desire, to broaden our horizons and expend our mind.

[Pages 99-101]

My Teachers

by Yisroel Levitau

When I was five years old, there was a great simcha in our home. My mother had specially baked a cake, taken out a bottle of Wishniak (cherry brandy) which she had set aside, and my father wrapped me in his great tallis, led me to the cheder, to R. Avraham Yossl the teacher on Dluga Street. My mother did not forget to bring along treats, nuts, candies, raisins, and almonds, to share with the other children in the cheder.

For the cheder children this was a double simcha. First of all, they received sweets, and therefore their schoolwork was also interrupted. They played in the courtyard with horse chestnuts.

The teacher readily took me from my mother and father, seated me by him near a huge alef–beys and with his pointer indicating the letters, taught me the alef–beys.

And this is how I first became acquainted with the cheder, with the teacher, and with new friends.

After I finished learning the alef–beys and Hebrew with him, I was brought to R. Yehoshua Yehezkel the teacher, where I undertook learning Chumash with Rashi. Each transfer from one cheder to the other was accompanied by new experiences. In this way I also learned with Reb Baruch–Meyer Without a Foot and with R. Avraham Esterdiner, with whom I studied Gemara, Mishnah, and Tanakh. Later I also studied with R. Fishele the teacher, the old scribe from Leshne Street. My last teacher was R. Ziske the teacher, with whom I studied Gemara with the Tosafists. With him I also celebrated my bar mitzvah.

Remembering all these teachers, who taught us to love not only the Torah, but also every Jew, I can see them before my eyes, filled with the love of Israel. I see before me Avraham Esterdiner, who had his cheder in Yoske Salti's house. He was terribly poor and had no coal to heat his own little dwelling. One shivered with the cold there. There were times when we saw him collect the crumbs of bread that the children left behind.

A tragic fate befell R. Baruch–Meyer the teacher. It was not enough that his chest rattled, that he was missing a foot, and was very poor, but God had struck him with an upsetting wife, Toveh–Rivkeh, who gave him terrible trouble. He was our neighbor and more than once came to sorrow through her. Among us we said that R. Baruch–Meyer suffers in this world and therefore it will be good for him in the world to come.

We saw the terrible trouble that his wife caused and we used to have great pity for him. It was a wonder that he still had a head for teaching the cheder children that people brought to him.

Speaking of my teachers, I see before my eyes also my friends from different cheders, dear trusty children: Yankele the rabbi's son, Avraham Edelson, Mordechai Weinbroom, the sons of Shepsel Katzav the butcher from Platkovski. Later on bigger boys, Ezriel Podberger, Moyshe Shtern, Shmuel Feigenboim, Shammai Boym, the rabbi's son, etc.

My Teacher R. Baruch_Meyer

My first teacher was R. Baruchl–Meyer With One Foot. He lived in our neighborhood, a couple doors away, by the blacksmith. Aside from what he suffered from the children, whom he called "rascals," he had a wife, Toveh–Rivkeh, who gave him such troubles that he surely lingered in this world for some sin. And we children also caused him more than a few troubles. For example, if we did not know the weekly portion in the Chumash, he hit us with his rod, so in revenge we would hide the rod when he fell asleep over his Chumash.

R. Avraham Osterdiner [1]

My second teacher was R. Avraham Osterdiner, in Yoske Solti's house on Dluga Street.

He was a good teacher. He taught Tanakh very well. I still can taste his sincere interpretations of chapters from Samuel the prophet. The better children of the city, the sons of the rabbi and the shochet, studied with him.

R. Yehoshua–Yehezkel and R. Ziske Freiman

I also had other fine teachers, for example, our neighbor R. Yehoshua–Yehezkel the teacher, who also taught older students, Gemara students. My last teacher [2] After we finished in his cheder, we knew enough to study a page of Gemara on our own.

Translator's Footnotes:

1. Spelled differently earlier Return
2. Text is defective here: one line is repeated and one is missing Return

---

[Pages 102-137]

Schools and Teachers

I don't have the strength to speak about all of the schools and all of the teachers who taught Jewish children in Wolomin. This is a snapshot of images and samples, who represent an accurate aspect of Jewish life in the shtetl. I will briefly describe the schools and the teachers that taught me from my earliest childhood years. The cheders, these schools, were my universities, in which I learned the basics of Yiddishkeit and mentschlichkeit. Let my few words serve as a memorial for them, who first planted in me respect for the Jewish spirit, for the written word, for the high principles and great ideals of the prophets and the Torah sages. The older I grow, the better I understand and appreciate the value of the learning, of the education, that we received in the cheder, the yeshiva, and the beis–hamedrash.

R. Avraham–Velvel

R. Avraham–Velvel was my first teacher. I was barely three years old when I was brought to him wrapped in a tallis, and on the very first day he started to teach me the alef–beis.

He lived with his family in two small rooms, a tiny place. In one of these little rooms R. Avraham–Velvel conducted his lessons. My first "welcome" that I received from R. Avraham–Velvel came in the words: "From me, Shammaiele, you won't get any special favors. Sit down and learn to be a Jew."

In this way he pretended to be strict and threatening. In fact he was a feeling Jew. He never, Heaven forbid, hit us or harmed us physically. It seems to me now that he was something of a child, just dressed and disguised as an old man.

We had tremendous respect for him. His teaching of the alef–beis and later of Hebrew was not difficult for children. He imposed no agonies. For every holiday he explained the meaning and purpose of the celebration, the heroic stories of the Jewish people.

R. Avraham Stardiner

After two years of studying with R. Avraham–Velvel, I transferred to the cheder of R. Avraham Stardiner. He was called this because he had come from the shtetl of Stardin. He seldom told anyone his family name.

His appearance remains in my memory, tall and thin, with a long beard and a long caftan. He was an angry man, and more than once we felt his heavy hand. But that did not stop us from overturning the classroom and playing all sorts of pranks.

Although I had certain privileges with him, as the son of an important man, I felt terrible when I saw how other children received slaps from his bony hands. His whip was always ready to carry out his sentence on a rebellious child, who had a deathly fear of him. The fathers knew about this and usually approved of the teacher's strictness. They saw in him a good intermediary for teaching their children, making them into men…When such a father asked how his son was behaving, he would get the answer: "I already took him by the "hoof'…" This meant that the poor boy had already felt the taste of the whip, which guaranteed, without a worry, that he would soon be a grown–up.

R. Shia–Chaskel

After my "term" with R. Avraham Stardiner I was brought to R. Shia–Chaskel, who taught Gemara. With him also we received our first instruction in writing Yiddish letters and composing a letter.

His cheder consisted of a single room, which was the bedroom, kitchen, and dining room. There R. Shia–Chaskel taught us the beginning of the Talmudic tract Baba Mezia. He wanted with all his heart to make mentschen of us, that we should be able to study and to write and to have a fine handwriting. In the shtetl he was considered knowledgeable. People said that he knew arithmetic and that he could have been a bookkeeper if he had only had a little luck.

R. Binyamin Shochet

That is what people called him, and no one was interested in his family name. It seems that he could not make a living as a shochet, so he had to turn to teaching. But even from that he gathered no honey. Want and need looked out from every corner.

R. Zushe the Teacher

He was considered a good teacher. He was brought from the "Yesodei HaTorah" school in another shtetl, and studying with him was an honor. At his cheder there were pretty smart students. Reb Zushe took great pleasure when he saw his students grasping the lesson that he taught, but the students used to give him trouble, playing all sorts of pranks.

It used to happen that he would doze off in the middle of a lesson, holding his head up with his hands, which were almost on top of the table. We would take a candle, pour out the wax, and stick his beard to the table. When he awoke, he could not raise his head, The pain was twofold: it pained him to tear his beard from the table, and he was ashamed that his students had lost respect for their teacher, who taught them Torah and wanted to make them good Jews.

These childish tricks never made him lose his temper and he continued to teach with generosity and love.

R. Avrahm–Baruch

A quiet, excellent Jew, who had been brought from another shtetl. He ate daily at different people's homes. He ate with us on Sundays, because it was a free day for my mother, with the businesses closed, and there was more time to serve a guest. On Shabbos he ate at Shepsel Katsav's, whose son was also his student and enjoyed certain privileges. He would not touch him even when he transgressed, at the same time that other boys felt his heavy hand for the same transgression.

R. Yehoshua the Teacher

He stands before my eyes as he did decades ago, when I studied with him. My parents, who wanted their son to be a scholar, sent their child to study with Reb Yehoshua the teacher.

He was brought to be the teacher by six families who were determined to have a good teacher for their sons. Until then he was occupied in the meat trade, from which he made a living. But the Jews knew that he was a great scholar and explained things well, so they convinced him to leave the meat trade and take up teaching.

R. Yehoshua began to teach with six students. In addition to teaching Gemara with profound argumentation, he also taught us Chasidism. He explained the Chasidic way and told Chasidic stories. He used to say that when a Jew explained a passage other than in its literal meaning, if he had excellent intentions, his explanation was as important as the Torah learning a great scholar.

Night and day R. Yehoshua used to sit over his Torah and his prayers and he expected the same devotion from us, his students. Being completely unbiased, he made no distinction between one student and another. By the way, our fathers, as was appropriate, valued his work, to which he devoted himself as if to prayer; they paid him a good salary for a teacher.

When I had my bar mitzvah, R. Yehoshua helped me to prepare the subtle arguments for the Torah speech that I had to give at the meal. I remember as if it happened today how his face shone, as if lit up by heat, when he cited the saying of the Talmudic sages that every day the Holy One Blessed Be He sits on His throne of justice and when He sees that the world is wholly guilty, he stands up from the throne of judgment and sits on the throne of mercy, and he added, if the world were run only according to the attribute of justice, it would not survive for even a single day.

It has been a long time since R. Yehoshua taught me how great is the attribute of mercy, and in all my journeys I have attended to his words and the fervor with which he said them.

Even today his passionate speech rings in my ears: "Knowledge, mercy, and the glory of God are the rungs on which a man climbs to the highest heights. Knowledge means learning the Torah without ulterior motives; mercy–not to wrong any man, to care for the other's honor, his property, and his health and to give tangible help to all who are needy; glory means to seem Godly, to conduct oneself in purity, order, beauty in dress, not to say foolish things, not to make needless outcries, not to quarrel."

From my earliest childhood years I felt the holiness of mercy. Almost every week we distributed collections of money and things for the poor, for the needy ill, for the hidden poor.

R. Yehoshua taught us the ideas of Chassidism and transmitted also the beauty of the rabbinic exemplars. Furthermore, what he strove to clarify, every year I grasped in more depth. In those years when I studied in the yeshivah, I increasingly considered and appreciated the depth of R. Yehoshua's ideas, which have remained in my mind, in the depths of my soul.

In the Yeshiva

My grandfather was reputed to be a great scholar in Wolomin, an uprooter of mountains, to whom the scholars would come with the difficult Talmudic passage. He would take the point of his beard in his mouth for a while and soon he would take it out and say: "I don't get what is so hard to understand…the answer is right there."

People called my grandfather R. Meir Sokolover, perhaps because he came from Sokolov. For as long as I can remember, he used to come to Wolomin for Shabbos. The whole week he spent in Warsaw, where he gave lessons in the Piasetchner Yeshiva.

After my bar mitzvah, when people thought of me as a grown–up young man, my grandfather took me with him to the yeshiva, which was at 16 Noviniorski Street, where I was at the beginning the only Wolominer among the yeshiva boys, who came from a variety of different provincial shtetls.

There for the first time I felt the transition from one era to another. Until then I had been a free bird in Wolomin, a child without worries, and I had pictured myself in the small, beloved shtetl among happy Chasidim and confirmed misnagdim and I thought that Wolomin was the whole world and the Master of the World sat over it, in Heaven, and regarded only us in the shtetl. In Warsaw, actually, I had no large worries, since my father had provided me with all the necessities. But there I had the feeling of homelessness, like an exile in the place of the Torah.

My eyes were opened and I saw before me new worlds, which seized my soul. As a resident at the yeshiva, I became friendly with all the other yeshiva boys, debated with them and spoke of all kinds of things, in order to show them that we Wolomin boys did not stand apart from others.

After finishing the terms in the cheders, my grandfather took me to the Piasetchner Yeshiva. Even today his voice and the tune in which he chanted passages from the Gemara, which touched my heart, ring in my ears, More than once I think back to those good student years, when I simply studied day and night, practiced Chasidism, and built palaces in the World to Come…Where is that now? Everything was so sweet, so good. In all my limbs it resounded with sweetness and with warm security.

I had a purpose in life. I would be a rabbi, one who fears Heaven; I would contemplate heavenly matters day and night. All my paths were sure and bright. All I had to do was grow up.

Learning and Insight

As the years passed, the desire to learn grew in me. I repeated over and over each childish day and night the Gemara, with the Tosafos [medieval commentaries] and arguments. This was no easy thing, to pass the hours sitting in front of the Gemara, busily going through page after page, trying to grasp a commentary. I used to love those Tosafos, although they were not terribly simple or clear. In them lie, like shadows, the secrets of the Gemara, and in the yeshiva we had to reveal those secrets, to uncover them, to make them clear, to unravel them as one unravels a huge, thick ball of string.

Years ago I was surprised when I realized how much I remember from those yeshiva years, how fluently I went over those tangled Tosafos.

Also in the yeshiva it happened that at one spot, a difficult passage, I was stumped, stopped in my tracks, and I did not know how to move on, even step by step–nothing worked. What could I do? I wrinkled my forehead, hummed a Gemara tune, and tried with all my might to find a way through this difficult Tosafos; I sought help in various commentaries, but nothing worked.

So I went to my grandfather, and oddly enough, the same words when spoken by him came out entirely differently. The mountain that stood in my way disappeared and it was now so smooth and light that it was like a shining, snow–covered road.

I envied him, my grandfather, for his sharp mind and clear thought, for his dedication to learning and praying.

It sometimes happened that with divine inspiration he would linger over a melody for who knows how long, but more often he would murmur and hurry through the prayers, instead of drawing them out in a banal way. When he was not the head of the yeshiva, people argued with him more about why he hurried through the prayers, but never on a regular Monday or Thursday, when he was so enthusiastic, as I have never been able to forget.

I was proud of my grandfather not only in the yeshiva but also at home, when we returned to Wolomin. In the beis–hamedrash he was the center of everyone's attention. The different groups of young men there, students, gathered around him seeking solutions for their questions and problems, which they had accumulated during the week. In my grandfather's face one could read the sheer joy of seeing the growth of a new generation of scholars in the shtetl, and he listened gladly to the difficult questions they posed and he answered them simply, leading the students from stumbling in the dark with each sparkle of his gaonic intelligence, with lightning–like revelations.

I remember, too, how I used to see him read the Torah portion of the week. With both hands he held the Torah scroll, and with his head held high toward the rafters he began to sing hoarsely, "Yehi ratzon milifney avinu shebashamayim"…, and in his voice was such sweet sadness that people could almost see and hear how the exiled priests cried by the rivers of Babylon, as their silent harps hung from the branches of the trees.

My Father's Music

A disposition for singing was even more strongly developed in my father, who was the cantor in the beis–hamedrash for the High Holidays and the festivals. He prayed before the altar with such sweetness as if he were pouring out his heart. I will never forget his moving melodies and how his eyes lit up during the prayers with pure sadness, with total involvement, as if he saw before him not only the whole congregation of Jews from the shtetl but as if at that moment he also wanted to be everywhere where Jews were in trouble or danger, on the sea or on the dry land.

I can see he face after he sang a prayer and he remained standing for a long time, contemplative and silent, with amazement frozen in his eyes, as if he would not yet return from wandering through the world together with the wandering Jews. The lengthy silence in the beis–hamedrash and the looks from the supplicants, who had turned to him, eventually woke him from his bleak thoughts, which stemmed from his feeling of great responsibility for the congregation, whose prayer–leader he was, with the duty of bringing their prayers to the Throne of Glory.

My father's singing, even his sadder melodies, always seemed pure and sweet in my mind. It was a music that exalted the spirit, captivated the thoughts, and refined the human being.

Chassidism and Kabbalah

By studying in the Piasetshner yeshiva, I gained status among the boys in Wolomin. On free days, I studied Chassidism with them and had a lot of fun. I had much to tell them about life among yeshiva boys not only in the Piasetshner yeshiva but in other yeshivas in Warsaw.

There were yeshivas in which this was the routine: early on, superficial learning, including the whole Talmud. Later, as they became more proficient in the Talmud, they began to go deeper, more thoroughly, and instead of simple argumentation they sought the true sense of each matter.

At that time I was at the level of proficiency. I wanted to be proficient in the Talmud, and afterwards, I thought, insight would come.

There were, however, students who loved to confuse themselves and others with minute arguments and complicated hypotheses. Often it happened that I had to wrestle with someone over a Tosafos about which I had a question. They poured on the commentaries, the Maharam, the Maharash, and P'nei Yehoshua. It became clear that they could not answer the question, but they wanted to show their cleverness. The result was that I had to go to my grandfather, who answered my question on the spot.

Asking questions was for me, unlike for others, not merely for the sake of asking questions. Some would sit for a whole day over a page of Gemara just thinking of questions. I thought that was a poor and impractical practice. That way, years go quickly and learning goes slowly, without progress. I also did not like running too quickly over the tractates and pages. They knew hundreds of pages of Gemara, but they understood it all superficially, and in later years they forgot it and sought ways to acquire the ability to go deeper, to object to an interpretation.

Thus I progressed little by little in independent learning under the influence and direction of my grandfather.

My grandfather for me was the exemplar of a total Jew, of a mentsh, who would not hurt a fly on the wall: of a mentsh who is not touched by the world's ugliness, and although his body is on the sinful earth, he is, with his heart, mind, and soul in the highest realm of heaven. But more than anything else I was impressed by his learning, his proficiency, his cleverness in study. My goal was to grow up as a scholar, just like my grandfather.

The new worlds that opened for me at the Piasetshner yeshiva I brought back to Wolomin. Every Shabbos I brought the news that I heard and saw in Warsaw to my friends in the beis–hamedrash. The boys from the Wolomin beis–hamedrash wanted to learn from me new approaches to learning and new practices of Chassidism.

Mussar

Aside from the Talmud and its commentators, in the yeshiva I studied by myself the Midrash, Chassidic books, and I took a look at the Kabbalah. I was greatly influenced by the Novorodok yeshiva, which was not far from the Piasetshner, at 11 Franziskaner Street. I used to visit there often. Their profound Mussar melody, their self–examinations, their immense, all–consuming religious rapture moved me and became part of me.

That was a period when I became carried away with the religious ecstasy of the Novorodok yeshiva students, with their ecstatic contempt for the world and their rejection of material things. An ecstatic trance for a bar–mitzvah boy could last for minutes or hours; for me, however, I found myself in such a trance for days and nights.

It appeared to us Wolomin Chassidim that the strongest religious feeling from childhood on was accompanied by a kind of innate "the Shechinah is in exile" sadness, with a feeling of responsibility for everything in the world that was not proper, that was an "evil matter to take part in"; every one of us was obliged to help the suffering, to rescue the pursued, to satisfy the hungry, to protect the homeless, to revive the sinful and to teach those who wandered without understanding!

Consequently the hours I spent in Mussar with the Novorodokers affected me greatly, as the yeshiva students did their mental gymnastics, contemplated, went into depth, with great force to free themselves from the surrounding mediocrity, from their own weaknesses and doubts, from the darkness of daily life.

In those days I did not know about the big Mussar controversies, which began years earlier in the rabbinic world, particularly in Lithuania, over whether Mussar belonged in yeshivas, as the prominent students of Reb Yisroel Salanter contended. By the end of the nineteenth century these debates had taken on an unfortunate character. The rabbis wrote articles in contemporary journals on this question, and there were yeshivas that were involved, thanks to their students, in a virtual war. The greatest war waged against Mussar–learning was led by the Slobodker and Telzer yeshivas. In Warsaw, in my time, no yeshiva allowed Mussar–learning. Only the Novorodoker stubbornly stood by this ideology.

I was then too young to adopt this path in its full depth, though it influenced my outlook, my ecstatic will to raise myself above daily life. I used to see in a dream how I suddenly raised myself up and began flying. I arose and flew, and I wondered why other people did not do the same thing.

When I told my closest friends about my dream, it seemed that they also had similar dreams. It seems strange, but such were the Wolomin schoolchildren and the older boys in the beis–hamedrash: they danced, they carried on, they played in the dirt, they played tag, hide–and–go–seek, but inside they had a passion, a longing, that later in their young manhood gave them no rest.

That is why they paid such close attention to what I told them about the Novorodok followers of Mussar. It seemed to me that my stories sharpened their fear of Heaven, but it also aroused their fantasies, perhaps because the road of Mussar lay so wide from their Polish–Chassidic environment and were so different from the customs and doctrines of the Chassidic prayer houses.

The Beis–Hamedrash

The beis–hamedrash was located on Leshna Street. From early in the morning men were there praying and studying. Books were always arrayed on the long wooden tables: Gemaras, a Yoreh Da–ah, a Shulchan Aruch, a Chaye–Adam, an Eyin–Yakov. Some people arrived only to pray and quickly returned to their work, merchants to their shops and craftsmen to their workrooms. Others sat in the beis–hamedrash the whole day praying and learning.

One of the perennial scholars was R. Ephraim Ivri, who used to wake at four in the morning, summer and winter, and run to the beis–hamedrash. He would sit and learn until three in the afternoon, when he would go home to eat something, but soon he was back in the beis–hamedrash, sitting and learning until late at night.

His wife and two daughters ran a little store that sold writing implements, from which they barely made a living. People said that when he was young, his father–in–law had warned him that he should find something to do. He wrote to him, "Pay attention to both food and to Torah–one has to live like all Jews and find a way to make a living." So he opened the shop. But gradually he became so involved in the higher spheres that his wife was left as the sole proprietor of the business.

His son, too, would spend all day and night learning in the beis–hamedrash, a young man with small shoulders and long sidecurls, which emphasized his long, refined face. After his marriage, he traveled to the Ger rabbi, even though like his father he was an Alexander chassid. He had the nerve to say in the Ger court that he had come to Ger because his father–in–law forced him to. But truthfully, he only had to travel to his own rabbi, that is, the Alexander rabbi.

Among the prominent Jews in the beis–hamedrash was also R. Leibush Farber, an adherent of the Agudah, a happy man who distinguished himself from the others. Although he listened to the very religious ones, who lamented modern times and who paid attention only to the Agudah faction, who wanted to bring an end to the attempts to bring redemption to the land of Israel before the messiah came, Reb Leibush openly sympathized with those who went up to Eretz Yisroel. When he learned that I intended to go to Israel, he earnestly said to me in a voice suffused with lovingkindness, "If you are near the Wall, remember, in God's name, to put in a note for me, too."

I reconstruct the beis–hamedrash because it seems to me that it occupied an important place for each of us, since that is where we learned the basic principle, "Hear O Israel" and "Moshe commanded the Torah to us, the inheritance of the congregation of Yakov" and other verses and blessings, even until the last years of our learning on our own.

Bound up with the beis–hamedrash is the memory of our fathers and grandfathers. And our mothers as well lived with the thought of the beis–hamedrash as a holy site, where their children and their husbands prayed and studied Torah. In each Jewish mother there was something of the rabbinical sage Yehoshua's mother, who, when he was an infant, would bring his cradle into the beis–hamedrash so that he would hear the voice of the Torah. From our earliest years, we grew accustomed to the sound of the Gemara–melodies that emanated from the beis–hamedrash.

Where did we children in Wolomin use to play? In and around the beis–hamedrash. That bound us by a thousand threads to the beis–hamedrash.

Good Students and Fiery Politicians

In my time, I remember, there were deeply devout young men in the beis–hamedrash: Moyshe–Feyvl Shtulman, a good student and a fiery politician who maintained that when the time came for action–put aside your Torah. That is, one may interrupt one's studying and hold in the beis–hamedrash a referendum for the Agudah. He also showed himself to be a fine orator.

Another fine student was Avraham Greenshpan, the scribe's son, who is today a rabbi, a slaughterer, and a mohel in Halifax.

Like an exemplar of a great Jew, the former Bobrowsk rabbi is engraved in my memory. He arrived in Volomin after the Bolshevik Revolution and he studied in the beis–hamedrash day and night. Always when I think of learning Torah simply for itself, before my eyes stands the figure of the Bobrowsk rabbi, as he sat bent over the Gemara and the commentaries from early morning until late at night.

Often I went through the shtetl with Reb Chaim–Aaron Bunems collecting money to support the great scholar, who breathed out the love of the Torah. His scholarship and gentleness had a tremendous influence on us beis–hamedrash boys. We saw how learning pervaded his whole being, so that he could no more stop learning than he could live without breathing.

In later years, when I knew that the word "philosophy" came from two Greek words—"philos," which means "love" and "sophos," which means wisdom–it became clear to me that so would the learned Greeks refer to the Bobrowsk rabbi, who embodied the love of Torah wisdom, who had a magnetic power for learning.

On the first Shabbos after Pesach, the study of Pirkey Avos began in the beis–hamedrash. It seemed that the younger Jews had, like myself, great affection for studying Pirkey Avos, which discusses great ethical principles and rules of conduct from the great Jewish characters of the past. My grandfather told me that studying Pirkey Avos went on over two thousand years ago in the great Babylonian yeshivas. From there the custom spread over the whole Jewish world. The six chapters of Pirkey Avos are printed in the bigger prayer books so that Jews can have them easily at hand. Actually I knew that Pirkey Avos is a section of the Mishnah and is printed together with all the Mishnahs and in the complete Talmud, in the Order Nezikin, and therefore it is also called "Tractate Avos." It can be found right in the middle of the Talmud.

R. Chaim Topol

An interesting character was also the shammos [sexton] of the beis–hamedrash, R. Chaim Topol, the grandfather of Yisroeldik the stage actor who is famous today throughout the world for his acting ability. He surely got the impetus for acting from his grandfather. Of course, his grandfather never entered a theater and never saw a stage with his own eyes. However, he had a spark of talent, which appeared in his humor, in the jokes he good–naturedly made about himself and others without hurting anyone, even when the joke had a sting. So, for example, without any anger toward women, he could say that the women's section of the synagogue had to have a floor because women were not worth enough for the ground to support them.

In his homespun, deliberate way of talking he often revealed simple everyday bits of wisdom, as, for example, that it is not worthwhile to chase after wealth or honor, because one who multiplies his possessions multiplies his troubles, and one who chases after honor, honor flees from him. And he had a story for every occasion. His jokes made the rounds, from mouth to mouth, and people held their sides from laughter.

The beis–hamedrash was a homey, popular prayer hall. Both ordinary people and rich Jews prayed there. People would take the opportunity to learn a lesson from the Talmudic page–of–the–day or to study a chapter of the Mishnah, to leaf through an old book or to study with excitement a page of the Gemara until late at night. In the early years it was a lively place. The young men would argue over a difficult Talmudic passage. But in later times, closer to the war years, it became quieter; for both the older and the younger generations, the beis–hamedrash was the best place for passing time in a spiritual fashion.

The shoemaker and the tailor, the wagon–driver, the small–time merchant and the owner of a larger store, the wealthy Jew and the pauper–at the hour of the afternoon and evening prayers, all left behind their businesses and their worries and were cut off from their outer lives, gathered instead for an enjoyable hour in the beis–hamedrash. No other gathering place existed for them. This sacred place was for the Jews in Wolomin a gathering place, a place for discussion of worldly matters, like politics or community affairs that interested every Wolomin Jew.

But the greatest pleasure that our fathers and grandfathers enjoyed was a page of Gemara, a chapter of Mishnah, an excerpt from Ayin Yakov or simply saying Psalms, each according to his ability and that of his companion, with whom he studied. One could hardly find in that older generation a single Jew who would not take part in some kind of learning or Psalm recitation. That was for people who were not from the community. Each person belonged in that framework, which gave him satisfaction, not only spiritual satisfaction but also pleasure and delight, the simplest sense of those words.

"It was a pleasure"–people used to say in Wolomin. In the beis–hamedrash they renewed and refreshed themselves, roused themselves, felt that they were not idle limbs but that they were part of a great people who had a God who had not abandoned them.

Preachers

Occasionally, when a traveling preacher would come to the shtetl, there was pleasurable anticipation. Everyone–men, women, and even children–took pleasure in hearing a good sermon. When one encountered a preacher with a nice voice and a pleasing cadence, who spoke sincerely, one's eyes welled up and even produced tears.

Wolomin Jews would forget their troubles for a while and taste the joy of the world. That was a greater joy than that feeling of purity one gets from rejecting worldly things. But at first glance, Wolomin Jews did not give the impression that they were sentimental. Rather, they seemed more serious, loving wisdom, a witticism, even something that cut them to the quick, but that was all superficial. In these preoccupied Jews–preoccupied with making a living, in sun and rain, in snow and frost, there always beat a feeling heart, which always responded to a warm word and longed for a sweet melody which exalted them, which led them to other worlds, more beautiful, higher.

Yes, now, for the first time, I feel more strongly the beauty of these beis–hamedrash Jews in our shtetl. The majority of these simple people, merchants, toilers, and shopkeepers–differed from the everyday people that we have encountered in our journeys and wanderings in different lands and countries. The simple people whom we have met among other people, end their days playing cards or with alcohol or with idle gossip and the like. They would dream a whole day of crawling out of their hiding places and their souls drained out of their bodies.

Different from these others is the path that our fathers and grandfathers paved in our old home. They did not leave their homes in the evenings seeking the yetzer–harah, only the yetzer–tov. They did not go out to unwind and to waste time, nor to seek frivolous adventures, only to exalt their minds and fill their souls with the highest feelings. The hours in the beis–hamedrash were, for the Jews of Wolomin, for generation after generation, a kind of spiritual purification. Those hours cleansed them of the dust of the day. They threw off a part of their material existence, and they returned home more spiritual, more in possession of themselves than when they left.

The Jewish "strings," which had become a bit loosened during the week, in the tumult of a whole week, were tightened up again in the beis–hamedrash. Once again the Wolomin Jew felt the supremacy of the transcendent, of the spiritual over the material, of the genteel over the boorish; and in such hours more than one began to regret his follies and became captured by thoughts of repentance.

Whenever I think about the afternoon and evening prayers in the beis–hamedrash, it comes to me that in our shtetl the day never descended to evening. Rather it was the opposite: the day rose instead of descending. In the evening, the Jew ascended, he rose to greatness. According to many accounts, our fathers and our grandfathers were people who were not satisfied with just praying. After praying, something seized them, in order to strengthen the body for the Torah, and they quickly turned to learning by the light of tiny lamps, or, in earlier times, of oil lamps.

They sat there by the notched and wax–covered tables and with a bolstering melody applied themselves to discovering the core of a "The rabbis taught…" and "Abaye said…" The melody was accompanied by bickering and sparring over the rightness of an argument and the difficulty of a Talmudic passage. One man tried to outdo another with a sharp word and a diverting argument.

At first they spoke about holy things and their conversation was casual. People listened to them as though they were authorities in worldly matters. But hardly had they opened their Gemaras before they took the paths of Nehardea and Pumbeditha, that is, they began to quarrel and wrangle. Here they question and there they answer, and here they think that everything has been answered, but then a new questioner arises, who poses in his melody a new problem. And then other voices sing out the problems and the justifications like weeping flutes. Others resounded and thundered with confidence, with malice for anyone who dares to disagree.

To this day I see before me the pale young men with their dreamy eyes and the grown Jews with their black and gray beards, and in my ears ring their Germara melodies in the beis–hamedrash. With the same melodies, we ourselves in our younger years sharpened our minds on each passage, saying, and verse.

Thus we absorbed the nectar of the Torah, of the Gemara with all its commentaries together with the nostalgic melodies. All my bones speak out, all my bones and limbs were shaped by them.

How clearly it teaches that a word is not simply what is written but how it is spoken. The melody is as important as the thought, the tone is as important as the style, the intention of a word is more important than the word itself, and now the beautiful melodies and pure intentions of the Wolomin Jews as they learned and prayed in the beis–hamedrash swim before me.

Let me mention something else. There were also those who learned quietly, swaying hour after hour over their Gemara, and one heard not a peep from them. But occasionally a melody arose from them, the old Germara melody with which our fathers and our grandfathers learned the same Gemaras, by the same tables in the same beis–hamedrash.

Chassidic Prayer Houses

Ger

On Leshne Street was the Ger prayer house, where about sixty Chassidim prayed. They were accounted in the shtetl as the sharpest and most excitable, ready to trample every opponent. It seems to me, however, that almost all of them were good, upright Jews, their glances suffused with the sheer warmth and light that they brought with them from the Ger court.

I see them on an ordinary Shabbos after nap time, as they enter the prayer house to read a sacred text and hum a joyful Ger melody, a melody without an end, with a lesson of spiritual awakening, just as people hum it in Ger.

At the time of the third Shabbos meal, one could hear through the windows the sounds of Shabbos songs, yearning, sung in the darkness, with closed eyes, unending, with supplications, with trust, with sadness, with joy, like a march, a military march toward the doors of the Throne of Glory. Soon the notes sound like tuneful caresses, nestling, poured out like sweet wine on the palate, moving and waking every limb. The Ger melodies never become worn out.

Some there were who spent their whole day in the Chassidic prayer house studying, swaying over their holy books, conversing, speaking about Ger, about new customs, behaviors, and laws.

Among the esteemed Ger Chassidim was R. Shia the teacher, who had traveled to the Sfas Emes and taught us how to reach a high spiritual level, guided us in how to serve the Name, blessed be He, and to study for its own sake. His son studied in a yeshiva in Warsaw and R. Shia the teacher every Friday would send him clean clothes to wear after he went to the mikveh.

Another esteemed Ger Chassid was R. Itshe Shpiegelman from the tannery, a scholar who used to come every Shabbos to the beis–hamedrash wearing his shtreimel and his silken jacket, to quiz the children.

The Chassidic prayer house was a world to itself. Unity between the powerful and the poor ruled there. Everyone said "du" [the informal form of "you"]. For the Chassidim the prayer hall was a second home, sometimes even more of a home than the first, for there they could escape from their worries and their heartaches. There they supported each other, helped with a piece of advice and with deeds, whether regarding sorrows, material difficulties, or spiritual matters.

Amshinov

The Amshinov prayer house could be found on Statsina Street. The Amshinov Chassidim had a reputation for being more worldly. Among them were wealthy merchants, some with trimmed beards. There were also simple, everyday people who showed great respect for the learners, listened to their Gemara lessons and Chassidic aphorisms, which the Chassidim repeated from their rabbi, whom they used visit in Atvotsk on the High Holidays, pouring out their hearts to the rabbi and believing in his power to help them.

Among the Amshinov Chassidim there were no very wealthy magnates. Those who often traveled to their rabbi would speak of the love for Israel that dominated his court. When a Chassid arrived there with a broken heart, hardly had he said "sholem aleichem" to the rabbi than he felt the gentleness of his glance.

Older Chassidim, who travelled to Rabbi Shimonl–Sholem, spoke about how difficult it was to approach him. He was always dwelling in Warsaw, in order to be prepared at all times to defend the rights and the honor of the Jews. Thus he did in Tsarist times and later, when Poland became an independent country.

Later, when the rabbi was not in good health, he moved to Atvotsk, but he was still in contact with Warsaw and was all his life the messenger and intercessor for Jews in times of trouble. The giants of Israel in Poland included the Amshinov rabbi and invited him to all the great local and world conventions and his word was often cited in important religious matters.

Wolomin

Wolomin Jews also had their own rabbi, who actually had his headquarters in Warsaw, but his faithful Chassidim in Wolomin had their own prayer house on Kashtshelne Street.

Unassuming and modest Jews were the Chassidim of the Volomin rabbi, although people used to pray with great rapture in their prayer house, with total devotion, "all my bones speak out." There was no lack of brandy at every opportunity for collective rejoicing, especially at Simchas Torah, when they would go through the streets, from one Chassid to another, eating and drinking whatever had been prepared. Chassidim in Wolomin especially loved to rejoice, to eat and drink in friendship, searching out the significance of the rabbi's words, which the Chassidim brought back after making a pilgrimage to him on a festival. One of the valued Wolomin Chassidim was Margolis, a great scholar and a God–fearing man.

The unity which prevailed in each prayer house did not exist between one prayer house and another, because they each had different attitudes toward community matters, which occasionally emerged with a special sharpness, led to controversies indeed in religious matters, such as hiring a shochet.

I considered myself a Sochotshav Chassid and more than once got carried away with ambition, which so interested a young boy. But now, when I go back in my memory to those times, all of those Chassidic prayer houses are near and dear to me, all the Chassidic melodies, the Shabbos songs in the Shabbos beis–hamekdash, when rapture mixed with gnawing homesickness. Jews would hold on to those hours with all their strength, not wanting to let Shabbos pass.

Cantors And Prayer Leaders

Actually there were no cantorial specialists and none of the cantors had a higher musical eduation. None had graduated from a conservatory. They were simple prayer leaders, but their prayers, the melodies and cadences possessed a peculiar sweetness, and the Wolomin Jews were delighted with their rather conventional voices as they welcomed them and prayed the morning and Musaf services, especially on the High Holidays,

The most outstanding prayer leaders were R. Yisroel–Mordechai the shochet and my father, R. Yehudah–Leib. In his way of praying and singing before the reader's stand, he did not adopt improvisatory recitative or "do–re–mi" or other academic practices. As he sang the prayers, his goal was to pour out his heart, and through his singing he could call forth tears–and not only in the women's section but also among the men. Mostly they were tears of great spiritual delight, but at the same time his singing caused a deep spiritual awakening.

My father had great musical strength, but he was not overwhelming. He was not aware of the lyricism of his own voice, but the congregation felt the refined and sweet ringing of his voice, which pierced the walls of the beis–hamedrash and spread over the streets of Volomin, which were so still on Shabbos and holidays, as if they wanted to hear the prayers.

Another prayer leader was R. Yisroel–Mordechai the shochet. Although I was jealous in regard to my father's singing and I was proud of his prayer before the reader's stand, I still felt with R. Yisroel how his melodies came from his heart. Going to the reader's stand, he felt himself to be a messenger for the congregation, who had to convey the prayer and the feeling for the whole congregation of Wolomin's Jews and display their bitter hearts to the Master of the World.

I will hear those melodies forever. Sometimes it seems to me that they burn holes in me. Sometimes they float far away from me and then return, like sounds and smells on a summer evening. They come together with the voices of the annihilated Wolomin Jews, about whom people testified that through the sweetness of their voices, they could bring the messiah. Such were those who prayed before the reader's stand on Shabbos and festivals or those who after the afternoon prayers recited a lesson for the shtetl's Torah students, astutely and sincerely, those who were simple Jews or great scholars. We should remember them all.

They were certain that their children would go along the same path, just as they had gone along the path of their ancestors.

The Agudas–Yisroel Youth

In my heart my affection for our elders' way of life never ceased, just as my love for their likeness never ceased. Now the memory of their end brings a deep sorrow, because our affection is suffused with a holy fire. So, too, is my membership in the Agudas–Yisroel Youth. With that same fire I devoted myself to the mitzvah of settling Eretz Yisroel.

The members of the Agudas–Yisroel Youth were mostly Chassidic young men who wanted to show that they were capable of more than just learning in the yeshiva or in the beis–hamedrash or finishing up the Talmud page–of–the–day or marking death anniversaries or melava– malkes.

When it came to elections, the Agudas–Yisroel Youth mastered election strategies and did not lag behind the young people in the free Zionist organizations and parties.

The Agudah was active in all the political and communal facets of the shtetl. They took part in the elections for the Polish parliament and senate, for the city council, and for the Jewish community, but the Agudah particularly devoted its attention to problems of strengthening the religion. The second generation of the Agudah movement, the young people, although they were like the old pattern of beis–hamedrash boys, still paid more attention to modern organizational techniques, showed initiative and ability in motivating the Chassidic youngsters and involving them in the task of lighting the fire of Torah and combating the currents of atheism and liberal ideologies that were spreading among the young people in the shtetl.

We began to distribute the Orthodox Jewish Press of Warsaw, organized lessons, spoke with the parents of young people and warned them of the danger of belonging to liberal organizations; we called gatherings of young people and furthered the program of the Agudah. We felt a communal and political power with which the other organizations and parties had to reckon.

From time to time speakers from the Agudah would visit our shtetl, and we, young followers of the Agudah, felt the power of arranging affairs, of discipline. Among the speakers who visited Wolomin, I most vividly remember Alexander Zishe Friedman, the general secretary of Agudas Yisroel in Poland. His articles in the Orthodox Press were full of emotion and logic. His style of speaking was clear and eloquent. Even the opponents of the Agudah had to reckon with him, partly because of his talent and partly because of his excellence. His insights into the Torah were appreciated by scholars. His book, "Kesef Mzokeyk," was pedagogical and learned. His anthology, "Der Toyrah Kval," was not about irrelevancies but was about everyday things, written with proficiency and acuteness.

His presentations and speeches in Wolomin made a strong impression on us, the Young Agudah followers. We were very proud of him and we were always on guard so that his opponents could not disturb his speeches.

Shabbos and Festivals

No fields, no palaces, no family coats–of–arms did we inherit from our parents. Consequently, we did not have to investigate the heroic chronicle of Sefer Yochasin down to our great–great–grandfathers. I always knew that they were religious and observant Jews and whenever they were not preoccupied with the problems of making a living, they never, not for a single hour, day or night, neglected the image of God, their Jewish and mentschlich dignity, and in the hardest times they never lost hope for better days.

What, then, did we inherit from them? What came down to us, their descendants, from our grandfathers and great–grandfathers? A deeply felt melody, a moral, a story from ancient times about wonderful people, about special events and about Shabbos and the Festivals.

A proverb says, "If you really want to know the people–go and see how they celebrate Shabbos and the Festivals." So, too, the character of our shtetl was revealed in its Shabboses and Festivals.

The holiness of Shabbos days put its seal on a Jewish child until his latest years. It framed his spiritual character, developed in him the enthusiasm for beauty and high–mindedness and also a sensitivity for poetry and music, for songs and hymns.

I tremble when I see passing before my eyes the holy moments of our pitilessly destroyed shtetl. Every minute of the day our fathers and mothers go before my eyes with their trembling love for the customs and commandments for sanctifying the seventh day of the week and each of the Festivals, with their anticipation of the approach of sacred days.

Each had according to his means the best food and the nicest clothing to honor Shabbos, for him and for his children. For the whole week, people were satisfied with whatever they had. There were homes in which people ate no more than dry bread and water, enough to survive on, but on Shabbos it was a mitzvah to prepare fresh challas, wine, and food.

For those who could not at all indulge themselves, there were always in the shtetl men with good hearts and charitable women who took care that the Shabbos angels should in mysterious ways make their way to every impoverished household and the blessing of Shabbos should rest on their tables.

There were homes in Wolomin where white tablecloths appeared only to honor Shabbos and Festivals. During the whole week their faces were gray and gloomy, but on Shabbos their faces shone and people found whatever solutions they could to prepare fish and meat. One could imagine the joy of the children in every home.

On Friday the shtetl took on another appearance. Beginning at dawn the streets were full of aromas from fresh baked goods to honor Shabbos. On Friday in the schools, we celebrated, because we knew that the school day was shortened today. In summer, right after eating we went out to play. When the sun got cooler, it revealed that people had gone to the bathhouse. People were not hesitant to enjoy this pleasure. But the approaching Shabbos hurried them on. People put on their clean clothing, and with wet beards and side curls they slowly made their way home, ready to greet the Shabbos Queen.

At the same time, the wives, with grease–covered aprons, placed in their ovens the cholent in clay pots. Then they started to wash their children, braid the girls' hair, and polish the candlesticks for candle lighting.

Thus stands before my eyes our home when it was suffused with Shabbos and over everything lay the grace of holiness. On the table are already the two challas covered with a cloth. On the polished silver candlesticks are the candles, and over them stands my mother, gentle and pale, slightly bent over, her outspread hands covering her face as she blesses the Shabbos lights.

Quietly her lips murmur the prayer. She prays for her husband and children, for the whole shtetl, for every Jew. Her hands, like twin birds, wave over the lights, full of pity and trust, and from my mother's eyes, sanctified by pain and sorrow, a tear falls on the white tablecloth.

My mother's soft, dove–like eyes, so sacred in the beauty of the blessed lights in Friday's twilight, accompany me all my days.

Step by step the Jews make their way to shul, to the beis–hamedrash and to the Chassidic prayer houses.

"Lecha dodi likras kallah, p'ney Shabbos n'kabelah"–the song is heard from all corners of the different streets, in all corners of the shtetl. In all the synagogues, everyone is immersed in the light of flickering lamps.

Shabbos, Shabbos! So earth and heaven sang in Wolomin. It was the song of generations that had in Wolomin their special grace and magic that remain with us today.

Where are you, Jews of my destroyed shtetl home, and where are the dreams of your young people, who learned about Shabbos from your example, the beis–hamedrash boys–with prayers and the music of hymns, the young people who joined organizations and parties–with the sound of discussion and lectures, with evenings of checkers and the music of Zionist songs?

Where are you, dear mothers, with your hands full of blessings? On the ashes of your hands grow new trees in Treblinka, in Maidanek, and in Auschwitz.

Where are those blissful hours of Friday nights, the fullness and riches of Jewish life in our shtetl home Wolomin?

Gone are the magical flames of the Shabbos lights in the narrow windows of our homes. Instead we kindle yahrzeit lights, flames in memory of a warm, pulsing, and beautiful Jewish life which once was and is no more.

The High Holidays

Preparations for the High Holidays were filled with awe. Certain people, my grandfather, for instance, and others like him, began to prepare starting on the fifteenth of Av. They began to examine their actions, to stay longer in the beis–hamedrash. In a letter to a relative in a distant city people wrote wishes for a good year and over all people were concerned with thoughts of repentance.

The real trembling began on Rosh Chodesh Elul. The blowing of the shofar and the collective recitation of Psalms early every morning darkened one's mood and filled one's heart with a gnawing sadness and a quiet fear. Thus began the days of accounting for one's soul and purification, of forgiveness and self–improvement. They awoke feelings of brotherhood and a desire to do good deeds, charity and righteousness. People were more careful about what they said. In Chassidic homes on those days people spoke more softly. Conversations in the beis–hamedrash were more courteous and subdued.

Many people in Wolomin held no worldly conversations from Rosh Chodesh Elul until Yom Kippur because in the whole world there is no better way to purify the soul than to keep one's mouth closed and speak no frivolity. Even more, such rejection of foolishness is good for a person when he considers the devotion of his prayers and he realizes that his pure devotion should not be mixed with other thoughts.

Even more powerful is the spiritual awakening of the first Selichos prayers, which are recited at midnight. There were some who directly after the melaveh malkeh went to the beis–hamedrash and sat and studied until midnight. Others walked slowly through the dark streets to the beis–hamedrash together with the children who had been awakened, silently and contemplatively.

Wolomin, my beautiful shtetl, now after decades I still hear the sounds and the stillness of that night. The moon and the stars spoke in their own secret language and I felt that the shtetl was full of shades.

On Erev Rosh Hashanah, people were not satisfied only with Selichos. They also said the whole book of Psalms before the Selichos and afterwards. They forgave promises, visited the cemetery, gave charity, fasted, some for a whole day and more for a half of a day. More strongly, with more ecstasy, they repeated the Thirteen Attributes of God, though the highest level was reserved for Erev Yom Kippur.

My pen is too weak to convey the mood, the experience, and the feeling of Erev Yom Kippur day in the shtetl. From dawn on, the Jews streamed to the mikveh. As I remember it, almost all the Jews, especially from the older generation, went to the mikveh on Erev Yom Kippur. Some would submerge themselves three times, before the morning prayers, before the afternoon prayers, and before the pre–fast meal. The only mikveh in town was certainly crowded, but that did not stop anyone.

At dawn began the atonement ceremony. Very religious Jews sought out a white hen, though in an emergency a brown one would do. The youngsters would say with great intensity the "Benei Adam" while their fathers swung the hen around their heads. They were sure that all their sins were transferred to the hens. This was the origin of the saying, "He looks like a hen during the "Benei Adam."

On that day all the Jews gave charity, each according to his means. In the shul and in the beis–hamedrash, people set up receptacles for various charitable causes and no one refused to contribute, both paper money and coins.

Several hours before candle lighting, the whole shtetl was prepared for the holiday. Mothers and grandmothers put on kerchiefs and scarves, and people went to neighbors and relatives, to friends and to those whom they had offended, wishing them a good year and a good inscription in the Book of Life, as well as asking forgiveness for cross words that had slipped out, for offending with slander and gossip. Wives embraced each other and from the houses arose laments and weeping. Children were clasped by mothers and fathers and were taught the importance of the Day of Judgment.

In the streets we saw people with tearful eyes. The fathers were dressed in white kittles and taleisim, and they blessed their children with voices choked with tears. Their mother had poured out her heart while lighting the candles.

Houses and streets were filled with dread. The mood was serious, holy, and fearful. With broken hearts people went to the shul, to the beis–hamedrash, and to Chassidic prayer houses for the prayers and the confession of Rabbeinu Nissim.

Soon, the tones of Kol Nidrei sounded through the whole shtetl. In the shul and in the beis–hamedrash the great yahrzeit lights were kindled in memory of deceased ancestors, of parents, who went to their eternal rest. The shul was full of light, with the men dressed in their white kittles.

Wolomin's Jews listened with dread and trembling to the mystical melody of Kol Nidrei. Many would stand for twenty–four or twenty–five or twenty–six hours before their creator and confess their sins, beat their breasts while they say "I have sinned," say prayers, songs, and praises to God amid rivers of tears. In the Memorial Service people recalled the dead, their ancestors from generations ago, who are at eternal rest.

When the cantor sang of the sorrow of our afflicted people in the prayer recalling the Ten Martyrs, old and young thought not only about those who were tortured by the Romans but about all who were killed amid great suffering in the Crusades, in the Inquisition, and through the rulings and persecutions through the centuries among all peoples.

Moving laments were heard from the women's section when the cantor recalled Rabbi Akiva, whose torturers flayed his skin with iron combs. Thus our mothers and grandmothers bewailed the dark Jewish fate in exile.

Finally the service ended with "Next year in Jerusalem."

After the evening service, people did not rush home to eat after the long fast, but they stayed to say the prayer over the new moon. The holiest day of the year had passed. Everyone felt clean, purified of sin and ready to begin a new year, a year for taking new steps in a difficult life, with a hope for better times.

Awesome and holy were the High Holidays in Wolomin, a way of life that was established over generations by Jewish sages, geonim and rabbis and was sanctified by martyrs through suffering and anguish.

Succos and Simchas Torah

Succos–so many ceremonies and commandments. But because of the compressed time, everything had to be done quickly. Many people had succahs prepared and had only to open the roofs and bring schach. Children helped to prepare the new succah. They decorated it with multi–colored chains and lanterns, but the greatest preparations concerned the esrog and lulav, which had to be supplied for the whole community.

The sexton used to go around to all the houses with the esrog so that the women could say the blessing. Fathers taught their children how to say the blessing and shake the lulav.

On Simchas Torah the children prepared paper flags with an apple on the point of the stick. For the children this was a great experience. In the apples they stuck a little candle. There were children who never had enough to eat, but for Simchas Torah they had to have a flag.

Jews in Wolomin made the Simchas Torah processions in the beis–midreshes and the Chassidic prayer halls. On their entrance into the shul, the girls would bend over to kiss the Torah scrolls.

During the day there were some Jews who made everyone happy by singing "Tzon–kodoshim," while young people circled them and held them up and their happy voices echoed all around.

Chanukah

Chanukah is one of those holidays when people can work, so the celebration was not drawn out. In every home there was a Chanukah lamp, which people received as wedding presents, some of silver and some of simple brass, some using oil and some using candles. People in the shtetl let themselves go, fried latkes, played a little cards, and in many homes people had cracklings with Passover schmaltz.

But for the children it was a real holiday. They received Chanukah gelt, played at dreidel in the beis–hamedrash and at home. Outside the frost cracked and the windows were covered with snow. Soon after blessing the Chanukah lights, having extracted from their parents all that they could, they ran to uncles and aunts for Chanukah gelt. Later they sat around playing dreidel and telling stories about the great hero Judah Maccabee and his heroic brothers, stories that they heard in school and that filled their imaginations with mighty deeds.

Purim

On Purim people were more worn out. The mothers made hamentaschen, meat kreplach, and other treats for shalach manos. Children made groggers and rattles for the megillah reading and especially masks to disguise themselves.

Grown–up Jews also disguised themselves, wearing different costumes and masks. Singing songs, they went from house to house collecting donations for various good causes, like supplying wheat to the poor for Passover, and others.

People dressed up as Ahashveros and the righteous Mordechai, as the patriarchs and Aaron the priest, as wicked Haman and others. They were welcomed into each home with drink and with the food that had been prepared.

The sending of shalach manos involved the children, who ran with runny noses from the frost delivering the shalach manos and in the process grabbing a nosh. A unique time of the year.

Pesach

Immediately after Purim, the season for matzoh baking began. Religious Jews only ground the wheat by hand and earlier they selected the wheat so that it would be free of any trace of chametz. Merchants brought samples to the rabbis so that he could put a hechsher on the wheat, kosher for Passover.

Usually the head of the household or his wife would come to the matzoh baking, chat with baker, and bring home the flour. The people who worked for the baker were hired, mostly women and younger girls as kneaders and rollers. Young men and boys would perforate the matzohs with a toothed wheel from a clock.

People brought the matzohs home in a bedsheet, tied with four knots, and hung them from a hook from the ceiling.

Then it was time to prepare the borscht, which was part of the work of preparing for the holiday. Then they put away raisins for raisin wine.

Having finished with these important tasks, which were handed down from parents to children for generations, they began a regimen of cleaning, scraping, , scratching, and koshering: airing out the books in the courtyard, emptying pockets in clothing, and koshering the pots. In the bathhouse were special containers in which people koshered their pots.

A particularly sacred task was baking the shmura matzoh for erev Pesach. This began the day before, when people set out water to sit overnight. This water, according to religious law, had to sit overnight in the house and with that water people kneaded the dough for the matzoh.

Often I went with the Chassidim to the well. One person held the bucket. Remember, it had to be made of wood. A second person–the earthenware dipper, and another–the strainer, and it was an honor for who would draw earlier and who later. When we had filled several buckets with water, we went home singing.

After the evening prayers we began the search for chametz. We often scattered breadcrumbs around solely so that we could make the blessing at the burning of the chametz. The ceremony was brief. But many of the homemakers were awake all night preparing for the holiday and it seemed to them that their work was never finished.

In the morning at the baker's, the baking got started. After handing over the sheet, the kneading began. One had to pay special attention to [the amount of time between] adding drops of water to the dough and when the kneading was done and at the right time he called out, "Take the dough." One of the rollers took the dough, divided it into sections and gave each roller a section, and then the work began.

The rolling was done on a long table, which was constructed of two broad boards which were scraped wondrously clean. The boards were laid on a wooden frame, which was called a "mare," and thus they became a table.

The rolled out matzoh, thin almost to transparency, was laid out for perforating so that they would not explode in the oven. From there they were taken and laid out in the oven, where in a corner a fire had burned continuously. A special person had the job of standing by the oven and counting the matzohs. The matzohs were placed in a special basket and distributed among the Chassidim.

My father prepared thoroughly for the seder. He prepared the seder plate, the four cups of wine, the Haggados for each person. After the asking of the Four Questions, everyone said together "Avadim hayinu, We were slaves in Egypt." There was no home in the shtetl which was not prepared for Passover with all its customs and in which the table was not prepared with fish, soup, and knaidlich.

Children anxiously prepared to open the door for "Pour out your wrath" and to see Eliahu the Prophet take a sip from his cup, which stood filled with wine on each table. But they never saw him because by that time they had fallen asleep. Almost every child in Wolomin had the same dream after falling asleep after the knaidlich. In our dream we saw Eliahu the Prophet, a little old man, kind and happy, with a silver white beard, in a white satin caftan embroidered with silver. He goes to the cup and sips so little that it was hard to tell. As people drank…

Every child had prepared requests and wishes to beg from Eliahu the Prophet, but at just the right moment, he became tongue–tied and could not say a word. Such were the dreams of the seder night for the beautiful, happy children.

The streets were silent except for the sounds of the Haggadah being sung, which lasted half the night. No one was seen in the streets, for everyone knew that on this night, Jews and Jewish dwellings were protected by holy angels. They float over the roofs, look in the windows, and stand like watchmen by the doors.

Preparations for the Passover Holiday
[This section, pp. 136–7] repeats in Hebrew much that was in the previous section.]

Shavuos

No special preparations were common in the shtetl, because the holiday commemorating the giving of the Torah is not bound up with special ceremonies, except that the milkmen were busy as the women prepared dairy meals, cheese–filled dumplings and baked goods with butter, cheese cake, cheese rolls, and so on.

In the prayer houses and in the beis–hamedrash, people decorated the walls and the floors with green branches, especially around the bimah and the holy ark, to remind us of the assembly at Mt. Sinai. Children went into the woods, as though there were no such thing as school or rabbi or whip. They brought home green branches, greens for the holiday, to hang over the windows and spread irises on the floors.

Thus were the traditions and customs observed in that inviting atmosphere of our shtetl, a homey Jewish and deeply humane atmosphere. Generations grew up sucking their life's milk from the inexhaustible source of Yiddishkeit, bound with every thread of their souls to the Jewish people, feeling their sorrows and their joys.

It was an epoch when many of the young people from our shtetl went away to seek culture from other people, allegedly. Many others went to other Jewish shtetls to seek more beautiful and better values. Disappointment came quickly, bitter and tragic disappointment, and the price was the most murderous in the history of mankind and led to destruction.

Seas of blood and tears have flowed and now, when we recall our holy martyrs, their treasures and traditions, judgments, laws, and customs are appear before our eyes. The more we think about them, the more we recognize their greatness and their beauty, their overall ethical behavior and the personal relations between individuals and the spirit of a higher morality that created the spiritual atmosphere of the shtetl.

[Page 138]

A life of purity and holiness

by Sara Baum

Translated by Sara Mages

Wolomin was typical Jewish town, like all other Polish towns, and although I was not born there I felt a connection with its people, especially with my relatives. There were Jews in it of all kinds: wealthy, beggars, merchants, laborers, craftsmen, observant and also free. However, the majority were Hasidim of all kinds and their opponents.

All the parties, which existed in Poland at the time, also existed in Wolomin.

The area of Jewish residence was the center of the town and in front of them, and behind them, swarmed anti-Semites of all kinds that the hatred of the Jews burned in them, even though the Jews created and built and also enriched their gentile neighbors.

In this atmosphere the Jews of Wolomin lived a life of purity and holiness and made a living from the labor of their hands. An insignificant percentage gained wealth. Many more lived a life of poverty and distress.

I knew the Jewish youth in the years before the war. Most of them were precious gems. They were always willing to do everything in their power for the homeland and for the people. There were those who learned and knew Hebrew, and the common characteristic of them all - the thirst to learn and to know.

This youth has not lost its image even in the days of rage. They proudly carried their sufferings and restrained their torture.

All were sacrificed on the altar of their Judaism during the Nazi Holocaust.

You are holy, the members of the destroyed community of Wolomin, we hear your last groans and together with you we turn to the Lord of Hosts:

"Pour out Your wrath upon the murderers, for they have devoured Yakov."

[Page 139]

My youth years in Wolomin

by Kalman Froiman

Translated by Sara Mages

"Yesodey Hatorah"

I spent eight years of my youth, from the age of ten to eighteen, in Wolomin, and devoted all these years to Torah study. I studied at "Talmud Torah" until its liquidation. *"Yesodey Hatorah,"* a more modern school, was built in its place. It contained four classes, in each class two hours a day were devoted to secular studies and the rest of the time - to Judaic studies.

After the student passed the intermediate-examinations he moved to a higher class.

My father, Yehoshua Froiman, was a teacher in the highest class. He was a Jewish scholar and, in addition to that, a simple man in his daily life. He was admired and loved by all who knew him, and he himself was humble.

When I completed my studies in "Talmud Torah" I was already, according to my knowledge, worthy of entering the "yeshiva," but it did not exist in Wolomin. My parents wanted to send me to Warsaw or to Wyszków to study in one of the large Yeshivot, but they were not able to afford it and I continued my studies in Beit HaMidrash.

Nine other boys studied together with me in Beit HaMidrash. We began with our own study and were assisted by older boys who had already made progress in their studies.

They only helped us in special cases when we met "obstacles" that we could not go through on our own. I mostly remember Feivel Stolman, a studious intelligent boy who was always willing to help.

This transition, from studying in the "*cheder*" to the study in Beit HaMidrash, where the boy was situated all day in a large hall among different people, young and old, studying and praying, was a tremendous event in the boy's life, an event that left its mark on the development of the youth and had a great influence on the course of his future life.

We studied diligently from morning to evening, we studied Gemara with interpretation. Our only entertainment was on Thursday nights when we brought bread and herring to Beit HaMidrash and had dinner together, chanting and singing ancestral melodies and Hassidic melodies in fraternity and friendship.

[Page 140]

That's how I reached the age of eighteen. At that time the young man in the town began to think about his future, and as the economic situation worsened and the persecution and economic pressure increased, so grew the yearning to leave the Vale of Tears in the Diaspora and immigrate to Eretz Yisrael.

The problem was not simple, because in order to reach Eretz Yisrael it was necessary to have a certificate, a permit issued by the British Mandatory government.

Indeed, we were members of "*Tzeirei Agudat Yisrael*," and each party received a certain amount of certificates at its disposal, but the quantity was too small and was not enough for all those who were willing to immigrate to Eretz Yisrael.

Wolomin was a pious town. Apart from the "*chedarim*" there were also Batei Midrash and Hasidic "*Shtiblach*" where they prayed and studied from morning till evening, on weekdays, on the Sabbath and holidays. The sound of Torah burst through the town from the throat of schoolchildren, small and big, from young men and yeshiva students. In this manner the spirit of the Jewish people was forged in the town and great scholars and proud Jews were raised there.

[Pages 141-145]

My Teachers

by Shmuel Zucker

The first day when I was led to school remains like a distant dream in my memory. It was a hard winter, and on the windows of all the houses the frost had woven flowers that filled our childish imaginations. It was Sunday. All through Shabbos everyone at home spoke about taking me to school. I rejoiced in the thought that soon I would be with the other children who ran out of the school with clamor and racket. It seemed to me that the school consisted of games and childish noise.

Even today it seems that I feel the warmth of my father's hand when he led me across the street on my first day as a schoolboy. Arriving at the rabbi's courtyard, he opened wide the door and a Jew with a long, white beard and glasses with golden frames gave us a heartfelt mazel tov.

The Wolomin teachers in their private schools and Talmud Torahs and pre–yeshivas were far from being pedagogues in the modern sense, but they created a profound influence on the creation of character in the Jewish children in the shtetl. Like most of my generation in Wolomin, I ranged through the whole gamut of school and I have so much to thank them for. I will cite several of my teachers as I thank them for my childhood:

Velvel Melamed

First is Velvel the Melamed, whose name and person I have known for a long time. Together with my father, I was ushered into a glazed terrace, and soon the rebitzin came in. She had left her kitchen to bring us refreshments, a glass of tea and some cookies. It seemed to me that the rabbi looked at me with love as he stroked his long beard. Soon on the table there appeared a silver tray with apples and almonds. The conversation became livelier. The rabbi sent me to sit by the window. From there I could see Waczechovski's garden, which the children used to love.

Waczerchovki's garden was full of tall, full–branched trees, on which the birds had built their nests, and their singing in the early mornings and the evenings sounded to my ears like the most beautiful symphonies. The garden was surrounded by prickly wires, and to our eyes it looked like an earthly Garden of Eden. All kinds of fruit grew there, and there were decorated areas for a variety of games. Children from the various schools in the shtetl would come to the garden, stand by the prickly wires, and look at the ripening fruit; and it sometimes happened that a child would work up the courage to squeeze through the fence in order to grab an apple that the wind had blown off the tree. More than once a child lost a piece of his sock with a piece of skin from his foot to the teeth of the big dog who served his master faithfully by roaming the garden and lying in wait for his victim, the Jewish schoolboy.

Fishele Melamed

Two winters and two summers I studied with Velvel Melamed. Having absorbed the rhythm of the alef–beis and of Hebrew, I had the foundation for further learning. Then my father turned me over to a second teacher, Fishele Melamed. He was more demanding. He used to sit by a new pupil, holding a hand and using a wooden pointer, which was sharpened to a point. With that he pointed to the Rashi, which he tried to stuff into the child's head.

If the child did not grasp the meaning of Rashi's commentary on the Chumash quickly enough, Fishele Melamed squinted with his small black eyes so that they looked like dark slits and immediately with his short, fat finger seized a piece of flesh from the frightened child and gave a pinch with a twist. He called out: "You get from me twisting pinch." Since the marks left by these pinches took a long time to disappear, many children from our shtetl carried these reminders of Fishele Melamed's pinches.

The pinch was not the only punishment that Fishele Melamed dreamed up for his students. To this day there is, on the small finger of my right hand, a sign of a blow that I received from his whip, which was wound around with thin wires. My transgression was that I was not listening to his teaching and therefore had my hand on my Gemara.

Meyer Melamed

I studied with Fishele Melamed for no more than a semester, that is, a half of a year. After that my father brought me to Meyer Shrek. Meyer Melamed's school was on Mikveh Street in the fall, when suddenly the rain caused the mud to deepen so much that people could get their feet stuck in it.

Meyer Melamed particularly liked to keep his students in the school until late at night.

We remember the names that his wife, Taube–Rivke, always uttered and sewed on her garments like amulets. When it was very cold out, she used to run into the schoolroom and bring with her the wind from the street. She was dressed from head to toe in black. She would hop around from the cold and murmur verses from the Torah. Often she would sit on the bench together with the students and say to us in a quiet but firm voice, "When there is no more wood in the school, then will come those souls who want to immerse themselves in the mikveh."

It is difficult to hide the fear that immediately enveloped our hearts. Full of fear, we left with our lanterns, which the wind quickly extinguished, and we were certain that that was the work of the souls who came out of the mikveh. In deathly fear we grasped hands, whispered biblical verses, so that the souls would have no power over us.

That fear seized our hearts and lies even today in my bones.

Shia–Chatzkl Melamed

My next teacher was Shia–Chatzkl. A thin, pale, sunken–backed man with a sparse beard, he liked to joke with the students that he was one of those teachers who had a reputation as a great explicator, could make clear a chapter of the Tanach, or a difficult passage of the Talmud, but if a student questioned him, he felt on his shoulders the sharp sting of his whip, which we called The Whipster.

More than once I felt that sting, and until now it is still hard for me to understand why that Jew felt so much anger and wickedness.

That infernal Whipstser he stored in his desk, which stood in his second room between the beds. When a student transgressed, Shia–Chatzkl ran into the next room, opened the desk, grabbed the Whipster in his hand, and brandished it with such power that it cut into the shoulders of the student.

The Whipster seemed to be three meters long. Whoever felt its bite had something to think about for a long time, to sit quietly, to look right at the rabbi and to do readily what he demanded.

The Melamdim Avraham–Baruch and Zishe

Two years later I became the student of Avraham–Baruch.

Between the two teachers Avraham–Baruch and Zishe in the Talmud Torah there was a wall with a damaged door, which was always closed so that they would not interfere with each other.

Both teachers had thick, gray beards, wore the same open smocks, through which could be seen their large tallis katan. Their teaching methods were also similar. They translated every word so they could make their way clearly through the densest thicket of a Talmudic passage.

They demonstrated shrewdness and wisdom and we regarded them with the greatest respect: They were "a plastered well that never loses a drop" [a quotation from Pirkey Avos]. They opened for us the door and tower of Gemara and Midrash, which became for us a beloved garden of learning. And that learning influenced our characters and morals.

So many years have passed since that time. Our horrible enemy finished off Volomin along with the schools. Teachers and students–I have never forgotten them. They taught us not only Hebrew, Chumash, and Gemara, but they also preserved our Jewish customs, our high morals, our love of Israel, and our love for our companions.

[Page 146]

The elementary school

by Tzipora Lewit-Grodzhitzki

Translated by Sara Mages

I received my education in a religious home. My grandfather, R' Moshe Grodzhitzki, was one of the dignitaries of the Jewish community in Wolomin and my parents followed his traditional path. In my time, there was already a compulsory education in Poland and Jewish children were forced to visit the elementary school every day. I managed to finish six classes at this school.

From the outset, this school was intended for Jewish children, but over time Polish children were also transferred to it. They had learning difficulties and the Polish schools wanted to be free of them.

The school principal, Mr. Zielinski, was indeed an alcoholic, but, it must be admitted, that during his tenure we did not feel discrimination. The situation changed radically when he was replaced by the new principle, Mr. Wilczynski, an outspoken anti-Semite who showed his hatred at every opportunity, always found reason to scold us and prove that the Jews are cheaters and cowards. If there was a quarrel between the children in the school yard, and the Jewish children did not remain silent and gave the abusers what they deserved, he cursed them and severally punished them.

A Polish student, Tomaszewski, was sent to our classroom and he terrorized the whole class. He beat the Jewish children with strong and vigorous blows, and when we tried to defend ourselves and give him what he deserved, the principle immediately summoned us to a meeting, opened with morality and rebuke and ended with the imposition of a punishment on us - "so you will know."

Tomaszewski the criminal was never punished.

On November 11, Polish Independence Day, each class chose its representatives for a celebration at the monument of the Unknown Soldier. In 1937 I was chosen as a representative of my class to participate in the celebration in which the principle, Wilczynski, delivered his speech. He said among others:

"You should know that the Polish Republic does not trust the Jews... There is no place here for your deceptive fraud. I and my teachers were appointed to teach wisdom to the children so that they can accept the good things we give them, but you, the Jews, cannot accept what is given to you. We aim to raise a generation that, in due course, will know how to defend our country. But, I know, that in time of need, not you, only Tomashevsky will be the one who would defend our country..."

[Page 147]

From an early age the activists began the pioneering education in our town, and this activity attracted a great deal of attraction, which also aroused the aspiration of the schoolchildren to immigrate.

We, the Jewish children, were astonished, as if he pounded on us with a club, and then I began to understand that we were strangers in this country.

Tomaszewski, of course, knew how to draw conclusions from the principle's speech and on the same day the criminal's fury rose and poured furiously on the children's heads like a roaring waterfall.

Some of our teachers were Jews and some Poles, and from them I remember fondly the teacher Zabroki, an honest man and an excellent teacher who knew how to bestow upon us his good spirit. He was faithful to his principles to which he always advocated: honesty, decency and a sense of responsibility. That's why we also knew how to honor him and appreciate his personality.

The teacher, Kanapik, was old and single. In Polish she was called: Kanifikovna, to emphasize that she was single.

She was lonely and bitter, and there was always a certain reluctance that we all felt, sorrow and indignation emanating from every word and sentence that came out of her mouth.

Bausch was a geography teacher and the smell of anti-Semitism also dissipated from him. He treated better students with Aryan faces, or Aryan names, and gave them better marks. He used to say to me: "Your face is Polish, you also have a Polish name, it's too bad you are Jewish ..."

I managed to finish six classes and the war broke out.

[Pages 148-151]

My Teacher R' Yehezkel Rubinshtein

by Chaim Rubin

Before I started studying with the teacher Yehezkel Rubinshtein I went through several other schools. Yehezkel Rubinshtein was an aristocrat among the teachers in Wolomin.

My first experience in school was in the Talmud Torah. I remember that I was four or five years old. The Talmud Torah was in Yoskes Laskovski's house on Langer Street, a three–roomed dwelling on the first floor. The nearest neighbor was Chavele Tziapkevich.

In the three rooms were three divisions. In the first room, in which I studied, was for beginners, who were learning the alphabet and prayers. The second room was for students who had gone further and learned Chumash with Rashi. In the third room were those who learned Gemara.

The students did not move from one room to the next every year. The students in the third room used to go to school throughout the year until they went away to study in yeshivas.

My first teacher was yellowish, but I do not remember his name. I only remember that we used to learn from early in the morning until night every day without exception. More than once we wished the teacher would take ill so we could be free.

After learning there for a year, I transferred to a second teacher, to Fishele on Leshne Street. There I studied Chumash. The rabbi, R' Fishlele, used to come to my parents often to praise me as a good student, as someone with a good head, as someone who would grow to be a scholar. Thanks to this praise, I received a larger allowance.

After three years of study, I had achieved my goal and I then went to study with Rabbi R' Yehezkel.

R' Yehezkel was my first teacher who gave me a general education. With him I began to learn writing and reading Yiddish, Polish, Hebrew, and arithmetic.

This striving for worldly education came about accidentally: when I was crossing a street, I saw people putting up posters with pictures, but I could not read the writing. Around the posters people had gathered and I was ashamed to ask what the inscriptions meant.

This happened after the Soviet invasion of Warsaw was repulsed.

At R' Yehezkel's, there were twenty students of different ages. His attitude toward us was more liberal than that of any other teacher of that time. Occasionally he would use a whip, but only for students who were disruptive. R' Yehezkel was for me the first teacher and the first school that made me interested in coming to study every day. He was the first teacher who taught me Tanach and made me acquainted with the historical past of the Jewish people.

His house was located in the center of the shtetl at the intersection of Lange and Wilensky Street. The room where we studied had two findows. We sat on both sides of a long table and listened with interest as he explained the chapters of Tanach, day by day. His enthusiasm and his scholarly approach to the chapters about King Saul inspired us students, so that long after we left for home we continued to talk about the Jewish kings.

R' Yehezkel had a very practical approach to teaching. I remember that he taught us beautiful calligraphy. We brought special notebooks and we concentrated on writing perfectly in straight rows.

R' Yehezkel was not fanatically observant. He went on his own path, He preached no sermons even though he knew about many of the Jewish failings of Wolomin.

He loved doing good deeds, and he had a reputation as a good writer of requests to the town council, to the local nobility, and to all of the other institutions. His requests were well argued in fine Polish. He also knew German, Russian, and he knew Yiddish literature. He often read us works by Sholem Aleichem, Y.L. Peretz, and others.

R' Yehezkel was not a Chasid, did not travel to a rebbe, and did not belong to a Chasidic prayer house. He was pedantically clean: always in polished boots and a clean and pressed kaftan, he would say and say again that we should take the example of people such as R' Moyshe Grodzhiski and his sons, from whom shone the fear of Heaven when they went on Friday evenings to shul.

R' Yehezkel understood the soul of a student. He never commented that we played ball in his courtyard. He often organized gatherings for us, especially for Chanukah, when his wife Simma made latkes in honor of his students.

He used to say that there were no better latkes in the world than those of his wife Simma. He would call them "famfuches" [I can't find a meaning for this] because they were thin, well–fried, and would melt in your mouth. It was said that anyone who then drank a glass of tea sweetened with sugar, his enemy should not know such pleasure.

R' Yehezkel was a very good father and worried about his children, even when they had their own families. Similarly he always took interest in his students, even after they were grown and self–sufficient.

R' Yehezkel understood the dilemma of Jewish young people, that there was no way for them to live in Poland. He used to say that for us Jews the only path was to go up to the land of Israel.

He loved the wonders of nature, and he used to go with us not only to Tashlich but he would walk with us in the surrounding fields and woods.

I remember in 1929 the massacre in Hebron, among whose victims was the Dubnikov family, whose son studied with us in the school. They were refugees from Russia and lived in Wolomin for a short time. He said Yizkor in shul and often mentioned Dubnikov's genteel bearing.

Shortly before the outbreak of the Second World War R. Yehezkel was still in good health. Had it not been for the barbaric Nazi murderers and their helpers, he would have lived to an advanced age.

[Pages 151-156]

The Talmud Torah

by Chaya Rubenshtein

The Wolominers built the Talmud Torah in the same courtyard as the beis–hamedrash.

The beis–hamedrash was a wooden structure that the Germans burned soon after occupying Wolomin.

The building of the Talmud Torah was a brick house that is still standing. Next to the Talmud Torah, they also built a school of five grades in which people studied secular subjects

The teachers of religious subjects all lived in the city, but the teachers of secular subjects came from Warsaw. After completing their work for the day, they returned home. The five–grade school by the Talmud Torah was created for parents who did not want to send their children to the Polish schools. After finishing the five classes, each student received a certificate, and if he wanted, he could continue his education in higher classes, but in other schools.

Many children continued their education in the Folk–School, the majority until the seventh grade. There were others who later studied in a gymnasium or in a trade school. Mostly those from the Talmud Torah went away to study in a yeshiva.

One of the teachers in the Talmud Torah was a young man from Wolomin, Shlomo Tabakman, who completed a teacher seminar in Warsaw and returned to Wolomin, where he took the position in the Talmud Torah. Before the war, he made aliyah to Israel, where he works even now as a school inspector in the Haifa area.

The Folk–School and its Jewish Teachers

At the time when Poland was occupied by Czarist Russia, before the First World War, it was very difficult for a Jewish child to study in a government school.

In Wolomin, actually, there was then a Folk–School, but not everyone could go to that school. There was an ordinance from the government that only children whose parents owned their own house could attend that school. No children of poorer parents could attend the school. The poorer children were therefore forced to study with a private teacher. But this was not always possible.

After the liberation of Poland, the ordinance was cancelled and all children, poor and rich, had access to the Folk–School. In the Folk–School, Jewish and Polish children learned together. Only in later years was a school created solely for Jewish children. The school was located on Varshevsker Street, in a house that was rented from a Jewish landlord.

The Folk–School in Wolomin had seven grades. The director was Polish. The teachers were a mixed group of Jews and Poles.

Many students, after finishing the Folk–School, continued their education in a Warsaw gymnasium or in a trade school.

One of the outstanding Jewish teachers was Mrs. Tiglovna, who successfully saved herself from Hitler's murderers and lives today in Paris.

Another outstanding teacher was Mrs. Necholsona, who now lives in America. Mr. Schneour lives now in Warsaw. The students, who occasionally still meet their surviving teachers, lived through moving times.

Most of the Jewish teachers were killed by Hitler's murderers. Among them was Mrs. Hellervona, who, with her whole family, lived in the Wolomin ghetto and who perished with the whole Jewish community of Wolomin.

The Beis–Yakov School

The Beis–Yakov shool was located on Leshnau Street, in the Kersh house. The school had six grades. The students began with the aleph–beis, learned to read and write Yiddish, studied Chumash, Jewish history, Jewish religious laws, and singing.

The girls in the Beis–Yakov school were very religious and observed the commandments that applied to Jewish women. When they finished with the school, they were well versed in Jewish knowledge. People referred to them affectionately as "little daughters."

When the school year ended, people organized performances based on biblical themes. Children from all grades participated in these performances. Children, along with their teachers, devoted great energy to these performances, painting and setting up decorations. Mostly these performances were a great success. Parents got a lot of nachas from their talented children, and teachers got real satisfaction from seeing the good results of their labors and energy.

Just like their mothers, these children, the young girls, the Beis–Yakov students, developed a refined and quiet modesty. Now we remain overcome by sadness for these dear and sacred figures, the Wolomin girls, cut off so young, separated from their parents, their teachers, their educators, on their last walk. Always they stand before my eyes as the exemplars of Jewish beauty and morality.

I remember the teacher Mrs. Borochov, who was sent to us from the central office of the Beis–Yakov–Schools in Cracow. She lived with the Zambau family, the son–in–law of the Wolomin rabbi. The children loved her. They saw in her the embodiment of true Yiddishkeit. She taught here until the last year before the outbreak of the Second World War.

In the last year before the war, one of our Beis–Yakov students, Dvorah Grodzhitzki, became a teacher in the Beis–Yakov School in Rodzhomin .

The Beis–Yakov School benefited from the moral and financial support of the town. Only the well–to–do paid tuition. The brothers Feivel and Dovid Shtulman gave outstanding support.

Unforgettable for the children were the Lag B'Omer excursions, the walks and the conversations that the teachers conducted with their students about the best chapters of Jewish history.

Beis–Yakov students used to come on Friday nights and early Shabbos mornings to pray in the shul. They took pride in their knowledge of Jewish studies.

Beis–Yakov Girls

The special qualities and the moral beauty of the young girls, which characterized the Beis–Yakov girls in Wolomin, showed themselves not only in religiosity and courtesy. They also loved Eretz Yisroel and they incorporated the nationalistic movement in their home life.

Among these simple Jewish girls were some who understood the depths of the principles and laws of the Jewish faith: how one should behave in all human situations according to Jewish principles, the commandments and the prohibitions regarding Shabbos observance and other areas of Yiddishkeit.

These girls learned a lot about Judaism, about the intent and style of Yiddishkeit. They knew that there was not one intent but many, that there is in Yiddishkeit a world of symbols which mirror the great truth of Judaism and which possess special secrets and intentions, which people cannot plumb to their full depths.

What did these young girls think when they went on their final path to their terrible deaths? Did they believe that the Jewish people was chosen to walk alone among the nations of the world, to be the first and to be unique in order to be evidence of the greatness of the Jewish God, of his Oneness, so that they should learn righteousness, the customs and ideals of the Jewish people? Why then does God look on indifferently while His enemies obliterate his troops? And where are the announcements of the great redemption which is supposed to redeem both us and them?

Perhaps they thought this must be the beginning of the Redemption; perhaps they justified the judgment, the frightful judgment on a people. They always held high the flag of Yiddishkeit and of idealism. They understood and knew from their experience that everything in life evolves through suffering.

With deep faith they lived and with deep faith they elevated their purity; in suffering they refined their souls.

Together with them, their teachers, leaders, and community workers drank from the bitter cup, murdered for the sanctification of the Name.

The Nazi killers obliterated the Jewish children, but they could not break them. Even the simple, religious, meritorious Jewish girls were as strong as oaks, and so they remained in those terrible days. Under Hitler's sword, which hung over their heads, they felt their responsibilities until the last minutes of their lives.

Such were the Jewish children of Wolomin, the Beis–Yakov girls. An example for us and for strangers, an example for our children and for our children's children, how to take a stand against the times and their storms and to remain true to the Jewish people and its higher morality.

[Pages 157-162]

Zealots in the Shtiebel and the Beis–Medrash

by Y.A. Weinbrom

In the Gerer Prayer House

Thinking back about my father, I see before me also the Gerer Prayer House: the Chasidim, their ardor in praying and learning, in dancing and singing on the holidays, and even in simple conversations and debates.

In the Gerer Prayer House I often used to listen to debates over the most sublime matters, over Hasidic ways and over Kabbalah, over the disagreements between the faction of the Kabbalah from the Holy Ari and the faction of Rabbi Moshe Cordovero. Words from the Talmud, from the commentators and from the Zohar, with their hidden meanings, were thrown around. People brought up ideas from the great rabbis, from the Rim [a well–known commentator], from the Sefas Emes [another famous scholar] and other great Jews, and people repeated holy words, rabbinic teachings, that dealt with heavenly matters and opened the eyes more clearly to see and undertake life on earth.

My father was one of the most distinguished Gerer Chasidim in Wolomin and also in the Ger court of the rabbi, where he was treated with the kind of honors that were reserved for the most important Chasidim.

I was still a cheder student when my father took me with him on a festival to Ger. The huge beis–hamedrash was full with Chasidim, who came from every corner of the country. Among the Chasidim were also rabbis, religious judges, and great scholars. It seemed as if the whole spiritual Jewish world would come together, in order to be near the rabbi. As in a true religious community, in Ger every distinction between poor and rich, between learned and unlearned disappeared. In Ger one felt oneself to be at Mount Sinai, with everyone equal.

Only at the approach to the rabbi's table could one first see the distinctions. From the thousands of Chasidim, only a select group, chosen by the rabbi, was allowed to sit at the table or to be called to the wine.

My father was one of those chosen Chasidim.

Every moment is etched into my memory. The congestion around the rabbi's table began at the door. Hundreds of Chasidim crowded one upon the other. Each wanted to be nearer to the rabbi, to see him and to hear him. A thick fog filled the air. Rivers of perspiration flowed from the men who hours earlier had grabbed a spot, and with every moment the congestion grew worse and more suffocating. Only the strongest could endure. The weaker lost their strength, and those who fainted were carried out of the line with great effort and had water thrown on them. After coming to, they tried again to struggle nearer to the rabbi's table. But around the table the men were clustered like roe in the belly of a fish. Even now they are before my eyes, like a sweaty, motley mass, fused together in the fire of great faith.

And yet it still seems new and surprising. Still greater was my surprise when in the surrounding stillness I heard the rabbi's gabbai call out my father's name:

"Avraham–Yossl of Wolomin."

Thus they called on my father to receive the cup of wine from the rabbi.

The huge beis–hamedrash was black with men, with an overabundant crowd of Hasidiim, one on top of the other, but only certain Chasidim were worthy of such an honor, to receive wine from the rabbi himself.

I went around in a daze. My respect for my father grew. I knew that men respected him for his great fear of heaven, for his status in the Hasidic world.

In Wolomin my father was not only the gabbai in the Ger prayer house. He also led the morning service on the High Holidays. He did not stand out because of an especially fine voice. He was no great musician, but he was chosen as the prayer leader in previous years because when he prayed at the reader's stand, people felt as if his prayer drilled its way into the highest heavens, as far as the Throne of Glory. This was prayer from a great Jewish heart, which could pray for the whole congregation.

The Ger prayer house was in the building of the Talmud Torah, where Rabbi Henech Goldvasser, my wife's father, was the director of studies. He also had the outstanding qualities that charactrerized our shtetl and with good deeds and good attributes served as examples for others.

In the Beis–Hamedrash

In the beis–hamedrash people prayed and studied. Poor and rich, Chasidim and Misnagdim, young and old. At afternoon and evening prayers, it would swarm like a beehive. Acquaintances got together and talked, but always the beis–hamedrash was filled with learning. From early in the morning until late at night, people were there studying.

There was a great Talmud–table, where people studied Gemara. My father used to sit at that table. In the morning, even in winter, when it was still dark outside, my father was already seated there together with other Jews, deep in Talmudic problems. The studying gave them strength and warmed their hearts.

Among these great zealots was also R. Chaim Aaron–Bunems. Night and day he labored in the Torah. Neither in praying nor in studying did he stay in one place. Rather he walked around in great rapture, here and there, shook, waved his hands, fervent, intense, "speaking with all his bones."

There were other zealots in the beis–hamedrash. total learners, but Aaron Chaim–Bunems was unique. It seemed that he had no home, to eat or even to refresh himself. He was quickly back in the beis–hamedrash, soaked in the fear of heaven and good deeds.

He excelled in showing great sensitivity to other's sorrows and needs. When people had to raise money for someone in need, Chaim Aaron–Bunems led the way, as though it were the most natural thing in the world. He often collected money in the beis–hamedrash and in the streets. People trusted him unconditionally and no one refused him.

"Happy is he who reaches such a degree"–so said Jews in Wolomin about him, and they treated him with courtesy and love.

Jews in the beis–hamedrash had a strong feeling for righteousness and charity. It once happened that a landlord wanted to evict a tenant. A commotion arose in the beis–hamedrash, and when each landlord arrived to pray on Shabbos, the congregation stood all together and would not allow the Torah reading to continue until the landlord openly, in front of everyone, was reconciled and came to a just resolution with the poor tenant.

Prayer Leaders

The Wolomin beis–hamedrash could not afford great cantors, but they were blessed with good prayers leaders. Such a one was R. Israel–Mordechai, the Shochet, who had a strong voice and whose praying before the lectern on the High Holidays and the festivals showed heartfelt sweetness.

With the approach of a festival, R. Israel–Mordechai shown with rays of holy flames. He put on his satin kaftan and on his head he wore a high velvet hat. As he stood before the lectern, a soft murmur ran through the beis–hamedrash. Soon a voice cried out "Ashrei" and everyone's heart trembled.

His selichos still ring in my ears, his "The soul is Yours and the body is Your work" in his melody went deep into the soul and called forth introspection.

His Modzhizer tunes combined with his manly voice and the Jews of the Wolomin beis–hamedrash regarded him as an unblemished source of beautiful song.

His singing, from selichos to the end of Yom Kippur, brought the congregation to another–worldly mood. When R. Yechezkel, the old sexton, stood by the door with his pushke after the first selichos, everyone threw in a couple of groschen.

[Page 161]

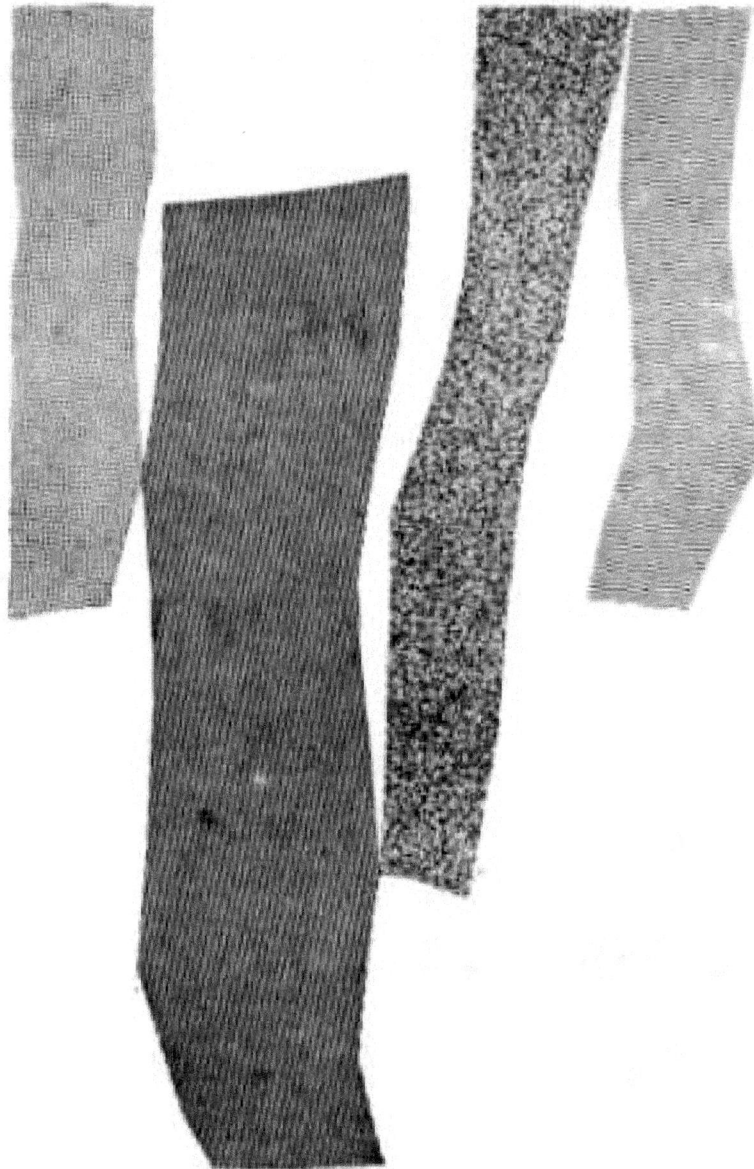

Parties and Organizations

[Page 162]

Blessed by activity
by Shimon Kantz
Translated by Yocheved Klausner

– Who knows and who would be able to describe the treasures of idealism, limitless energy and deep love of homeland, which the pioneers of the Jewish renaissance in Wolomin invested in their work, and was not mentioned in any of the official reports! All of the pioneers were fiery enthusiasts, blessed by activity, dedicating to the Zionist Organization the best of their lives and devoted to serve it fulfilling ideas and projects and organizing practical work. Whatever they did was accompanied by the sound of pure gold, which touched every heart and was kept there, and was sung on the lips as a holy choir.

Happy is the generation that heard these sounds! Woe to the generation that in sadness was forced to mourn the loss of these sounds, quieted forever.

The Zionists of Wolomin, young and old, felt that they were an integral part of the great Jewish people, who was welcoming its renaissance and redemption and was not ready to give up its particular revival. Their lives were active, full of struggles between new opinions and beliefs, which began to push aside the old ones; between new parties that suddenly grew upon the ruins of the old ones, in the process of revival and redemption. The articles that described these processes were written by the party organizers, who had full freedom to relate the histories of their respective parties from their own points of view, leaving for the reader the task of discovering the common qualities between the parties as well as their differences concerning their political struggle in general and in Eretz Israel in particular, and the ways they chose to win the hearts of the Jewish population of Wolomin, which soon would go up in flames.

[Page 163]

The Zionist Movement

Zionist Activity and Pioneer [halutz] Training

by Elka Shamir–Grizhek

Translated by Yocheved Klausner

My shtetl, Wolomin.

A small town, and yet it was able to give expression to all ways–of–life, all kinds of ideology, all kinds of organizations and youth movements: *Hashomer Hatza'ir*, *Gordonia*, *Hehalutz*, *Hehalutz Hatza'ir*, BEITAR – and all were devoted to the idea of pioneer training and Aliya.

As was the custom everywhere, in our shtetl too we had sailings and outings, assemblies and parades. I remember the festivities on *Lag Ba'omer*, when the pioneer youth would go to the forest carrying flags, trumpets and drums. At the head of the parade walked Eliezer Bergzin; the discussions were about the State of Israel, active in their minds as an accomplished fact.

Toward evening we returned. As we neared our town we formed straight rows and entered the town at the festive sound of the drums and trumpets.

Each of us hoped to see the State of Israel in a positive way, without shadows.

Oh, holy and pure sacrifices, I wish you could see that your hopes were fulfilled and the State of Israel was established, sovereign and independent, with its wonderful Army to protect it. You, together with all the Jews of the world, would be proud of the Israel Defense Army!

With the rise of Anti–Semitism so rose the will to make Aliya and the young people began to join the Zionist Movement, asking to go immediately to the training camps, in spite of their young ages.

[Page 164]

The Young Pioneer [*haluts*]

In those days I was he secretary of the *Hehalutz* branch. The young people devoted their whole energy to the pioneer work, hoping to receive an agricultural education, in order to be able, when they go to Eretz Israel, to work the land and make a living by the labor of their hands.

The youth of the town, in particular the *Hehalutz Hatza'ir*, introduced in our town an atmosphere of Aliya.

Hehalutz Hatza'ir

A group of Hehalutz Hatza'ir in Wolomin

[Page 165]

We had lotteries, lectures and theatre performances, the income being devoted to the Aliya Fund for pioneers who were in training for Aliya but were not able to cover the expenses.

We managed our cultural activity with great enthusiasm. Often we had a Literary Evening, with the active participation of the young people; but of course, the main purpose of all activity was to give the youth a "pioneer" education.

Many of the members of *Hehalutz Hatza'ir* indeed went to the training camps, but unfortunately not all of them succeeded to make Aliya, due to the War. Few of them are with us in the Country.

A group of Hehalutz Hatza'ir

Keren Kayemet LeIsrael [JNF, the Jewish National Fund]

It was a great and important project: our purpose was to put in every house a "JNF Box" to collect money, but it was not easy, because there were many who opposed the project.

But we did succeed, and once a month we went to the families who agreed to collaborate and keep on their shelf at home the box. We would empty the boxes and our hearts filled with pride and happiness. All hesitation disappeared, and we felt that our movement was turning into a serious power among the young people in town. Hebrew songs were heard at our meetings which we held almost every evening, and the dances never tired us.

[Page 166]

The assemblies and the lectures enlarged our knowledge in all areas. Our ideas penetrated the hearts of the parents, and they understood that our purpose was not to incite the children against the parents but against the empty life in the exile [Diaspora] and to educate the youth to building the homeland and creating a new Jew–Pioneer. Our actions were not in vain. Until the great enemy came and destroyed it all.

Leibele Herman

Tens of young people would gather every evening in the room of Leibele Herman. He was one of the first members of our movement and he was a real personality.

First and foremost in his thoughts was the worry for the fate of his nation and the national matters were the main purpose of his actions. He was a working man, who lived by the labor of his hands and devoted all his efforts to the Zionist idea. He worked tirelessly and quietly, with much devotion, never stopping.

Leibele was not privileged to see the establishment of the State of Israel. He perished, with all the Wolomin Jews, in the death camp of Treblinka.

The Committee for "The Working Israel"

A group of young people from Hehalutz Sitting: Miriam Mandelberg, Goriner, Elazar Berg

[Page 167]

On the Roads of Aliya

Translated by Yocheved Klausner

My hand is trembling. How can one write about the Jews of our town, the town where I was born and grew up, and now it is destroyed, with all the dear and beloved who perished in the ghetto and in the death camps?!

I left Wolomin in March 1939. I left my home with a heavy heart and a pressing feeling that I will not see my home any more, that terrible times were approaching, but I could not think that such a horrible tragedy was near – the destruction of my family, my town, my nation.

My parents died many years before the destruction and had a Jewish burial. I was left an orphan, without father and mother. Together with my two sisters, Feige and Gitl, we went to live with my sister Frida who was married and had three children.

Soon she was widowed. Her economic situation was bad, she worked hard and with the sweat of her brow she earned the bread for her young children. The life conditions worsened from day to day, and I could not see any hope for the future in the anti–Semitic Poland. From my early childhood I was active in the Pioneer movement and with all my heart I hoped for Aliya.

I was the secretary of JNF and later the secretary of the local *Hehalutz* branch. My activity in the pioneer life gave me much satisfaction. In 1933 I went to a training camp to prepare for Aliya.

After six months of training, the Aliya gates closed. I remained six years in camp and after a great effort and many dangers I succeeded to reach our country through the illegal Aliya.

I went straight to Kibbutz Ashdot Ya'akov, where I made my home, and I am living there until this day.

Meanwhile WWII broke out and I did not receive many letters from my sisters, which caused me much worry. In 1941 I received their plea through the Red Cross: "Our situation is very bad; if you can, please help us."

I knocked on every gate, but all were closed.

I was left the only one to eulogize those who have perished, Frida and her three children: Feige'le, Yeshaya and Rose'le; Feige and her husband Yosef Grosskopf and their baby; Gitel and her husband and child.

[Page 168]

The Joy of Youth at the Hashomer Hatza'ir Branch

by Zahava Weinbrom – Golda Goldwasser

Translated by Yocheved Klausner

The *Hashomer Hatza'ir* Branch in Wolomin was located on Daluga Street, in Leiba'le Berman's apartment. The first counselors were Moshe Weinbrom and Moshe Platkovski z"l and the writer of these lines.

Every evening we gathered, boys and girls, some of them from very religious families. The reaction of these families was severe; they opposed the youth movements' programs, fought with their sons and daughters and forbade them to participate in the activities; however, little by little we overcame the difficulties. Those youths, who connected their fate with the Zionist movement, have found here, at the *Hashomer Hatza'ir* youth movement, a home. The activity proceeded and sprouted deep roots among the Wolomin youth, who found great joy and satisfaction in the activities.

A group of Hashomer Hatza'ir members

[Page 169]

A group of Hashomer Hatza'ir members
In the center, sitting: Zahava Weinbrom

We conducted ideological counselling activity, we learned about the historic relationship of Judaism to Eretz Israel, we strengthened the collaboration between the branches and we arranged frequent meetings – in the form of camps or seminars. Our branch was blessed by a number of very devoted members who, in addition to their activity in the branch were active among the general public as well as in the Scout Camps.

We made every effort to keep our place of meetings clean and beautiful, decorated with pictures, slogans and a "wall newspaper" that appeared regularly. In the effort to create an image of a true "*Shomer*" – a devoted and fitting member – we had to overcome difficulties stemming either from the family situation of the youth or from their cultural environment, since our members – those who were interested in hearing about Aliya – came from all social strata

Our Branch excelled in collecting money for the JNF. We were active in *Hehalutz* and *The League for Working Eretz Israel*. We had meetings in the forest, every group wits its flag, we sang Hebrew songs and danced Eretz Israel dances.

The *Lag Ba'omer* outings were particularly impressive. The outing [*tiyul*] has become an important event in town. By the end of the day, old and young went out of town to meet the walkers, proudly carrying their flags. The proud scouts made a great impression on the Polish population.

We are carrying with love the memory of those days, when the members of the movement became adults hoping to make Aliya, but were murdered by the Nazis.

[Page 170]

The Youth in the Zionist Movement

by Zev Nadvorny

Translated by Yocheved Klausner

The town Wolomin was located 18 km. from the capital Warsaw. It was not famous, just one of the small towns in Poland, similar to so many other towns, and it had a very small train station. No famous names of rabbis or poets are connected with it, great leaders or magnates have not lived there and stormy events did not take place there; but the thing that did distinguish the town and constituted its pride – was its Jewish youth, who was active and lively, and its heart and soul were open to the love and devotion for our nation and our far homeland.

The Wolomin youth knew that the first thing to do was to acquire knowledge and to understand what nationality meant. It was not an easy thing, since this was not a simple science. It was not enough that the Jewish people possessed a strong will to live, that they fought for their existence, longed for redemption, created, along the generations, a great literature in the ancestral language and suffered terribly during many years; theoretical proof was needed as well, in order to show that this was indeed an existing nation. The youth in our shtetl began to participate in discussions, went to lectures, argued with opposers and became more and more convinced of their ideas and rights.

The best of the young people gathered around the Zionist movements: *Gordonia, Hehalutz Hatza'ir* [the Young Pioneer], *Hashomer Hatza'ir, BEITAR, Hehalutz*, etc. The young boys were polite, and at the same time full of energy and joy. Those youth movements brought a new spirit of life into the small town. To this day I can hear the common singing, and I remember the "horah" dance in the house and around the bonfire in the forest.

[Page 171]

One of the most beautiful festivities took place on Lag Ba'omer, when hundreds of young boys and girls marched through the central streets of the town wearing their festive costumes – blue, white or gray shirts and carrying the blue-white flags over their heads. Even the weather collaborated mostly and we had blue skies, just like the sky in Eretz Israel.

The young people walked, singing and dancing, toward the Mironova forest on the hill, from where the entire town could be seen. The dancing had no end.

After the dancing we ate sitting around the bonfire, singing and playing on instruments. Most of the songs were Israeli and traditional songs and we were excited like little children.

But the day was devoted to discussions as well. Every group would talk about life in Eretz Israel, about the development of the Pioneer movements, the importance of the training camps and the preparation for Aliya.

Among others, there was the question of educating the members according to the aims of the movement. Even during discussions of such serious subjects it was possible to feel the atmosphere of satisfaction and happiness. When learning about the wonderful past of our nation, during moments of spiritual elevation, we fully believed that the day of redemption was near and that we will take an active part in rebuilding the land.

But when night came and we were on their way to our homes, we met on the road the reflection of the foreign land – the ugly face of anti-Semitism, which was present in Wolomin as in all the other Polish towns and carried the hints of the coming disaster. The young Jewish people in town were the first to fight it.

The anti-Semitism was expressed by acts of violence, as attacks on Jews and public quarrels and clashes with incited Polish youths. Vocal and written propaganda against Jews was conducted, largely supported by the Polish authorities. The Christian population in Wolomin was full of hate and it happened more than once that Christian youths attacked Jews.

[Page 172]

I remember one Sunday, at noontime, some of my friends walked on Daluga Street, one of the central streets in town, where most of the residents were Jews. Suddenly a group of Christian youths came from one of the alleys and one of them took out a gun and began shooting toward the Jews. One of my friends, Avraham Teitelbaum was hit. Fortunately he was not severely wounded and soon was out of danger; the bullet remained in his body to this day.

I also remember one evening, as I came home, I found my father z'l sitting in the chair and his face was full of blood. My mother was washing his wounds and relieved his pain. He said that he was walking on one of the side streets to the house of one of his clients. A few young Christians attacked him with sticks and stones, and only thanks to his courage and composure he managed to escape.

Those events angered us and we organized, aiming to help whenever there was an attack on Jews. Mostly we succeeded to chase away the hooligans.

Those attacks showed us how vital, important and necessary self-defense was, and we realized that it was our duty, since the authorities did not react to the attacks and did not help.

The young people began to think about their future and only one solution seemed real: Aliya to Eretz Israel. The various movements began to make practical preparations for that purpose – the first thing being the establishment of training camps, where young people were trained for manual work, in particular working the land. The life conditions in the camps were not easy, but the aspiration to make Aliya gave the youths courage to complete the training and go to Eretz Israel, whether through legal or illegal Aliya. In Eretz Israel, they very soon became an integral part of all branches of the economy – agriculture, industry, commerce, crafts, medicine etc. But many of them did not have the chance to reach Eretz Israel – they perished in the Holocaust.

We remember what our enemies did to the Wolomin youth.

[Page 173]

We shall never forget the dear and devoted young people who remained forever loyal to the eternal Jewish people and to the vision of rebuilding the Nation in Eretz Israel, and were murdered by Hitler.

We shall remember the wonderful youth movements that were destroyed before they could fulfill their dream of Aliya to Eretz Israel and help with its rebuilding.

Their memory shall be kept forever in our hearts. May God avenge their blood!!

[Page 174]

"*Hakhshara*"

by Kalman Fruman

Translated by Sara Mages

In order to obtain an immigration certificates we had to go through "*Hakhshara*" [training], meaning, we had to work for a certain period in agriculture and all kinds of other jobs.

In 1933, "Agudat Yisrael" organized the first "*Hakhshara*" group in its history, in an agricultural farm near the town of Chorzele.

Among the fifty members of the group there were, in addition to me, three others from Wolomin. Most members of the group came from Frankfurt, Germany.

For half a year, from Passover to Sukkot, I worked on the farm. It was an interesting period that played a role in shaping our spiritual and mental image.

Zionist youth marching on the streets of Wolomin

[Page 175]

We did our arduous work with enthusiasm. In our free time we studied and debated, sat and enjoyed a page of Gemara, but more than any other great Jewish sages, we were enthusiastic by the *Tannaim* and the *Amoraim* who were craftsmen. Our heroes were: Yochanan *HaSandlar* [the shoemaker], Rabbi Yitzhak Nappa?a [the blacksmith], Shemaiah who said: "Love the craft and hate the rabbinate," and R' Yehudah, of the earlier sages, who left a teaching: "Any father who does not teach his son a trade teaches him banditry," and it is told of him that when he went to Beit HaMidrash he carried a pitcher on his shoulder saying: "Labor is great, as it brings honor to the laborer who performs it."

We searched and found in the sacred books all the words of praised said in them about craft, like: "The merit acquired from labor may be helpful even when the influence of one's ancestors is not," or: "Lest a man say, I am the son of the patriarchs of the world, I am from a large family, and I do not deserve to do a job and be humiliated." They say to him: "Fool, your creator preceded you, who did the work before you came to the world, as it is said: "From all His work that He did."

Sometimes we listened to lectures. One of the lecturers, who came to us from time to time, was HaRav Yitzchak Meir Levin, a leader and speaker, who stirred up our emotions with his speeches and encouraged us to face the problems of our time.

I got married after completing the training period. I received an immigration certificate for my wife, and I and we immigrated to Eretz Yisrael.

Affinity to Eretz Yisrael

Life was difficult in Israel at that time, full of worries and pains and there was almost no livelihood. We worked in all kinds of arduous jobs solely to ensure our basic existence.

We overcame the difficulties thanks to our affinity to Eretz Yisrael which was also the ideological cause of our immigration.

I was raised and educated in a religious home and absorbed within me the affinity of our people to their homeland. In the Torah there are two *mitzvot* that can only be observed in Eretz Yisrael. Therefore, the preservation of the Jewish constitution in its entirety is conditional on the Jew's residence on the land of his ancestors.

The affinity of the Jew to Eretz Yisrael accompanies the course of his life, as *Hazal* [Our Sages, may their memory be blessed], said: "Anyone who resides outside of Eretz Yisrael is considered as though he is engaged in idol worship" (*Ketubot* 110b:23). In the same place, Rabbi Yochanan said about the *mitzvah* of living in Eretz Yisrael: "Anyone who walks four cubits in Eretz Yisrael is assured of a share in the World to Come." The spiritual superiority of Israel found expression in the words of *Hazal*: "There is no Torah like the Torah of Eretz Yisrael and not wisdom like the wisdom of Eretz Yisrael."

[Page 176]

The Midrash expresses the affinity between the people and their homeland in its commentary on the biblical verse in *Shir Hashirim* [Song of Songs 8:14] "And liken yourself to a gazelle": "This gazelle walks to the end of the world and returns to his place, the Jews, even though they scattered all over the world, might return in the future."

The holiness and affection of Eretz Yisrael did not end in the studies of the worshipers of Beit HaMidrash in Wolomin. The yearning grew stronger from year to year but to our great sorrow only a few were able to fulfill their aspiration.

A group of Tzeirei Agudat Yisrael

They absorbed the spirit of Judaism and tradition and remained faithful to the path of the Torah and *mitzvoth,* and the immigration to Eretz Yisrael was the highest stage in their thinking. These young people were sensitive, and their hearts told them even then that a Holocaust was approaching and coming upon humanity, especially upon Judaism.

My parents' home

I had someone to learn from. I learned the affinity for our country and also other good virtues.

My father, Yehusua, was a teacher at "*Yesodei HaTorah*" and acquired love and admiration from many. He knew how to instill in his sons the treasure of piety and virtues.

My mother, Masha of the Newman family, was endowed with a warm Jewish heart, with vigor and the spirit of a true "Woman of Valor," Together with that she contained a treasure of patience, modesty and humility.

My eldest brother was a scholar and fulfilled God's work in faith. He nurtured a warm and traditional Jewish home, was a devoted husband to his wife and a compassionate father to his five children. He was twenty eight when I left Poland.

My sister Ester was beautiful and a devoted daughter to her parents. She was gentle, kind-hearted, listened to the words of others and knew how to help in good faith and emotion.

During the German occupation she supported the family by smuggling food from Wolomin to Warsaw. She was blonde with blue eyes and looked like a Pole. The Poles betrayed her, handed her to the Germans who murdered her.

My young brother studied at "*Yesodei HaTorah*" and continued his studies at Beit HaMidrash. With joy and excitement he carried within him the desire to immigrate to Israel and join us. He knew his destiny in life but he was not able to do so.

[Page 177]

My sister Rivka was twelve years old when I left Poland, a charming girl, beautiful and modest. She was our pride and joy and everyone who saw her, saw a graceful rose.

My youngest brother, Avraham, was young and innocent. He was ten years old when I left the town. Here I see him playing a childish game and his childish words, full of love, ringing in my ear. He was so intelligent, so developed and so sweet.

Their memory will not leave my heart forever.

When I remember them, I feel as if something is about to explode in my mind and my heart is torn to pieces. I cannot express on a paper everything that I feel, everything that is raging in my soul. May HaShem avenge their blood!

[Pages 178-179]

The First Zionist Organization

by Shmuel Vinogoro (Argentina)

It was in 1916, in the middle of the summer, in the month of Av. We were a group of several friends, men and women, who came together with the goal of fashioning a Zionist organization. With us were: Binyamin Nodvarni; Chava, Manya, and Feige Vinogoro; Itke Moroko; Feige Lichtman; and others. Avraham Tenenboim directed the cultural activities.

We were full of enthusiasm for the Zionist idea, and we threw ourselves passionately into the activities of clarifying the idea and attracting new members. We arranged meetings, lectures, and referendums on various subjects.

There was already a library in the shtetl, and we took it over, buying new books and giving it the name "Haskalah."

The first Zionist organization, which called itself "Hatikvah," assumed an important place in the life of Wolomin. Our cultural evenings were very successful and we were forced to rent a larger venue.

Discussion evenings were added to the original cultural accomplishments. We discussed literary and political questions, national and cultural problems.

Quite important were our evening courses for learning the Hebrew language.

In the club we also formed a drama circle, which through its performances threw light on our collective future and conferences. We also arranged performances in the city auditorium that attracted huge audiences among both the young and the old.

With the outbreak of the Polish–Russian War, almost all of the Jewish young men entered the army, and our work was interrupted. We stored the archives and the supply list of the first Zionist organization in the home of Chaim Rodziminski.

Later on, Chaim Rodziminski also entered the army, from which he never returned.

After the war, activities resumed on a larger scale. Until the dark night overtook us and the Wolomin Jews suffered the fate of the six million horribly–killed martyrs. Among them were my nineteen martyrs, my mother, my brothers, my sisters, and their families. May the Lord avenge their blood!

[Pages 180-185]

The Organization

by Y.A. Weinbroom

The first Zionist center in the shtetl forty years ago was "Tarbus". The local "Tarbus" chapter included all those who felt a connection with Zionism. Generally the Zionists were the upper–householders. The idea of creating a party called "The Organization" arose because the comrades who wanted to lead the party's activities ran into opposition from the general Zionists. It happened that on a certain Friday evening when there was a gathering of the "Association"–comrades, the general Zionists came out against them and the conflict spread so widely that the local police came and forbad the local to hold meetings.

This and similar difficulties confronted the first steps of the "Association" in Wolomin. They had to fight for every greater enterprise, such as organizing a chess evening, a lecture, a get–together, or a meeting.

The guiding spirit of the Association was Leibele Berman, who was tireless in his activities and showed great initiative in organizing the association's efforts and in dealing with the difficulties caused by the conflict with the other Zionists. Leibele Berman was a family man and also businessman who had to worry about making a living, but nevertheless he often neglected his business, telling his wife that he had to take care of something important. These important things consisted of going to the meeting hall of the Association, finding out what was going on, if anything needed organizing, leading a meeting, planning an evening or an election. The party activities were to him the most important things, and activities for the population, especially for the young people of the shtetl, were for him more important than his business.

The day finally came when the Association in Wolomin received from the Hechalutz Center three certificates. When the first three members from Wolomin set out on their aliyah to Eretz Yisroel, it was quite an event. It gave impetus to the organization. It increased the number of members. It led to creation of the youth organizations "Gordonia" and "Hechalutz Hatzair." Diverse political and cultural activities developed. Young people began preparing for life on kibbutzim, and the dream of making aliyah to Eretz Yisroel seized a majority of the shtetl's youth. A portion of these young people was thereby saved from Hitler's murderers.

Keren Kayemes For Israel

The initiative to organize a fund drive for Keren Kayemes for Israel in Wolomin came from the general Zionists, who were also the first collectors. In the beginning it worked this way: early on Shabbos, people would come to the Tarbus Hall to pray, and when they were called up to the Torah, they promised a contribution for the Keren Kayemes. Keep in mind that this system did not have the appropriate status or the educated character that the collections had to present. The collections were private and lacked the reputation of openness. No one undertook to distribute pushkes from the Keren Kayemes in homes. There were also many other better known causes, and therefore the idea of the Keren Kayemes collection did not resonate among all the sectors of the population, both among the young and the old.

With the coming of the Association, came also a change of direction. The idea of Keren Kayemes began to come to life and the consciousness of its importance began to grow. The cause left behind its narrow confines of the party hall and people began to speak of it openly.

For the first time a flower day was declared. People had to have permission from the authorities so that the comrades, male and female, could go out into the streets with the blue and white pushkes and collect money. This made a strong impression. For many people it was a new thing and it created enthusiasm.

But people also had to take into account that they could not be satisfied just with that. First, they could not declare "flower days" too often. Second, it wasn't a matter of just more less money. The psychological moment was also important, awakening the feelings of the Jewish populace, making positive people's attitudes toward the Keren Kayemes. Keep in mind that the unique "flower day", with the impression it had made in the shtetl, still could not solve the problem that confonted the young idealists and supporters of the cause.

The importance of distributing the Keren Kayemes pushkes was clear and understandable, but at the same time there were various disturbances. What started out as the cause distributing pushkes turned into a difficult and responsible task. The Zionist idea was not yet popular enough in all sectors of the Jewish populace in the shtetl. It was the time of the Fourth Aliyah, when Eretz Yisroel was going through a huge crisis, and many who had gone there were returning, which made a bad impression in the shtetl. All of this made the undertaking of the Keren Kayemes more difficult.

With this situation in mind, the leadership of the Association in a joint meeting with the general Zionists decided to create a special committee that would devote itself to the Keren Kayemes and give it their full attention, strength, and initiative. The writer of these lines was put in charge.

We went to work with great intensity and began to distribute the Keren Kayemes pushkes among the Jewish homes. Clearly this was not among the easiest jobs. We had to plead with people, persuade, influence, clarify for them the significance of our cause for the Jewish people throughout the world and for each individual Jew.

To be absolutely truthful, not every household required such exertion. There were Jewish homes in Wolomin who happily encountered the people who came to them with the Keren Kayemes pushkes, openly showed their enthusiasm and good will to the collectors in regard to future activities.

At the same time we organized lectures and readings which took place either in the Tarbus Hall or in the beis–hamedresh, in which the speakers clarified for the audience the great importance of the Keren Kayemes and the duty of each Jew to take part in the cause. This approach was direct and fruitful.

We made a promise that we would not be exempt from our great duty to the Keren Kayemes. We did not separate the idea of the Keren Kayemes from the larger Zionist ideal, from the greater Zionist activities among the Jewish populace in Wolomin. Helpful to us was the newly formed pioneer organization "Gordonia," which provided enthusiastic activities to popularize Zionist ideals among young people. Soon after, the youth organization "Hashomer Hatzair" was formed, which included many members of the Association. Zionist activities increased and became more intense and involved more sectors of the population. Hechalutz Hatzair was formed. Since it had so much strength, we committed ourselves to Keren Kayemes with more diligence. School children also were involved in the cause. They distributed pushkes not only in their own houses but in those of neighbors. The cause took in almost the whole Jewish population of the shtetl. There was barely a dwelling that could deny the children's requests. It was hard to oppose the children's enthusiasm for Eretz Yisroel. In their eyes burned a holy fire for the building of Eretz Yisroel. Their faces burned with the joy of actively participitating in collecting money for the redemption of the land in Eretz Yisroel. They saw before them the realization of the dreams of generations in exile. Hardly anyone could withstand the devotion of the children.

The results were tremendous, psychologically, politically, and also practically. They spiced up the Zionist propaganda. The young people were filled with the pioneering ideals; they took preparatory classes for kibbutz living, getting ready for the hard work in Eretz Yisroel.

This great success attracted the attention of the Keren Kayemes central office in Warsaw, and they sent us greetings and awards for our hard work.

That was a time when the Jewish youth in Wolomin lived spiritually, developed culturally, broadened its horizons, and adopted all the Zionist colorations.

Our shtetl did not lack adherents of any of the existing Zionist youth organizations and parties in pre–war Poland.

But all lived with the hope of being redeemed from exile and of living free, Jewish, and human lives in their own land.

But it turned out differently———

Terribly differently.

No more the sparkling youth, the rebels against the government, who participated so eagerly in Zionist activities; those who dared to bring into the observant shtetl the first cabinet with secular books and called it a library; those who dared to march in the streets with blue and white banners, singing Hatikvah, and who were ready to sacrifice themselves for the idea of national and social liberation, and who with Chasidic fire and devotion threw themselves into the battle for the thousand–year–old dreams of Jews and of human beings.

[Pages 186-189]

Gordonia
by Shmuel Zucker

Just as in other shtetls in Poland, so in Wolomin there was a chapter of the youth movement Gordonia. This was a reaction to the other aspirations of different youth movements like Hashomer Hatzair or Hano–ar Hatzioni. The Gordonia movement appealed to the working and student youth to join their ranks and adopt their new approach to the daily problems of working youth. The youth organization Gordonia had its own way of enlightening and appealing to Zionist young people.

At that time Jewish life in Wolomin sparkled with diverse social activities, for a single Jewish life, for a better future: the young people sought new ways to achieve their huge aspirations.

I remember the long winter nights when we used to come to the meeting room of the Zionist organization the Association. We were a group of young people who were determined to organize the Gordonia in our shtetl.

One winter night I was invited to the Association meeting room. The room was small and cold. The weak gleam of the naphtha lamp fell on the faces of the young people, a group of friends who gathered with the aim of organizing in Wolomin a chapter of the youth organization Gordonia.

The idea of Gordonia had captured us. It was new and captivating, and we threw ourselves wholeheartedly into the work, together with a group of young men whom we thought of as candidates to be pioneers.

Our first step was to create a bond with different young people in the shtetl and work out the forms of organizational work. In the cold little Association hall, we began to breathe with a new spirit. The young members approached the activities with energy and zest. The work was not easy. The economic state of the Jewish population was difficult and the idea of Gordonia was foreign and strange. We were not frightened. We debated with our opponents and clarified for our followers the words of the new movement. Little by little we overcame the crisis and felt that with each day the pioneer spirit got stronger among our members. New young people joined us. At the beginning they were only from the working classes, but as time passed young people from the schools also joined us.

After a short time the Gordonia organization decided to rent a larger and nicer meeting place where we could gather every evening to conduct conversations and lectures on different topics.

Our instructors had to confront peculiar problems, which were not easy to solve. Most of our members came from the folk–class. Many did not have the opportunity to study, but they had a thirst for learning and education. In our organization these young people had their first meeting with the wider world, with the problems of the Jews in Poland and the problems of Jews in general, with Jewish workers in exile and in Eretz Yisroel, with our place in the Zionist and in the socialist movement. There were some who learned for the first time through our organiztion to read a book and understand the ideas and problems that were expressed in them.

We conducted our enlightening work through words and deeds, led private conversations and held lectures, helped form the thought of a national home in Eretz Yisroel. That thought gave a sense to the young people that the life of the shtetl and the organization had a significance for life, infused with the aspiration to make aliyah to Eretz Yisroel.

There were some young people for whom the Zionist idea seemed distant and strange, and it was not easy to explain it and bring it into their minds and hearts.

But together with our logic, our enthusiasm and deep convictions also convinced them that we had chosen the right path.

At first the working–class young people came to us, people who were imbued with the idea that the Jewish people in their own land would be a working people, a free people, who would combine the material with the spiritual, with toil and mind, a people without oppressors or oppressed, only partners and comrades in work and in economic life.

In this way the young working people of Wolomin accepted the idea of Gordonia. Then came the more educated students. Our membership increased and we acquired a big and attractive meeting place where we came every evening, discussed and conversed about various topics, literary, political, and social.

Gordonia grew in quality and quantity, blooming like a beautiful blossoming garden. It became an effective factor for the young people in the shtetl.

In our organization the Jewish young people of Wolomin developed and prepared a new path. The Jewish young people in Wolomin for the first time faced the need to take its full place in society, to bear collective responsibility and to participate in the reciprocal help between one young person and other and all together with their leaders.

Gordonia blossomed and grew. In the shtetl people began to feel the influence of the Gordonia youth. At work people began to sing songs about Yisroel, which they learned in our organization. The spirit of Gordonia was felt in many Jewish homes. Mothers sang their children to sleep with a song that was sung in the evenings at the Gordonia hall.

On Lag B'Omer the Gordonists would march through the streets of Wolomin. Their parents would stand on both sides of the street with smiling faces as they watched their children.

Young people with talent to organize, expound, and educate grew in the ranks of Gordonia.

When I was 34, I left Wolomin and left behind Gordonia and all it did, full of aspiration and hope. The young people worked sincerely and passed on their message. But that did not last long. The horrible war came and cut off everything.

The majority of the activists in Gordonia did not merit to see their ideals fulfilled, ideals for which they were ready to give their lives.

Blessed be their memory!

[Pages 190-193]

From Wolomin to Tel Aviv

by Menachem Tayblum

Decades have passed since I lost my shtetl, Wolomin. Who could conceal it,, since I exist always with my shtetl, with my large, many–branched family, with all the dear and friendly Jews, who lived in an environment of hatred, with their warmth in joy and in sorrow, with their help for the poor and sick and their great generosity to each other?

I was born and raised in Wolomin. My parents were well–to–do, ran a lumber business and belonged among the most distinguished families in the shtetl. My father was one of the founders of the Merchants' Bank, one of whose goals was to help any merchants who couldn't get on their feet and needed a loan. My father, a fervent Alexander Chasid, became the chairman of the bank, and at home I often used to hear how he spoke with the members about impoverished merchants who needed help. Often people came to us for donations for poor, beaten down Jews. Wandering preachers and ordinary guests would come. Our home was open to anyone in need and to anyone whose heavy worries pressed on his heart so that he sought from my father a word of advice on how to get out of trouble.

In general the Jews of Wolomin did not lack for problems. They were always oppressed by heavy taxes. There were times when the Poles conducted boycotts, a bitter agitation, so that the peasants and the workers would not buy from Jews. The government, the tax office, the magistrate all helped to oppress the Jewish shopkeepers.

Although our home belonged to the upper–class world, more than once I saw my father worried and predicting hard times for the Jews in Poland. More than once I heard my father groan over me, over someone whose head was full of stories and games and who could not conceive of what would come. My job, I knew, was to learn. Where can one learn serious business if not in the Gemara? There, the people of Wolomin believed, lay the whole of a man's luck, the best that one could achieve in life.

Jewish children in Wolomin, poor and rich, were lively, vivacious, and happy. Yet those years quickly passed. The children quickly faded and became, at a young age, little Jewish adults, with thoughtful, worried faces. Even their fun and their pranks were serious and calculated, although done with heart and soul

Early on I was enrolled in the Zionist youth movement and in 1933 I went to a Zionist preparatory course in Bialystok that was organized by the "Gordonia" youth organization.

At home they were worried whether, for the sake of the Holy Name, I would pray every day. I must confess now that every encouraging speech of my parents resonated not at all in my heart. My dream was already to become a pioneer, to make aliya to Eretz Yisroel and build a Jewish land.

Being young, I was not proficient in all the problems of Jewish social life, but I realized that for Jews in Poland there was no future.

This fact was proven when a non–Jew shot my brother. This caused a great commotion in the town. My mother lost her power of speech from fear. She became ill and died in that very year.

I was then in Bialystok when I received a telegram about my mother's condition. I went home right away, but when I arrived in Wolomin, my mother was no longer alive. I was only in time to go to her funeral.

Good, dear mother of mine, you have stood before my eyes through my whole life. I hear your good words, warm, comforting. You had a good word for everyone and you felt every sorrow that befell the Jews.

Your heart, dear Mother, even in the hardest times never failed to believe that better days would come, as the Master of the Universe would avenge the wrongs done to the Jewish people.

Even before Wolomin became a valley of destruction, of holocaust, you were already a sacrifice for the murderers of Jews.

You, dear Mother, were an omen that dark clouds were moving in over the Jews in Poland.

Soon after, I left Wolomin with the feeling of leaving a tottering house, like an ark, struggling against stormy waves, which at any moment could sink. My only hope was to go to Eretz Yisroel.

For a long time I was in Kibbutz Givat Chaim. From early in the morning until late at night the day was filled with different kinds of labor. I loved life in the kibbutz, despite the constant toil. As soon as my work was finished, I became involved in the social and cultural activities in the kibbutz, in the comradeship among the members, in the idealism which pervaded all of us.

Once, when I was working on the road, I saw Rodl Ostroviak, a Wolomin native, who had already lived in Israel for several years. She recognized and called out teasingly: "Look there, Tayblum's son working on the road."

That she had seen my proud bearing and had swallowed her own astonishment attracted me to her. At that moment once again the shtetl swam before my eyes and I felt even more strongly the desire that all the Jews of Wolomin should live in Eretz Yisroel and there help to build a new land.

This remained a dream. Only a few succeeded and are now with us in Israel. We are united by the memories of our old home, the memories of our nearest and dearest, the holy martyrs of Jewish Wolomin, which once was and is no more.

[Pages 194-195]

The "Maccabee" Sports Club

by Shmuel Fierovitch

The social life in the "Maccabee" Sports Club remains in my memory like a bright dream of active youth.

The sport club gave birth to an intense life among the young people in Wolomin. I remember the 29th of May in 1929, when we, a group of friends, sat in a poor, dark room and discussed the gloom that affected the youth of the shtetl. That was when the idea arose of creating a sport club that would include all strata of the Jewish youth in our shtetl. The founders were: Yisroel Grossinger and Yisroel Lichtman, and also Ch. Kver z"l. We went out into the shtetl and began to mobilize young people around the idea of creating the "Maccabee" Sports Club. Although we had no location for gathering together, Chaver Zucker invited us to the "Gordonia," where we held our meetings. In a short time we were legally certified to use our own locale and we proceeded to create a gymnastics division and to join the global organization "Maccabee." Soon after we created the soccer division and we appeared in competitions with other sports clubs. And then our troubles began. As the goalie for the

Maccabees, while guarding the goal, I always had to be careful of the stones that were thrown at us by the anti–Semitic Polish youth.

Our sport club also fostered a warm cultural life. We had a drama group, took part in different Zionist activities, and worked diligently for such Jewish charitable organizations as Keren Kayamis and Keren Hayisod.

In this way we went about our business until the outbreak of the Second World War.

[Pages 196-199]

The "Maccabee" Sports Club

by Malkeh Yellen–Greenberg

The grown–up youth who, at the time of the German occupation, led the community cultural and organizational activities, had at the outbreak of the Polish–Soviet War entered the army. When the war ended and life slowly became normal again, these young people started to contemplate the knowledge that they had gained about the wider and broader world and a social life began to simmer and ferment with discussions, speakers, and lectures.

Even before the First World War ended, when Wolomin was taken by the Germans, we heard the repercussions of the October Revolution in Russia. There were young workers who were suffused with the socialist ideas of that era and who believed that with the October Revolution had come the liberation of the working class and the redemption of mankind.

There were young people in Wolomin who were not simply dreamy idealists but who were also filled with strong wills and aspirations towards action and who enlisted in the fight for a better life. Many dreamed of traveling to Russia and joining the ranks of the communist fighters.

These seeds fell on fertile ground, and later, in the Y.L. Peretz Club a leftist group was established that people called "The Reds."

The activities of this group were illegal. The members stood out for their extraordinary enthusiasm and spirit. Not worried that they were being persecuted by the police, they expanded their underground work with their full youthful idealism.

The young Jewish communists were in close contact with the Polish communist workers in the glassworks. They had collective get–togethers and meetings, where Jewish and Polish communists presented talks about the situation in the country, about strikes and other painless [?] topics.

Among the communist activists were some who came from deep within the masses, from poverty, while others came from well–to–do homes but had arrived by different paths at the ideals of the revolution and with idealistic impulses through themselves into the illegal activities, studied historical materialism, Lenin's writings and other illegal works, books, and pamphlets.

During the nights, the young communists used to plaster the fences and walls with communist slogans for communism and throw red pennants over the high telephone wires.

It seemed like the very air was filled with revolt and idealistic young hearts made me feel the highest ecstasy.

The Oyfkum [Awake] Drama Club

The members of the Oyfkum Drama Club in the Y.L. Peretz Library came from different organizations, from the working class and the intelligentsia. I remember the two brothers–in–law Moyshe Zissman and Lippa, with their wives, from Katchelna Street, who had a radio store; Aaron Demski, who lives today in Brazil, Tuviah Weinberg, Shoyme Flotkowski, I and my sister Beiltshe, and others, whose names I forget.

The drama club went through crises, especially when a portion of its membership left Wolomin, whether for Warsaw or for Paris.

But the club came to life again when people got to work: Tuvia Weinberg, Leibl Radziminski, Noson Wolfovitsch, Yechiel Zucker, Yankev Markito, Shloyme Flotkowski, Kapelushnik with his wife, Freidke Greenshpan, Zhenya Asman, who lives today in America; Esther Friedman, now in Brazil. I and my sister Beiltshe were active participants in the drama club.

We began to rehearse Yakov Gordon's play "God, Man, and Devil." The rehearsals lasted for two months. The participants were enthusiastic.

The first performances of Peretz Hirschbein's "Neveylah" [Infamy] and Yakov Gordon's "God, Man, and Devil" took place in the hall of the Peretz Library. The audience was large, and later on we performed in the Adria movie theatre in the marketplace.

The audience exceeded expectations. The performance brought together a significant gathering and the profit went to the library to buy new books.

After the presentations in Wolomin, we went on a tour of the neighboring shtetls, like Rodzimin, Tlushtsh, and others. These performances also attracted large audiences, and the profits also went to the library.

Everywhere the halls were full and we, like true actors, suffered from stage fright. These memories have lived long in my mind. When it became dark in the hall and the curtain went up, there was such silence that you could hear a pin drop on the floor. Our hearts stopped beating. We gave each other courage and strength.

Part of the way through the first act, we heard the first applause, and our hearts became lighter. The second act was more soaring, livelier.

When the curtain went down after the last act, the people in the hall rejoiced and our hearts were full with joy and pride. Backstage, people came to thank us and to praise the performance.

In Wolomin people talked about our drama club, about certain members, as they talked about actors and actresses. Wolomin was raised to a new height and was moved to greater endeavors.

We tried out one–actors, recitations, music. We put on Mark Arnstein's "The Eternal Song," Sholem Aleichem's "Mazel Tov," Anski's "Dybbuk," Goldfaden's "The Two Kuni Lemels," Yakov Gordon's "Mirele Efros," "The Intellectual," and others.

Our drama club had a reputation beyond Wolomin, in the other shtetls where we toured. Every new production was a holiday for the public and for the actors.

We regarded our work as serious and even sacred. We put so much strength and effort into our productions so that they would maintain a high standard. The star of our club was Noson Wolfovitsch, who is today a famous actor and director in Israel.

The comrades: Shoyme Flotkowski, Tuvia Weinberg and Kapelushnik painted the sets. Meyerovitsch was the prompter.

The drama club allowed people in Wolomin to feel culture, and it brought to the shtetl a holiday feeling and joy.

The members of the drama club were young people who worked all day–in the glassworks, in workshops. In the evenings they came to rehearsals, often tired, worn out, but full of enthusiasm and energy, and, as opposed to professional actors, they never thought about earning money through their appearances. In fact, they often made up for box–office deficits through their own few groschen.

The drama club enjoyed a moving reception from the Jewish population of Wolomin, and they all perished together.

[Pages 200-202]

The Peretz Society

by Yakov Rosenblatt

Wolomin, people used to say, was a town crowded with people from every corner of Poland, as was the case in every town and shtetl, full of a variety of Jews; religious, liberal, Zionist, progressive and all manner of others. As the proverb says, "Ten Jews and fifteen parties." Overall Jewish life in the shtetl was both religious and cultural, modern. I will, however, not write about all the different partisan societies in the shtetl, because I do not know so much about them, but I will take this opportunity to say a few words about the Peretz Society, where I was for several years a member, and try to commemorate its workers and activists who were, for the most part, killed by the German beasts.

The Peretz Society had its own beautiful library, where workers used to come to take a book to read in order to acquire a little knowledge and clarity. The directors of the library used to bring different speakers, organized readings, crossword puzzle evenings, as was then the custom, organized a variety of literary and political debates, as in the old times. In a word, it was good cultural work.

The managing committee of the library: Mlienek–chair, Meirovitsch–secretary and librarian. Liffa, Moyshe Zusshman, Leah Asman, Feyge Burtchevski, Yitzhak Krasutski, the writer of these lines, and others whose names I cannot remember.

It is worthwhile mentioning other members whom I remember: both Meinemer brothers, Rochel Goldwasser, Helya Budny, Toyvah Jagoda, Moyshe Grosinger, Shepsel Zilbershtein, Gitl Manga, Neshe Kahn, both Greenshpan sisters, and scores of others, whose names I have forgotten.

I must mention Meir Falkovitsch, who later went to Paris in 1940 and who fell in the war against the Nazis.

In the Peretz Library there was also an active drama group that presented different plays, and not badly. The director, a unique fellow, a Wolomin native, was Tuviah Weinberg. These are the participants I remember: Yechiel Zucker, Shoyme Flatkovski, Yosl Flatkovski, Yankl Mankita, Zhenya Hasman, Malkah Yelien, Shmulke Manga, Freyda Greenshpan, and others.

The Framian Sports Club

Also in the library there was a sports club–"Framian," whose members participated in light exercise and a football division. The directors: Zhenya Katz, Avraham Rosenberg, Shimon Wishnievski, Karol Jagoda, Shloyme Trosterman. The members: Chana Chofkovitsch and Rochel Chofkovitsch, Rochel Flatkovski, Rivkeh Bartchevski, Chaika, and others. Players in the football division were Moyshe Butz–Bramkacz, Shimon Wishnievski, Shoyme Blumenkranz, Shulke Topol, and others. All of the above and others whose names are not listed were for the most part killed by the Nazi criminals.

Yet, regardless of the great cultural work of the Peretz Society and its contributions to wresting the young workers from ignorance and darkness, to everyone's great sorrow and grief, they bled fruitlessly and many of them ended up in Polish prisons for defending a false idea, even though they themselves fully believed that this idea, for which they gave away their lives, would bring salvation both for Jewish workers and also for the Jewish people, so that, albeit not with bad intentions, they led the young Jewish workers astray on a false, bloody path.

Today, in view of the events of recent years, as we are replanted in the historical land of our ancestors, we see at every turn the falsehood of that path, it is sufficient to point out the great prejudices against the Jews among the same "progressives" and "peace"–advocates to whose ideas and directions the leaders of the Peretz Society clung. It is sufficient for us to shout out the famous verse from the Song of Songs, "They made me keeper of the vineyards, but my own vineyard I have not kept…"

In all my travels in states and lands, enduring the worst experiences, always before my eyes are the ideal patterns of the Jewish youth in Wolomin. Their loud voices ring in my ears, arguing in the union, in a club, over matters that seemed to have universal and national significance. It was not their fault that they were so bitterly deceived.

[Pages 203-206]

Philanthropic Societies

by Chaya Rubinstein

Translated by Theodore Steinberg

All of the philanthropic societies that existed in Jewish shtetls also existed in Wolomin and were occupied in helping the poor and the sick. The Linas Hatzedek [Lodging of Righteousness] was such an institution. It was occupied with helping sick poor people who lacked the ability to call a private doctor or to buy medicine.

The Linas Hatzedek would lend the ill a hot water bottle, a thermometer, an electric lamp, and other things that they needed and could not obtain in any other way.

There was no hospital in Wolomin, and therefore the Linas Hatzedek served as a primary resource for those in need and was a true helping organization for the poor who were ill.

The members of Linas Hatzedek used to go and watch over the ill, sitting awake near them for a whole night and performing the functions of a nurse.

The poor Jews in Wolomin knew that the Linas Hatzedek was a place where they could find their first help for the ill.

Linas Hatzedek was on Dluge Street in the same building as the Amshinav Chassidic prayer house.

In the same area was the Gemilus Chasadim [Deeds of Lovingkindness] window, where in times of need, people could get loans without interest and pay them back in small monthly installments.

I remember one case when an older woman became ill and she had no way to get treatment. Her condition deteriorated daily and the fear of death hovered over her. The doctor held firmly that she should go immediately to the hospital in Warsaw, but this poor sick woman could not cover the expense of a trip to Warsaw.

I went to the Gemilus Chasadim window and told them about this case, that the woman needed 150 zlotys. That was the cost of getting this sick lady to Warsaw and to the hospital.

I described the situation to the leaders of the Gemilus Chasadim, and I assured them that I could gather that sum, but it would take me several days. The leaders of the Gemilus Chasadim took me at my word and immediately gave me the money. On that day I took the woman to Warsaw, where she stayed in the hospital until she was well and could go home to Wolomin.

I kept my word and, together with my friend, collected the money and returned the full amount to the Gemilus Chasadim so that they could help other people in need.

I tell this story as just one representative of scores and hundreds of other cases in which the Gemilus Chasadim was the only place that people knew to go to for help.

Wolomin did not lack for needy people, merchants and workers, from whose bones the tax offices sucked out the marrow. At the Gemilus Chasadim window they could always borrow a sum sufficient to help get back on their feet. Most of them were able to repay the loans. The installments were reasonable.

The Cooperative Bank

Wolomin was one of the newest cities in Poland and it developed very quickly. Over a short period of time, many new houses and streets were built, and it became a modern shtetl.

But not everyone could keep up with such growth. Many who had created businesses or workshops ran out of breath trying to face crises, and a moment arrived when it became clear that it was necessary to create a bank that would help the inhabitants at a time of economic crisis.

The merchants and the craftsmen then created in Wolomin a branch of the Warsaw cooperative bank, of which they were members.

The bank was established on Pshechadnya Street, in Baruch Shulman's brick house, for which he was compensated and which contained all the facilities necessary for a bank.

The bank truly became a real source of help for the Wolomin merchants and craftsmen, who could there get a loan of up to 1,000 zlotys at a low interest rate. It was enough to have two guarantors who would guarantee that the debt would be paid.

The members of the bank chose a committee that supervised the giving of loans.

The loans had tremendous significance and truly helped many merchants and craftsmen keep their jobs, enlarge their stores, their workshops, and pay off their debts in order to expand their businesses.

The bank prospered. It attracted new members. I must mention the discipline of the members, who punctually made their payments, worried that the bank should grow, because they saw in it an institution that served their interests.

The situation of the Jews in Wolomin, as in all of Poland, was like that of a ship that is about to be flooded by evil waters, without a today or a tomorrow. As in every small shtetl, everything was out in the open. Everyone knew each other and each other's business, either by seeing it or by hearing it. The Jewish merchants' groschen were earned through sweat and blood. There was always pressure from a lack of money, which was made worse by the vexations and persecutions of the Polish government, which did all it could to worsen the situation of Jewish merchants, leaving them not even air to breathe.

Consequently, every little bit of help was terribly significant, and such was the cooperative bank.

The shops, workshops, and businesses of the Jews in Wolomin barely survived, and each loan that was successfully obtained, helped them get on their feet, helped them survive and hope for longed for salvation.

In short, when a city is being built, there is work for different kinds of craftsmen. But as time passes, a crisis arises and the Jews strengthen themselves by filling small shtetls. Families without income increase, and their situation becomes worse each day so that they require aid.

Let me praise Jewish creativity, energy, and vitality, that led to the warmth with which Jewish Wolomin responded to every appeal.

These are only a few hints about the greater philanthropic institutions in Wolomin. Certainly I have not accounted for all the people who took part in organizing these efforts, who were active in bringing help for those in need. I beg pardon and understanding, because I am writing all of this from memory, since I have no written sources.

That is why I have not presented just plain facts and events that should be recounted, because I am not sure of their accuracy and I do not want to get things wrong. They gave away so much and got so little in return and were so tragically murdered.

[Page 207]

Because we were Jews...

by Henia Knopf

Translated by Sara Mages

I was born in Wolomin and also grew up there. I was lucky that in my time there were already elementary schools for girls and I was given the opportunity to get a thorough education and as a result to broaden my horizons. During my time, political movements also arose in the town.

I belonged to Gordonia. This movement instilled in us political views and also helped us to broaden our horizons. From time to time we heard lectures on political, biblical or just current affairs. In the movement I made social connections. I keep some of the connections to this day.

Of all my friends the image of Leah Mendelson, a girl with blue eyes and brown hair, was etched in my memory.

I also remember an incident related to this girl: unlike most of the city's Jews, who lived in the center, Leah lived in a Christian area and we, the members, accompanied her to her home in the evening after the lectures.

The school students with their teachers

[Page 208]

Once, when we accompanied her, and we were near her home, a gang of Polish children attacked us and beat us with murderous blows. From all the beatings I lost consciousness and when I woke up I was lying alone in the street. I could barely get up and somehow got home. For a long time I was broken and depressed.

Why did the Poles beat us?

Because we were Jews…

For this reason the buds of revival in our town have found an echo deep in our hearts. The activities of the pioneering youth organizations, which began to influence us already at school, expanded and deepened the aspiration for a political revival in Eretz Yisrael.

This activity created an atmosphere of glowing hopes instead of despair and melancholy, of exaltation instead of disappointment and apathy, of lofty aspirations instead of distress and doom, the belief in small and big deed brought a great change in the life of the people.

This is how branches of "*HeHalutz*," "*Hashomer Hatzair*," "*Gordonia*," and all other Zionist organizations, parties and institutions, were established in our town. We were able to overcome various elements of opposition and unified the aspirations and actions for the idea of the settlement in Eretz Yisrael.

A group of primary school students and their teacher

[Page 209]

[Page 210]

Figures of our town

[Page 211]

Shimon Kantz
Translated by Sara Mages

The past has disappeared in a shocking calamity that sanctified us forever. We remained its sole guardians and we must bequeath to our children the light that was in the town, the sublime virtues, the devotion and greatness that were there, the beautiful Judaism. The present of us all is built on the same vibrant and active way of life. As we get older, we feel the need to go back to it, to knock on its doors. And if the bustle of the days and their troubles come and remove the past and its figures from our hearts, the dreams of the night and its nightmares come and revive them before us. Then, we go back and visit our parents' home, the *heder* or the school, where we studied, Beit Hamidrash where we prayed, and in the morning we wake up with a sense of loss. Yes, we are the last generation for whom the Holocaust is not a chapter in the chapters of the martyrology of our people, a chapter taught in schools or read in books, but part of our history, the personal biography of each and every one of us – our loneliness, grief and pain. We carry the Holocaust not in our memory, and not in our imagination, but in the cells of our aching living flesh. In that place we grew up; there we embroidered our dreams; there we fought for our truth; there we loved our first love; there we built our image. All the uniqueness within us, which determined the foundation of our soul and created the pattern of our inner being – came from there. There the seed was sown, and there our spiritual image was carved. What can we do? what are we commanded to do? Not to lock them, our annihilated fathers and brothers, in books, but to sow them as a living seed in the blood of our children and grandchildren, a growing seed that bears a lot of fruit. We will not only inherit but also bequeath.

If only we could attach the living heritage of our ancestors to the values of our children until they will blend together.

[Page 211]

A distinguished man and a beloved rabbi
To the image of HaRav R' Zev Bergzin

by Dr. Sara Hamburger–Mandelberg

Translated by Sara Mages

R' Zev–Wolf Bergzin was elected Rabbi of Wolomin at a young age. Until then he had not serve in the rabbinate. He devoted himself to his studies and excelled in his talents and sublime virtues. He used to get up at five in the morning to study various lessons, engaged in his studies and renewed Torah innovations. He used to demand the same from the students of Beit HaMidrash, to study a little every day in reading, and to innovate something in the Holy Torah.

He used to write dozens of letters to different people on various matters, and was known in his agility in replying to letters to any claimant. He was calm and treated others with respect.

He was an exemplary rabbi, excelled in his comprehensive biblical knowledge and noble personality. He was accepted by the public as the town's rabbi that all the affairs of the town were entrusted to him. Everything was done modestly, and for this reason created a quiet and pleasant atmosphere around him.

He was gentle and noble–minded, inspired all the Jews of Wolomin, those who surrounded him, and they were many and good.

HaRav Bergzin was polite, a man of distinguished character, vision and action, and also his power of action stemmed from his nobility.

He had a broad–minded imagination, but was not absent from the reality of the town, its worries and limitations, in the term of "A ladder set up on the ground and its top reached to heaven" [Bereishit 28/12]. His sky was always bright, clear and pure, as his mind was clear and his heart pure. From here his tendency for over–optimism, optimism leading to action, building and creating in all spiritual and material areas, because the rabbi also cared for the town's poor. He helped not only with a good advice, but also with financial support in time of need.

His belief was great and strong, deep and complete belief in the Divine Providence, but he also believed in man, because he is part of God from above and was created in his image, hence his positive and kind attitude to every person.

Friendship constituted an important chapter for the rabbi and he was always surrounded by friends and admirers. His love for the people of Wolomin was impartial, and it was rooted and based on a deep responsibility for everything done in the Jewish community and on sincere friendship.

Love, without sincere and true friendship, is not enough. Pure and simple love means to take, while friendship means to give. This is what characterized R' Bergzin. He was always willing to give without anything in return. This was known to those who were close to him, and those who came in contact with him, in private matters and also in matters concerning the general public.

And so he used to say: "A man sees the world as if his half is entitled, and half must, and he is the deciding factor" [*Kiddushin* 40b].

Therefore, he always looked for new ways to correct the order of the community, the relations between the parties, between person and person. He was not frightened by any mishap and obstacle, and so he said: "If a river flows and encounters an obstacle on its way, it finds a new route." Life flows and does not stand in one place, therefore one must strive for renewal, as it is written about the attitude to the Torah: Every day will be a new day for you!

His heart ached for every split in our town, and he saw in the split the source of all failures and inability to change. Therefore, he always made bold efforts to bring about a dialogue, to reconcile and make peace between opposing parties, find a common language and work together, because he did not suffer quarrels and disagreements and tried not to be involved in it.

Many were his good deeds, acts of charity and kindness of the rabbi of our town that need to be told and told about. He was gifted with a good heart and advocate by nature, brought people together and tried to help them.

He also took care of matters of religion and *kashrut*, and as in every field of his work as the town's rabbi he was highly appreciated.

R' Bergzin preached in pleasant words of kindness and love, not in the manner of the preachers of his time who threatened with hellish torments. For this reason he often spiced his words with beautiful parables taken from life and reality, according to the comprehension ability of those who listened to his words.

His admirers repeated a story they had heard from him about a Kotzker Hassid who hid behind the rabbi's door to hear how he reads the weekly Torah portion. When the rabbi reached the verse "Love your neighbor as yourself," the Hassid heard him reading in bewilderment: as yourself? as yourself?, and only then he calmed down.

The rabbi explained: the command "Love your neighbor as yourself" is a difficult problem. If the reference is to a person very close to me – so be it, just like you, and many times more than that, because a person may be more attached to another fellow–man than he is to himself. The life of a fellow–man may be more precious to him than his own life. But, if the intention in "neighbor" is for every Jew, or for every person – could it be possible? could it be real? It seems that this command, which is a great rule in the Torah, is about giving direction: the intention was to love your neighbor.

The main problem – the rabbi said – is not in "like you," but in the difficult task of being open and also directed to love. This is a huge difficulty, and the content of the great rule is to overcome that difficulty. It is difficult to be directed towards love and together with that to be real, that is, to beware of pretending, and it is important that the person knows how to stand up to this difficulty.

With inner peace he dispelled the anger of others, welcomed his rivals, showed tolerance for their views, pursue peace and did kindness to his name, and was ready for any role, difficult and easy alike.

He settled misunderstandings, or disputes, between people sharing similar ideas, and in his cleverness influenced both sides.

During the terrible Holocaust he went through all the torments of hell, but did not stop his work. He did not leave his congregation and was with the Jews of Wolomin until the last moment. He gathered them and encouraged them, guided them and prepared them for what to come with love and devotion to his last day.

First from the left: Rabbi Bergzin with R' Yisrael Mordechai Shohet (Tentshe)

[Page 214]

Hot embers

Childhood is a homeland, and it makes no difference where we saw it, whether here or there. It is the core of the open space, the morning of our lives and the center of the world. Therefore, it is also no wonder that we all carry in our hearts the town of our childhood, because it is the station from which our first journey to the best of our plans departed. It remained in our hearts like a burning fire, restrained in our bones, and our duty is to dig deep and write about it, about its people and institutions, and all those who lived around us and influenced our lives from their spirit.

"You grew up in a cultural environment" – my fellow–townsman once told me.

True, I grew up in a cultural environment and I must mention it, tell about it.

My father was Avraham Nehemiah Mandelberg, my mother – Chana Kuna of the Zagorodsky family. Both came from different backgrounds.

My father was born in the village of Sztabin in the Suwalki province. His ancestors were born and lived in this village. They were farmers back in the time when the rule over the villages in Poland was in the hands of Polish noblemen. One of his ancestors, Avraham Nehemiah, was murdered by a Polish nobleman, more precisely, by his messenger. Why? Avraham Nehemiah spread a rumor that the Russian Tsar, Alexander II, was about to free the villagers from their slavery in the hands of the landowners. The landowner, Count Bezostowski, was arrested and brought to Grodno in chains, and was later released for lack of evidence that he had murdered the Jew.

I was very close to my paternal grandfather, R' Yehudah Leib Mandelberg. My grandfather was a symbol of goodness and fairness.

At the age of six I contracted severe rheumatism. I lay completely swollen, unable to make a slight movement. I thought about death. I see my grandfather sitting next to me and putting a spoonful of food in my mouth, and every time, when I was sick, my grandfather was by my side taking care of me.

And when I was a medical student, and had to prepare for exams, I studied at my grandfather's house because no one bothered me there. I knew that my grandfather would watch over me, and wake me up at the right time to get to the exams, because I had to travel by train to Warsaw.

I knew that my grandfather was a philanthropist, but I learned about the extent of his philanthropy while I was staying at his home. My grandfather spent more money on alms than on his own family, and all this was done in secret, in accordance with the Jewish tradition of giving in secret. My father followed my grandfather's footsteps.

Besides that, my grandfather and my father were completely different types: my grandfather was blond with blue eyes. My father was a brunette with gray eyes. My grandfather was gifted with technical talents and my father was a man of the book.

[Page 215]

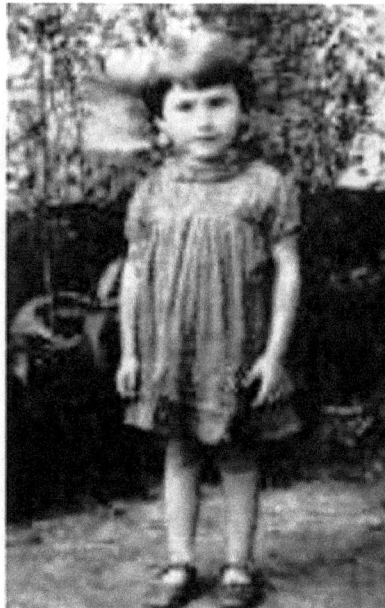

**Miriam–Azia, the eldest granddaughter
of Nehemiah and Chana Mandelberg**

My father's soft gray eyes revealed a secret of an innocent, gentle and leaning soul. Leaning on what? On creative work that embraces the world in its simplicity. He was a simple and good Jew, decent in his actions, helpful to the weak and loved by all who knew him.

In those days every father aspired to give his son a broad religious education. My father studied in yeshivot in Suwalki and Grodno, and in Yeshivat Slabodka. The result: my father was a scholar, well versed in *Shas* and *Poskim*, so much so that only a few were able to compete with him. He was also well versed in Hebrew literature, especially liked to read Bialik and Tchernichovsky, and if a new word was introduced into literature he knew its exact origin. He was also a mathematician, but he had no opportunity to exploit his talents. Although in the town we were considered to be "rich," we barely made a living.

Indeed, we had a house, but only some of the tenants paid rent. To be more precise: those with means paid, and the poor lived for free. The poor tenants knew that Nehemiah Mandelberg would not evict them from the apartments and will not file a lawsuit against them. In this my father was not the only one.

When I finished my medical studies I was a young doctor. Our tenant, Mrs. Shmitanka, went and gave money to her relatives so that they would invite me as a doctor, and Mr. Hershel, who worked as a gardener for the Poles, took advantage of his connections and said that I was the best doctor.

My father by nature loved people. He was willing to help anyone even though he treated the Admorim [Hassidic leaders] indifferently. He had an understanding for all types of people, even those with completely opposite views.

I remember an episode: one Saturday afternoon, my father and I sat at the table. As usual, my father's head was bent over the Gemara. A number of people, of the town's dignitaries, entered. R' Nehemiah – they turned to him – you are a man of Torah and labor, join us, the people of "Mizrachi."

In my heart I am with you – my father replied – but I will not join any party because once I belong to a certain party, I will treat the members of other parties in a negative way and I want to love them all."

[Page 216]
The members of "Mizrahi" rightly described my father as a man of Torah and labor. His life was not easy. We had a workshop for thin planks, kind of shingles made of wood. The shingles were made with primitive tools and it was arduous work.

My father's money went in two main directions: tuition and taxes. At that time there was no compulsory education, it was only the domain of the rich. I studied at the gymnasium, then at the university and the tuition was not cheap.

And with regard to taxes, it was known that in Poland the Jews were the main taxpayers. My father paid, and paid, far beyond his means. At home they never bought new furniture, never went on vacation, just worked and worked.

My father had one goal: Torah and labor. In the middle of the night, when I woke up from my sleep, I saw my father sitting at the table, leaning over the Gemara to the light of a simple kerosene lamp, and heard the characteristic melody: "*Tnu Rabanan*"– I could understand that, I did not understand the rest.

My father died of typhus in the ghetto, on 27 Av. May his memory be of a blessing.

My mother z"l was from a completely different area. She was born in Davyd–Haradok, a town in the Pinsk Gubernia, to a special family. It was known that there were only writers or teachers in this family, and not a single merchant. My father called them the "Shimon tribe."

Seated: R' Yehudah Leib Mandelberg with his second wife Yehudit
Standing, from the right: the couple Krasotzki and the couple Koren

[Page 217]

My mother's grandfather, R' Yehudah Leib Resel, was the head of a yeshiva in Mir. Of my mother's four brothers the eldest followed his father's footsteps and continued to teach in his birthplace, Davyd–Haradok. The rest advanced: one earned a doctorate in agronomy in Berlin, and one devoted himself to journalism, worked for the newspaper *Ha–Tsfira*" and later for the Yiddish newspaper "Moment" in Warsaw. The youngest was a clerk.

My mother was orphaned from her father at the age of thirteen. She did not have the opportunity to study because she had to take care of her elderly mother (my mother was the youngest in the family).

I remember my maternal grandmother, Zipora Henia, as very religious tall woman. She prayed from a very big and thick Sidur, which was printed in Rashi script, and aroused the admiration of all the neighbors in the building.

My mother learned sewing to support herself and her elderly mother. Her brothers also supported their elderly mother.

R' Nehemiah Mandelberg and his wife Chana née Zagorodsky

My mother worked hard. There were five daughters in our family, only daughters, and I was the second. Admittedly, each of us felt as if she was the only daughter to her parents.

In the darkness and despair, which accompanied my life in the Diaspora of Poland, life in the bosom of the family constituted a ray of light that I will remember to my last day.

My mother was very musical. Only the youngest of us, Hania'le, had a talent similar to my mother. But, Hania'le also did not use her talent for music.

My mother was a symbol of nobility and gentleness, she knew how to suffer without complaining, she had tremendous endurance, and knew how to work and love.

My mother and her family members were murdered by the Germans. The Jews of Wolomin found their death in Treblinka. My mother was probably murdered on the night of the ghetto's liquidation, on the eve of Simchat Torah 1942. May their memory be blessed.

[Page 218]

The way–of–life in Wolomin

Not much is known about the history of Wolomin. It's possible that a village named Wolomin existed for a long time, but Jewish Wolomin, and that's what interests us, was established at the end of the 19th century.

The Russian government constructed the railroad connecting Warsaw with St. Petersburg (today Leningrad). Stations were set along the railway tracks, about every 18 kilometers, and the first station (on the Warsaw side) was Wolomin.

Geographically, Wolomin is located about 17 kilometers northeast of Warsaw in the Mazovian Lowland. The geographical definition of "lowland" was correct – and every resident of Wolomin can attest to that. It was enough to dig at a depth of a meter to reach groundwater. The mud and dampness, which were always plentiful, also testified to this.

I mostly remember Wolomin as a town where the residents knew each other well. And not just got to know each other: everyone knew their neighbors' problems and shared their joys and worries.

In those days, when there was no national insurance, social assistance, WIZO, etc. – I cannot remember a single case in which a Jew starved to death or lay sick without help. In place of modern institutions was "the Jewish heart," and the meaning of Jewish heart is the desire to rush to the aid of others at any time.

There were those who especially devoted themselves to caring for lonely patients, and have done their job with real devotion.

Almost every Jew with means gave interest–free loans – it was called *Gemilut Hasadim*. This mutual help was expressed in various directions, and constituted a ray of light in the difficult life of the town's Jews.

The life of the town's Jews was difficult, government and municipal jobs were blocked for them. Their scope of making a living was very limited. Some owned small grocery stores and barely made a living. Relatively there were a lot of craftsmen. The painting profession was almost entirely in the hands of the Jews. There were many tailors, shoemakers, carpenters and factory workers. The porters were all Jews. Most of the roads in Wolomin (as far as there were roads) were paved by Zelig. I see Zelig, short and bearded, wearing a Jewish hat and a thick rope around his waist. The Jew stretches ropes and paves, and paves and paves. In summer and winter you always saw Zelig on the road. Who planned the paving of the roads? Not an engineer, but Zelig himself.

The conditions in the town were also very difficult. The town did not enjoy any inventions of modern technology: there was no gas, no sewage, electric lighting was introduced only in 1930, and only a few homes enjoyed it.

[Page 219]

Housework required a lot of physical strength. For example: boiling water was involved in a rather complicated process: it was necessary to bring water, sometimes from great distances, chop wood, thick and heavy, and to light them. Then it was necessary to add ordinary wood, then break coal stones and add them to the fire so that it would not go out. It was also necessary to take the ashes out of the stove. It is amazing that despite the elemental inconvenience, the town was clean – a lot of work was invested into keeping it clean.

Most of the houses in town were built of brick and there were also wooden houses. The structure of the town was coincidental because its builders did not need a license and did not seek the advice of an engineer. The houses had courtyards which were separated by wooden fences. The Amur Cossacks, who camped in Wolomin in the winter of 1914–15, probably considered these fences as an unnecessary nuisance. They demolished all the fences, and one courtyard was created from all the courtyards.

During the period described, that is, until the First World War, the town's cultural life was concentrated mainly in the field of religion: more precisely – around the synagogue. They prayed in the synagogue on the Sabbath, holidays and also on weekdays. There, the townspeople had the opportunity to hear the cantor sing, or a sermon from a preacher who happened to be in town. There they also studied the Gemara and talked on current affairs.

The boys studied in the *heder*. The *heder* was a primitive school, usually in the teacher's private apartment. The teacher was called "*melamed*." Over time Talmud Torah school was established in Wolomin. In Talmud Torah the level of education was higher than in the *heder*. There was also a rabbi, but the rabbi lived in Warsaw on Kopitzke Street. It was all for men – and only for men.

On the other hand, the social life of the daughter, and the wife, were generally very poor. Every girl's ambition was to know how to write a letter in Yiddish and an address in Russian. But few have been able to fulfill their aspirations. If a girl wanted to write in Yiddish she had to turn to Avramcze the teacher. Avramcze's school was in his kitchen where a long table stood. Avramcze sat at the head of the table and the girls around him. And if a girl just wanted to know how to write an address in Russian, she had to attend a school with one class under the management of Mrs. Salomea Lvovna Shachnowitz, who was helped by her son Alexander and her daughter–in–law Anna. There, they learned Russian and also arithmetic.

In the second period, with the establishment of independent Poland, primary schools were opened in Wolomin and children, boys and girls, studied there at no cost. This greatly aided the intellectual development of the girls. Most finished elementary school and some were able to complete their studies in Warsaw.

[Page 220]

Because of the shortage of apartments in the capital city of Warsaw, many people lived in Wolomin. They had nothing to do with the town. Wolomin was a kind of hotel for them because their workplace and their area of entertainment were in the capital city. These people lived mostly in its suburbs. The central part of the town kept its character. There was also a change in the life of the Jewish youth. Organizations of a political, cultural or sporting nature were established, and the horizons of the youth have expanded considerably.

Unfortunately, I remember very little about this period. I hope others will write about it in detail.

Chevra Kadisha

In the town of Wolomin was an institution that instilled terror and fear in those who did not belong to the poorest strata.

The name of the institution – Chevra Kadisha [Jewish Burial Society].

The death of a rich man constituted a cause for a lively controversy in the town. People argued: how much should be taken from the grieving family, and why should more be taken from others.

Sometimes the required amount exceeded the family's ability to pay, then, a lengthy negotiation took place and meanwhile the deceased waited for his burial ceremony.

The Polish government set a certain price for a grave, but could not force Chevra Kadisha to provide its services at a fixed price.

People believed that the deceased, to whom this honor was not given, did not know rest and may appear in his family's dream and disturb their rest. This belief gave immense power to the society and everyone surrendered to it.

We had a tenant and his name was Pinchas Burstein. He was called "Pinya." He fell ill without hope and he knew it. He feared that after his death the family would have to give Chevra Kadisha all the money he accumulated throughout his life. He began to build a house for his only son, who was married and the father of a girl. "There will be no money – Pinya thought – they will not pay and in the meantime my son will have a house."

After Pinya's death it turned out that his calculation was wrong. The society demanded a lot of money and the son was forced to pay.

During the negotiations, the grieving family heard different opinions from the tenants. One advised to pay, others advised to refuse and place the responsibility on the members of Chevra Kadisha. Fear prevailed over the contempt of the dead, and the son paid the full amount.

[Page 221]

There was a wealthy family in Wolomin called "Komorna," which means rent in Polish. Once, this family had a house and the landlady used to forcefully demand "Komorna" from the tenants, hence the nickname. The head of the family, a quiet and good man, died and his body was laid for three days because they could not reach a compromise with Chevra Kadisha.

Tamari relates: "My uncle Moshe had influence in Chevra Kadisha. The widow turned to him and asked to lower her husband's burial fees. R' Moshe explained to her that they would not lower the price by even a single penny. The widow saw that she had no choice and agreed to pay, and she had only one request: R' Moshe, this amount will also be considered a payment for me, so that after my death I will not have to wait three days for my burial.

To the credit of Chevra Kadisha it must be said that it used the money for constructive purposes. It also built the building of "Talmud Torah."

In the Second World War the Germans completely destroyed it.

The epidemic

It was during the First World War, in the years 1915–1917 the Germans were in Wolomin and they maintained order. In spite of it we suffered a lot. We did not have enough food and there was a period of hunger for bread. White bread was the lot of individuals. We also lacked a lot of essential goods, especially soap. The sanitary conditions in Wolomin were not the best, there was no sewage, and water had to be carried from afar. A box in the yard was intended for garbage and waste water, it was called "garbage dump." The garbage accumulated and waited weeks for it to be emptied.

No wonder that under these conditions a typhus epidemic broke out that killed many of the townspeople. There was usually one funeral a day. Sara'le, the only daughter of our tenant Fanya Burstein, died at that time. In our thermometer, which was used by Sara'le, the mercury reached up to 41.9 degrees celsius. Sara'le was 18 and was considered to be the most beautiful young woman in town. After her death her mother, Pera'le, claimed that her daughter had died of the evil eye.

There was no doctor in town. We did not receive any hygienic instructions. People began to consult how to overcome the problem, and came to the conclusion that the epidemic would stop only if they erect *chuppah* in the cemetery.

The director of the synagogue, Esther'le, managed to pair a couple who agreed to get married in the cemetery.

[Page 222]

She, the blacksmith's daughter, was not among the successful girls and in addition had a paralyzed arm. He, the matchmaker's stepson and stepbrother of Ola the water porter, was a normal boy, but apparently did not have an easy life in his stepfather's house.

As mentioned, the wedding was held at the cemetery. There were two funerals on the day of the wedding and the epidemic continued to rage. With the end of the war, and the improvement of conditions, the epidemic ended.

The double life of Shimon Schlachter

I don't remember R' Shimon Schlachter, but the townspeople talked a lot about him – and rightly so.

He was considered a respected man, knew how to study a Gemara page and also how to behave in society. He was among the followers of the Rabbi of Wolomin and visited his home.

What did he make a living from? It has been said that he traded in pig hair, an important material for making brushes.

Every Sunday he traveled a long distance, and returned home on Sabbath eve and on the holidays.

Once, R' Shimon did not return home and the residents of Wolomin no longer saw him. The matter turned into a riddle. No one knew how to answer the question: what happened to R' Shimon?

My grandfather, R' Yehudah–Leib Mandelberg, solved the riddle by chance. When he was in Nasielsk he saw a police guard leading a prisoner whose hands were chained. My grandfather looked at him in amazement and fear. The prisoner was R' Shimon Schlachter.

Needless to add what an impression it made on my grandfather, he began to investigate among his circle of acquaintances and was given details that seemed strange to him, but they constituted the absolute truth: R' Shimon, a respected Jew, lived a double life.

In Wolomin he was a decent man, and outside Wolomin he was one of the talented thieves in Poland,

And so the man lived for many years, and for many years he was very successful – until one night success turned its back on him.

And so it was: on Sabbath eve, after dinner, a young couple decided to pay a visit to their parents. But when they were already on the doorstep of their parents' house, the husband decided to return home. He had some unrest in his heart. They both returned home and saw that the door was open. A shadow of a man was moving in the dark, approaching the sideboard and rummaging through it.

The young man attacked the "shadow," grabbed his throat and knocked him to the ground, the neighbors were summoned, the police arrived and arrested the thief.

The thief was Shimon Schlachter.

Shimon Schlachter was no longer seen in the town. He spent the rest of his life in prison because he was accused of many thefts.

[Page 223]

I remember his wife. His second wife was a quiet and nice woman.

It was said in town: he was lucky as long as he was married to his first wife. Things changed when he married his second wife, because success depends on the wife…

The rise and fall of Alter Friedman

When my grandfather, R' Yehudah Leib Mandelberg z"l, wanted to marry off his son and daughters he looked for a pedigree, and so he also behaved when his eldest daughter, Bilha–Malka, reached the age of marriage. He married her to Alter Friedman, the only son of the Rabbi of Trzcianne, Rabbi Shmuel–Daniel Friedman.

Alter's real name was Chaim–Gershon, but when he was critically ill his name was changed to Alter.

As mentioned, he was the son of a rabbi and probably the rabbi's home influenced the shaping of the young man's character, and something personal of his own, that no one could decipher, was inherent in him.

When he was at his father's house young Alter did not know shortage, did not work to earn money, and probably because of this he did not know how to take his financial affairs seriously.

For example: after his marriage to Bilha–Malka he received from my grandfather z"l a big fabric store, and later a decent sum of money in order for him to travel to Grodno to pay his bills.

Alter did not travel to Grodno and did not pay his bills. Instead, he sent letters to his family, first from Berlin and later from Hamburg. He informed in his letters that he decided to use the opportunity and see the world.

His wife, Bilha–Malka, was not happy about it, because paying the bills was more important to her than her husband's visit to Germany.

Alter, like his father, loved people and more than once demonstrated it in his actions. Reuven Mandelberg relates: once, Alter was hosted by the Mandelberg family in Sokolska, suddenly he disappeared and appeared a few hours, later sweating and tired. It turned out, that a Jew, a passerby, asked Alter for directions to a nearby village. Alter did not content himself with a literal explanation, when he saw that the Jew laden with a heavy load he took it from him and carried it to the Jew's destination.

Sztabin, Alter's place of residence, was destroyed during the First World War. He loaded his wife and daughters on a cart, and also did not forget the fabrics, and moved to Wolomin.

He is standing before my eyes: a tall man, with a bent stature and a pointed beard, pale, wearing a short coat, and a hat, which was called then "Melonik," on his head.

My mother used to tell that the same pale Jew was a hero in his youth. In the days of the pogroms gentiles attacked his store to loot it, but Alter wounded some of them and they left the store.

[Page 224]

At the beginning of the war Wolomin was still under Russian rule, the Germans entered in the summer of 1915, and when the war ended an independent Polish state was established. In those days, the currency continually changed its form: first there were Russian rubles, then German marks, then Polish marks. The common denominator of these banknotes was that their value diminished. People still believed that this money was s stable and they only thought the goods were expensive. Alter belonged to those who did not reconcile with the "price increase." If he had merchandise, which cost him many years ago three rubles per meter, and his wife sold it for twenty rubles per meter, Alter argued that the profit was excessive, and it was enough to take four ruble per meter. Most often he found a way to return all the money to the buyer, except for four rubles for a meter which, in his opinion, belonged to him.

The result was that the amount of merchandise in the store slowly disappeared, because, when he came to buy merchandise from the wholesalers in Warsaw, he had to pay the full price.

In the town Alter was considered to be a *tzadik*. He knew to find the poor and the sick and help them above his means. Reuven Mandelberg recounts: once, we were hosted at Alter's home. Bilha–Malka cooked fish for the Sabbath and when she wanted to serve them to the guests, she found out that the fish had disappeared. Alter managed to take them out of the pot and brought to the poor. Every Friday Alter collected groceries and brought them to needy families.

Alter's family lived frugally, but he was always in a good mood, always smiling and surrounded by many friends. In the big store there were three stalls on which bearded Jews sat and listened to Alter's stories, and his stories were many and interesting. He knew to tell about Wilhelm the Emperor, about Bismarck, about Jews and Christians, the priest in Sztabin, and also about the village teacher, Shmuel Graenum, who was so smart that he was called "Shemad–Graenum."

Once he told about Moshe Montefiore, how he traveled to the Russian Emperor, Nicholas I, and asked him to alleviate the bitter fate of the Jews of Russia. He knew to tell how the emperor tried to poison Montefiore but he found a way to avenge the cruel emperor. He organized France and England against him (The Battle of Sevastopol), and in the end the emperor himself took poison and committed suicide. For a nine–year–old girl, this was the first opportunity to hear about Sir Montefiore, and it may have been the first opportunity for many of the townspeople.

This was Alter's golden era.

[Page 225]

During this time he loved to arrange marriages and came up with surprising results. Very few professional matchmakers have been able to pair such a large number of couples like Alter, and there was a reason for that: people knew that Alter did not engage in it for a profit (he sometimes lost his expenses) but solely for the sake of a mitzvah, and they trusted him more than they trusted the professional matchmaker.

I remember how Alter made a match between the son of our tenant and a girl from the town of Rajgród. Alter said to the groom's mother: "Mrs. Perla, talk to the bride in Hebrew and see how fluent she is in the holy language" Poor Mrs. Perla did not even know the shape of a Hebrew letter.

As mentioned, all these happened in Alter's golden era – and that glow ended almost tragically. The situation in the store was getting worse. He had no money left to buy new merchandise and started taking out loans at ten percent interest per month. The townspeople brought him money, they thought he was a *tzadik*, a man of wonders, and he borrowed to pay the interest, until there was no one to borrow from, and he went bankrupt.

A commotion broke out in the town. Different and strange things became known. Among those who gave money to the Alter were Jews who did not suspect him, Jews who did not have a penny in their pocket, sometimes even beggars. Overnight the *tzadik* became a deceiver. The money belonged to the "simple people," and this was the most tragic thing in Alter's bankruptcy.

Alter sat alone at home with a bleak soul, forsaken and miserable, and in his heart a feeling of unbearable grief and bitterness. Alter was lonely and hopeless, without blessing and happiness, and his soul was like a book of morality and awe, full of repentance, pain and sorrow.

*Miriam, daughter of Nehemiah and Chana
Mandelberg with their eldest granddaughter Miriam–
Azia*

[Page 226]

All his admirers left him, only a few remained loyal, and he was lonely until the end of his life.

Alter and his wife died in Sosnówka Ghetto to which the Jews of Wolomin were deported by the Germans. Many Jews died in the ghetto: some from starvation, some from illness, and some were murdered by the Germans. Alter and his wife died of starvation.

Decades separate us from Alter, and during that time I had the opportunity to talk to many people who were with him – and all of them were in complete agreement that he was a man with a heart of gold, who loved people and was willing to share his last slice of bread with others, only the events, or the conditions, caused him to engage in trade without any commercial sense. May his memory be blessed.

He and She

They both got married at a very young age. Although he had gotten married and divorced before, he was still young. And since it is impossible to be without a wife – they decided to get married.

Mendel was offered a lot of matchmaking, among others, Chava'le. How was the matchmaking carried out? Simple, the carter harnessed the horse to the cart and together with Mendel traveled to see the bride.

"I saw her and did not want to marry her," Mendel once told me. "Why," I asked, "maybe she was not beautiful?" "She was beautiful – answered Mendel – but she made an impression on me that she was spoiled, and a working man must not marry a spoiled woman." "So, why did you marry her?" I asked again.

"It was not me; it was the cart owner" Mendel answered. "When I told him to quickly harness the horse so we could leave the place, the carter answered me firmly: "I am not leaving unless you agree to marry her." "Under such a situation, having no choice, what should I have done? That's why I married her."

The impression Chava'le made on Mendel was correct. Chava'le was really spoiled, because all of her parents' children died and she was the only one left alive. They turned to the advice of the *tzadikim*, and they decided that Chava'le must not stay at her parents' home. Therefore, Chava'le grew up in her grandmother's house and there Mendel saw her.

Life, too, proved how right Mendel was. After the marriage Mendel opened a dairy shop in the city of Warsaw.

Once, Mendel went shopping, Chava'le stayed in the store and when he returned he saw Chava'le sleeping soundly.

Then I realized – Mendel told me – that I have no one to rely on and I must take on the burden of our existence, on myself and only on myself.

And indeed, he took on himself the burden of earning a living. He was a quick and talented professional, but his work was seasonal, from Passover to Sukkot, and meanwhile the family has grown and he had to support a wife and nine children throughout the year.

[Page 227]

Mendel worked hard and did not lack troubles and distress, and I remember the time when he had heart failure.

He was not old yet but the illness confined him to bed, his lips turned blue and he breathed heavily. His bed was placed by the open window and it helped him a little.

Whoever saw the sorrow of the family, whose sole breadwinner was confined to a deathbed, had to draw the conclusion that I drew: the burden of earning a living for a family must not be placed on the shoulders of one person, no matter how talented he is, the wife must also help in the burden of earning a living.

She was not a homemaker, and although there was no cleanliness or order in this house, we, the town's children, liked to gather there because of the small furniture that suited our size. Tea was served in cups, but without saucers (it seemed very logical to us) and, occasionally, the eldest daughter would open the buffet door and take down battalions of "*zarfatim*" [roaches] and we, the children, ran over the "*zarfatim*" and listened to the characteristic squeak as we as we ran over them.

How the children were raised? The older raised the little ones. The second daughter especially excelled in her diligence and ran the household until her wedding day. Together with that, Chava'le was a talented woman, knew how to cook, bake and embroider, she also knew how to pray from the Sidur, but preferred not to cook or bake. She also did not pray much, simply out of laziness. Chava'le was a smart woman. For years and years, when the town was without a doctor, she was our doctor. With a decisive voice, and complete confidence, she made the diagnosis and performed all kinds of medical treatments, including bandages, cupping, etc. In one area she surpassed doctors and professors alike: she knew how to expel the "evil eye." She was a good woman and was willing to teach me how to expel an evil eye, but she had two conditions: a) I had to be under the age of nine. b) Be the eldest.

I was able to fulfill the first condition because I was six years old, but not the second because I was the second child, and so, unfortunately, I remained ignorant in this area and to this day I do not know how to expel an "evil eye"…

The couple, Mendel and Chava'le, was an exemplary couple. If Mendel had not returned in time from work, Chava'le would have gone looking for him all over town.

And once, when Chava'le had a nerve breakdown, Mendel hit his head against the wall, the first and last time I saw a man hitting his head against a wall.

Mendel died of heart disease when I was already in Eretz Yisrael. Chava'le remained a widow and at the outbreak of the Second World War fled with her children to Russia. A small part of the family survived.

[Page 228]

I observed this family a lot. Just as I came to the conclusion that the burden of existence should not be imposed on the husband alone, I also understood that the wife should not be assigned only one role: housekeeping. A woman, who does not like housekeeping, can be useful in many other areas, and the road to these areas should not be blocked for her.

R' Yoske Sultis

When I was a little girl I played with the children in the yard. One of the children emphasized at every opportunity: Yoske Sultis is my uncle, meaning: my uncle is a respectable man, that's why you also owe me respect.

As far as I know, there were very few Jewish Sultis [village head], and one of the few was Yoske Sultis whose surname was Laskowsky. In the course of time, Wolomin became a town and the title Sultis, a rural title, was abolished, but for all the years of his life Yoske Laskowsky was called: Yoske Sultis.

He was good–natured and showed affection to the townspeople, and even though he came from the simple class, the speech in his home was calm and noble, and everything he dealt with for public needs was his main concern. "An urgent matter – R' Yoske used to say – should not be missed or rejected, and its importance should not be measured to a small or large degree, and when a person thinks that the work is heavy, he should make an effort and do it when the time is right."

Yoske Laskowsky (Yoske Sultis) with his wife

[Page 229]

Yoske Sultis was a tall man with a blond beard, blue eyes and classic facial features. He was blessed with a beautiful wife and many children, most of them boys. He was very respectable in the town and no one questioned his honesty and kindness. Therefore, all the responsible duties of that period were assigned to Yoske.

For example: the town's Jews greatly suffered from the burden of taxes imposed on them. The Polish government was democratic: it included the citizens in the imposition of taxes. It was called "committee." There was a committee for income tax, tax for the turnover of funds, etc. Yoske participated in all the committees, or almost all the committees. He did not have an easy life. He fought, with his heart and soul to protect the livelihood of the town's Jews. He was so honest that even the Polish officials treated him with respect.

Yoske had many buildings, and the buildings had a lot of apartments, many tenants lived in the apartments but no one paid rent. They simply lived for free. As a landlord, Yoske had one and only duty: to pay out of pocket the taxes for the houses and for maintaining the cleanliness. Yoske's fate was the same as the fate of almost all the town's Jews. he was murdered by the Germans.

Aunt Necha – a noble figure

When I was a girl aunt Necha lived in our house. That's what the Tayblum family called her (she was probably their relative), and we also called her by the same name.

Aunt Necha had a husband named Motel Rozevikviat, which means in Hebrew: pink flower.

Now, when the heart is full with happy and painful memories, I see aunt Necha before my eyes – a middle–aged woman, with a wig, pink cheeks and small wrinkles around the eyes.

We all loved her. She portrayed a character with moral strength. Her life was not easy. In addition to her daughter's farm, she ran a grocery and vegetable store and her livelihood was not plentiful. Battalions of goats attacked the vegetables and ate them indiscriminately and with great appetite.

Aunt Necha never complained and never said a word of insult or curse. She was content with little and all her worries were directed at others, that there would be no starving Jew in Wolomin and that he would not remain ill without help. She donated to the benefit of the poor and also collected donations from others.

I remember the Sabbath candles at Necha's. She lit more candles than in other homes. Lighting candles was one of the three *mitzvot* imposed on a Jewish woman, and aunt Necha knew how to fulfill the *mitzvot*. They constituted the content of her life.

May her memory be blessed.

[Page 230]

The home of R' Yankel the baker

I mostly remember the town of Wolomin from my childhood. Then I lived the life of the town more than at home. I spent days and nights at our neighbors, and I remember R' Yankel the bakery owner and R' Mendel that I used to visit their homes.

A fence separated my parents' house and R' Yankel's house, it had an opening which served as a passage from yard to yard. The lifestyle and concepts of the neighbors were like the lives and perceptions of all the town's Jews. Every morning they went out to work. R' Yankel had a bakery and also a store where he sold bread and other groceries, and for me it was an experience to help R' Yankel and his wife. I delivered loaves of bread from the bakery to the store, a job I really liked, and to this day I love the smell of fresh bread. I also helped with other tasks in the store, I filled sugar bags and handed them to R' Yankel's wife, Mrs. Mirka, and she weighed them and pack them nicely.

I watched every move she and the shoppers made, how a woman opens her purse, how the shoppers greet each other, and how they turn to the shopkeeper.

At the home of R' Yankel I also watched his family's lifestyle, which was greatly different from the lifestyle at my parents' home.

They worked hard all days of the week to earn a living. For us, the children, the most enjoyable pastime during the cold winter days was on top of the huge oven. On this "*piekarnik*" we did not feel the severe Polish winter. In the summer we had a shed, in which logs were kept, and they were comfortable for various jumps and games.

R' Yankel and his wife had four sons and four daughters. His wife, Mirka, was a woman of valor, a reserved woman who engaged in the daily business matters and in negotiations. She was a tall and upright woman. Her diction was sharp and rhythmic. The merchants respected her for her integrity and talent to run a business. It was possible to trust her. R' Yankel himself did not work hard and preferred to rely on his wife and his family.

At home, Mirka had no time to rest. She worked, worked endlessly. From morning to evening the house turned like a giant wheel which gnawed all hours of the day and evening with its teeth. Everything was swallowed up in the worry of existence.

And I, a six year old girl, admired Mirka's thinking ability. To me she was really knowledgeable in arithmetic. I was amazed how she calculated the bills, which were complicated in my eyes, without a pencil because, even though the ruble was the official currency, the trade with the Polish farmers was done in zloty. Then, according to the accepted rate, the ruble was six zloty and twenty groschen, and Mirka had to divide and add according to the ruble.

[Page 231]

R' Yankel's sons were not of the same material. His two older sons devoted themselves to Torah study and R' Yankel was satisfied from them because, like all the town's Jews, he aspired to raise his sons to Torah and good deeds. They studied in the *heder* and in Beit HaMidrash, and also studied the Gemara at home. They were diligent.

The third son, Shmuel, showed little interest in studies and preferred to work in the bakery, to take care of the oven, etc. and he tried to convince me that it was better to be a boy than a girl. I could not understand, because I knew that boys must study in the *heder*, a matter that I never envied. I also knew that when they grew up they would have to serve in the Russian army and I imagined how difficult it was…

Over the years I sometimes remembered Shmuel's words and then I realized that he was right…

The fourth son was still young and it was not known where he would turn and what would attract his heart.

Of R' Yankle's daughters I remember the eldest, Fradel, she was tall and upright like her mother and also as industrious as her. She was a loyal helper at home and participated in all the worries. She was always willing to help, knew that life is not an answer of living without special intention… Therefore, a wonderful bond has been formed between mother and daughter, a bond of love and mutual admiration, and both constituted a solid foundation for the home.

Every girl's ambition in Wolomin was to know how to write a letter in Yiddish and Russian, but it is doubtful whether Fradel reached this level of education. In contrast, her sisters already knew how to read and write, because in their time elementary schools for girls had already been founded.

I loved R' Yankel's family and the atmosphere at their home. The big room was always well organized. It also served as a dining room for the men – the apprentices who worked in the bakery ate together with R' Yankel and his sons and, at times, also a "guest" that R' Yankel brought with him from the synagogue.

The women, Mirka and her daughters, sat and ate in the kitchen, and there we also played together.

Fate separated us. My parents sent me to a gymnasium in Warsaw and later to university. But when I remember them, a sea of longing rises in me to the smell of the fresh bread, to the warm and pleasant atmosphere, to the small town in its joys and sorrows, it's wealthy and poor inhabitants, a precious corner, which enveloped my childhood days in a holy aura.

[Page 232]

Hospitality

by Zev Nadvorni

Translated by Yocheved Klausner

The former residents of Wolomin remember with love and longing their shtetl. It was a small and simple Jewish shtetl, with low houses, where a mixture of people lived: merchants and shopkeepers, artists and artisans, not unlike so many other towns in prewar Poland. The members of the community of Wolomin were not different from other communities in their dress, in their customs and not even in the education of their children; their lives were intensive, they included a large intelligentsia and their way of life was full of ideology and spirituality. True, they did not have old synagogues, palaces or large houses built of precious stone; it was a town of working people – builders, ironsmiths and other craftsmen, but great was their thirst for knowledge and Torah and their readiness to do good deeds.

The town had another precious quality: it was the town of my childhood. A man has only one homeland in his life – only one town of birth, and even when one is in a distant place one feels its existence. Even if you ignore your past, it lives inside of you, and for many years it remains part of your being. As a child I have walked on the soil of my shtetl, and with a child's eyes I have seen it and have grown up in it. I accepted it as it was, with its market place and narrow alleys, its streets and its beauty. I absorbed its taste and its style – and we became one.

The town and its people were marked by their simplicity, but one of their particular fine qualities was their hospitality, which was so special that they were called "*voyle men*" which means "good people." Indeed they were good people and acted toward guests in a polite, helpful and welcoming way, and fought for the privilege to be their hosts and share with them their bread. Not far from the synagogue there was an inn, where every guest could find a place to spend the night without having to pay. No guest from out of town would remain without a warm meal; the guests were divided among the residents of the town and every head of family was proud to bring home a guest. On Friday night, every Jew came home from the synagogue with a guest for the Sabbath.

[Page 233]

On Fridays, when in every home they prepared for the Sabbath – cooked, baked, cleaned and set the tables – a place was reserved for the guest. The poorest house would become a holy palace where one could rest and rightfully recite the blessing "To make the seventh day a holy time," as it deserves.

The Sabbath nights became etched in our hearts, as the weekday work in every corner in honor of the "Queen Sabbath" was finished. On the table, covered with a spotless tablecloth white as snow, two *halot* (special Sabbath bread) were ready. Mother, wearing a Sabbath dress, stood near the table and fixed the candles in the two silver candlesticks. She prepared an extra cup of wine for the guest who surely will come. To this day I can hear her soft voice welcoming him with "*a Gut Shabes*" (a good Sabbath) – two words that were enough to make the guest feel at home, part of the family.

Some of the "guest–receivers" in our town have become famous in the entire neighborhood, among them the family of Chaim Yakov Nadvorni, whom they called "the miller" since he owned a flour mill and in the shtetl people were called by their profession rather than by their surname; this was how the name Chaim Yakov "the miller" persisted.

The Nadvorni Family

Chaim Yakov the miller's house was always open to any guest or passer–by – a person on the road, with the sun beating on his head, stones hurting his feet, dust blinding his eyes and his whole body being tired; he was thinking only of the distance to the house of R'Chaim–Yakov "the miller" knowing that he will find there a place to rest, to wash up and to eat – and he praised the one who opened his home for him and prepared all that he needed. R'Chaim–Yakov's house was indeed open to anyone who needed help in food or dress, in money or advice – to eat breakfast and continue on the road or to stay a few days. R'Chaim–Yakov was modest and would speak to the guest as to a friend, and if he came home late and the guests were already asleep he would walk on the tips of his toes in order not to wake them.

[Page 234]

R'Chaim–Yakov's house was an example to others. How pleasant were the Sabbath evenings, when the synagogue was full of people and the children surrounded the cantor saying Amen after him; I was seeking with my eyes the guests – the handsome old man whose eyes followed me tenderly, and was hoping that he would be our guest, feeling that he would have much to tell about his adventures, as did all those who kept wandering from town to town. The Shabat guests in our house were simple people but had sharp tongues and knew how to tell stories and legends. They had tender souls, some of them had daughters waiting to be married off, but they didn't have the means to do that and grooms could not be found; so they went from town to town trying to collect money for this purpose, waiting for a good match. Our guests would tell all kinds of strange stories, which I do not intend to repeat; but I shall tell just one story about hospitality.

There was once a very wealthy man, who always managed to avoid taking a guest to his house for Shabat, and if he was forced by the Gabay of the synagogue to take one, he would do it with an angry face and would not respect him. The guests would complain that while the host was receiving fine food, they would be given only meager leftovers. Once, one of the guests, who was smart, decided to "fix" the miser rich man when the latter was served a rich soup while he was served a plate of hot water, he began to tell a story about the earth and other stars, about the sun and the moon and showed the host how the stars were moving, by using the soup plates as examples. He moved the plates around and around, until the plate full of good soup rested in front of the guest and the plate of hot water in front of the host. As he started eating, he became angry with his wife and began shouting at her and reprimanding her, arguing that the food was fit for dogs. She was offended and a strong argument broke out, which continued during the entire Shabat. Since then, they stopped the discrimination between the host and the guest. This is only one of the stories about hospitality in our town Wolomin, where the guests were an integral part of the way of life, especially on Shabat. Our sages say that the Sabbath protected the people of Israel more than the people kept the Sabbath.

[Page 235]

All week long people talked about the Sabbath and on Thursday the preparations began – for the people of the town and for the guests who were expected for Shabat. A special atmosphere reigned in town. The residents who were away all week – to the villages, to the fairs or to various exhibitions – returned to their homes to prepare for the Holy Sabbath. I saw my mother lighting the candles, and it seemed to me that her eyes shone like the candles as she covered them with her hands and recited the blessing in a clear and sweet voice.

Her entire face was shining through her fingers and a tear, like a pearl, fell from her eyes. After lighting the candles her eyes filled with light and her eyelashes trembled in the glow of the Queen Sabbath. These images and many similar ones will never fade, and for me they are an unending source of reminders of good things – holy feelings that I am keeping deep in my heart since the days of my youth. My eyes are weeping for the loss of our shtetl Wolomin and for the holy Jews who were murdered during the terrible tragedy, among them our parents, brothers and sisters. We shall always keep alive the holy memory of the people of our shtetl.

The "*Gut Shabes*" will never be heard in our shtetl again, neither will the voices from the *Bet Midrash* [house of learning] or the voices of the little children from the *Heder*. No more stories about receiving guests…

The shtetl is empty of its Jews and its Jewish character – only the mute walls are crying the cry of mourning for the town which had lost its sons.

May these lines serve as an eternal light to the memory of the holy and pure people, who have sanctified the Holy Name, in their life and in their death.

[Page 236]

This is how we became Wolomin Citizens

by Arie Brisker

Translated by Yocheved Klausner

My parents were born in Ukraine; however, after the Bolshevik revolution they did not want to remain in Russia. They sold all their belongings, bought a horse and wagon and left with a convoy for Kiev.

We were a family with seven children, five boys and two girls. On the way, a little orphan girl joined us. Our parents adopted her and we all treated her with much love. She stayed with us until she was eighteen.

We traveled during the day, and at night we "parked" in the open field until we reached Warsaw and from there we went to Wolomin.

The Wolomin Jews welcomed us warmly and helped us settle. My father obtained work in a glass factory.

This was how we became citizens of Wolomin.

Sabbath Evenings

Together with all the other Jews of the town, we were happy with our way of life. My home was a traditional one, and I remember in particular the Sabbath evenings, when Father would sing the special Sabbath songs and we would join him in loud voices, happy that the Holy Blessed One has given us such a big and holy day.

We were sitting at the table listening to Father's voice:

"Come and see – Father would say – the fine qualities of the Holy Sabbath: a person lights a Sabbath light, it sheds light on both his worlds. A person prepares a beautiful meal for the Sabbath, the Sabbath provides him with all his needs. A person keeps the Sabbath in the present world, his body is not only preserved in the other world but he is also protected from all troubles".

Once he told us about a very poor Jew who did not have the privilege to keep the Sabbath in a proper way, because he did not earn enough money for his sustenance, and when Sabbath Eve arrived he did not have enough money to buy what he needed for the Sabbath. His candlesticks would stand without candles and his plates without meat or fish or any other food for Sabbath.

[Page 237]

His wife, with a sad face, said: "Woe is to us, we have nothing for Sabbath".

The man went into the other room and came back with seven pieces of copper in his hand. He bent them here and there (he was a goldsmith), and created seven coins, and nobody could have seen a difference between them and real Empire coins. But somebody informed the authorities and soon he was chained and arrested and taken to prison. However, a miracle happened and the same day a royal order was received and he was released and engaged to work at the royal palace as a great artist.

To end the story, Father added:

"He who keeps one Sabbath in poverty, merits to keep many Sabbaths in richness."

Father would sometimes lead the prayers (serve as cantor) and we, the children, would help him with our choir.

All his life he hoped to make Aliya to Eretz Israel and he would say that Aliya to Eretz Israel is equal to all the other *mitzvoth* (commandments) together. But he did not achieve that.

These were the Jews of Wolomin and this was our town, where we were born and raised, where our beloved have lived and which was destroyed among the other Jewish communities in the European *galut* (exile).

My parents, my elder sister and her family were murdered in Treblinka.

My brother and his family were murdered in the Warsaw Ghetto. The other four brothers and one sister are living now in Israel.

Near the Memorial Stone
Standing: Noah Brisker, Tchortak, Mordechai Silberstein

[Page 238]

The Grodzhitzki Family

by Miriam Feigenboim

Translated by Yocheved Klausner

In 1900, my parents Moshe and Shifra Grodzhitzki were among the first settlers in Wolomin. At the time they had three sons. In time, three more sons and three daughters were born. I was the youngest.

From the stories my parents told, I know that they had a difficult time, in particular during the First World War; the children were young, the economic situation was bad and calamity followed calamity. But they did not despair, and courageously they fought the war of sustenance.

In time, their economic situation improved. They founded a factory of soda-water and lemonade, but work was primitive and difficult and they worked hard from dawn to night, all week. But as the Sabbath came, came the much awaited rest. I loved the reception of the Sabbath in our house and in the street. I loved watching the street on Sabbath eve at dusk and feel how the Sabbath took the place of the weekdays – slowly but insistently, until it got full control.

At dusk, the people began to walk toward the synagogue. They walked slowly, in order to keep the Sabbath commandment "do not walk fast on the Sabbath".

I remember my father and my brothers wearing their Sabbath clothes and going to the synagogue. All were tall and handsome, and the townspeople would look at them and say about my father: "This is one of our people who have a pure heart". My father was proud of his sons, although he was very modest.

In the shining light of the Queen Sabbath, Mother would greet us with a holy feeling and say: "A Good Sabbath". These two words, of a sad sound, are echoed in my memory to this day and will not leave it forever.

In our home, we used to bake *matzot* for Pesach. Moshe Grodzhitzki's *matzot* were famous in all neighboring towns, for their taste and their Kosher quality. Jews would come to us to buy *matzot* even from Warsaw. And in addition to all their work, my father and my brothers found time to study Gemara (Talmud). The sweet melody of their learning, early in the morning before they went to work, is still sounding in my ears.

[Page 239]

When primary schools were established, my father was one of the first to send his daughters to school; he was always interested to know how his daughters were doing in school.

Almost in every class there was a Grodzhitzki girl from our family; in some classes there were two or three Grodzhitzki daughters or granddaughters.

My parents' home was always full of guests and friends, some coming to see them and ask how they were, some to ask for advice and some just for a regular friendly visit.

My mother, a short woman, was of a good nature, always ready to help, always busy cooking and baking.

Years passed, and we grew up and became adults, and I still remember the days of Sabbath and Holiday, as the sons and their wives and children gathered in our home. All were sitting around the table; although it was not large enough, all felt comfortable. The conversation was around matters of Torah and also regular chat. My mother would serve her delicacies and smile her sad and pleasant smile.

Oh, dear Mother, how much you loved us!

The noise that the children made did not bother anyone. Father would say: I do not hear the noise; to my ears the voices sound like music.

R'Moshe Grodzhitzki and his sons

[Page 240]

Chaya Gitl, R'Moshe Grodzhitzki's daughter

With the eyes of my mind I see my father working happily for the Community; he helped founding the "Talmud Torah" school and the "Bet Ya'akov" school for girls and helped with the needs of the synagogue.

He would always avoid honors, but he would honor others as one would honor a king. He was asked once:

- Is not honor one of the three things that end a person's life?

He replied:

-This was meant when one seeks honor for himself; but you should honor others as much as you can, since this is what we were ordered to do: to honor our fellows.

My father was in touch with many people and had many friends. He felt close to every Jew, as if he were a member of his family. He was gentle in his relationship with his fellows, but very strict in his behavior concerning matters of commandments from heaven; he had no fear, and spoke the truth in front of any person; therefore his opponents treated him with respect and honor.

During my childhood, as well as an adult I heard many times people praising Father's good heart and deep understanding. He knew how to grasp the situation of any person and understood his needs; he always tried to help as much as he could, in body and in spirit.

My father died in 1934 after a grave illness. He was taken to his eternal resting place by his wife, his nine children, daughters-in-law and sons-in-law, grandchildren, friends and admirers.

My mother was murdered by the Germans in the ghetto, the day after it was destroyed.

The others perished in the concentration camps and in the gas chambers. Of all my brothers only Yakov survived, since he made Aliya before the war.

I managed to sneak out of the ghetto the night before its destruction and to obtain "Arian papers."

The little daughter of my brother Yakov was hidden during the war by a Christian family. In 1946 she arrived in Eretz Israel and here she fell in the War of Independence.

Zlata's Sabbath Tea

Every shtetl had its characteristic figures, so had Wolomin. One of these figures was Zlata, the wife of Shmuel-Aizik Pletkovski. She was a quiet woman, religious and the symbol of a good heart.

[Page 241]

She was always busy. She had a large family: 8 children and a sickly husband. She managed a store selling textiles. When there were no buyers in the store, she would hold in her hand a *siddur* [prayer book] and pray.

Zlata remembered all the people who were in need. She knew in what house there was nothing to eat and she would take some food to that house. During the cold winter days she would remember the women in the neighboring shops and bring them hot tea, to keep warm.

The "guests" who came to town – Jewish poor people – were directed to Jewish families, where they would receive a hot meal. In case there were more guests than host families, the solution was simple: they sent the people to Zlata, where there was always room during weekdays. Whoever came in hungry left content.

This was during weekdays. When Sabbath came, Zlata's home turned into a Tea House. In Poland in those times, they did not have "warming plates" (that don't cook, but keep the food hot), and the custom was that every Sabbath morning a Christian woman would come to the Jewish houses and light the stoves; but not everybody could afford that, therefore they went to Zlata to have hot tea.

On Wednesday the preparations for the Sabbath tea began. They had to prepare a certain number of cans of water – and the water was brought from afar, from a well with tasty water, since Zlata would not serve just plain tea, but only the finest tea, with sugar.

Every Sabbath, starting early in the morning, people would flock to Zlata's house to drink tea. There were some, who were not happy with one glass, and would sometimes drink up to five cups. With the patience of an angel, Zlata would serve the tea, finding room for all the visitors.

People would take home full kettles of boiling water – at Zlata's home tea was abundant. Thus, the drinking of tea would continue until the end of Sabbath.

When all good Jewish people rested or slept the Sabbath sleep, Zlata had no time to rest, because people came to her house all day long. With every cup of tea she served, she welcomed the guest friendly and politely. This was Zlata, all pure and gentle, and her Sabbath tea became a drink of hope and spirituality.

From my entire family only two sisters remained: Rachel Grossinger, who fled to Russia and Hendel, who remained in Poland and hid in the attic of a grain storehouse. Both are now in America.

[Page 242]

My home

by Altke Grinszpan–Tamari

Translated by Sara Mages

My father' Dovid–Tzvi (Hirsh) Grinszpan was a descended of the Aleksander Hassidic family. He was born in the town of Wegrow. His father, Yehudah–Leib Grinszpan, a Strykower Hassid, was a God–fearing scholar. In his last years of his life he lived in Wolomin and served as a teacher.

He had six sons, my father was his firstborn.

My father was short, skinny, had big blue eyes, his face was alert, immersed in spirituality and adorned with a long beard and high forehead. He was a scholar, a righteous and innocent man, a scribe.

He woke up early in the morning and went to the "shtiebel" to pray *Tefillat Shacharit*. Then, he returned home and strengthened his weak body a little with a light meal and sat down at his table, his working table.

For whole days he held duck feathers in his hand and wrote Torah Scrolls, *tefillin* and *mezozot*, in holiness and purity, in his elegant and rhythmic handwriting.

The Grinszpan family

[Page 243]

The Torah scrolls written by him were famous throughout Poland, and well–known wealthy families (like Prywes in Warsaw and Poznanski in Lodz) ordered Torah scrolls from him.

Countless Torah scrolls were left after his death.

My father was quiet by nature, focused, introvert and humble. He had a wonderful sense of humor, a warm heart, was hospitable and greeted every person with kindhearted smile.

Every day he brought home many guests from the "shtiebel" and took care of their needs.

He was also a well known reader of the Torah in the city, and when he read the Torah in the synagogue before the community, he brought great pleasure to all his listeners. His pleasant voice, which came from the heart, entered the heart and evoked soul–stirring emotions. On Purim, the neighbors gathered to hear the reading of the Book of Esther. Great enthusiasm and inner peace merged within him.

My father had a deep rooted faith, and when he was debating a certain crisis, he traveled to the Aleksander Rebbe to consult with him. He believed, wholeheartedly, that only the Rebbe, as the messenger of *hakadosh baruch hu* could bring him salvation.

His opinion was, that only by the power of deep and sincere faith there is meaning to life, and without faith life is empty and lacks any content and meaning.

He brought an uplifting mood to our home. On the Sabbath and holidays he sang the hymns in his pleasant and emotional voice and shared it with the whole family.

On the Sabbath and holidays he wore a silk capote, black and shiny, and on Simchat Torah he wore a *shtreimel* on his head. He invited all the men of his "shtiebel" and they danced in circles and on the tables.

We kept the tradition at home in its original form, warm, rooted and touching the depths of the heart. My father, in his usual manner, was humble and righteous, loved truth, pursued peace, and was imbued with love for the Jewish people. He carried in his heart the kindness of a man who knows how to instill his love in everyone who comes in contact with him. He behaved humbly with God and with people, cultivated in his heart respect for every person, even the simplest.

He fulfilled the *mitzvoth* of the joy of life: eating: drinking, singing, dancing and everything allowed to him and his body to enjoy in this world, out of the refinement of joy and seeing it as a reflection of the Supreme joy.

This joy did not come just for the sake of material joy, but the joy of the spirit, joy in the inwardness of life in their holiness. He lived and enjoyed this world and, at the same time, prepared himself for the spiritual life in the next world, embodied the simple, natural, and innocent Judaism, which protects its hidden light secretly and quietly.

[Page 244]

My mother

My mother, Sheina–Feiga, was the daughter of Matityahu Blumenkrantz from Kosów Lacki near Sokołów, a lessee of a flour mill and a power station who was known by his nickname "Matis the Miller" (Matis der Milner). He was a descended of the Aleksander Hasidic family and initially served as a ritual slaughterer. He was handsome, wise and accepted by all and therefore often served as an arbitrator in merchant disputes. For years served as chairman of the community committee in Kosów.

A diligent woman, short with black hair, brown eyes, gifted with a wonderful and juicy sense of humor, a strong character and inexhaustible vigor. She was very sociable, imbued with the love of people, was interested in everything that was happening in the world, ran businesses to contribute to the family's livelihood since the income my father brought as a scribe was not enough to cover the many household needs.

Her desire was to give her children an excellent education. She woke up early every morning to make breakfast for the family and get the kids ready for school. She especially got up early on the eve of the Sabbath and holidays to bake challot and cakes. On the Sabbath and holidays she dressed in her best dresses and knew to create a sweet warm atmosphere throughout the house. She lit the candles in the elegant silver candlesticks. Her face glowed through her spread fingers in a supreme glow, a teardrop fell from her eyes, and she uttered the pure blessing in a clear voice: "*Lehadlik ner shel Shabbat.*"

My brother, Avraham, chose his way of life according to our parents' values. He studied at yeshivot in Bialystok, Lubawicze and Mesivta in Warsaw, and was among the outstanding students. He was a member of "Agudat Yisrael" and a fan of HaRav Yitzhak Meir Levin. For 36 years he served as a rabbi in the city of Halifax, Canada.

The eldest daughter, Alteka, was always active in the field of culture among the local youth. She regularly attended meetings, lectures, parties and conferences. She immigrated to Eretz Israel in 1935 as the pioneer of the family so that she could organize their aliya, but the plan did not materialize because of the Holocaust.

For the past twenty years she has been working as a coordinator of the Working Mothers Organization, at first in Bnei Brak and later in Kiryat Ono. Her main role is the management of children's institutions and care for low–income and disadvantaged families. She married Tzvi Tamari, a lawyer, a legal aid officer in the Israel Defense Forces.

The second daughter, Fraida, had big blue eyes and golden hair. She was kind hearted, gentle, quite, and active in the socialist movement. She always cared for others, for justice and honesty.

[Page 245]

The daughters of the Grinszpan family: Hanna, Sara and Alteka

The third daughter, Sara, had a strong character and a lot of energy. On her own she graduated from the Faculty of Law of the University of Warsaw, married an engineer and at the beginning of the Second World War served as a teacher in a gymnasium in Kletsk.

Hanna was beautiful, full of grace, humor, wisdom and intelligence. She graduated from a trade school in Warsaw and worked as a bank clerk in Wolomin. She was very sociable and involved with people.

The last daughter, Gittel, was active in "Gordonia" and aspired to immigrate to Israel. She was very popular and well–liked in the youth circles.

Our home was like a public institution. There was always a big commotion in it. Friends, from school and youth organizations, came in and out at all hours of the day. Among them were Zionists, socialists, revolutionaries of all kinds, and there was no end to the heated debates that took place between them. Things often led to outbursts of emotion even among the family members.

In this turmoil and quarrel of opinions, my mother's opinion was always accepted by everyone, no matter what their view was. Although she kept the *mitzvot*, prayed every Sabbath and holiday at the synagogue, she was very patient with others.

Of all the family members, who perished in the Holocaust, only the son Avraham and the daughter Alteka survived.

[Page 246]

The Tepper family

by Penina Tepper-Grossman

Translated by Sara Mages

Of the whole family I am the only one left.

I was not yet five months old when my father passed away, and I only knew a stepfather whose love to me was not less than the love of a true father. In daily life he was known in the town by the name Gudel. He had a good soul, was not angry at anyone, and was God-fearing and observant. He worked hard all his days to please God and people, asking only for the wages he earned from his hard work for his existence.

My mother, Chaya-Beila, was a loving and working mother. I had three brothers and a sister, and she gave us all the feeling that we were her whole life.

All days of the week she was busy, from early morning until evening, in the poultry and dairy trade and the customers loved her for her honesty. Her moral principles were deeply, deeply rooted, and she was careful not to offend a person's dignity.

Jews and Christians visited our store, and there were times when my mother noticed that someone put something in his basket and did not pay, but my mother did not respond so as not to cause shame to the person.

Many people owed my mother money, she never reminded them and did not demand repayment of the debt out of concern that they could not pay.

I remember the case when Shiye the butcher demanded from my mother a debt of ten zloty for a chicken that I myself paid him, therefore I claimed that we did not owe him anything. But, he swore on the lives of his children that I did not pay. My mother immediately gave him the money, and gave me a slap in the face and said that I made a Jew swear by his children's lives.

Members of the Tepper family

[Page 247]

All days of the week they worked hard and made do with crumbs of subsistence, all so they could provide for their family honestly and fulfill the *mitzvot* they received from their ancestors, as stated: a man is born to work, work for a living, and work for the fulfillment of the *mitzvah* of helping others, and so she used to help by giving charity in secret to the needy, to the poor and the sick.

Sabbath came, rest came.

The preparation for the Sabbath began on Thursday evening. Thursday evening was devoted, among others, to the washing of the children's hair and the kitchen. My mother started early so there wouldn't be too much to do on Friday, on a long day in the summer and, of course, on a short day in winter.

My mother was active and agile, a symbol of boundless devotion, devotion that knew no bounds of fatigue and health, and taught us the basic rules of obligation and human purity.

Avraham Tepper

Shmuel David Wilenski and his public activity

In Wolomin everyone knew Shmuel David Wilenski, or as he was simply called with affection: Shmuel David. He was of medium height, had a small black beard and two wise eyes which radiated kindness and love for others. His face expressed nobility and his appearance was orderly. He respected every person and treated even the simplest Jew with affection.

Shmuel David engaged in carpentry all his life. There were many Jewish carpenters in Wolomin. Almost all of them were learned, polite and sociable and Shmuel David was their loyal representative. He has done his work out of the joy of life and, at all times, received the divine judgment with love.

[Page 248]

Zipora Wilenski, Chaya Lustigman-Schneiderman

He was imbued with the belief that God directs human life down to the smallest detail and distributes, in justice and mercy, joy and sorrow. He saw the Torah as the most important thing.

He had nimble hands and knew how to help the townspeople even in areas outside of his professional work. The reference is mainly to the medical field because there was no one better than him for assembling cupping, a cure that was very common then in the town.

The local doctor, Dr. Chaplizki, appreciated the knowledge and virtues of Shmuel David, and sought his help in performing serious and complicated treatments.

By the way, the doctor's work in his town was quite complicated and difficult and he had to know all the pains and diseases. Among others he was also called to deliver a baby, and the matter was not easy considering his working conditions and the living conditions of the town's Jews. Women gave birth in their homes where there was no electricity, gas and sewage. Water had to be brought from a well or a pump, sometimes from a considerable distance. Shmuel David performed his medical activity with astonishing simplicity and without pay, out of love for people and for the sake of a *mitzvah.*

The townspeople returned love and respect, appreciated his sincerity, his willingness to help and the wisdom of his life, and sought his advice.

He was pleasant and affable, spoke quietly and in inner peace, and loved to quotes the words of *Hazal* [our Sages of blessed memory].

His most notable virtues were his gentle soul and noble approach towards people. These virtues paved the way to the hearts of the townspeople and also to the people of the Polish authority, including the judge and the head of the council.

[Page 249]

Shmuel David Wilenski

And here he had ample opportunities to help the town's Jews in their distress. The Polish officials, who ruled in the town, listened to him, admired his loyalty and showed understanding for his requests which were always related to the concern for others. We saw him walking from office to office in order to expedite the help to the needy. Shmuel David has done good deeds to the inhabitants of the town.

Many were his concerns for those who needed help, and he provided it with a full heart, with special devotion, and in his home he was a good husband and a devoted father. The love of the family, which illuminated his eyes, was full of softness and tenderness.

Although he always had a job and did not know poverty, he aspired, in his heart and soul, to immigrate to Israel, and was privileged to fulfill his aspiration and also bring here part of his family.

In Israel he was surrounded by many friends and admirers, his circle of acquaintances was wide and he got to see his grandchildren.

Shmuel David belonged to the type of people we see in public activity, in providing material and moral relief.

His son Mordechai relates: "In Wolomin there was a poor family whose daughter had reached the age of marriage but they lacked a dowry of one thousand zloty. The rabbi called Shmuel David and instructed him to collect the dowry. He made a list of the ten richest men of the town and each was asked to donate one hundred zloty. My father was successful in his action, in every house his request was granted, and along with the donation he also received their blessing that a groom will be found and the couple will get to see an honest generation from him. Shmuel David answered Amen, and said: may we be privileged to hear comfort and salvation with all the Jewish people, Amen, and may we be privileged to see the Redeemer who will soon be revealed, Amen.

But, in one house, which was known for its stinginess, the rich man set a condition before my father: he must know where the groom is from. My father answered: from Wyszków. And the rich man immediately said: I do not agree that a girl from Wolomin will marry a man from Wyszków.

[Page 250]

In the glow of our ancestors

by Malka Carmeli

Translated by Sara Mages

My father, Yitzchak Dancziger, was called in the town: "Itchele from the beer," because he engaged in the production of black beer, a profession he studied in addition to the production of paper bags for packing goods in the shops. In his youth he studied in yeshivot and excelled in his studies, but his talents were not utilized because the paths to development were blocked for the Jews of Poland.

We, the parents and their eight children, lived in one room. The kitchen also served as a factory, and despite the great overcrowding my mother never complained about her bitter fate, and thanks to her diligence there was an atmosphere of security and hope for a better future at home.

My mother deprived herself of anything that seemed to her a luxury and waste. She knew how to live modestly, but at the same time in good taste, in appreciation of pleasant and fine.

Yitzchak Dancziger, his wife, their son and daughters

[Page 251]

There was something sober and practical in her, and in tense moments of fatigue and exhaustion she found peace in the book "*Tz'enah Ur'enah*" [the Women's Bible], which gave her the understanding of the human soul, while having great love for him.

Yes, the book and the Sidur brought her rest and relaxation, enriched and filled her soul and gave her strength, confidence and faith.

Who will measure the strength of her faith along with her concern for the well-being of her children?

Ester Dancziger

The love for grace and beauty merged in her with the kindness of our mothers from all generations, who knew how to inspire out their love on everyone who came in contact with them.

My father was affable and pleasant, people fully trusted him and when he needed money there was always someone to lend him the amount he needed. Once it was R' Avraham Goldwasser and once someone else. Everyone knew that my father would repay the debt on time and on the due date.

His favorite topic of conversation was politics. In this area few could compete with him. In turbulent and peaceful times, people came to him to ask his opinion on matters of the utmost importance in politics between the countries.

He had a pure and gentle soul and listened to others. As a committee member of "*Kupat Gemilut Hasadim*" [Interest-Free Loan Fund] he invested a lot of effort into expanding and increasing the assistance to the needy. When he came to know about a Jew in need of help, he went out to collect donations for "secret giving," and secretly offered the help to the needy so as not to embarrass him.

On Sabbath eve he brought a guest to eat at his table and was kind to him all the time. There were guests who told interesting stories, and we, the children, listened to their stories and took pity on their families who remained in their far away homes.

And here it's worth noting my father's work at *Chevra Kadisha,* in which he was a member and cared for the honor of the dead. He was agile in his work because from the day of his adulthood showed his willingness to make an effort and never had an hour of rest.

I was the only one from the family to survive. My brother's son miraculously survived and lives in France.

[Page 252]

My mother

by Alter Carmeli

Translated by Sara Mages

My beloved mother, my light, was diligent, kind-hearted, innocence and righteous. All her days she shone with the purity of her anguish, the anguish of a widow who was left alone with her three children, orphans without a father, and on her own she made her way through the surges of life, which were cruel to her when they took her husband from her.

I was twelve years old when my father passed away and felt that the light of day was taken away, that the light in the sky was damaged. My mother was left without any assets, without profession, and so that the children would not starve for bread, she got up at four in the morning, walked to the nearby villages, bought fresh milk from the farmers and delivered it to the townspeople.

She has done this work in summer and winter, in autumn and spring, every day, in the rain and in the snow. She left the town with empty jugs, and on the way back carried jugs full of milk.

Her legs got used to walking, but the income was too meager. She did not eat enough, her body weakened until her legs barely carried her.

My mother also learned to produce dairy products and sold them to the stores, when that was not enough to support her children, she found herself another job. She chopped wood into thin sticks, packed them in bundles and sold them to her customers.

Despite the difficult conditions she knew how to provide help to anyone who approached her, and did so stubbornly with efforts to the end.

The neighbors testified: to come to her with a request, was like coming to a good and kind sister.

Her payment was, when she saw her children grow up to be honest and decent people.

She died at the age of 48 of typhus that often afflicted the town.

May her memory be blessed!

[Page 253]

Early days

by Tzvi Silberstein

Translated by Sara Mages

I was born in 1892, one of the first to be born in Wolomin. At that time the number of Jewish residents in Wolomin was small. They did not have a cemetery. According to my father, R' Yitzchak Silberstein, there was time when the Jews led their dead for a Jewish burial in the city of Stanislawow [Ivano-Frankivsk], a distance 35km from Wolomin. At that time the whole settlement was owned by Wojciechowski.

Wolomin started to be built after the paving of the railroad track from Warsaw to St. Petersburg (today Leningrad), because Wolomin was the first stop near Warsaw.

Wolomin's proximity to a big city aided its development. People began to settle in Wolomin because of the density of housing in Warsaw.

Great help in the development of the town was its proximity to the summer resorts in the great forests in the south, and Czarna in the north.

However, at that time the tram was harnessed to horses who took the passengers to the trains, from there to the town, and to the resorts which served as a source of livelihood for the townspeople.

Immediately after its founding, the town began to develop at an accelerated pace. Many houses were built. The first to engage in construction was Lipshitz, and after him R' Herschel Kut who excelled in his vigor.

It's impossible to say that there was a kind of economic paradise in the town, but there were opportunities for people with initiative to make a living and also to get rich.

A few lines should be devoted to the description of the atmosphere in the first days when the rabbi, R' Wolf Bergzin, was appointed to the rabbinate of Wolomin where he lived until its destruction.

At first he had opponents because of matters of no importance. The unsatisfied turned to the Rabbi of Szmulowizna and asked him to settle in Wolomin. Indeed, he did not want to get into the conflict, but a special delegation managed to convince and reassure him on the grounds that the conflict would end upon his arrival.

The rabbi complied with their request and agreed to accept the rabbinate. It did not take long and the controversy erupted with greater vigor. The quarrels between the supporters of Rabbi Bergzin and the supporters of the rabbi from Szmulowizna, even reached a scuffle.

When the rabbi from Szmulowizna passed away, the residents of Wolomin decided not to invite a new rabbi. HaRav, R' Wolf Bergzin, served as the town's rabbi to his last day and was loved by the townspeople.

As I mentioned, Wolomin was built at an accelerated pace. The lots were purchased from Wojciechowski at a price of five kopecks per cubit, but later he raised the price to three rubles. The closer the lot was to the train station, the price was higher.

[Page 254]

Haim, Tzvi Silberstein's son, was a soldier in the US Army and fell in the invasion of Normandy, and so lies the deep connection between his heroism and the sanctity of the silent heroism of Wolomin's Jews who perished in the Holocaust. Like them, he knew fear and moments of weakness, but he knew how to take the decisive step at the right moment. Haim had a well-developed sense of responsibility and willpower, and was capable of risking his life to live heroically.

Such was Haim, whose father, Tzvi Silberstein, is one of the first to be born in Wolomin. He absorbed within him the atmosphere of the sanctification of God's name out of love for the people, love for Land of Israel, for which he was willing to sacrifice his young life. Haim knew how to live and die heroically.

[Page 255]

The blessing after a meal
at my grandfather's in the town

by Rachel

Translated by Sara Mages

My grandfather, Yisrael Mordechai Tencza, was the "*Shochet*" in the town of Wolomin, Poland. As I remember him, he was an upright and handsome man with an elegant beard, and a proud and friendly Jew whose face always smiled with kindness and love of humanity.

His home was open and warm for all the townspeople, and there were ten children in it that my grandmother Leah, his humble and pious wife, gave birth to and raised.

My mother, Dvora, recounts memories from her family home:

Our house was full with people, laughter and joy of life, all days of the week, but was at its peak when *Shabbat HaMalka* arrived. The men returned from the synagogue, the candles were lit in the silver candlesticks, and the set table shone from the whiteness of the tablecloth and the luster of the dishes. Father sat at the head of the table like a king and around him his children, like a crown to the heads of those gathered for the Sabbath meal. And my mother, small and nimble, a Shabbat wig on her head and a festive apron around her waist, served noodle soup, fish, and the rest of the delicious Shabbat dishes she had prepared the day before on the large porcelain stove in the kitchen.

They ate and blessed, and then came the great moment of Shabbat songs. They broke out in songs, songs of thanksgiving to God, songs for welcoming the Shabbat and songs for the uplifting of the soul. Grandfather led in his loud voice, his sons and daughters accompanied him in their pleasant voices which burst into the town's streets and stopped people who listened to their jubilant voices.

And I, his granddaughter, remember: I came with my mother, and my sister Yehudit, for a visit after a stay of a few years in Israel. I was about eight years old and, of course, I already spoke the sacred language. The big house was empty. All of them got married and scattered here and there. Only their youngest daughter, Rachel, remained to live with them. The encounter with tradition, the problems of kosher slaughtering, anti-Semitism, the strictness to maintain uniqueness - it is forbidden to speak Hebrew on weekdays, and forbidden to speak Polish on the Sabbath - revealed to me a new and foreign world of Jews in the Diaspora which, despite my eight years, left a strong impression on me.

But I remember one Sabbath: in the morning grandfather went to the synagogue, and grandmother sat and read chapters in *Tz'enah Ur'enah*, her good face was immersed in the book, she read the words in a soft melody and occasionally wiped a tear from her eye. For me it was time to go to the baker to bring the good cholent.

[Page 256]

Grandfather came and we sat down to eat, at the end of the meal I asked permission to say the blessing. With the Sidur in my hand I read the blessing after the meal in simple and clear Hebrew, there was silence and only my voice was heard.

I finished and raised my head, grandfather sat excited and tears welled up in his eyes, and grandmother ran to the kitchen and back as she was giving me plenty of kisses, nuts, almonds and candies.

I thought a lot about those days. It was so strange to see him in his weakness, as it was strange to someone, who did not know him well, to see him in his strength. The same Jew, who conquered the love of us all, had supreme courage and was able to gathered strength in time of disaster. When I grew up I thought a lot: where did he get such peace and such strength?

I did not understand then what the special excitement was about, but many times, for many years, I remembered this event and thought that they were tears of happiness, that his granddaughter, who was only eight years old, read before him in the sacred language, in a language that for him was a language of longing for something far away, a dream for the land of the forefathers.

It is a pity that my grandfather and grandmother, their sons and grandchildren, were not able to reach a state of rest in our country. They were not able to because they were annihilated together with the rest of the Jewish martyrs in the great Holocaust. Only a few survived from this large and beautiful family. May their memory be blessed.

[Pages 257-264]

The Wolomin Rabbi

by Tz. Volominer

Translated by Theodore Steinberg

Until the First World War, the Wolomin rabbi lived on Szcienkevitsch Street in Wolomin. The Wolomin rabbi was the son of the Kuzmir rabbi and was known as a greater sage. The rabbi's court had a special attraction and was a center for Torah and Chasidism. It drew to itself both young and old Jews from surrounding shtetls and from Warsaw. Among them were some with keen minds, but the ruling principle was the striving for peacefulness and wholeness.

The Wolomin rabbi based everything on truth. Chasidism, the rabbi said, means wholeness, the harmony of spirit and body, both in the service of the Creator.

But not only the learned came to the Wolomin rabbi. So did random Jews, for a simple page of Gemara or a chapter of Mishnah or a chapter of Psalms; they came to the rabbi to feel the radiance of his personality. The rabbi shared with everyone, showed his love and sincerity, and spoke with each person according to his need.

A Chasid told me:

"I was pretty young when I first came to Wolomin to the rabbi. In welcoming me, the rabbi asked if I knew how to study. I answered that I had to help my father in his store. On the rabbi's face I saw a hidden pity and he quietly murmured, 'So why has he come to me?'"

"I was suddenly taken aback. The rabbi noticed my embarrassment and quickly responded:

'It doesn't matter…If you transact business honestly, it is as if you studied. The whole purpose of study is in order to know how to excel in dealing with God and with one's fellow…Nu, and one also has to be good to oneself, not to be a fool and be taken up with misconceptions, with arrogance, simply to be a Jew, an outstanding Jew. Do you understand? That's why you've come to me, isn't it?'

"That's the truth," said the Wolomin Chasid–since then I have undertaken every day to learn a page of Gemara and I have felt the peace in my soul that the rabbi brought to me."

Thus Wolomin became known in the area as a center of Chasidism, which was as accessible to the simple Jew as to the scholar.

In the Wolomin prayer house, which was on Varshevski Street, in R. Yakov Margulis' house, men prayed and learned and had meals. There developed there an authentic system, a system that stressed the essence rather than quibbling or hair–splitting, to clarify the law according to its deeper intention. This system spread among the Wolomin Chasidim in Warsaw and other shtetls.

Understandably, life in Wolomin adapted to the rhythm of the "court." In scores of houses, men ate their Shabbos evening meal quickly so that they could get to the "tisch" [the rabbi's public meal]. So, too, did those who were not Wolomin Chasidim, who did not pray in the rabbi's prayer house but in the beis–hamedrash or with other groups. Young students were curious to see the Chasidim from other shtetls gathered together, among whom were well–known scholars, and Wolomin people were proud of their celebrity. In Wolomin there were many bright students and they eagerly spoke about their learning with scholars from other cities.

In times of trouble, God forbid, people hurried to the rabbi. If someone needed advice, he went to the rabbi's home. With good news, too, people ran to the rabbi, because people knew that the rabbi rejoiced with every joy of every Jew.

On a festival or a day of leisure, when a large number of Chasidim went traveling, Varshevski Street and surrounding streets were full of strolling groups who wandered here and there speaking of their studies. The sound in the shtetl was loud, like when a family gets together for a joyous occasion, though courtesy ruled everyone and kept the abundant joy under control.

The Wolomin rabbi's Chasidic prayer house also served as a window to the greater world. Chasidim from Warsaw brought with them big city ways and, sharing them with the Chasidim from other, smaller shtetls, provided familiarity with remote places, with poor and with rich. People met each other, befriended each other, and often arranged marriages, sometimes between a Wolomin householder and a visiting Chasid, sometimes with a prodigy from a Warsaw yeshiva.

You have to understand that this often affected the income of the Jews of Wolomin. Traveling Chasidim needed lodging in which to stay for a night or two. Many householders earned a few rubles on festivals by providing Chasidim with food and lodging.

The rabbi had seven children, sons and daughters. When the oldest daughter got married, the whole shtetl went as one. Everyone rejoiced in the rabbi's celebration.

I was still a child, and since then much time has passed and many things have happened, but each wedding is engraved in my memory and remains there until this very day.

Several weeks before the wedding, things started cooking. You could feel in the air that something big was coming. Everyone felt that the wedding of the rabbi's daughter had a personal meaning. Seamstresses and dressmakers were swamped with work. Although the actual wedding garb was made in Warsaw, still there was plenty left for the local seamstresses to do. The clergy anticipated the fees they would collect. People provided fowl, eggs, and other products for the wedding. There was turmoil in the shtetl, and everyone knew the latest news and what was about to happen.

The groom, people knew, was a glorious person, though still young, who had, however, rabbinical permission to be a teacher and who came from a rabbinical court. In the shtetl people regarded him favorably. We would acquire an ornament in our family, where Torah and greatness go together, and he would advertise Wolomin's Chasidism to the world, at the eastern wall with his silk and satin and high sable shtreiml.

Clever young men sharpened their wits so that they could discuss their studies and learn a lesson. Wolomin's beis–hamedrash boys rejoiced with every arriving scholar, especially when it involved that brat the rabbi's son–in–law.

The bride one did not see in the street except for when she went to the seamstress together with her mother or with a younger sister. When she appeared, people stood still and watched after her. Her genteel face beamed, and later on at home people spoke about her grace and modesty.

More than one young woman envied her because of her beauty and breeding, and many young men envied her intended, who would be getting such a beautiful bride.

In the last days before the wedding, the doors of the rabbi's house were not still for a minute. Some went in and some went out. Chasidim willingly volunteered to be waiters, porters, and to do whatever tasks were necessary. Chasidic wives who were known to be good cooks offered their help in preparing the food and beverages for the wedding. Tailors and shoemakers brought the clothing, shoes, and undergarments. The gentle rustling of satin and silk could be heard and the new boots of the rabbi's sons squeaked.

The rabbi's intimates sat with the gabbais and drew up a list of the important guests who had to be invited. Others made plans for how to set out the tables and benches, including rooms for the visiting in–laws and a room where the bride and groom could be alone after the ceremony.

The kitchen was full of visitors and helpers. From the courtyard one could hear the shrieking of the fowl, and the rooms were full of the smell of baked goods, filled with raisins and preserves.

Everything was fussed over, everything was elaborate. Faces shone and eyes took on a special look…

Only in the rabbi's private room nothing disturbed the usual daily routine. Despite the tumult all around, the rabbi was sedate and comfortable. He prayed, he studied, he welcomed Chasidim, he gave advice, and he conferred blessings.

Finally the wedding day arrived. The shtetl was in an uproar. One saw the silk caftans and high shtreimls of the arriving in–laws, distinguished guests, and Chasidim. Poor folk from other shtetls came seeking some income. People had celebrated a special meal for the poor and afterwards put a piece of cake for their children in their pockets and a donation in their hands.

Meanwhile, the Chasidic waiters and assistants had had something to drink and had become talkative and had started to yell and shove to get people out of the way, so that people would not interfere with their work, which they regarded as a sacred service. Is it a small thing, after all, that the rabbi is marrying off his daughter?

Others congregated around the bride, asking her how she felt while fasting and whether her heart was going so fast that she felt faint. She was the most important person in the house, and everyone was on tiptoe to fulfill any request that came from her mouth.

When evening crept in, the festival seized every home in the shtetl. From the windows in the rabbi's house blinker scores of lamps that lit up all of Varshavski Street, which radiated light and joy. R. Yakov Margulis had given over his whole house to the celebration. In one room the young girls danced, friends of the bride, darkly beautiful daughters of Wolomin, in their white silk dresses. In another room the young men of the Wolomin beis–hamedrash and the Chasidic prayer house came to the groom, eating cake and drinking wine and discussing their studies.

The other rooms were packed with the in–laws and their families, with important Jews of all kind, dressed in silk and satin caftans, each according to his taste. They sat not only around the table but also on benches, chairs, and stools around the walls, or they paced back and forth around the room, casting a glance into the other rooms.

In the air there was a warm murmur, accompanied by the pleasant aromas of wine and fragrant cigars.

In the middle of an ordinary week the Jews threw off the yoke of having to earn a living, of business, and got caught up in the rabbi's festive rooms, a wedding with such spirituality that it elevated the soul.

Together with the other children I stumbled among the feet, but like a grown up I felt the importance of this wedding.

Suddenly the whole world seemed, as if in a wave, to turn toward the door of the room where the groom sat with the young men. The music suddenly turned into a march. People led the groom to the chupah.

The throng was so great that no matter how I pushed, I could not break through to see the groom. Only when people sat down for the meal could I see him sitting at the head of the table surrounded by the in–laws from both sides of the family. In the bright lights shimmered the silk and satin. The big candelabra sparkled. I saw the young pale face of the groom that looked out from under his high, broad shtreiml. Quiet reigned as people listened to his words of Torah. So the groom delivered his commentary.

The men gathered closer, not wanting to miss a single word. The rabbi, who was sitting on the right side, rocked back and forth with a serious face and in the silence he repeated the words, at first quietly but then in a louder and more audible voice. The gemara melody filled the whole house.

When he finished, everyone swayed and you could hear cries of "Mazel tov, mazel tov!"

People congratulated him, extended their hands, and pressed forward as though it were each person's own celebration. People began to remove the stoppers from the bottles and pour wine into the cups and glasses. Later on people spoke about wealthy Chasidim who used to bring really expensive wine from their cellars.

Then the dancing began. Chasidim held each other's belts or hands, threw back their heads, closed their eyes, moved their feet, higher, more lively, dancing ecstatically.

Individuals, lively and happy, performed tricks: tying their coats with belts, bending their knees, their yarmulkes held down, their heads to the side, they launched into a Cossack dance and then another Russian dance, with the clapping of hands and loud laughter from the younger boys and girls who stood around them, wanting to see the Chasidim dance.

With the outbreak of the war, all of this ended. Chasidim stopped, since in war time it was dangerous for the rabbi to live in a small shtetl and the rabbi had moved to Warsaw, where he lived on Kupietski Street.

The Chasidim traveled further to Warsaw. From Wolomin, too, people traveled there and, when they came back, repeated the words of Torah that they heard from the rabbi, but there were some who complained about the big city, who lamented that the rabbi had settled in a metropolis. Truly, they said, it's more ostentatious there. It lacks the heimishkeit [hom;iness] of the shtetl.

This kind of talk sounded foolish to me, comical, but in time I came to understand those Jews. In the big city, Jewish life lacked that hominess, the spaciousness, the commonality of a religious voice in the street, the surrounding nature, as it was in the shtetl.

The old customs did not have the same status in Warsaw as in little Wolomin.

Coming to Warsaw, the Chasidim felt more strongly the exile of the Shechina. There were beautiful shuls there, wealthier Chasidic prayer houses, the best lulavs and the most kosher esrogs, great cantors and valuable shofars–everything that could be bought with money, nice fruit, expensive Torah covers, artful embroidery. Only one thing was missing–the openness of the street, the freedom and heimishkeit that Judaism and Chasidism had in little Wolomin.

In the Wolomin beis–hamedrash the prayers and sighs and melodies were not confined by the four walls. They mixed with the noise and the stillness of the shtetl. They travelled between heaven and earth with the tunes from the other Chasidic prayer houses, harmoniously and quietly, out to the fields, to the woods, and they blended with the still, nourishing melodies of the surrounding nature.

All of the joyous occasions, all of the Jewish customs and festivals in our little Wolomin had spaciousness, air, hominess, and so it was, too, with the Chasidim of Wolomin.

It seems that the rabbi felt this, too, and from time to time he would come to Wolomin and stand together with his Chasid R. Melech Levita.

When a Wolomin Chasid married off a child, he would invite the rabbi, and the rabbi would come to celebrate with his Chasidim, because a Chasidic wedding in Warsaw seemed far different.

The rabbi was killed by Hitler's murderers.

May God avenge his blood!

[Pages 265-267]

The Wolomin Rabbi, Rabbi Wolf Bergozin

by Chaya Rubenstein

Translated by Theodore Steinberg

Before Rabbi Bergozin occupied the rabbinical chair in the shtetl, there was a sharp dispute among the Jews. They had brought in a rabbi who did not please part of the populace. So they brought in a second rabbi who did not please the other part.

For a while there were two rabbis in the shtetl, and each rabbi had his adherents and his opponents.

But the city could not maintain two rabbis, so the community decided to find a rabbi about whom the population could be unanimous.

They searched for a long time until they discovered that the Ruzhan rabbi had a son-in-law living in his house who had rabbinical ordination. A delegation immediately headed for Ruzhan to speak with the young man, who made such a good impression on him that they immediately decided to invite the young rabbi to Wolomin.

He became our rabbi, Rabbi Wolf Bergozin.

Rabbi Wolf Bergozin came from Nazhelsk, near Warsaw. His wife was the eldest daughter of the rabbi of Ruzhan. Her sisters were also married to rabbis. One sister was the wife of the Dlugazhad rabbi, Rabbi Pomerantz. Another sister was the wife of the rabbi of Radom, Rabbi Kestenberg.

There was also a sister whose husband succeeded her father in the rabbinical chair of Ruzhan after the father's death.

The young rabbi, Rabbi Wolf Bergozin, pleased the inhabitants greatly and was unanimously chosen to be the rabbi.

In the same year that the rabbi arrived in the shtetl, people started to build a new beis-hamedrash.

Rabbi Bergozin had all the virtues of a local rabbinic authority: he was a pursuer of peace, a commanding but subdued man who demonstrated abundant wisdom in leading the Jewish community. The Jews used to flock to the rabbi for advice, whether in family matters or business matters.

When a disagreement arose, with great wisdom he brought peace to the disputants. His house was open to every Jew in the shtetl.

Also his wife Rachel excelled with her sincere friendliness and her sensitive heart, with her willingness to encounter every needy person with advice, with a comforting word, and also with tangible help.

They had eight children, five sons and three daughters. All of their children were born in Wolomin.

The eldest son, David, got married and emigrated to America, where he still lives.

The oldest [text says "second"] daughter, Itta, married a Wolomin boy, Moshe, the son of the Wolomin shochet R. Yisroel Mordechai.

The second daughter, Sarah, married a Wolomin boy, Leibl Zemba, who had rabbinical ordination.

The third daughter, Perl, also married a Wolomin boy and settled with him in Warsaw.

The son Elazar married a Wolomin girl, Chava, the daughter of Perl and Mattis Teiblum.

The three youngest sons did not marry. They were named Gadol, Yakov, and Binyamin. They studied in the yeshiva and were loved by their friends in the shtetl.

In the difficult days of Hitler's occupation, the rabbi remained with the Jews of the community and encouraged them, giving them confidence and hope that better times were coming.

The Jews of Wolomin merited something that other Jewish communities in Poland did not: usually the Nazis took the rabbis as their first victims, putting them either in the ghetto or the concentration camps.

When the Germans ordered the Wolomin Jews into the ghetto, the rabbi went with them. The ghetto was in Sosnavka, three kilometers from Wolomin.

For two years the Jews were held in the ghetto, and the whole time the rabbi was with them, suffering all the difficulties which pervaded the ghetto, until the dark days of liquidation arrived. The Germans surrounded the ghetto and ordered all the inhabitants into the square. There, too, the rabbi was with the Jews and went with them on their last journey.

The Wolomin Jews were taken to Radzomin, where the Jews from Legyanuv were also brought, and together they were taken to Treblinka.

[Pages 268-271]

Yechezkel Shammos

by Yosef Eisenberg

Translated by Theodore Steinberg

People called him Cheskl Shammos. He was a tall and big–boned Jew, had a long and thick white beard and bushy gray–white eyebrows which concealed his small but lively eyes.

He had a deep voice, and when he used to awaken the Jews of the shtetl early each Shabbos morning to come say Psalms, his deep bass voice filled the streets with strength and warmth.

His whole store of knowledge consisted of reading the "Shevat Mussar" in archaic Yiddish and of saying Psalms. When he woke people up to say Psalms, he infused his tune with his whole sense of reverence, of the fear of Heaven and the love of Israel. He sang these words: "Little Jews, dear and beloved little Jews, holy little Jews, wake up to serve your Creator."

He rested a bit and then continued singing with his warm bass voice: "Get up, little Jews, get up to say Psalms. It's already six o'clock!"

The words and the melody in which he sang them had a holiness to them that invaded the hearts of those who heard them and did not allow them to go back to sleep, made them get out of bed, even in the cold and frosty dawns.

Yechezkel earned his livelihood by working in the beis–hamedrash. He also provided an escort for the rabbi in the shtetl. On Fridays he went with him to the bathhouse. Early on Shabbos he accompanied him to the beis–hamedrash.

Before the arrival of the High Holidays, Yechezkel the Shamos would knock with his wooden hammer on the shutter of the Jews' doors and windows, calling the people to Selichos, the penitential prayers.

Throughout the year he made sure that everything in the beis–hamedrash was in order. He collected any papers that had the divine name in them and put them in the attic, treated them like holy objects, put them away with the torn prayer books, protected them so that the children would not tear the pages.

Chaskl Shammos also helped the rabbi by summoning a Jew to a rabbinical court and many other matters that were important to the community.

Over time, he was not satisfied with only reciting Psalms. His routine broadened to include a verse: "Akaviah son of Mehallel used to say" all the way to "the King of all Kings, blessed be He."

He lived on what the Wolomin Jews would give him every week, a few groschen in salary, but thanks to his widened routine, he asked for two groschen.

I remember once when he came to my father to collect the groschen and asked, "Reb Berl, do you want an "Akaviah son of Mehallel?"

My father, who had not consulted with the leaders of the shtetl, gave him the coins.

No one knew where Chaskl had ever come up with Akaviah son of Mehallel. Later on it turned out that the secret was really quite simple. One time, he had come into the rabbi's home and had complained that the Wolomin Jews were late and failed to wake up for saying Psalms, and he begged the rabbi to teach him some new words to rouse everyone, so the Wolomin rabbi thought a bit, went to the bookshelf, took out a book and opened to the passage, "Akaviah son of Mehallel said: Know whence you came and where you are going and before whom who will stand in the future for judgment and reward–before the King of all Kings, blessed be He."

R.' Chaskl learned the verse by heart. This took him a whole week. A week later he came to the rabbi and repeated the verse together with a tune that he invented. The rabbi was quite pleased and on the spot he translated the verse into Yiddish. R.' Chaskl was taken with this and immediately began to use his "Akaviah son of Mehallel" with his usual fervor.

Once there was a heavy frost in the shtetl. All Friday night a blizzard raged. At that time we lived in Schuchman's houses on Statziner Street. Soon the strong bass voice of Chaskl the Shammos: "Little Jews, dear, beloved little Jews, wake up…"

At the same moment we heard a fearful outcry. It was R.' Chaskl screeching: "Gevald, Jews! Help!"

My father and I ran out into the street. Yoske Saltis was already outside, with a copper shield around his neck, which signified that he was a representative of the authorities. Leibush the Lame and other Jews were also there.

Before our eyes we saw an amazing sight: Two non–Jews were holding R.' Chaskl by the shoulders and yelling at him in Polish that he should sing his little song again, because they liked it so much; but R.' Chaskl could not understand what they were saying and was certain that the non–Jews had attacked him and were going to kill him.

The other Jews quickly grasped what had happened and calmed R.' Chaskl down, making him understand what had happened.

Frozen through, dressed in five kaftans and a bunch of scarves, which he had wound around his neck and face and over his beard, R.' Chaskl stood with his arms stretched out, as if he were at the cantor's table, and began his song with a drawn out tune, from "Holy people, little Jews" to the whole "Akaviah son of Mehallel."

In the street a deep stillness reigned. The non–Jews stood there happily the whole time, like strings sympathetic to the tune, which sounded powerfully over the whole shtetl.

When R.' Chaskel finished, we recognized a deep emotion on the faces of the non–Jews. Both of them took out coins and presented them to R.' Chaskl and could by no means understand why Chaskl turned away from them as if he had been scalded and only said a single word:

"Shabbos…"

To the assembled Jews he said, "I'm going into the beis–hamedrash…Tonight I won't wake anyone else…"

The people remained standing silently. With wonder and amazement they looked after the bowed figure of R.' Chaskl, whose step from his reddish boots echoed in the frosty stillness of the Shabbos morning.

R' Yisrolke Feldsher

He was a short man who wore a long kaftan, and in winter he also wore a cotton jacket. His thick black beard covered his whole face practically up to his eyes. He worked as a doctor, healing sick people, even though he had no medical studies. His patients were only men. When he was called to attend a sick person, he came into the house like a wind and immediately asked, "Nu, nu, where is he?"

His patients mostly suffered pains in their sides from constipation or catarrh.

When R' Yisrolek arrived, he took a look at the sick man, put his ear to the man's heart and listened, through the man's clothing, to how his heart was beating, told him to hold his breath, cleared his throat, and soon came out with a diagnosis and then gave orders: apply leeches, smear on French turpentine…well.

If someone was suffering from constipation, R' Yisrolek ordered him to stick out his tongue, which might be, for example, white as milk. He held the tongue, wiped it with his hand, saying, "Aha…white…" which meant that he would cure the man in no time. He would order an enema for the man, castor oil, and sour milk.

If the sick man complained about a sore throat and needed a special treatment, R' Yisrolek always had with him a wad of cotton, which he ripped out of his cotton jacket. He rolled the cotton onto a stick, dipped it into iodine and…the sick man was quickly cured. Just like with the cotton, so with the sticks: he did not have to carry them around in a valise for first aid. It was not necessary. The cotton he took from his own jacket and the stick…in which home in Wolomin would there not be a broom? R' Yisrolek would take a straw from the broom, wrap the cotton around it, and done…

If it happened that the condition of the patient became serious, R' Yisrolek would consult with the patient about whether to call a doctor. R' Yisrolek would give his opinion about whether to travel east, that is, to Yadova, or west, that is, to Warsaw. The patient himself had to decide.

In Wolomin people used to say that in his youth R' Yisrolek had served in the tsarist army and was assigned to work in a military hospital. There he developed some medical skills and represented in the shtetl both a public health officer and a doctor. He never demanded that people pay him. Whatever anyone gave him was enough, and if someone gave him nothing, he never said a word of complaint.

Slaughterers and Cantors

The Wolomin beis–hamedrash on Leshne Street did not have a designated cantor, but everyone knew that R' Yisroel–Mordechai the Shochet had a claim on the reader's stand. On an ordinary Shabbos or Festival, he led the prayers without helpers or assistants, but with the approach of the High Holidays he put together a choir, which consisted of boys with sweet–sounding voices who helped him with singing the High Holiday prayers, the different tunes and marches.

R' Yisroell–Mordechai the Shochet was a prayer leader who quickened people's hearts with the warm tone of his praying and who enchanted those who heard him with his beautiful voice. When he sang a tune from Mordzhitz, he put his whole body into it. He would lead the Kol Nidrei prayer as well as the Musaf and Neilah services, and music lovers would come from other minyanim on the chance of hearing R' Yisroel–Mordechai sing a new tune from Mordzhitz. Anyone who ever heard him sing never forgot it. Even today I can hear R' Yisroel–Mordechai's tune. Before my eyes I can see his stately appearance, his long, fair beard, his thoughtful glance and the dreamlike look on his face. When you saw him walking in the street, his appearance demanded respect and honor. Even those who did not know him felt immediately a servant of holiness.

R' Yisroel–Mordechai was a clever Jew. No one ever heard him complain and he had a good and a loving smile for everyone. Everyone in the city, big and little, right and left, loved him. Hardly anyone knew his family name, Tentshur, because everyone called him R' Yisroel–Mordechai the Shochet, and in this name stood his pedigree and his pride.

There were only two shochets in the town. R' Baruch Rotshanzer was a Ger Chasid. People called him Rotshandzer because he came from the shtetl of Rotshandz, which was on the other side of the river. He spoke with a hard "r". On the High Holidays he led the morning prayers. Some in the shtetl called him "the black shochet," because, as opposed to R' Yisroel–Mordechai, he had a pitch black beard. He was welcomed in Wolomin after the previous shochet, R' Chaim Binyamin, became old and his hands began to tremble. He did not cease being a shochet altogether, but confined himself to slaughtering fowl.

R' Baruch the Shochet was selected in his thirties, along with Moyshe Gutvetter, as a delegate to travel to Israel to buy soil for the Wolomin householders. This was after the Ger rabbi had called on Jews to travel to the land of Israel and had in Jaffa and other places bought large tracts of land.

R' Baruch the Shochet was an unassuming man, honest and dedicated to every undertaking he assumed. I remember him together with my young friend Moyshe Ko–ohr and R' Moyshe Gutvetter as we travelled to various places buying soil.

Moshe Ko–ohr was shot by the Nazis in a village near Paris, Valerien Siren on February 21, 1942.

R' Baruch the Shochet was killed together with all the Jews of Wolomin by the Nazi murderers.

R' Moyshele the White

R' Moyshele the White was called that because he was a whitewasher. He had a scraggly beard and spoke with a thin, womanish voice. One of the shtetl's wits once asked him, "R' Moyshe, can't you speak a bit more gruffly?" R' Moyshe snapped back, "Why not? Meanwhile, kiss me in the…If you do, I'll speak more gruffly…"

Always I see him as if he is holding in his hand a ladder, from which hangs a pail with pain and in his other hand a brush with a long handle. In earlier times when there was no work, the householders in the shtetl gave no thought to whitewashing the walls of their poor dwellings, he used to wear a vest, to which was attached a thick chain of white metal. On the chain were hanging a pair of horseshoes, the head of a horse, a rifle, a compass and other such trivial things. R' Moyshele prided himself in this equipment, and if someone asked him a question, "R' Moyshe, what is that?" he slowly and with great solemnity he removed the chain from his vest pocket until there appeared a heavy silver box, round, with a little top. This was a watch with double doors, on which were engraved the heads of Russian czars.

R' Moyshel then sighed into the box and opened one of the doors, and then R' Moyshe announced in a declamatory voice, "Now it is exactly two o'clock."

If someone brought to his attention that the train to Bialystok had already long departed, he paid no attention and immediately responded, "That shows that the train was too early…My watch shows the exact time."

R' Moyshe had two sons who helped him with his work on those days when he was swamped with work. Soon after Purim, when the snow started to disappear and the leaves in the shtetl became greener and thicker, R' Moyshel became more important in his own eyes, almost a field marshal, because the pre–Passover days in Wolomin marked the assault of the housewives, who flocked to him from every corner of the shtetl, just like, you should pardon the comparison, Chasidim to their rabbi, with their demands and requests, each one in his time, and began to bargain with him, some with feminine coquetry and some with motherly pleas. Each housewife wanted R' Moyshel to come first to her, before others got to him, besieging him with their demands.

In those days R. Moyshe valued himself highly. Seeing himself surrounded by so many women, who depended on the goodness of his heart, he self–importantly gave them to understand that in the previous year he had promised this and that housewife that if they waited for year, they would be first this year…

Secondly, this year he had only a single color that could cover that color with which he had previously for the other housewives.

Seeing that the women were entirely in his hands, at the same time he added something else, which was always a bit difficult for him: "You must know," R' Moyshele said to the women, "this year I will not stand for any nuisances. I have no time to waste with such foolishness." The women began to mutter unhappily: "What's he talking about? Not to be a nuisance?"

R' Moyshel remained firm despite the women's unhappiness. He spoke firmly, quickly, and simply: "Whoever agrees, fine. Whoever doesn't, so be it…"

Since they had no choice, the women agreed and R' Moyshel began his work, his painting.

In the courtyards, all kinds of furniture began to appear–different styles from different generations, furniture that the women placed before their doors in order to free up the rooms for whitewashing. People began to scrub, to brush, to pour, to cleanse. The noise in the shtetl became a racket. The straw which was taken out of the mattresses and spread out in individual stalks flew around the shtetl along with the colored papers that had been stuffed between the double windows for the winter to keep the cold out of the houses. In the air there were feathers from the pillows and featherbeds.

R' Moshel did his work whitewashing the walls, soaping them up, going from courtyard to courtyard, carrying his ladder with his pail of pain and singing a variety of cheerful songs.

Thus did people live in Wolomin, sometimes quietly and idyllically and sometimes in a tumult and an uproar. There were happy days and sad, evenings noisy with singing and gatherings of people and unhappy evenings, when people were consumed by longing and from the desire for a bigger and better world, and people did not realize how much beauty and depth could be found in their own shtetl, with its scholars and simple Jews, gabbais and Chasidim, shammoses and workmen, beis–hamedrash students, who spoke only about their learning and about large, distant yeshivas, and young people, who discussed the problems of our national exile and the salvation of the world, who studied Ahad Ha–Am, Nordau, probed Hegel, Kant, Marx, and Engels, got all excited about every election–they all had their own aspirations, and they are all dear and holy to us now.

\[Page 272]

Slaughterers and Cantors

Translated by Theodore Steinberg

The Wolomin beis-medresh on Leshne Street did not have a regular cantor, but everyone knew that the place before the cantor's stand belonged to R. Yisroel-Mordechai the Shochet [the Slaughterer]. On ordinary Shabbos days and holidays, he led the prayers before the cantor's stand without assistants, without a choir, but with the approach of the High Holidays, he would assemble a choir made up of young men with sweet-sounding voices who helped him sing the High Holiday prayers, the various tunes and marches.

R. Isroel-Mordechai the Shochet

[Page 273]

R. Yisroel-Mordechai the Shochet was a cantor who could move people's hearts with the warm tones of his praying and who enchanted those who heard him with his beautiful voice. When he would sing a melody from Modzhitz, it suffused everyone's limbs. He would lead the Kol Nidrei service, Mussaf, and Ne'ilah, and music lovers would come from other services when there were breaks to hear R. Yisroel-Mordechai sing a new melody from Modzhitz. Anyone who ever heard him never forgot. Even today, I can hear R. Yisroel-Mordechai's singing. I can visualize his stately appearance–his long, fair beard, his thoughtful glance, and the transcendent look on his face. When people saw him walking in the street, he showed courtesy and honor even to those from foreign towns. Even people who did not know him recognized in him a holy aura.

R. Yisroel-Mordechai was a clever man. No one ever saw him get angry, and he had a good word and a loving smile for everyone. His family name, Tentczer, was little known. Everyone called him R. Yisroel-Mordechai the Shochet, and it was with that name that he gathered fame and praise.

There were two other slaughterers in town. R. Baruch Ratshanzer was Ger Chasid. He was called Ratshanzer because he came from the shtetl of Ratshandz, which was on the other side of the Vistula. He pronounced his "r's" differently. On the High Holidays, he led the morning prayers in the beis-medresh. Some people in the town also called him "the black slaughterer," because in contrast to R. Yisroel-Mordechai he had a dark black beard. He was accepted as a shocker in Wolomin after the former shocker, R. Chaim Binyamin, grew old and his hands began to tremble. He did not abandon slaughtering altogether, but he confined his work to fowl.

R. Baruch the Shochet was chosen, in his thirties, along with Moshe Gutveter, to go to Israel to buy land for the people of Wolomin. This came after the Ger rebbe had called on Jews to go to Eretz Yisroel and had purchased in Jaffa and other places large tracts of land.

[Page 274]

R. Baruch the Shochet was an artless man, earnest and devoted to the job he had assumed. I recall how together with the friend of my youth, Moshe Ku-ohr, along with R. Baruch Shochet and R. Moshe Gutveter, we traveled to different spots to buy land.

Moshe Ku-ohr was shot by the Nazis in a village near Paris, Valerien Suresnes, on February 21, 1942.

R. Baruch the Shochet was killed together with all the Jews of Wolomin by the Nazi murderers.

[Pages 277-281]

R' Yisroel–Mordechai the Slaughterer

by Noson Gingold

Translated by Theodore Steinberg

R' Yisroel–Mordechai was a slaughterer and a cantor in Wolomin, a unique personality who deserves a broader and longer article. Perhaps others who knew him better will compose one, people who know more of his personal and social life and have more material to recount about him.

I do not know the year in which R' Yisroel–Mordechai came to Wolomin, so I must be satisfied with drawing a picture of him and his family beginning in 1931, when I became acquainted with them, and ending with the outbreak of the Second World War.

I knew that R' Yisroel–Mordechai came from the shtetl of Stack and at an early age undertook to learn to be a shochet, that he had a great devotion to Yiddishkeit and good deeds, and that he was zealous about learning, so that he developed a reputation as a shochet, a scholar, and a fearer of Heaven. His intensity and attraction to knowledge were revealed not only in study, in repeating the Torah insights of the Amshinov rabbi, but also in music, in rejoicing in public. He had a beautiful voice and over time he became a cantor. Thus he became both a cantor and a shochet in Wolomin. People used to say that a cantor and a shochet go together like Vayakhel and Pekudei [two Torah readings that are often read together].

R' Yisroel Mordechai had ten children, five sons and five daughters. The oldest sons were quite observant. The oldest later became cantor–shochet in the shtetl of Vishkov. The younger children were more modern, more attracted to the Zionist movement.

I came to their house in 1931 because their fourth daughter, who was the ninth child in the family, became my wife.

Consequently I was able to observe more closely this ideal family. R' Yisroel–Mordechai was of average height, a little heavy, with a broad face, which was made even broader by his beard, which did not hide his permanent smile and the gentleness of his face. He never complained, always had a funny comment ready, and the Jews loved him. Even young people who were not so observant showed him great respect. He never moralized, and he never listened to those who thought of themselves as God's Cossacks.

On Shabbos, many citizens had the tradition of coming to R' Yisroel–Mordechai's to eat kugel. His wife's kugels, kishkes, and milts [spleen] were renowned in the town.

I once happened to hear someone from Volin, one of the "fine" Jews, who warned R' Yisroel–Mordechai that he should pay attention to his children, because people said in the shtetl that they took the train to Warsaw on Shabbos. R' Yisroel–Mordechai responded: "My children? God forbid…People should not say such things…Incidentally, I wonder whether you've given a thought to your own children? Pay attention so that what the sages won't apply to you: 'He submerges, but the creeping thing is in his hand…'"

The better that I came to know this excellent Jew, the more my respect for him grew.

R' Yisroel–Mordechai liked for his sons–in–law to sit at the table together with his sons on Shabbos and Festivals. He particularly liked the two youngest sons–in–law because they had once been yeshiva students and knew how to converse and learn with him. I remember one conversation when R' Yisroel–Mordechai said to us: "Two things I learned from the Amshinov rabbi: love of God and love of Israel. The author of *Yismach Moyshe* derives an idea from the word 'love,' which has the gematria value of thirteen. When two Jews love each other, their love is double thirteen, that is, twenty–six, which is also the value of the Living Name [i.e., the Tetragrammaton]. In other words, the love between one Jew and another creates the Ineffable Name."

In dealing with the laws of slaughtering, R' Yisroel–Mordechai tended to the lenient side, especially in cases of a large loss [if something were to be declared not kosher]. R' Yisroel–Mordechai therefore did everything he could not to declare an animal unkosher and not to cost the butcher a large sum of money. He therefore consulted the *Yoreh De–ah* and other books about the laws of slaughtering until he found a reason not to declare an animal unkosher.

R' Yisroel–Mordechai was also famous as a cantor. When he was a young man, he studied music and developed his voice so that he truly became a famous singer. People in Wolomin told many stories about his singing, about his strong voice, and about its sweetness. I will retell one of them:

It happened on Rosh Hashanah, when R' Yisroel–Mordechai said the prayer "Hineni…" At the words "trembling and frightened" he gave such a yell with all his might that a pregnant woman in the women's section miscarried through fear.

People also used to say that in the early years when he first came to Wolomin, the Radzimin village elder, along with other Christians, would come to Kol Nidrei and Neilah so they could hear R' Yisroel–Mordechai sing and pray.

Most of his children inherited his musical talent. Most notable was his youngest daughter, Freida–Rochele, who sang so beautifully different piyyutim and helped her father to sing Shabbos songs. She also sang opera arias. She had a superb coloratura voice. But she never sang when people asked her to, only when she wanted to. Then she would take off. Usually it was on a Saturday evening, when outside darkness was falling and in the house lights had not yet been lit because the father was still at the third Shabbos meal. Often I would hear her magical singing on a Shabbos evening and it would transport me to another world, a world where everything was good…R' Yisroel–Mordechai's wife, whom people called Leah the Shochetke [a feminine form of Shochet], played a huge role in helping to create the enlightened atmosphere of the household. I often wondered at her refinement, at her good soul. When I met her, she was middle–aged, a bit weak, but she was never stingy with help or with money when she had to deal with someone who needed help, whether it was someone who was ill or someone dealing with poverty.

People in the town knew that if they had to help someone in need, they would go first to Leah the Shochetke. She never allowed a poor person to leave her home empty handed.

It once happened that a poor person came to the house begging for a donation and Leah the Shochetke accidentally had no small bills at hand and the poor man could not give change for a large bill. Seeing her embarrassment, the poor man left, but Leah the Shochetke quickly recovered. She snatched some pieces of sugar and other dry foods and ran after the poor man, begging him to take them so that he would not leave her home empty handed.

R' Yisroel–Mordechai used to bring home from the slaughterhouse milts, kishke, liver, and sweetbreads, and Leah the Shochetke would sell them. Poor women knew Leah's "weakness," that she had a heart full of compassion for the poor and they often used that weakness, begging her to give them a little piece of kishke on the side. There were also always people who lacked a few groschen to pay. They knew that Leah the Shochetke would never take back even a little piece of the meat. And she would never write down the debt. R' Yisroel–Mordechai used to lament to the children that he didn't know what their mother did with the money. "Today I brought home so much meat from the slaughterhouse," he would say, "and there is so little money." R' Yisroel–Mordechai truly never knew the secret of what his wife did with the money.

R' Yisroel–Mordechai died several days before the war in his seventies. On the day of his funeral, almost all of Wolomin was in mourning. The whole town demonstrated its love for this refined, goodhearted Jew.

Leah the Shochetke was killed together with her children and grandchildren, either in the ghetto or in the camps. The only survivors were two daughters who had gone to Israel before the war. These two daughters with their children and grandchildren represent the continuation of this ideal family, and there, in Israel, they add on to the golden chain of this beautiful Jewish home, the home of R' Yisroel–Mordechai the Shochet.

Leah the Shochetke belonged among those figures who enlarged every Jewish shtetl. She was one of the righteous women who were not satisfied with going over a chapter of Psalms or praying on weekdays when it was emotionally difficult and eyes dripped with tears, falling on the old prayer book pages. Her religious goodness consisted of what she did in her home and in the street, in her sorrows, so that a Jewish home should not go without challas and fish for Shabbos, poor sick people should not go without the help of a doctor, without the warm supervision of an attending person.

Wolomin was a poor shtetl, but rich and magnificent with personalities like R' Yisroel–Mordechai and his wife Leah.

[Page 282]

Our Courtyard

by Shmuel Zucker

Translated by Theodore Steinberg

It's been so very long
since from you I went away;
so many names have slipped my mind
since that long ago day.

I still can taste from Yosef's shop
his fresh–baked bread and rolls,

which could not relieve the hunger
of our poorer neighbors' souls.

I remember Meyer Treger,
whose heart was free of greed,
as he used his little piece of rope
to lug a sack of seed.

His daughter by the window stood,
glancing from side to side,
hoping there to see a man
who'd take her as his bride.

There was Rosa, who made shoes–
her children she would hold,
who often cried themselves to sleep
from hunger and from cold.

Chanah the milk lady
was bent over by her years,
trying to earn a dowry
for the daughter she held dear.

Yankel who made challah
also lived in greatest woe,
always ready to fall asleep,
weary from head to toe.

Itschele who made our beer
never lacked for sorrow,
though he always held out hope for
a better tomorrow.

The hands of Zvi the sewer
I will forget no more.
He used those hand to make the shirt
That on my back I wore.

[Page 283]

Hospitality

by Shmuel Zucker

Translated by Theodore Steinberg

The well–trod path that led to the wooden steps of the shul was decorated with yellow leaves that that fallen from the scrawny trees. Closer to the shul, you could sense the stagnant air from the well–worn Gemaras with their torn spines and of the other books that sat in the bookcases covered with dust. The doors of the beis–medrash stood half–opened and you could hear the plaintive Gemara chants. Two rooms were also there that were known as "hospitality."

Jews with white beards, genteel faces, and the wise looks of Talmud scholars stayed there together with simple Jews, with worn out and worried faces with black, tangled beards and downcast eyes, that glanced around nervously. There were also Jews with trimmed beards or no beards at all who came from distant lands, from faraway towns and shtetls. In the evenings you could see them entering with their bags with a little clothing, a book, a siddur. They appeared to be deep in thought, lost in other worlds. They went quietly, accompanied by the feeling looks of the Wolomin Jews.

A whole day they had gone from house to house, adding a groschen to a groschen, which they laid aside and sent to their families, which they had left in their distant homes.

The hospitality rooms were over the beiso–medrash. Inside, the air was heavy with different smells. On winter evenings, the round iron stove filled the rooms with a choking smoke blocked the faces, so that two people in conversation could not see each other.

In the evenings, I used to sneak in and listen to the conversations of the strange Jews, to their fantastic stories. Each one had his own life history, which described distant places, in towns and shtetls with different adventures. Many of these stories stayed with me for days and nights, in those years when I sat in the neighboring schoolroom, where I studied my lessons. Their talk rang in my ears, their nostalgic voices. There were some who had left their homes years earlier, in the First World War, leaving behind wives and little children. When they returned from the war, they found nothing. Their shtetls had burned down. Many Jews were slaughtered in the pogroms.

There were also some who had left behind in their home towns established households. Good business disappeared in confusion, in the terror of the Cossacks. When they returned home, their businesses were pillaged and their homes in ruins.

It seemed to me that all Jews were victims of the World War. There were also some who served at the front, had become invalids and were not capable of any kind of work, which forced them to wander through the world. From town to town, begging for a piece of bread to sustain their lives. They had descended to such poverty that they could barely survive. They had no good fortune and could not support their families.

The hospitality rooms were for them a luxury and a cure. It used to be that when a Jew in his wanderings by foot managed, with his last strength, in great pain, often with a high fever, to arrive at our hospitality rooms, Yankl Blecher would take him in hand, Yankl who worried about the poor Jews and would call a doctor or a health worker, seeing to it that his bed was clean, with a white sheet and a blanket. He hovered over the poor man like a good mother, dressed him, reassured him, wished him good health.

The Jews of Wolomin spoke about the hospitality rooms with great warmth, thinking about them as a great mitzvah, and mothers would say, "Even the birds who have lost their nests get on the roof where they see the smoke from the hot stoves curling up and they can warm themselves."

Secret Gift

I remember how Moyshe Oyslander once told me that he had once seen in a dwelling where a whole family was hungry. The parents could not bear to see the suffering of their children and were in despair [literally: they hit their heads against the wall].

In our courtyard, too, there was such a family, with seven children. Their crust of bread was gone in an instant, and soon you could hear through the broken windows the cries of the children: "I'm hungry!"

It happened that in the same courtyard, Yosef Baker had his bakery, and the smells of fresh bread and rolls would permeate the homes, which only increased the hunger in that poor dwelling.

In that dwelling, both the adults and the children went hungry.

Moyshe Oyslander said that their poverty gave him the idea of creating hospitality and "a secret gift" for poor Jews in Wolomin who were distraught and without incomes.

He gathered regular members who would give money each month and with the money buy a variety of items: flour, rice, sugar. They also got coal in the winter and they took it to the homes of people who were too ashamed to ask for charity.

These people would sit locked in their homes, ashamed of their own distress. They were like forgotten poor folks in the town, and concern for them called forth "the secret gift," which Wolomin's Jews considered a great mitzvah, something holy. They never spoke openly about those needy ones. They made sure that no one knew about their poverty so that they would not be embarrassed.

Leshne Street

If it had not been for the heavily laden horses and wagons that used to arrive on Thursdays from the surrounding villages for market day and disturbed the water and mud that had accumulated from the rains, the wooden houses, together with the beis–medrash, would have sunk in the standing water and mud from Rosh Hashanah until Pesach.

More than once it happened that someone's galoshes got stuck. More than one schoolboy ran home with a sad cry because in the deep mud he had lost a shoe that was too big for him, since he had borrowed it from an older brother so that he could go to school.

Leshne Street was small and narrow, with scattered and inferior houses were green and decrepit and bore witness to their age and lineage from the time of grandparents and great grandparents.

On Leshne Street there were also fences that always had milk cans and washed out pots hanging from them, as well as diapers and laundry.

Around the mud, hens, geese, and turkeys gathered, picking up with their beaks the corn that had fallen from holes in the sacks on peasant wagons. The corn sat there, soaking in the water that was always covered in green slime.

A mixture of voices and tunes always arose from Leshne Street, from Aaron Bynum's heartfelt Gemara chant that broke out from the broken glass in the beis–medrash to the tumultuous voices from the noisy courtyard where the building of the Yesodei Hatorah stood, where scores of students swayed over their Gemaras and argued over difficult passages in the Talmud or in the Tosafos. These voices mixed with the neighing of balking horses who had torn loose from their carts.

To this was added the bleating of the white goats that enjoyed munching on the grass in the little bit of a field that bordered the beis–medrash.

Aryeh Braude

Suddenly the cries of Ephraim Zilbershteyn were heard, as he stood wringing his hands over the fallen body of his horse, who was his sole source of income. Ephraim's eyes were blood–red from anger and protest against this great injustice that had befallen him.

No one could help him. His cries and pleas were drowned out by Tzalke the kasha maker's mills, that had been operating all day and deafened the whole shtetl.

Only Aryeh Braude was attentive to Ephraim's cries. He didn't just throw up his hands, but he put on his cotton jacket and big boots and blew out of his dark room like a wind, moving quickly across the street to the disaster where Ephraim stood with his horse.

Aryeh threw himself across the belly of the dying horse and with his strong hand he pulled open its mouth that was clamped shut. He poured into that mouth a bucket of salt water and said, as if he were a doctor, "That should help!"

It actually did help, and when Aryeh stood up and straightened himself out, he stretched his hands toward the sky and said, "Master of the Universe, would you take away someone's livelihood?!"

It happened that the anti–Semitic Polish young people decided to attack the Jews in the shtetl, Aryeh Braude gave orders like a general. He gathered young people around him and armed them with iron bars and rods. He stationed them strategically in the streets, and in the shtetl there was a new feeling. Jews comforted themselves and felt secure that nothing would happen to them because Aryeh Braude was watching over them.

Aryeh had a large Jewish heart. When he found out that some Jew did not have the wherewithal to make Shabbos, he put on his black kaftan that he had received for his wedding, so that it was old and full of stains, tight and too short. He ran his broad fingers through his beard and set out through the shtetl to collect a few groschen for the hungry people in that poor household.

On hot days, when children swam in the clay pits, we would hear that someone had drowned. Immediately Aryeh Braude would appear, wearing a colorful flannel shirt and his big talis–katan. He quickly threw them off and jumped into the water to pull out the drowned boy.

A conflagration broke out in the shtetl, and Aryeh was the first one there. He did not wait for the fire brigade. Instead he immediately ran into the burning house and saved what he could, bringing out a very sick woman and little children and then some other things.

On his broad face and ruddy cheeks there always shone a childish naivety and a good–hearted willingness to help everyone with no thought of reward but just for the sake of helping people.

[Page 289]

Erev Shabbos

by Shmuel Zucker

Translated by Theodore Steinberg

Erev Shabbos in the Shtetl

On Friday the shtetl put on another face. From early morning the streets were full of the aromas of fresh–baked goods, for Shabbos and the whole week; smells of baked challas, of kichele, with blackberries that grew abundantly in the surrounding forests. The peasants brought them in big earthenware pots and sold them in the market for groschen.

In the school everyone was happy, because they knew that the school day was short. In summer we quickly went outside the village and played games.

When it got cooler, fewer people were in the streets. The noise was less. People shuttered their doors in the stores and workshops. The last horse and wagon had already left the shtetl for the village. Jews appeared with little brooms in their hands on the way to the shvitz–bath. All day long a black smoke appeared, and through the windows we could hear the voices of overheated sweat–ers on the highest bench.

Jews didn't enjoy these pleasures for long. The approaching Shabbos interfered. After the shvitz–bath, people had to go immerse in the mikveh, three times in honor of Shabbos. Then people put on their clean clothes, and with groomed beards and payes and heavy trousers they went home to greet the Shabbos queen.

At the same time, the wives, with tightly tied kerchiefs, brought to the baker their cholent in lime–smeared pots. They hurried back quickly to get home. It was already time to go to shul, and in the home there was still much to do. One had to wash oneself and the children and prepare the silver candlesticks for candle lighting.

On the road came a solitary Jew, from the villages, from Warsaw, a business traveler, and then there went the last Jew. Yechezkel the Shammos, with his long white beard, leaning on his cane, goes through the streets and with his big hammer knocks on the shutters and the walls and calls out, "Shabbos, Shabbos…"

Meyer the Porter, with his stiff boots, goes home tired and puts away his padded shirt, which is covered with meal from the sacks he carried all week on his broad shoulders to Yosef Kressever.

Shiala the Shoemaker removed from his nose the broken glasses that are held together with a bit of string. He has already cleaned up his workroom, where he sits all week from early in the morning until late at night.

Migdal the Tailor has already washed the floor on which lay the mud of a whole week, brought in by the peasants' boots.

Ephraim from Leshne Street has already emptied from his sack the straw in which his children sleep. The straws serves both to lie on and as a cover, in the summer heat and the winter cold.

Bashke, the poor woman who has moved from place to place all week with her bag of rags and has nowhere to sleep at night. Now she has taken Yosef the Baker's dark hallway, where she will rest until after Shabbos, when he will have to start baking the bread and rolls for Sunday morning.

Freidele from the market place has already packed her flattened pillows behind the broken windows so that the wind will not extinguish the Shabbos candles that she is about to put on the white tablecloth.

Happy were the horses of Ephraim and Chaim Zilbershtein, who were unharnessed and stood in the broken wooden stalls, wondering at the stillness that lay over the straw.

Young girls with newly washed hair and braids and red ribbons run around in their courtyard holding in their hands freshly baked kichele, from which they take occasional bites.

Soon each dwelling will be full of Shabbos, and over everyone will rest the favor of holiness. On the tables are two beautiful challas covered with a cloth. In the shiny silver candlesticks are candles, over which the mother stands, gentle and pale, with light, spread hands, and soon she covers her face with them and blesses the Shabbos candles.

Her lips quietly mouth the prayer. She prays for her husband and children, for every Jew. Her hands, like twin wings, pass over the light, full of mercy, security, and trust, and from the momma's eyes, holy with sorrow and pain, a tear falls on the white tablecloth.

Mother's mild, dove–like eyes, so holy in the glow from the blessed lights on Friday evening, accompany me everywhere, through my whole life.

Jews with black satin caftans, with shined shoes and socks, go to the beis–hamedrash to welcome Shabbos, leading children by the hand, the older children walking behind. They enter the beis–hamedrash to welcome Shabbos.

So, too, goes Yisrael–Mordechai the Shochet, all dressed up in his silk caftan. With his soft fingers he strokes his reddish beard. He walks with slow steps on the way that leads to Leshne Street. In the brightly lit beis–hamedrash, the reader's stand waits for him. There he will soon sing Lecha Dodi with a new Modzhizer tune.

Between Mincha and Ma'ariv

The wooden beis–hamedrash, which the German murderers destroyed and sent up in smoke, still stands before my eyes. Deep in my memory are the winter evening when we, schoolboys, after studying Chumash with Rashi, ran home and together with our fathers went to the beis–hamedrash to say the afternoon and evening prayers.

The beis–hamedrash was a warm home for all the Jews in the shtetl. Gathered together were great scholars, merchants, and workmen, porters in their grain–covered clothes, bakers, who brought with them the smells of fresh bread. Each one found his place there and davened mincha and ma'ariv set away in the corners with their particular groups. Some conversed while others learned; some argued while others told stories from the Gemara and the Midrash; others talked politics.

I see Chaim Aaron–Binum's, the dream interpreter, who always sat alone, swaying over his volume of the Talmud. The more he learned, the more his face lit up.

There were also scholars who learned with others. They sat here and there around a table and listened to each other's sharp arguments. There were also shy men who were eager to hear a new interpretation of the Gemara, and even when that interpretation did not appeal to them, they sagely nodded their heads, not demonstrating their astuteness, so that everyone thought they were great scholars.

It sometimes happened that in these warm surroundings suddenly would be heard a lament from an unhappy mother whose child was seriously ill. Then everyone would immediately begin reciting Psalms. We could feel in the air a great Jewish unity and care for each other.

Near the western wall, which bordered the women's section, young men in oversized coats sat around tables and swayed over their Gemaras. Whether they studied alone or with a friend, from time to time they would get up and go to the stove, which was seldom too hot. Having felt the cold tiles, they went back to the Gemara on the table, immersed themselves in a difficult passage, indifferent to whatever was going on. Thus the young men would sit by the dripping candles until late into the night.

The beis–hamedrash became even more ardent later in the evening when the Hasidim came from their rabbi and with great rapture recounted his sayings about the Torah or sang a new tune that they had heard by the rabbi's table.

[Pages 293-302]

My Little Shtetl of Wolomin

by Yisroel Levita

Only a few of us are left from Wolomin, so it is the duty of each of us who can still hold a pen to describe and lament the horrible abrupt ending of our near and dear, the martyrs of our shtetl. In the first chapter of Job is a passage that reads, "And behold, a wind came from across the wilderness, and it struck the four corners of the house, and it struck the young people and they died."

This passage applies also to Wolomin. Job's troubles fell upon our shtetl. There are so many families, from which no one survived to tell about their parents. For me, it was a miracle that I survived. One of a large family, I lost my parents, four sisters, their husbands and families, and I feel the obligation to memorialize them, so that their stories, and their names and their memories should not disappear.

My father's real name was Mottl Kover, but he was called Melech the Watchmaker, on Dluga Street. My mother was called Ester'l the Watchmaker. Melech the Watchmaker was one of Wolomin's finest Jews and Chasidic citizens, an excellent and clever Jew, a member of the Shomrei Shabbos fellowship. Every Friday in the late afternoon, he, along with R. Leibush Farber and R. Shmuel–Dovid Burshteyn, would go out to announce that it was time to close up the shops, Some of the businesses liked to stay open later than others, but when they saw these fine Jews, they were quick to close up shop.

My father also belonged to the Chevra Kadisha. Aryeh the Shammos would come to my father and tell him that someone had died in the town, and my father immediately set his work aside and went to help with the preparation of the body, just for the sake of the mitzvah. He prayed at Yankl Margolis' in the prayer house on Warshavski Street. Almost every Friday night he would bring home a guest for dinner.

At Yankl Margolis' in the prayer house my father was the Torah reader. On the High Holidays, he led the Musaf service and Kol Nidrei. His prayers were always said with a broken heart, and he pleaded with the Creator of the Universe on behalf of all Israel.

As someone who cared deeply about the needs of the community, my father was also a member of charitable organizations. When someone was ill, people would call him to spend the night with the sufferer. My father would leave us and go to the sick person in order to provide some comfort.

People called my mother Esther'l the Watchmaker. She also loved to do good deeds. She would take our neighbor, Tovele Shultz, the wife of Aharon Bunem from the fur store on Dluga Street, and they would go to distribute money to poor young women so that they would have a dowry and be able to marry.

And who did not come to Melech the Watchmaker in his shop? Young and old, a schoolboy who needed a battery for his lamp, a Christian young man who needed a string for his guitar–everyone came to us. From his small business, he managed to arrange marriages for his four daughters. He never promised what he could not deliver. But fine Chasidic young men took Melech's daughters without dowries, just as they were, because Melech the Watchmaker had such a fine reputation.

Shabbos With the Wolomin Rabbi

The Wolomin rabbi, R. Eliezer Shoyme Taub z"l, lived all year in Warsaw at Kufietze 5. Every summer he would come to Wolomin for eight days, and he would stay with us. My father would turn the whole house over to the rabbi, while we slept in the shop.

I will never forget the joy of the week that the rabbi spent in Wolomin, especially Friday evening. Young men would arrive from Warsaw in order to spend Shabbos with the rabbi. There was such joy on Friday night when the Chasidim would begin to sing zemiros, particularly with the Modzhitzer melodies, since the Wolomin rabbi was the nephew of the Modzhitzer rabbi. Young and old, including women and girls, would come and stand beside the window of our home in order to hear those fine tunes. Even those who had long ago distanced themselves from Yiddishkeit would come to hear the singing.

The whole Shabbos was full of great music.

While the Wolomin rabbi was in Wolomin, people discussed matches between the young women of the shtetl and the young men who had come to spend Shabbos with the rabbi. Every time the rabbi came, a match was made. In this way my father made matches for his daughters without dowries, gaining fine Chasidic sons–in–law from Warsaw.

And all of this has become ruin, ash, gone with the wind. How can we find consolation for the destruction, for our dear ones cut off in their youth, the life of our dear shtetl Wolomin. If all the woods became pens and all the waters became ink, there still would not be enough to describe the destruction that befell us. Is it possible for a human hand to describe it? How can one comprehend that the whole world simply looked on as children, young people, and the elderly were murdered so cruelly and no one stopped the murderers from their killing? No one came to help us. The crematoria of Auschwitz, Maidanek, and Treblinka burned our beloved ones and no help came. As long as we live, we will remember.

Our Neighbors

Our neighbors, dear, good Jews–so much tenderness, love, nostalgia, and longing your memories call forth.

Alter Friedman from the sewing store–a fine, observant beis–medrash Jew, he had good children, daughters; our neighbor Markreich, a good–hearted man who would run out at night to cup the ill, often without taking any payment from the poor.

We even had a Christian neighbor, a baker, Wladerski, with whom we lived on good terms and who never showed any enmity toward Jews.

R. Ephraim Ivri

Ephraim Ivri lived by Yechezkelo–Yehoshua in a house at 16 Dluga Street. His dwelling consisted of two small rooms with a tiny kitchen–the rest, a shop. The merchandise in the shop was pencils, notebooks, shoelaces, and paper. Through most of the year, boys and girls seldom appeared to buy anything there, but at the beginning of the school year Ephraim Ivri did a lot of business, since the non–Jewish school was opposite his shop. From his little business, Ephraim Ivri had to support a sick wife and two sons and two daughters.

One son, Moyshe, was an idler; the other was a yeshiva student named Yiroel–Ezriel–Chaim–Yechezkel. Both daughters, Sara and Dvorah–Leah, were quiet souls. I remember when their mother suddenly died and the cries of the daughters broke my heart. Soon after, I heard their brother Yisroel–Ezriel come to them and say quietly, "Dvorah–Leah, you know, in the holy Torah is written that a Jewish child should not complain so bitterly about death. Thank God, our father is still alive."

This little speech worked. The girls' mourning slowed down and became quieter.

Their father, R. Ephraim Ivri, did not know what to do in the store. The real storekeepers were his wife and daughters. He did not even know the price of the smallest merchandise. Rising before dawn, he would take his tallis bag and go to the large beis–medrash on Leshne Street, pray, read a book, take a nap. At noon, he would go home, wash before eating his meal, which consisted of rye bread and the head of a herring, washed down with bitter tea. Then he said the grace after meals, asking, "Dear God, don't let us be in need of sustenance" and thanked Him for the favor of a satisfying meal.

Then he studied a page of Gemara, until the time for the afternoon service. He returned to the beis–medrash for the afternoon and evening services and then he learned for two hours. Then he sat down for his big dinner, which consisted of some soup with a piece of rye bread and a little meat, accompanied by a cup of tea and with great devotion he praised and blessed God who had shown him favor for the entire day.

Despite his poverty, he brought up fine and religious children. They all behaved righteously, got married to fine men, and had grandchildren. For all of that, Ephraim every minute praised the Lord of the Universe for the great kindnesses that He had performed.

R. Shmuel–Eizik Flotkowski

Shmuel–Eizik Flotkowski owned a sewing goods store on Dluga Street. He had good children, daughters and sons, and was blessed with a good heart. It was tradition every Jew on Shabbos mornings hot tea. Everyone came to his kitchen, a big one, in which large kettles were set to boil water. It worked like this:

On Shabbos mornings, Jews would go from the ritual bath to Shmuel–Eizik's for a glass of tea, especially in winter when it was cold. The Jews really enjoyed their glass of tea, with milk, or hot coffee. Sugar stood in little bowls on the table. Also plates with lemon slices. R. Shmuel–Eizik went around dressed in a silk housecoat, making sure that everyone had a warm drink.

It was not only men who came to R. Shmuel–Eizik but also women with cups or jars for a little hot water. R. Shmuel–Eizik's wife stood in the kitchen with a huge ladle and distributed the hot water.

Thus it went until Havdalah.

Who could forget them?

"And tell it to your sons!" We should pass this story down through generations so that those who follow us can know from whence they came, so that they can continue the beautiful customs and pass on the good deeds of our forebears.

Yisgadal v'yiskadash sh'mey raba…

My Grandparents

I remember when I was a small child and my grandfather, R. Leybl, was a teacher in Wolomin. He taught older students, who showed him great respect. When Friday evening arrived, my grandfather put on his silk kaftan, which was worn with age, his velvet hat, a broad belt, took his old Eyin–Yakov prayer book, and went to the large beis–medrash on Leshne Street.

My grandmother Chaya meanwhile put on her large headkerchief and her new linen dress, put on the table five large silver candlesticks with wax candles, the old silver wine cup with its saucer, put out two brown breads in the place of challas, covered them with the challa cover, and turned on a bright lamp.

Later on she stood by the lights and blessed them in a loud voice. She prayed for sustenance and health, for good fortune for her children, that they should have good futures, that they should be virtuous and observant Jews.

My grandfather stood in the beis–medrash praying the afternoon service with total devotion and then recited the Song of Songs.

R. Yisroel Mordechai the Shochet then went up to the reader's stand to welcome Shabbos. He sang L'cha Dodi with a sweet, heartfelt melody.

After the evening service, everyone wished each other "Good Shabbos," as was the custom, then "Good Shabbos" again, and started for home.

The Poor

As was the case in all the little shtetls, poor people came to Wolomin. They would come to warm themselves by the oven in the beis–hamedrash. After the evening prayers on Friday nights, they would stand by the doors and wait for someone to invite them home for Shabbos dinner.

My grandfather would wait until everyone had gone home, and when he saw that there were two poor people whom no one had invited home, he would bring them home for Shabbos dinner.

When my grandmother saw the guests who came with my grandfather, she was a little sad as she contemplated what she would give them to eat. She had no challas and no fish. But she was a righteous woman. She said nothing, had no bitter words for my grandfather. She simply divided things into smaller portions so everyone could have some.

My grandfather sang "Shalom Aleichem, mal'achei hashalom," said Kiddush over the breads, since he had no wine (for where would he have gotten money for wine, since he was only a Gemara teacher for young men, who paid very little?). After Kiddush, my grandfather and the guests washed for the brown bread, dipped it in salt, and ate. My grandmother filled the plates with fritters and pasta.

On my grandfather's face there was not the slightest sadness. His face shone with a pure spirit, and he sang "Kol m'kadesh" with a calming melody.

When it came to the meat course, my grandmother gave the guests larger portions than to my grandfather. Mostly it was less expensive meat, but we should not forget the carrot tzimmes that combined a thousand flavors.

After eating, my grandfather said the grace after meals with great devotion and when he came to the verse, "Let us not need anything from hands of flesh and blood," a tear would appear in his eyes. He prayed that he should never have to be dependent on any man and that he should always be able to perform the mitzvah of having guests.

Chevra Kadisha

The members of the Chevra Kadisha performed their duties like sacred work for which there was no reward. The members were Chasidic Jews, learned people who held Heaven in awe, some of the most respected citizens of the shtetl. Among them were: R. Dovid the Shochet, Eidelsohn, R. Yankel Margolis, R. Melech Levita, R. Shmuel Burshteyn, R. Chaim Schultz, R. Shmuel–Eizik Flotkowski, R. Moyshe Graditzki, and others.

The head of the Chevra Kadisha was R. Aryeh, who was also the gravedigger. He was a simple, fine Jew. When someone died in the shtetl, he immediately contacted the membership so that they could come to perform the purification rituals in the home.

In the shtetl there was no need to send out an alarm. As soon as someone died, the whole shtetl knew. People could tell from the black wagon with two horses, covered in black cloth up to their eyes. Aryeh brought the boards on which to lay the deceased to the house.

When the funeral procession went down Dluga Street or Koshczelna Street, everyone stopped working a paid homage to the deceased.

When the procession came to the great beis–hamedrash on Leshne Street, a large crowd would be there with the Chevra Kadisha. People took the casket out of the wagon, put it on the staircase of the beis–hamedrash, and the rabbi, R. Zev Bergazin delivered a eulogy.

If the deceased was a Chasid, a learned man, he was brought into the beis–hamedrash, seven circuits were made in the sanctuary, and the rabbi eulogized him there..

From there the deceased was carried on people's shoulders to the sacred spot, which was an area two kilometers from the shtetl.

On the road, many people followed the procession, accompanying the deceased to the sacred spot.

The Chevra Kadisha took care of all the necessities and for the honor which the dead required. They also took care of placing a grave marker.

Righteous Women and Community Leaders

Dear and wonderful were the righteous women who dedicated their whole lives to taking care of the needy, the poor and sick, widows and orphans. I remember how selflessly they did their work:

Estherl the gabbai's wife had no children, but she devoted all her years to helping needy people. Her help was always discreet, so that no one would ever feel shame.

Estherl the watchmakers' wife, Tovele from the butter shop, Reyzl Margolis, the wives of Shmuel–Dovid Burshteyn and Shmuel Eizik Flotkowski–they were the women leaders of the shtetl.

On Friday afternoons the righteous women would take baskets to the homes of the wealthy , where they collected challas, bread, eggs, meat, cooking oil, and other items, which they then distributed to the poor.

There were numerous people in Woomin who appeared to be honored householders, but at home they lived in squalor, having nothing to feed their children and no way to heat their homes in winter. When Estherl the gabbai's wife appeared in such a home with a basket full of food, it was as though the sun suddenly shone. The children felt as though they were visited by an angel from heaven who brought them good things to eat.

The righteous women also helped poor girls who yearned to be brides.

There were in Wolomin many families where girls were being raised but who lacked money for dowries so they could get married or buy appropriate clothing. The righteous women kept watch over every poor household where daughters needed to be married, and they took care that no young woman should remain unmarried.

In the evenings they would gather together, and in the early mornings they would go to businesses and collect money for poor brides.

First they would go to the rich, to the factory owners, to Dr. Frank, to the barber–surgeon Markreich, to the Tayblums, to Mintz, and so on.

The righteous women also undertook to buy outfits for the brides, furniture and other things that were needed for the home. There were often cases when they would rent a room for the new couple and prepare the wedding so that everything would be right and the family would not be embarrassed.

At the wedding, they would act as the servers and busied themselves taking care of the guests as if they were relatives of the bride.

There was in Wolomin no lack of homes where fathers or children suffered for years with tuberculosis. The disease accompanied poverty. Tubercular fathers could bring no income to the home. Sick children were bedridden from malnourishment because they lacked the food that they needed.

There were homes in which great human tragedies were played out. The mother was the only breadwinner. She had to leave her sick husband with the children and go to the homes of the rich, where she would wash laundry, clean, cook, and in return receive a little food, a hand–me–down, or a pair of shoes for her children. Coming home after a day of hard work, she had to make a little soup for her family, though there was not always something there to cook. When a child became ill, there was no money to pay a doctor or to buy medicine.

The righteous women oversaw such poor homes, sympathized with their problems and did all they could to alleviate their woes.

[Pages 303-305]

Our Shtetl is Unforgettable

by Shimon Wishniewski (president of the Wolomin Society in America)

We first settled in Wolomin in 1925. My father had a sister in town, Sheva–Sarah Mindel, who took us in and helped us get things in order. We fit in right away and became familiar and close with the Jews in the shtetl.

Those were very pleasant years, long, sweet shtetl years, filled with dreams of great deeds, with images of a great big world; attended with Chasidic tunes, with the prayers of religious Jews, with the excited singing of young pioneers, of idealistic dreamers, who saw visions and were filled with expectation.

A small, poor shtetl, but so rich in grand moments, when even the poorest, whether materially or spiritually, felt greatness and were taken up with the possibility of realizing high ideals.

Always I see before me God–fearing Jews, scholars with deeply furrowed brows, Chasidim in religious ecstasy, and simple merchants with everyday wisdom; the teachers, who taught the children from their first aleph–beis through Gemara and Tosefos, sharpening their minds and imbuing their hearts with Jewish beauty.

Religious Jews

In my ears ring the old Chasidic tunes that filled the air of the shtetl, from Kabbalas Shabbos until the melaveh malkeh, the tunes of "Atkeynu Seudata" and "Kol M'kadesh," and every time that I remember them, it occurs to me that thus sing people who are freed from their earthly worries and concern themselves with heavenly matters, with pure spirituality.

Shabbos filled the homes of Wolomin with the angels of grace [mentioned in "Shalom Aleichem"], with an extra soul, with the Shabbos Queen, with guests, who helped to fulfill the great mitzvah.

Unforgettable were the Days of Awe, and Pesach, which tasted of the four cups of wine, of sweet–and–sour Pesach borscht, of long spring nights and a sea of streaming light; Shavuos, which arrived in the shtetl with joyful greenery, with the magic of the giving of the Torah; Succos, when the streets and courtyards of Jewish poverty were adorned with green roofs and inside with the rainbow colors of paper chains and lanterns.

Oh, those Days of Awe, when the gates of mercy opened and Jews brought their please to the Master of the Universe, begging for forgiveness for their sins.

So many years have passed from that time to this, but still I see before my eyes the bent over, cherished Jews of my shtetl. For what sins did they beg forgiveness? For the whole year they had worked hard for a piece of bread–tell me, what sins did they commit? Still, the more God–fearing were the Jews, the more intense was their regret over uncommitted sins.

In the fearsome days, Wolomin was beset with fears and duties. Jews went around deep in thought, studied Torah fervently and prayed in holiness. The Creator had sent a soul, and each person had to make it pure, free from the sinful passions that troubled it.

The Idealistic Young People

There was so much beauty in the young people of Wolomin. Who can forget the bright faces in the heat of discussions over idealistic stances? Young people with earnest looks on their faces, on their entire being, took on themselves the burden of the people, of all humankind. Beis–hamedrash young men with beautifully trimmed sidecurls and pressed white collars secretly read secular books, strolled outside the town, listened to fiery speeches in the woods and were later caught up in the storyâ€¦

Since that time I have experienced a whole world, seen huge, beautiful things, attended great theatrical performances, but be assured that nothing can compare to the performances of the Wolomin drama circle.

An overwhelming joy seizes me when I remember the Peretz Library. Such a valuable treasure of books, and how the young readers benefited from it.

The lectures, readings, and discussions in the evenings erased the grayness from the preceding and upcoming workdays. Young blood sang a great dream about a happier future–for the people, for all humankind.

Who can forget it, my dear shtetl of Wolomin?!

[Pages 306-307]

My Father's Responsibility

by Yehoshua Edelzon

People in Wolomin knew my father by the name R. Binyaminl–David Shochet. He was a great scholar and an ardent Jew. As a young man he had studied in "Yismach Yisroel," and the Jews in the shtetl always showed him great respect. In his dealings with people he demonstrated tact and wisdom.

We, his children, from our earliest years absorbed the virtue of showing respect for people, even if they had a lower social standing than we did. If a child came out with a word that in my father's eyes seemed impertinent, my father would sit the child next to him and calmly make him understand how distasteful it is to be impudent and dignified is the man who shows respect for others, even those who are younger and poorer.

Ah, how I miss that time when I was old enough to understand what was going on in our world, when I began to know the people around me, to understand who was who, and I seemed to have such a many–branched family on both sides, grandfathers, grandmothers, uncles, aunts, cousins, and other relatives.

My grandfather on my mother's side was the rabbi in Stock. My father boarded with him for a while, sitting and learning all day, becoming industrious and showing a sharp mind. But a time came when he wanted to be independent. but he did not intend to make of the Torah an axe for chopping [e.g., he didn't want to use the Torah for monetary gain], so he travelled to Volomin, opened a shop, and went into business.

Be assured that the yoke of the business fell on my mother. She valued my father's learning and held him in honor. She strove not to disturb his learning and did everything she could to help with the business, from which they eked out a livelihood until disaster overtook the business and our household was reduced to poverty.

At that time it happened that one of the shochets in Volomin had left and people came to urge my father that he should assume the position of shochet.

My father agreed to become the shochet, but with a heavy heart, and he was always occupied with the idea that he had taken on himself a heavy responsibility.

With his idealism, his love for creatures and for simplicity, my father won the sympathy and love of the people of Volomin.

Dear Father, your great sense of responsibility became for me an example for all times and all my endeavors.

I always see before my eyes your great Jewish and humane behavior, at home and in the street, in the beis–hamedrash, which was full of people studying, young men, children and old Jews, whose whole spiritual life consisted of stiudying Torah, righteousness, and religious behavior.

I can see you entering the beis–hamedrash with slow steps, smiling at the small and the large, the smile of love of Israel and love of humanity.

[Pages 308-313]

The Kover Family

by Itta Kover

Distant, sweet shtetl years.

As I write about the Wolomin train station, which, until its downfall and destruction, pulsated with colorful Jewish life, what comes to my mind is the variety of Wolomin Jews, leaders and everyday Jews, merchants and tradesmen, who built and shaped the lost Jewish Wolomin. One of the first pioneers among those who laid the foundation for the Jewish community in Wolomin was Reb Motl Kover.

He arrived in Wolomin in 1905, when he was in his energetic years, full of initiative and energy. He was thirty–something when he learned that near Warsaw, by the Wolomin train station, the Jewish settlement was beginning. He did not think long about abandoning his prosperous merchant station, and he told his young wife, Feige–Zisl: "We're going!"

Arriving in Wolomin, he quickly befriended the local Jews who established with him a small but tightly–knit Jewish society, in which they helped each other and lightened each other's affairs, and he easily went through what we call the birth pangs of absorption.

On the first days he walked around the shtetl, looked around, observed the streets and the houses, which looked poor and needy, lacking sidewalks, lacking paved roads, though that did not surprise him; rather, his imagination was stirred, and he saw before him a bright field in which to apply his energy.

He made connections with the householders of the shtetl, the official power brokers, and laid before them his project to build up the shtetl, pave the streets and the sidewalks, and cobblestone the roads.

To come before the town magistrate at that time with such plans took a lot of boldness. Reb Motl did it with the greatest self–confidence, adding:

"I am prepared to see it through myself, to build, to bring order. From you I require only official go–ahead, permission for everything."

It was remarkable: Here was completely new man in town, not known at all in the shtetl, and he showed so much proficiency and integrity. Everyone approved of him, both Jews and Poles.

Possibly what helped is that he used his outward appearance, his patriarchal bearing, his dignified bearing, which, from the first day, drew everyone's attention to him.

He was tall and slender. From under his wise–looking forehead looked out two clever eyes, which either glittered or bored through one, and he radiated gentleness and wisdom. His long black beard hung down as far as his heart.

In his words everyone felt the cleverness of an experienced entrepreneur who could do a lot for the shtetl, and he quickly assumed the leadership in Wolomin society. The magistrate had endorsed all of his official undertakings, promised to pave the sidewalks and the Wolomin streets, to fix and improve the old, to improve the external appearance of the shtetl.

Reb Motl eagerly applied himself to the work.

But in the shtetl there was also a subversive element. Everywhere people spoke about the Jew, who came from Kosov Podloski, who settled in the shtetl and before he even really knew the people, he had taken over the shtetl. All of the streets were full of workers, revived, spurting with building, with creating.

It wasn't long before Reb Motl Kover was a contractor building houses. They had to enlarge the station, they had to bring in more workers, more Jews to move into the city. Wherever one turned, one felt Reb Motl's young enthusiasm for building the shtetl, for building house after house. He quickly developed a reputation as an experienced entrepreneur with many plans.

New residents came, Jews and Poles. The ties with the big city of Warsaw were broadened and strengthened.

It was not Reb Motl's custom to stand still in one spot. His impulsive nature prompted him to even more buildings, houses, streets, and sidewalks, whole neighborhoods.

And suddenly there came a crisis.

One morning Reb Motl disappeared from Wolomin.

This was right after he received a letter from his family in Kosov Podoski telling him that three kilometers from them a nobleman would sell his court, a large estate and all the grounds. This was in the village of Albenovo.

He got an idea. At just that time, a Christian had offered him a good price for his house in Wolomin. He did not think long about it, and quickly concluded the transaction.

The Kover family moved to Albenova.

Reb Motll became a true prince. In the area around Kosov, everyone spoke about the new Jewish prince with his long black beard, about the Jewish princess Feige–Zisl, the daughter of an old Kotzker Chasid, who later travelled to the Sfat Emes [a famous rabbi].

The Jews in the area prided themselves in them, commented that the Prince and the Princess travelled in a coach pulled by four horses over the streets of Kosov. They excelled in uniting themselves with the Jews of the shtetl, devoting a lot of money to charitable causes. Just as in Wolomin, there dwelling was open to anyone who was in need, they gave huge donations, supported the Jewish community, and on every holiday sent around wagons filled with potatoes and grain to distribute to the poor. The goodness of the Jewish Prince was known in the entire area, and Jews prided themselves in him, seeing in him an example of a devoted Jew, who used his wealth to help those in need.

When the First World War broke out, the district, the shtetls and villages, were turned into the front lines. When the Russians abandoned the district, they destroyed and burned cities and villages. The same fate befell Albenovo. The Russians there burned everything. This severely affected the scores of homeless in the poor district who hid at the home of the Jewish Prince, having there found protection and sustenance. The Russians turned their full fury on his estate.

Reb Motl Kover took this as a heavenly decree and quickly packed up his remaining possessions and left with his whole household, his oldest daughter Chana–Golde, Chayele, Moyshe, Yehudis, Rochel, and Dovid. They all returned to Wolomin.

In Wolomin, Reb Motl Kover had another house, a remnant of his former great possessions. Now it became a necessity. He lived there with his growing family.

His long, patriarchal beard had gone silver, with snow–white hair. In the wrinkles on his forehead, one could see the experiences he had lived through, though he was still full of strength and energy and had gotten right back to work. The Jews of Wolomin welcomed him with great warmth. In addition, the Christians showed him great respect. He was back in his element. He became a contractor and started building.

It was not long before he was chosen as a member of the city council, or, as people then called it, a councilman.

A Celebration to Dedicate the Sefer Torah

Among the moving experiences of the Kover family was the imposing celebration to dedicate the Sefer Torah in Wolomin. This was the first such celebration in Wolomin. This took place after Reb Motl had moved to Albenovo. The whole shtetl participated in the celebration. People walked through the streets with burning torches, people sang Chasidic melodies with accompaniments. Young and old joined together in leading the Sefer Torah to the beis–hamedrash.

This was an experience that engraved itself in the memories of all the Jews of Wolomin at that time. For years and years, people spoke about that celebration.

THE FIRST PIONEER

Magnificent was the banquet that the Wolomin Jews put on for their first pioneer, Moyshe Kover, on the occasion of his leaving for Eretz Yisroel. This was in 1925, when Jews in Poland had not thought, except for a select few, of going to Israel with the purpose of building their own land. They saw the threatening clouds that were gathering in the Polish skies over the heads of the Jews.

To these select few the Kover family, with Reb Motl at its head, had paid attention. They gave earnest thought to making aliya to Eretz Yisroel.

First Reb Motl sent his son Moyshe, who was to be the vanguard, the pioneer and scout to check out whether there would be a place for his whole family.

Shortly after Moyshe, daughter Yehudis went. She now lives in Tel Aviv with her husband Avraham Rozenblit and their daughters.

Soon Reb Motl himself began preparations for going to Eretz Yisroel so he could be together with his whole family. He had not reckoned with the cautionary letter that he received from his children in which he could read between the lines that life in Eretz Yisroel was not so easy and that people had to be prepared for hard physical labor. He was not dissuaded and he decided to take the decisive step.

For him there was no question about a certificate, because he was able to travel as Capitalist who owned over a thousand pounds sterling, as the British mandate–power then required.

Jewish Wolomin decided to thrown a going–away banquet to honor the Kover family. Everyone took part in this banquet, every layer of the shtetl, all the parties, beginning with the most religious to the most extreme Zionists and all the other factions. In their orations, they all praised the great services that the Kover family had provided Wolomin, their contribution to the building of the shtetl and for supporting the various Jewish institutions, and, above all, for building the shtetl's beis–hamedrash.

The impression was overwhelming. The Kovers were the first family at that time to travel to Eretz Yisroel. They awoke both hope and longing.

For many years people in the shtetl spoke about this banquet, which was engraved on everyone's memory.

Reb Motl Kover with his wife Feige–Zisl merited arriving in Eretz Yisroel and lived their last years in Tel Aviv. At this time his daughters still live in Tel Aviv: Yehudis with her husband and her daughter Rachel with her husband. All the other children, Chana–Golde with her husband Pinye, their children and grandchildren, Chaya'le with her husband and children, and their son David were killer in the awful slaughter together with all the Jews of Wolomin.

[Pages 314-317]

Moshe Kover

by Shmuel Vinagoro

שבכם חתפן

From his earliest youth was Moyshe Kover bound up with our shtetl, with its society and cultural traditions, with Zionist activities, with drama. In all of his deeds, Moyshe demonstrated his wonderful qualities and high moral character, his deep empathy for all and his warm understanding for each person's sorrow and worries.

Always energetic and full of life, he found time for everyone and never grew tired. In 1922 we were both delegates to the Keren Ha–yisod Conference in Warsaw and I had a chance to observe how he was completely absorbed, heart and soul, in the Zionist idea. I saw his respect for the Zionist leader Nahum Sokolov, which came from deep within him.

He devoted a great deal of time and toil to his Zionist work in Volomin. When the young men were away in the Polish army, he took on himself alone the responsibility for the work, for the various Zionist activities that took place in Volomin, and it demanded great selflessness to overcome all the hardships of his daily tasks.

Because he was a friend to everyone, he showed with his attitude to people and his readiness to do a favor, his social activities focused not only on the demands of Zionist party work. He also participated in other activities from all facets of Jewish life in Volomin.

When, among the Jewish immigrants from Russia there arrived also illegal refugees, he often intervened with the police and through his interventions prevented many Jews from being sent back to Russia.

Moyshe Kover was a good person and a good friend. I was one of those who was bound to him by a thousand ties. I saw in him my closest friend and when he made aliyah to Israel, I corresponded with him. His letters overflowed with deep friendship and also with great idealism, which was the chief feature of his character and which led him to the killing fields of the Spanish Civil War and later to France, where he was killed by murdering hands.

In his letters he would describe his explorations and his principles, and in my eyes he was always a mentsch who was bound with all the passion of his soul to a bright beginning in his spiritual life, which swam before his eyes always in a world which tried to extinguish that light.

I often used to ask him: Where did he get such idealism and righteous generosity.

The answer comes to me whenever I think about our destroyed shtetl, where together with hard work and the chasing after income there was so much love for other people. Material life was poor and flimsy, the streets shoddy, dusty, and muddy, the shtieblich shabby, faded, and in them dwelled men who belittled material goods and counted not on physical wealth but only on the treasures of the spirit and their greatest desire was to be a simple hard–working Jew with the glory of the Shechinah.

Moyshe Kover was a son of such Volomin Jews, the foundation of whose souls was "love that has no limit." Moyshe had absorbed the spirit, the ideal, the belief. There had arisen his love for people, for Jews, and the sparks of that holy fire he carried with him for his whole life.

Molocz–The Great Host

I left Volomin in 1932, but the Volomin Jews engraved themselves in my memory, and I remember them always with love as good and sincere Jews, simple Jews of every age and education, scholars, working people, and merchants. They prayed three times a day, and when something bad happened, they turned to the Master of the Universe through the words of King David, through his Psalms.

There were also Chasidim, who constantly told wondrous stories that they heard from their rebbe while learning and judging with love, through joy, and they rejoiced in the rebbe's teaching licked their fingers after every word.

Moyshe Molocz was a simple Jew, but gifted with a big heart, a good heart, with sympathy for every sadness, ready to give his last morsel to a hungry person or a donation to a pauper.

In those days there was no organized way of providing hospitality in Volomin, so Moyshele a special room so that a stranger who came to the shtetl could have a place to sleep and a meal. He would run among his neighbors asking for a bit of food or warm water. A poor person could have the pleasure of performing the commandment of refreshing the soul. And at his own table there was always a guest.

At the time of the First World War, bread was scarce in the shtetl, but from Moyshele's dwelling no poor person ever went away hungry and no stranger ever went without a place to sleep.

Everything has its test, through which people can prove whether it is real, just like with gold and silver. The test by which people can determine if someone is Jewish is love of Israel, because by as much as a Jew shows love for another Jew, by that much is he a real Jew.

Moyshele Molocz passed the test of love of Israel. If there were a Nobel Prize for nobility and goodness, they would have to award it to Moyshel Molocz.

Through his heart went all the sighs of the Jewish poor who somehow had arrived in Volomin. Through his eyes ran all the tears of sadness in the shtetl.

His nobility and goodness attracted the attention of the home owners in the shtetl, and they saw how important it was to create and institution for hospitality. Consequently at the beis–hamedrash they organized a hospitality committee.

When the First World War broke out, Moyshel Molocz was already old, but having seen a Russian soldier, he volunteered at the military commission, but they refused to take him because of his age.

Moyshele responded: "I wanted to help….I didn't want to shirk my duty…but if you don't want me, what can I do? Who am I and what am I that I should oppose the will of officialdom?"

During his whole life he interpreted things for the best, "gam zu l'tovah" [a Talmudic saying: "this, too, is for the best"]. Nothing he did was for a reward, but it was simply from his great goodness and sympathy for the poor and the sad–alnd for His beloved Name.

[Pages 318-321]

Lights From Hearts

by Mordechai Freedman

Each of us has in his heart a golden threat that binds us to our old home. In each of us smolders, like a fire that neither wind nor rain can extinguish, deep memories of our native shtetl, of the quiet streets, of the beis–medrash, and of all the people who prayed and learned there.

The beloved, dear beis–medrash Jews all live in my memory. Often it feels to me as if I just lost them yesterday.

Now I see a hot day in Tammuz. The air in the beis–medrash is thick, full of prayer and drawn out Gemara chants. Near a long table are sitting simple Jews who sway back and forth over their Gemaras. Over there sits R. Yakov Margulies, a fervent Ger Chasid and a distinguished scholar. He studies with everyone, explains a difficult passage and everyone listens to him with pleasure, rejoicing in his sharp intellect, in his shrewd way of disentangling a knot with probes and questions. His eyes shine with a light that seems to come from a sacred world.

When he ends the lesson and everyone has gone away, he remains sitting there, sunk in his thoughts. You can see how a passion boils in him for the highest realms. But the ladder on which he tries to climb will not hold him…

Into the beis–medrash comes R. Chaim Topol. People called him Chaim Kosover. He sits down at the same table as R. Yakov Margulies. He opens a Gemara and tries to immerse himself in a passage, begins to hum a quiet tune, but nothing comes out. His thoughts are scattered, flying off to a distance or perhaps focused on the everyday problems of earning a living.

From these thoughts he is torn away by R. Yakov Margulies. his constant adversary. Now he has raised his eyes from his Gemara, looked at R. Chaim with a thoughtful glance and said quietly, "It must be pretty hot outside."

"Yes," says R. Chaim curtly.

R. Yakov continues to speak, half to himself and half to R. Chaim, "In the beis–medrash you don't feel the heat so much, do you?"

R, Chaim again offers a brief "Yes," as if he does not want to talk, but R. Yakov is not dissuaded by his reluctance and becomes more talkative: "It's already the three weeks [before Tisha b'Av]…In another week it'll be Tisha b'Av. Summer is passing and soon the days will be cooler. Soon the Holidays will be here…"

Normally R. Chaim is not so quiet. On the contrary, he would seek to respond with a witticism, a joke. He particularly enjoyed contradicting R. Yakov, with whom he would tangle in his gentle way, but on that day in Tammuz it was too hot to do so. His head hurt and his temples throbbed, and I was sitting in the beis–medrash, quiet in a corner, where I could hear the quiet conversation between these two Jews for whom I held a hidden love in my childish heart, particularly for R. Chaim, who embodied the warmth of an ordinary person and who would even behave foolishly with children, laughing and talking with them. unlike other Wolomin Jews who believed that such behavior was inappropriate. People should have respect for their elders and children should not fool around in their presence.

Totally different was R. Yakov Topol, the grandfather of the famous actor in Israel who bears the name of his Wolomin grandfather, the wise man and sharp wit, who had riches in his heart, poverty in his pockets, and squalor in his home.

I remember: I have seen him on winter nights stoking the fire in the oven. Another time I saw him recounting the Temple sacrifices with great devotion. But more than these, I remember him standing there with his gentle smile in the space between his mustache and his beard. And always he brought with him cheerfulness and joy.

When R. Yakov Margulies died, R. Chaim went to the funeral. Everyone knew that they were not fond of each other and watched R. Chaim with wonder. Some even murmured, "How can it be…?" R. Chaim could not refrain from joking, "I can't believe that he died…I have to see him buried."

Everyone loved to hear R. Chaim's jokes. Only R. Yakov could not bear them. He would take his red handkerchief out of his pocket and noisily blow his nose as a sign that if everyone loved the joke, because everyone was a fool, he, R. Yakov, had had enough buffoonery. But on that hot day in Tammuz, it seemed as though he would gladly engage in a conversation with R. Chaim about holidays: how long was it until Pesach? Soon the beautiful holiday of Shavuos would be gone, the time of the giving of the Torah, that greatest of gifts, which the Jews received at Mt. Sinai. People had surely felt the greatest joy, which he also felt and which shone through his speech, but R. Chaim, as if he were angry, said, "Truly, the Master of the Universe went to all the peoples in the world with the Torah, asking if they would receive it, and no one wanted it. Only we yelled out, 'We will do and we will hear.' So what makes the poor Kishinev sexton guilty? Why does he come to the shul and bang on the Holy Ark with nails? How has the poor man sinned?"

When R. Yakov heard this, he was enraged, so that he jumped up and yelled in a strange voice, as if the earth had sunk under him, and then said wildly, "Shush, shush…If you were not Chaim Kosover, I would say that you were a non–Jew, a disgrace to the Jewish people…You shame the holy Torah, the life of the universe…"

R. Yakove screamed in such a tone that everyone in the beis–medrash trembled: "He will sink to the deepest depths–he will fall to Gehenna…"

These exclamations did not excite R. Chaim, and as if he did not understand why R. Yakov was so inflamed, he shrugged his shoulders and said, "What goes? One dares not ask? Even the tanaim and amoraim [Talmudic sages] asked probing questions."

R. Yakov made a dismissive gesture with his hand and began to sway over his Gemara. R. Chaim also became quiet, as if the dispute displeased him, since he had meant no offense. As he bent over his Gemara, his chant blended in with the other chants of the young men and boys at the neighboring tables.

Generations old Gemara chants, thin and hoarse voices, and the words came together like flames, one with the other, yearning and joyful, intense in themselves and piercing other worlds, higher, lighter, like the thoughts that travel with fluttering wings, like birds who sing songs to the Creator of all worlds.

Dear holy figures of our destroyed home. I am bound to them by a thousand cords, by blood and flesh. Their destroyed lives will be with me to the grave.

[Pages 322-327]

Our Parents' Home

by Pesse Feige Wengraver & Esther–Malkeh Borokovski–Shteinberg

Our home was always open for the hungry and the needy. They knew that in our home they would find a outstretched hand ready to help them. Our parents, Chaya and Leibl Borokovski, may their memories be a blessing, took upon themselves the yoke of making sure that in the shtetl no poor person would go without challas and meat for Shabbos. They gave on their own, and they made sure that others should not forget the needy.

In earlier years, our father had commissioned the writing of a Sefer Torah for the Wolomin synagogue. When people brought the Sefer Torah into the synagogue, it was a great holiday. Young and old rejoiced together. The whole town was lit brightly every evening, and the police walked around keeping order. Jews sang and danced along the whole path of the procession.

Great was the sadness when some time later the Sifrei Torah were stolen from the synagogue, along with other Sifrei Torah.

As an Amshinaver Chassid, our father often used to travel to the rebbe, but this did not prevent him from being an energetic and capable businessman. His guiding principle in business was "Be careful in what you say," and he therefore kept his word in every transaction. He was well known for being true to his word. Those who knew him best knew that despite his devotion to Chassidism, he was no idler. He had mastered a number of languages.

In our courtyard could be found the Amshtinaver Chassidic prayer house, where people prayed and studied. After our father died, our mother fulfilled all the commitments he had made to the rebbe. The rebbe lived in Otvotzk, and I remember travelled with me to the rebbe in Otvotzk. It was not easy to get in to see the rebbe in Otvotzk. There were times when a person had to wait a whole day, but my mother was an exception and was quickly welcomed in, and I remember how enthusiastically she spoke about the holy rebbe, about his sparkling eyes, with which he looked so softly and mercifully at his Chassidim.

Our parents capably managed the warehouse for wood and other building materials, as well as the wine business and the brandy concession, which we had until 1937, when it was taken from us as a result of the growing anti–Semitism.

For his position as councilor in the community, and for his membership in the Chevra Kadisha, our father was beloved and honored by all who came in contact with him.

I remember one incident that involved Councilor Zitovski, who had a tannery near the cemetery. He and my father were close friends. When, after the First World War, the tannery stood idle, with no way to get it moving, Zitovski proposed to my father that he should become a partner and devote his energy to reopening the tannery. With this opportunity, the Polish councilor confirmed our father's excellence, and the partnership lasted through the final years of Father's life.

Throughout his life, our father was a fervent Zionist and thought of making aliyah to Eretz Yisroel. But he did not live to do so. But he planted his love for Israel in our hearts and raised us in the spirit of wanting to be in our sacred land.

After my marriage, in 1934, together with my sister Malkeh and her husband applied for a certificate, but we fell victim to a hoax. In 1939 we left for Argentina. There, too, we raised our child in the pioneer spirit, and when he was 22, my son went as a pioneer to Kibbutz Ayin Hashloshah.. For ten years he lived without us in the kibbutz. In 1965 we liquidated our business in Argentina and made aliyah. My older sister, too, along with her whole family, came to Israel with the full intention of being part of the Jewish state. This was the spirit of our father, who raised us with foundational love for the idea of the return to Zion.

We also had two brothers: Gedaliah and Chaim. Gedaliah was killed together with my mother in the great catastrophe that befell all of Polish Jewry. Chaim died a half year before Father, in the month of Elul. He left behind a year–old son, who lived until Hitler began the slaughter of six million Jews.

In our house lived a woman named Hinde Bartshevski, who ran a sewing goods store. She had several daughters and a son, whose name was Yidl. The oldest daughter Leah became friendly with us and borrowed books that we had checked out of the library. Yidl also liked to read books. They had to do it behind their mother's back, who was quite religious and did not want reading secular books. It happened that the mother came upon those books and angrily tore them up. Our parents knew about this, but they always showed understanding both for her and for us. Our parents were also religious and observant, but they had not forbidden us to read such books; they showed us tolerance, and they understood that we could not be backward, that we had to know what was going on in the world.

Hinde's daughters and son later became communists. They left for Paris. After the war, Yidl became co–editor of the *Volksstimme* in Warsaw.

I remember what we used to do in the library. I ordered the books. There were organized lectures and readings, discussions and game evenings. Melech Manne was the secretary and Yakov Zucker was the treasurer. I was the librarian. But when the communist group formed, they took over the library. They expelled members for no reason, refused to call meetings, and did whatever they felt like. Our opposition was fruitless. The communists cared nothing about feelings, although they knew how much effort and energy we had invested in the library. When there was no bench to sit on, I took a bench from the Amshinever prayer house that was in our courtyard. That turned into a scandal. When people came on Shabbos to pray, they had nowhere to sit. I did not lack problems. In the end, we had to give up on the library, which had been hijacked by the communists.

But we were not defeated and we immediately formed a Zionist organization, which was called Tarbus. There we had lively activities, and we organized classes to learn Hebrew. The teacher was Wolfawitz, the father of the actor Nathan Wolfawitz, who lives today in Israel. There were also lectures and readings on various topics. On other evenings the young people arrived full of questions that were on their minds. There were also some who spoke Hebrew without difficulty. People greedily threw at them newly learned words and rejoiced in enriching their language so that they were able to converse in Hebrew.

In order to collect funds for Keren Hayisod, Keren Kayemes, and Shekalim–Farkoyf, the young people of Tarbus conducted many activities. On Flower Day, which we organized, I used to go with Golda Salage, and it often happened that Christians, too, contributed to our cause.

Our home was also a meeting place for scholars. Chasidim, students, and ordinary Jews were often in our home. My father's best friends were: the shochet Yisroel–Mordechai Tentsche, Mandelberg, Moyshe Manne, Margulies, and many other dear and hearty Jews.

May their memories be blessed!

[Pages 328-332]

Our Home

by Zahava (Golda) Goldvasser–Veinbloom

My Father

We lived on Synagogue Street. Our apartment differed little from all the other rented apartments in the shtetl that were constructed in the old way. My father, R. Henech Goldvasser, a religious Jew. a Ger Hasid, had dedicated his whole life to Torah and service. Ever since I can remember, my father in the very early mornings, summer and winter, while it was still dark outside, would go to the beis–hamedrash to study, and only after davening Shacharis would her come home. Then he would undertake his hard work, studying Torah with the children of the shtetl.

My father was a teacher in the Volomin Talmud–Torah. He loved introducing children to the blessings of the Torah, and the Jews of the shtetl had great trust and confidence that their children would receive from him a good Jewish education. People showed him great respect and honor.

My father worked hard at his job, but he barely had an income, so that we lived in a rented apartment with an exemplary family life.

A warm Jewish dwelling, which exuded an atmosphere of high morality. The children were devoted and bound to their parents and particularly felt the sorrows of their mother, was a weak and ill woman who often needed our help. We consequently learned to worry about her, while our father was so involved with community matters, with mitsvos, with doing good deeds for those in need.

My father was also a trustee of the chevra kadisha. This was a job full of righteousness and truth, for which not everyone was suited. There were some who only attended the banquets that the chevra kadisha used to sponsor every year on Purim and other minor celebrations. Anyone who observed the activities of the chevra kadisha up close felt the sacredness of their work. Not everyone merited being able to do the work of the chevra kadisha. My father undertook this work with heart and soul, and he felt great responsibility both for the daily labor and for the special solemnities which often were observed in our home: the post–funeral meal, a Kiddush after the fast. Our father communicated his devotion to us, and in honor of our father we often helped him prepare and organize the solemnities. Our father saw in the activities of the chevra kadisha a great mitzvah and strictly observed all their customs. which he did not waive even in the ghetto.

In the ghetto, the Germans decreed that the dead should be buried not in burial shrouds, only wrapped in paper. My father saw in this a shameful desecration of the dead and responded that as long as he lived, he would not tolerate that people should bury the dead in paper. For that he was put in prison.

He remained true and devoted to his duties until the last minutes of his life and he merited dying in the ghetto without suffering the pain of the concentration camp and the crematorium.

Our Mother

People called her Reb Henech's Wife. Even when speaking directly to her, people used this honorific rather than calling her by her given name, Leah.

She was a careful Jewish woman. She davened three times a day, and she knew all the prayers by heart; but because of her devotion, she feared making an error, so she davened from the "Korban–Minchah–Siddur." I still see her before my eyes with her glasses on, low on her nose, with tape in the broken spots. She also put on her glasses in order to knit various things for her children.

My mother was an expert in keeping house and raising children. I remember her great joy at the marriage of my older brother Hershel, who had a fine wife and who raised his children in the spirit of our household. Later my sister Esther–Gitl got married; my brother Avraham–Yitzchak attended yeshiva, , sang well, and served in the Polish military, where he became an invalid. He married Shimon–Noson–the teacher's daughter, a fine woman, with he had sweet, dear children and built a beautiful family life. Yisrolik also led such a beautiful Jewish life with his wife. All were killed, gassed and cremated by Hitler's murderers.

Shabbos

Unforgettable was out old Jewish home with its rich Jewish life, the customs, Shabbos and yuntuf, that filled our lives with such heartfelt warmth.

Even now I feel the holiness of Friday evenings, when my father and his sons returned from the beis–hamedrash and in our home was heard the beautiful tune of "Shalom aleichem, malachei hashalom." Father's Kiddush sounded beautiful to our ears, which he would not say if one of the children, even one of the daughters, was not yet in the room. It used to happen that one of us, one of the girls, lingered in the street, but one she realized that the men had left their davening, she would hurriedly run home, knowing that Father would wait with his Kiddush.

Our Shabbos food, with the Shabbos tea, which had to be absolutely, perfectly kosher, had a special place in our household. From early on neighbors would come with a scoop to take tea from us, which they would carry off with friendly greetings. In addition, Father's friends would come to drink a glass of Shabbos tea, which was brewed according to the strictest laws.

Holidays

Similar, too, were the yuntufs with the following of all the laws. For Rosh Hashanah our father hastened to the mikveh. On Yom Kippur he went to the mikveh in the morning and in the evening after eating. Back at home, he put on his white kittle, blessed his children, and instilled us with holy awe for the Day of Judgment.

After Yom Kippur, people quickly started to build a succah, a job in which my brothers were busy. The girls helped our mother prepare good foods. My mother always worried lest she be embarrassed in front of others for not having enough food in the succah.

The first night of Succos we all went to hear our father's beautifully sung Kiddush and to have a sip of wine.

Early the next morning we had to get up early to bentsch esrog, because later our father and his sons went to the beis–hamedrash and took the esrog with them. After the prayers, women whose husbands had not bought esrogs came to us to allow them to bentsh esrog. I can still hear their questions as they arrived at our home: "Reb Henech's Wife, can we bentsch esrog here?

My mother answered, both happily and righteously: "With great honor and pleasure!"

In my memory also is the reading of the Megillah at Purim. My father used to read the Megillah at home for us, and we used to invite the neighbors so that they could hear the Megillah. As they left, they would say to us, "God willing, we should hear the reading of the Megillah again in a year."

Especially light and beautiful was the holiday of Passover. The cleaning and scrubbing would begin, updating clothes and shoes; but the nicest part was the seder, reciting the Hagaddah. Father interpreted each verse for us and we relived the great miracle of the exodus from Egypt. We sang "Bimhayrah b'yameinu" and "Chad Gadya."

The mood, the holiness, and the exaltedness of each day remain engraved in my memory and in my spirit to this very day.

[Pages 333-334]

The Nisnkron Family

by Shmuel Nisnkron

Reb Dovid Nisnkron died in 1937. He left four sons and two daughters and grandchildren. In the war, Hitler's forces killed the whole family, except for two sons who, by a miracle, escaped their murderous hands. Yossel today lives in Paris and Shmuelâ€"in America.

Reb Dovid Nisnkron belonged to the distinguished homeowning families in Volomin. He was an Amshinever Hasid and he guided his children on the Hasidic path. His son Aaron was shochet. The others studies in yeshivas and his two daughters were Beis–Ya'akov students.

Reb Dovid's wife was an excellent and kind householder, welcoming to guests, and their home was open to anyone who was in need, for anyone who was travelling to do a mitzvah. Although Reb Dovid was not wealthy, he was always ready to do a kind deed and to give charity with an open hand.

Reb Dovid was an employee in the glass factory. When the glass factory closed, Reb Dovid went into business with blue dishes in the market. From this business he earned his income with dignity, and he was not stingy about spending money on education for his children. He sent them to yeshivas, one to Warsaw, to the Toras Chaim Yeshiva, and one to Baranovitch to the yeshiva of Rabbi Elkhanan Vasserman.

The daughters, students at the Beis Ya'akov School, were always part of a circle of Hasidic daughters.

He was one of those who never sought honors, remaining simple and modest. He was a baal–koreh in the Amshtinever shtiebl, undertook studying lessons in the beis–hamedrash, where each evening between minchah and ma'ariv people studied a chapter of Mishneh or a page of Gemara.

Being happy with his portion, his greatest desire was to guide his children in the paths of righteousness, and he was delighted to have a son who was a shochet in a small shtetl near Kelz.

After Rebb Dovid's death, his wife and daughters continued his business and continued to go on the path that their father had shown them.

When the war broke out , I was in Boronovitch, which was on the Russian side. I continued to study at the yeshivah, having no opportunity to travel to Volomin, even though I desperately wanted to see my mother, my sisters, and my brothers, whom I never saw again. They were murdered, just as all the Jews of Volomin were murdered in the ghetto. None of them escaped the murderous clutches. They struggled to stay alive, but the fate of all the Jews did not avoid them.

My older sister Chantshe in Paris, a married woman with three children, also did not escape the dark fate and she was killed at the savage hands of Hitler's forces. Only I and my brother Yossel remain, the survivors of that large, wonderful family.

[Pages 335-336]

The Wedding in the Ceremony

by Noach Schultz

My father Aaron–Binem was one of the earliest residents in Wolomin. My brothers Chaim the shochet and Shlomo were, together with their families, killed as martyrs. They shared the fate of all the Jews of Wolomin.

At the beginning off 1919 there was a typhus epidemic in Wolomin that claimed many victims, young and old. The first victims were: Sarah Burshtin, a beautiful young woman; the son of Henoch Hinde, Leibl Borokowski; Selig Katzav; the daughter of Yakov Czabak, a young girl.

At that time in the shtetl a conflict erupted between the rabbi and the shochets, who held that they did not earn enough and were not required to support the rabbi. The shochets contended that the householders should bear part of the obligation to support the rabbi. It went so far that the rabbi had put an interdiction on the shochets. This caused terrific unrest among the Jewish population in the shtetl. People sought ways to put an end to the typhus plague. The choice fell on Uleh the water porter, who was chosen to marry Zindl Koval's daughter and to hold the wedding in the cemetery.

The whole town helped to prepare the wedding. Everyone felt like an in–law, and all the Jews of the town came to the ceremony.

Shmuel Vingoro had suggested to the rabbi that they should do a redemption of the spirit. That is, everyone who entered the hall after the wedding should buy a ticket and the money should be given to the newly married couple.

This idea pleased the rabbi, so Shmuel Vingoro and Yitzchak Brotshtein were stationed by the door.

The gathering was truly startling. Everyone wanted to go in and take a peek at the bride, who stood near the Warsaw baker. The Jews happily contributed, for they believed that the wedding in the cemetery would bring salvation from the epidemic.

[Pages 337-341]

Traditions of Shabbos and Weekdays

by Devorah Grajinski

Translated by Theodore Steinberg

Summer. On Friday evenings on the long street of the shtetl there is a crowded movement. It is only the train coming from Warsaw, the last train before candle lighting. People hurry home. Those are the Jewish passengers who are hurrying home, eager to be with their families before darkness arrives and the Shabbos Queen arrives.

Wolomin's Jews lived hurried lives. Rushing was a normal part of their existence. Life in the shtetl was bound up with the big city, Warsaw, which was only nineteen kilometers away. The merchant might travel several times a day, whether with a few zlotys to bring merchandise for his little store or to seek other business. The worker traveled every day to his job, there and back. The students studied in Warsaw, in the gymnasium or the trade schools. Others went to take care of various matters in government offices or institutions whose headquarters were in Warsaw.

In contrast to most Jewish settlements in Poland, Wolomin was a relatively new shtetl, and as a new settlement it grew around and focused on the train station. As time passed, the shtetl spread out, taking up a greater area, and new neighborhoods were formed, though they were settled by non–Jews.

Around the train station, on the long street and in the smaller streets such as Warshavski, Kosczcelne and others was the business district, where the Jewish merchants had established their businesses and shops.

Also to be found there were a few huge factories owned by Jews—the glassworks, the foundry, the factory for iron beds–which employed hundreds of people.

During the week, the area was in tumult and chaos. But on Friday evenings, the tumult quieted. The shops closed, the merchants and workers hurried to be home earlier in order to welcome the coming Shabbos.

From the homes wafted the aromas of cooking fish and other Shabbos delicacies. Through the open windows you could see the sparkling lights of the Shabbos candles, which conveyed that Jewish homes had thrown off the everyday world, the gestures and the tumult of making an income, along with all the weekday worries, and they put on instead their Shabbos comforts, their Shabbos souls, so that over the whole shtetl, covering everyone, floated the special rest of Shabbos.

The Jews of the shtetl kept Shabbos.

"Good Shabbos! Good Shabbos!" the Jews greeted each other.

Good Shabbos greetings filled the summer air like the fluttering of wings from the birds overhead.

Adults and children streamed toward the beis–hamedrash. All the Jews went, tall and short, thin and not–so–thin. They went slowly and quickly, old and young Jews with heads held high, long beards, with large and small deeply–sunk eyes, walking majestically. They were going to pray, and meanwhile they considered God's world.

Then in the beis–hamedrash Jews again wished, "Good Shabbos. Good Shabbos!" Bliss shone from their faces. Their voices mixed together like bees on a blossoming branch. The entrance way opened and closed. More and more Jews arrived, prayed. A mixture of voices like a disorganized choir filled the shul. The atmosphere became heavier. The heat became laden with the odor of God's name. The leader of the prayers stood by the prayer stand, and soon was heard the "Lechu neranena," and the congregation responded enthusiastically. The contact between silk and fabric of the Shabbos garments rustled like corn stalks in the summer breeze. The Jews prayed, rocked back and forth, some with their heads and shoulders, others with their whole bodies, some silently and some in full voice.

Arriving back at his bright home, the father says a loud "Good Shabbos" and soon he strides across the room, with his hands behind his back, and begins to say "Shalom Aleichem, malachei hashares...." The father says this as though the angels should walk around his house. When he arrives at the wall, he stands still, sticks out both hands, and says, as if he is speaking to the angels, "Go out in peace." He warmed himself up with the angels. Later he broke up the silence and began to sing "Ayshes chayil mi yimsta," drawing out every word with his tune. Then he went to the table and poured the wine for Kiddush. The wine cup was a family heirloom, a gift for my parents' wedding. My father closed his eyes and said, "Yom hashishi, vayechulu hashamayim ve'ha'aretz v'chol tsva'am." He said it word by word. The words filled the stillness with warmth and sanctity.

The children were already impatient, but they listened politely to Father's Kiddush as they sat around the table. My parents ate slowly. Between courses my father sang, "Kol m'kadesh shevi'I k'raui lo." He sang a Chasidic tune, rocking back and forth as he sang. The house was full of music. Three–quarters of the Shabbos candles were already burnt out. One light began to drip. The wax dripped on the silver candlesticks. The children's faces beamed. We all sat bent over our plates and ate. Finally we sang again, "Menuchah v'simch or laye'hudim." As the youngsters grew older, they became more impatient. They had no time. They ate quickly and went away, seeking to relieve the spiritual malaise that existed so strongly among Wolomin's young people, especially in the thirties. There were at that time intensive community activities. Some went to gatherings of Zionist organizations, like Hashomer Hatzair, Hechalutz, Betar, Gordonia, and others, where the new type of young Jews were formed with pioneering spirit, where the dream of a Jewish renaissance was woven, of a national rebirth in a Jewish homeland. There they danced the hora and sang songs of national redemption. They could talk about how they would realize their intentions to make aliyah.

Others went to the Beis Yakov School on Leshne Street, in Kershne's house. There they studied and commented on the week's Torah portion . The beautiful Torah stories kindled their youthful imaginations. Calling forth feelings of pride in the glorious past, they awakened strength and hope for a better future.

In the Beis Yakov School many of Wolomin's young women received their traditional education. The organizers were the leaders of Agudas Yisroel: Moyshe Gradszitzki, Yitzchak Shtulman, Yehuda–Leib Baum, Shmuel–Eizik Klatkovski, and others. The teacher who ran the school was Chana Gilevska–Garfinkel, the daughter of the head of the Mir Yeshiva. She lives today in New York. Herself quite observant, she instilled in us a love and devotion to Jewish tradition and Jewish values in all of their aspects. After she left Wolomin, her position was taken by Leah Merzer, the daughter of a Chasidic family in Warsaw. She undertook the job with tremendous devotion, taught the young girls the principles of Jewish ethics, of human dignity. The last teacher was Sarah Borochovitsch from Zhelikhov, a gentle and refined soul. She was young enough that she also became our friend, someone in whom we could confider. Because of the strict educational methods, children also had a strong need for a warm friendship with their teacher. It is no wonder that we felt so close to this teacher, Sarahle. She earned our greatest respect, this beautiful person, and we give honor to our memory of this beloved friend, whose friendship had such an influence on me and on the other girls. Sadly, she shared in the fate of our martyrs.

Awakening the memories of the Beis Yakov School and the later B'nos Agudas Yisroel requires that I recall the students of that time, whose beautiful lives were cut short in their early years by the murderers. I always see before my eyes the honored Dinah Zilberberg, the sweet Fradl Boym, who had such a gorgeous voice; the refined Bluma Schwartz, Chaya Flotkowski, Chana–Golda Shtulman, Leatsche Taub, Rivka Filzman, Rivka Tzirl, and so many others whose names time has erased from my memory.

I should also remember the young people of Agudas Yisroel who made so many contributions to the activities in the Beis Yakov School. The organization of Agudas Yisroel Youth gathered in the modern Talmud Torah in the rebuilt wing of the beis–hamedrash, which people called "Der Binyan" [The Building]. This Talmud Torah was led by Moyshe–Feyvel Shtulman, who had studied for many years in a variety of yeshivas and who excelled thanks to his extraordinary dynamism. Friday nights were also joyous in the Peretz Library. People read, talked, and discussed, or they just spent time there. There also the revolutionaries gathered, those who believed that only a revolution could bring salvation. Observant Jews did not regard the Peretz Library favorably, regretting that their children were infected with enthusiasm for the ideas of socialist justice and brotherhood, for freedom, equality, and our highest ideals, that resonated so strongly among Wolomin's young people.

There were meetings and gatherings where people considered actual problems, and always these evenings were filled with song, with Jewish folksongs, with nostalgia and a hope for a better tomorrow, for a world of righteousness and justice.

Afterwards the young people would go for a walk around the shtetl. In the houses the Shabbos candles were burned down and the streets were slowly enveloped in a serene Shabbos sleep.

[Pages 342-343]

Zlateh

by Miriam Gradjitzki–Feinboym

Translated by Theodore Steinberg

Like every shtetl, Wolomin had its own unique types and characters, who stood out for their specialness. One such figure was Zlateh, the wife of Shmuel–Eizik Plotkovski. She was a quiet and pious woman, an exemplar of goodness. She was always occupied, with a large family, eight children and a sick husband. By herself she ran a manufacturing business. When there were no customers, she sat and prayed from her siddur. She always thought about the neediness of the shtetl. She knew in which houses people went hungry and when to bring something to eat.

During the cold days of winter she worried about the women in the surrounding shops, bringing them a glass of hot tea to warm them up, sharing with each a kind word, whether of comfort or encouragement.

Poor people often arrived in the shtetl, and if it happened that there was nowhere for them to sleep or eat, there was always a place for another person at Zlateh's.

Thus it was for the whole week, but when Shabbos came, Zlateh's home was transformed into a tea house. It was the custom in the Jewish shtetls in Poland that on Shabbos a Christian woodsman would come early in the morning to light a fire in the oven, but not every home could afford to light a fire. But in every home they knew they could come to Zlateh for a glass of hot tea.

Please understand, this required boiling many kettles of water, and the water had to be brought from a distance, because people sought a well with the best water. Zlateh's tea was famous throughout the shtetl, because what she did came entirely from the goodness of her heart. Therefore, in the middle of the week people began to anticipate the Shabbos tea. They bought sugar and prepared glasses and cups and tea ingredients.

From early in the morning on Shabbos, people began to come to Zlateh for tea. Many were not satisfied with only one glass. These were passionate tea drinkers who would drink five or more glasses of tea at a time. Zloteh showed everyone great patience, calming down those who had to wait for a place until the earlier arrivals were all drunk out.

People didn't come just to drink a glass of tea at that spot, but they came with teapots to take tea home to their children. At Zlateh's, no one went without tea, and thus it proceeded for all of Shabbos. While others took their Shabbos nap, Zlateh remained on her feet. She had no time to rest while people went in and out, and she did it all with heartfelt warmth, as if every glass of tea that she served gave her great pleasure.

Such was Zlateh.

From her large family, only two daughters remain, Rachel Grossinger, who survived the war in Russia, and Hendl, who hid in a village with a shepherd. Both daughters now live in America.

[Pages 344-345]

Jewish Livelihoods

by Malkeh Grinberg–Yellen

Translated by Theodore Steinberg

Between the two world wars, Jews in Wolomin, just like in all the other Yiddish shtetls in Poland, were mostly in business. In the later years, the war against Jewish businesses intensified. In addition to high taxes, a boycott was declared against Jewish businesses, and picketers were sent out. At that time the peasants and the workers liked shopping in Jewish businesses. The newly arrived Christian merchants were stiff, withdrawn, and showed no special courtesy.

The customers simply did not feel comfortable in the Christian businesses. They did not dare to touch any merchandise with their hands. They had to take off their hats, but most of all the prices in the Christian businesses were higher than in the Jewish ones. And they could not haggle. The prices were fixed.

In the Jewish businesses and shops, the Christian customers felt free. They could touch the merchandise as much as they wanted, go back and forth on the prices, get credit, and pay in monthly installments.

The Jewish merchants and shopkeepers were informal, familiar, not distant, took an interest in the private worries of their Christian patrons and understood their problems, their customs, and their habits in buying and business. The Jewish merchants also dealt in local products that the peasants brought to sell in the village.

The shops and stores were fairly primitive, often lacking even doors, so that the merchants used to suffer from the frost and wind during the long winters, and they would warm their frozen hands over firepots.

Such were the poor shops. There were, however, higher class merchants with better appointed stores who conducted business on a larger scale, though their number was small.

Jews in Wolomin were represented in the following professions:

Manufacturing: Shmuel–Eizik Flotkowski, Yoske Laskowski, Shprintze Boym, and others.

Leather and shoe accessories: Mottl Rubenshteyn and Abba Fromm. Shoe manufacturing: Listfogel, Yungerman.

Glassworks and kitchen containers: Mordechai and Chana Grodzhitski. Iron manufacturing: Nisn and Pesse Vagman. Coal storage: Mandberg. Bookseller: Shtatman.

I try as hard as I can to remember more names, but it is not easy. I remember the Radziminski food shops on Warsaw Street, Shmyentanke on Dluga, Shachna, and others whose names I have forgotten

---

[Pages 346-347]

Our Home–A Fortress of Goodness

by Yisroel Manne

Translated by Theodore Steinberg

I see before me my father, Chaim–Noach Manne, speaking to me his heartfelt and intelligent words. I see this scene constantly before my eyes. He rises from his unknown grave in the ghetto and reminds me of the goodness in the world.

He was down to earth and good not only with his wife, our mother, Chaya–Rachel, for whom he had such great love; with his children–four sons: Moyshe, Yechezkel, Yisroel, and Melechl–and two daughter: Freida and Dvorah–but also with his friends and acquaintances.

He was a great jokester, and there was a lot of laughter when people spoke with him and he shared jokes and witticisms that also contained much wisdom, an understanding of human weakness, and hopes for better times.

In 1930, when the handworkers' union was formed, he became the chairman until it was shut down, and everyone felt that he was a support in hard times.

Poor people who journeyed through Wolomin knew of him. Hungry people came to him with the assurance that he would provide them with something to eat. As a trustee in the "Welcome to Guests" fellowship, he worried about whether they would have a place to lay down their heads and rest from their travels.

I remember "Welcome to Guests" the way people remember emotional things from their childhood years. The office was found in the beis–hamedrash on Leshne Street.

On the upper floor there were two rooms. In one room was a Holy Ark, and a minyan prayed there every Shabbos. In the other room were several beds where every stranger could be an honored guest and could spend a night, or more, without paying.

He always stuck out his neck for others. Just as a year is divided into seasons, so for him it was divided into mitzvos Shabbos and weekday, by day and by night. The hardest were the ones at night, when, God forbid, something happened in the town and one had to run out in all conditions to advise or to help.

His favorite mitzvah was welcoming guests, which he did wholeheartedly, by day or by night. He used to write memos to this or that householder saying that he should take in a guest for Shabbos.

When the Germans burned the beis–hamedrash building, for my father it was a many–sided blow, because in the building were the guest rooms and he could no longer help the poor people who flooded into Wolomin.

I was not in the ghetto. I escaped and experienced Siberian labor camps. When, after the war, I returned to Poland and visited our shtetl, which was ruined and bare, people told me that also in the ghetto my father's house was a gathering place for people to pray, which meant risking their lives.

His fate was bound up with that of Wolomin's Jews, for ever and ever, and his home was always a fortress of goodness.

[Pages 348-350]

Our Glasswork Workers

by Xenia Katz–Manne

Translated by Theodore Steinberg

We were nine children when we were left alone with our mother Rachel because our father had been drafted into the Russian army.

The First World War had broken out.

Our mother tormented herself to feed her nine children, to clothe them and to educate them. She worked beyond her strength in order to pay teachers. When Matthis, Yankel, and Moyshe were young, she sent them to study at the Voldova Yeshiva.

When in Wolomin, as in the other shtetls, a typhus epidemic began to rage, it struck our overworked mother and she died.

We were orphans.

Our father was at the front, and we prayed day and night for his well–being. We hoped and waited for his return.

Meanwhile the older children assumed the roles of parents, cared for the younger ones, made sure that they ate and studied. But it was not long before our youngest brother, Berl, fell victim to typhus. Shortly after him, the oldest sister, Chanah, died. She had been married shortly before and left her husband, Sholem, with a two–year–old daughter, Kailtche. Later she came to live with us.

Later our oldest brother Yankel passed away. He also had a wife and a child.

Six of us remained, without means to live, without supervision, abandoned, lonely.

How I rack my brains trying to reconstruct how and with what powers we six orphans managed to sustain ourselves in such hard times.

But you should know that even in such sad times there were brighter moments of Jewish compassion and sympathy shown by the Jews of Wolomin. They helped us through those difficult times, until our father returned from the army.

The horrors that our father had encountered took a toll on his strength. The changes in him were obvious. He did not fall totally into despair, but the responsibilities of life and for his helpless children wearied him. From being a religious Jew with a beard, he became a "freethinker."

Our father worked at the Vitrus Glassworks, where he held a position as a "puffer." He was among the first Jewish workers in the glassworks; and later, when many young Jewish men and women wanted to work in the glassworks, my father did them many favors, helping them get hired and showing them how to excel in the work.

My father's help for these young people had great significance, because the leadership of the glassworks, even the Jews, often did not want to hire Jews, because that often caused antagonism among the Polish workers, and they did not want to cause conflicts. My father's ambition was to show that Jews could be outstanding workers.

My two brothers, Itzik and Sholem, also worked in the glassworks. Their jobs were to take the hot glass to the molds. They were apprentices and became masters. They were the only Jews in this trade, not only in Wolomin but in all of Poland, where at that time Jews were not hired for this difficult industry.

Wolomin was a successful place. Wolomin's Jews, young and middle–aged, had broken through the wall of prejudice not only among the Polish workers but also among the Jewish bosses, the higher–ups. The Jewish workers did not lag behind the Poles. They often surpassed them in their professional knowledge and qualifications.

The Jewish working people in Wolomin did their work conscientiously and with confidence. They conducted themselves with an attitude of reciprocity and courtesy.

In time, professional work also developed in Wolomin. Even the bosses organized a handworkers union.

Eventually the work became a contentious element. From time to time speakers came from Warsaw for readings and lectures. People started reading newspapers, brochures, and books.

The natural surroundings of the shtetl were gorgeous. Thick woods, fields, and a flowing river. Summer arrived, young men went walking with young women, they sang songs, some openly and some secretly so that their parents would not know.

Everywhere the young people were active, ebullient, full of life and energy, deeply convinced that there would be brighter future under the influence of high ideals, along with the traditions of their fathers and grandfathers.

From the distance of the years that have passed, I see these Jews in their full beauty. How much fairness, how much feeling for social justice these young people felt! What a holy sense they had of a fine working life, but it was so horribly cut off!

[Pages 351-352]

Jewish Youth in Heavy Industry

by Yakov Rosenblatt

Translated by Theodore Steinberg

In 1927 I arrived in the shtetl of Wolomin, which lay by the train line that led from the Vilna Station in Warsaw. Through Wolomin, which was eighteen kilometers from Warsaw, ran about forty round–trip trains daily, both regular and express. On this line also ran a daily express train to the Soviet border shtetl of Nigarelyana.

Wolomin Jews made daily journeys to Warsaw and back: these were Jewish merchants and workers who either worked in Warsaw or sought work there. Warsaw was to Wolomin like a house was to an attic: one jump and one was in Warsaw, or back in Wolomin.

There were two glass factories in Wolomin: one, "Vitrum," with its Jewish owner Flanzreich and his partner, the apostate Renglevski. There the director was Aharon Hersh Gortnkraut. Later his place was taken by a German. The Vitrum glassworks were always free of Jews. They wanted to hire no Jewish workers. Later on, two Jews came to work there. One, Yerachmiel Zbertchuk, a cousin of the poet, became general overseer and chief sorter of faceted glass. The other, Ephraim Katz, had worked in the warehouse. These two Jews did a lot to pave the way for other Jewish men and women to work in the glassworks. How much more did these two help the Jewish workers in the factory.

Ephraim Katz's two sons, while they were still young, helped to tend the fires in the ovens. They were the only such Jewish workers in the factory: over time, Itzik and Sholem became masters. It was very rare in all of Poland to see Jewish glassworkers in such positions.

Another Jew, Likerman, was overseer over other kinds of glass. In the warehouse worked Zanvel Gortnkraut, the former director's brother. At the iron molds worked Dudtsche Latke with his younger brother, Aharon Latke. The poet worked as a sorter. Both of Katz's daughters also worked in the glassworks. Zashe worked at painting glass, while Zhenia had a number of jobs. My two sisters, Zelda and Dvorah Rosenblatt, along with Malkeh Zitzbank and Beila Demski, worked at wrapping the glass in paper and bags. Beila Fiasetzka worked at a variety of jobs, like shaping the glass. Malkeh Yelyen had earlier worked at fusing glass and later as a sorter. Other workers were Zhenia Asman, several Trosterman sisters, Chaim Veynrib, Hershel and other Jewish workers whose names I cannot remember. Thus Jews entered the Vitrum glassworkds and became a good support for their elders.

There was another glassworks, a cooperative, called Fratza. Only Poles worked there. Two steel plants, one bed factory owned by, I think, Veynman. A Jew was the bookkeeper there. There were also several Jewish workers, among them Moyshe Fostalski. In another steel plant worked Leon Buden. I don't know whether other Jews worked there.

From those days, when Jewish youth from the town and the shtetl had little employment, because even the big Jewish–owned factories did not want to hire Jewish workers, was the achievement of Zbertchuk and Katz noteworthy, for they helped many young men and women from Wolomin at a time when most Jewish young people struggled with making a living and had to travel to neighboring Warsaw to find jobs, which was like splitting the Red Sea.

[Pages 353-357]

My Home Shtetl

by Helle Goldvasser–Budni

Translated by Theodore Steinberg

At the beginning of the eighteenth century, Wolomin was still a small settlement in the midst of woods and swamps that were teeming with all kinds of creatures. The elders of the shtetl used to tell stories and legends about how people lived in earlier times in the surrounding areas, carrying axes out of the fears that threatened them, so that people called the place "Woleh–amin," which means, "Chase away the fear with axes."

My grandfather, Mottl Griziak, with his wife and children, was among the first inhabitants of Wolomin. Wolomin at that time bore little resemblance to the Wolomin in which my sisters and I entered the world. Our childhood years passed by in a Wolomin which had grown with time and changed its appearance. There were two glass factories, two iron factories, two tanneries, and many workshops.

The owners and partners in the factories were Jews. All around were large living quarters for the workers. The population in Wolomin grew quickly. A portion of the young people found employment in the established factories.

Among the Jewish population in Wolomin, the greatest majority were handworkers in the old Jewish crafts: shoemakers, tailors, carpenters, brushmakers, tinsmiths, and textile workers.

But there was no lack of poor people in Wolomin's Jewish population. Many Jewish families lacked even bread and potatoes.

The Budni family, Dovid and Rivkah, were also among the first Jewish inhabitants of Wolomin. He had a tailor shop from which he earned a living for his growing family.

In our home, all the holidays were strictly observed, according to tradition and law. Yom Kippur is most deeply etched in my memory. Even today it remains so vividly in my mind, and I cannot free myself from the great terror that befell us in the evening before we went to the Kol Nidrei service. My father wrapped himself in his tallis. ready to go to shul. He called each of his children individually, laid his hands on their heads and blessed them. These were very moving moments, and with loud voices we wished each other a good year.

Later on my parents went with my brothers to shul while we, the girls, stayed at home. We sat by the burning candles and waited, with fear in our hearts, for our parents to return from their prayers.

In general, people in Wolomin took pride in the arrival of the High Holidays, those fearsome and holy days. The preparations were different, more spiritual than those for other holidays, For certain people, the season of trembling and fear began on the fifteenth of Av. Chasidic Jews stayed in their study houses through the night. Already if one parted from someone from another town, he wished him a year sealed for good.

When the month of Elul arrived with its shofar blowing and psalm recitations early every morning in the beis–hamedrash, even we girls felt that the days of self–examination and purification, forgiveness and repentance, good deeds of righteousness and charity had arrived.

It appeared that every day the people of the shtetl became more careful with their words. People spoke more quietly, in more refined ways, and I believe that also in business dealings people behaved in more seemly ways.

The first selichos services began in the middle of the night. Young and old felt it. In the dark streets people made their way to the beis–hamdedrash, and even though I was sleeping at home, it seemed to me that I could hear the voices of those praying dries to the Throne of Glory, begging for themselves and for all Israel.

In my childish heart I could feel the awakening of Erev Rosh Hashanah and when the Jews in the shul recited Psalms and went to visit the cemetery, but the culmination of the season was Erev Yom Kippur.

My pencil is too feeble to record the mood, the drama, and the feelings of Erev Yom Kippur. That mood dominated every year until the Disaster, even when a large part of the Jewish young people became more worldly and some of them had abandoned their faith.

Almost all of the Jews in Wolomin on Erev Yom Kippur were pervaded by that fearful mood. Some people went three times that day to the mikveh, before morning prayers, before afternoon prayers, and after the concluding meal. The women also immersed themselves.

On that day Jews gave charity generously. Several hours before candle–lighting time, the whole Jewish population was dressed for the holiday. The women wore mostly white headscarves or shawls on their heads. Everyone went to neighbors, friends, and acquaintances to wish them a good year, that they might be inscribed for good.

We, the young girls and boys, were affected by the mood of our parents, so that we also asked forgiveness from each other for whatever offenses we might have committed, for angry or incorrect conduct.

From many homes came sounds of lamentation, indications of broken hearts. Jewish mothers lamented the fate that awaited their children and with tears wished for a divine decree..

Children clung to their mothers. Men went through the streets with tear–stained eyes. Even those who did not cry had tears in their voices.

The mood was sincere, holy, and fearful.

With broken hearts, full of fear and trembling for the great day of judgment, people went early to the beis–hamedrash, to the prayer houses and Chasidic prayer houses to say the special prayers and the confession to the Master of Miracles, before the chazzan began Kol Nidrei.

We hear so many tunes and melodies throughout our lives, but no melody is etched so deeply in our memories as the melody of Kol Nidrei.

The melody echoed through the stillness of Wolomin's streets, entered our house, where we, the girls, remained alone by the light of the burning candles. We did not then grasp the meaning and did not understand the sense of the words, but we felt, in this still and deep night, that the melody expressed the prayer of all the Jews in the world, from all places and all generations.

As I write about this small aspect of our home, the memory tugs at me of our grandfather and grandmother, my zayde and bubbe: Mottl and Friveh Griziak, z"l; our parents, Rivkah and Dovid Budni, who were killed in Treblinka, my sister Dara, who was at the war's outbreak the miother of two daughters. With her husband and children, she was killed at Treblinka.

My brother Noach, who was an active member of Gordonia, in 1939 went illegally to Eretz Yisroel. He was a member of the Mishmar–Hasharon Kibbutz. In 1940 he died tragically. He drowned in the Sea of Tiberias. My brother Leon also died suddenly in 1963 in Israel. My aunt Esther and uncle Shoyme and my cousin Darkeh Schultz.

From our large family, the only survivors are the authors of this article: Helle Goldvassero–Budni and Fellah Indershteyn–Budni.

[Page 358]

Noah Bodni's Grave

by Shmuel Zucker

Translated by Theodore Steinberg

In the woods at Mishmar-HaSharon
Stands a stone among the stones
Engraved with words in memory of
Young Noah Bondi's bones.

Early on you left your home
To lead the way for those who stayed,
But then the Jordan swallowed you
Before your words could be conveyed.

You dreamed about a clear blue sky
While on your lips was borne
A song of sprouting fields
And flourishing corn.

And then the flowers blossomed
That you sowed with loving care,
But faithfully they wait for you,
Though you can't return from there.

Of your family there is no one left,
No parents, wife, or child,
And your grave in hams, rain, and wind
Is subject to elements wild.

In the woods at Mishmar-HaSharon
Stands a stone among the stones
Engraved with words in memory of
Young Noah Bondi's bones.

[Pages 360-361]

Ulla the Water Porter

by Rachtshe Asch

Translated by Theodore Steinberg

Everyone called him The Matchmaker, though no one knew whether in his whole life he had actually arranged a match. People knew that he was extremely poor. Together with his wife and two sons he lived in a dark hole where poverty shrieked from every corner.

Both sons, Shloyme and Ulla, grew up free and wild, showed no fear of their father, were always hungry, and went around in torn clothing.

Their mother used search among old discarded clothing for something for them to wear. She sat with a bowed head and searched, listening while her husband taught us girls how to pray. After a while she would start to hum under her breath one of the prayer tunes.

There was great sadness in that tune, a plea that sent a cry to the Master of the Universe asking why He had forgotten her. I heard her murmur, "People live, they have apartments, enough bread to eat…"

My friend Doveh Budny and I learned to pray with The Matchmaker. When I remember the poverty of his home, I get very sad. In my home I used to lie with open eyes and wonder why people were afflicted with such povetrty.

When Ulla grew up, he became a water porter, carrying water to Jewish homes. When I would see him go by with his pails and mutter to himself–I would think of his mother, how she would sit in a corner of the room where her husband taught girls to pray and she would murmur about people who lived with apartments and enough bread to eat.

[Pages 362-364]

Our Home

by Esther Tayblum–Kornfeld

Translated by Theodore Steinberg

A thousand threads bind me to my home–shtetl Wolomin. My father, Shmuel Tayblum, was the very first of the Tayblums to settle in Wolomin. Right after him came his two brothers, Pinchas and Mendel. All three of the brothers were involved in the wood and building material trade.

Wolomin was still a small settlement with just a small number of Jews. At home I often heard stories about those early years, when the earth was slowly transformed from woods and swamp and started to be arable. Winter corn and spring grains. Houses sprung up in the town and the population grew.

Our family, too, grew. There were fourteen children in our house. I was eight years old when my father died, but his ways of acting are engraved in my memory, our religiously observed Shabboses, the bookish depths with which he approached everything. He was an observant Jew, an Alexander Chasid.

As was the custom among Chasidim, we made early matches for the children. But at my father's death, there were still eight unmarried children. They were still quite young, and it was difficult for my mother to raise them.

What was then a greater joy than for a mother to see her sons studying day and night? "For what," my mother murmured with a sigh, "for what do I work if not so that my children will be fine Jews, to learn and to walk in God's paths?"

For that, day and night she prayed to God and praised him for His help in raising her children, and as they grew, things became easier for her. She derived so much nachas from them, and she made marriages for all of her children aside from Mina, who was the youngest and still awaited her intended.

Ah, Mama, how well you raised your children. In your quiet glances we could see the emotions in your motherly heart. You felt each child's pains and rejoiced in each child's happiness. For each of us you found the right words to comfort us in difficult times.

Always, dear Mother, you were with us, and your blessings washed over our heads with promises of plenty, with hopes for a life without sorrows.

With your fervent wishes and blessings, it was easier for us to go through life, surviving hard times and hoping for better.

You nourished us with heartfelt prayers when we were little–and when we were grown, as well.

It seems to me even today that I can feel your hand on my forehead when I had a high fever.

Your great worry was that we should, with God's help, be healthy, commit no sins, and always follow the laws of kashruth.

My dear mother, the bloody war put an end to all of your hopes. She was killed, together with her children and grandchildren, together with all of Wolomin's Jews who were sent to Treblinka.

From our large family, from all my brothers and sisters, I alone remain alive so that I may mourn their gruesome deaths.

My brother Moyshe was still a young man when the Second World War broke out. From his earliest years he demonstrated good–heartedness. He never refused to do a kindness or a good deed.

Early on, Moyshe began to think about Eretz Yisroel. He was a thoroughgoing Zionist, and he spent a great deal of money on Zionist causes. He always showed an open hand when it was time to collect money for Keren Hayisd and Keren Kayames.

My mother got great nachas from him. The lumber warehouse that he managed and the business in which he was a partner made him an influential man. In partnership with my brother Itshe he built houses and became like a true father to his sisters, and he always took care that his mother should lack nothing.

My brother Moyshe was fated to be the first victim that the Gestapo arrested in Wolomin. After seizing his business, they came looking for the boss. When they could not find him at home, they took his wife Chana and declared that when Moyshe appeared, they would free her.

Everyone knew that his appearance would not free Chana. The Germans and their deceptions were already well known. But Moyshe could not work at hiding while his wife sat in prison, so he turned himself in to the Gestapo, with only the slightest hope that they would release his wife, the mother of his children.

They immediately sent him to Dachau, to the well–known concentration camp, from which he never returned.

And the Germans never freed his wife Chana.

The two of them were the first victims among the people of Wolomin, already in 1939, even before the ghetto was created.

Already at that time our way of life was beginning to disappear and the way of death began, until it turned into the full catastrophe.

[Page 365]

Idealism

by Esther Blumenkranz

Translated by Theodore Steinberg

Not far from the big city of Warsaw, Wolomin had all the advantages of a shtetl, ringed around by villages, fields, and woods. All sorts of threads bound together the shtetl and the villages. Jews traded with peasants. They went to the villages, and on market days the peasants came to the shtetl with their wagons full of produce and greenery, with hens and ducks, cows and calves.

People were also bound up with Warsaw. There was mutual trade, marriages were made, family and social relationships. Our proximity to Warsaw gave our shtetl a big–city coloring, invigorated the activities of young organizers, who arranged readings and lectures on literary and political topics. People sang and danced and dreamed about a better life, the dream of exile.

With sorrow we remember the pulsing life in our shtetl and always will be carry in our hearts the love of idealism of our youth, the fine qualities of our parents, the great passing on of traditions of our scholars and teachers, the Jewish doctors and dentists who showed such consideration for the poor who became ill.

How wonderful were our older people who carried their age with dignity and love for the young, who showed their elders the traditional Jewish respect and learned from their rich experience. So, too, from their teachers and religious scholars and from everyday Jews whose humanity became apparent as people got to know them and see into their souls.

Unforgettable holy martyrs, your memory will always be engraved in our hearts.

[Pages 366-369]

The Young People of My Shtetl

by M. Fotograf

Translated by Theodore Steinberg

There was a shtetl in Poland called Wolomin with a thousand Jewish souls. The shtetl is now empty of Jews, without a single Jew. There were Jewish streets and alleys that were engraved with their distinctive life, with prayer, with learning, with work, with dreams, with songs, and with the struggle for a more beautiful and better Jewish life.

This was all once–upon–a–time, when Jews in Wolomin worked, traded, built, created, raised new generations, and hoped that better times would come.

Today, after the bitter storm of the Nazi murderers, all hopes are gone, together with the lives, and Wolomin remains without Jews.

Now I write for the Memory Book, which must serve as part of the inscription on the tombstone that we, the living, spread over the whole world, set up for the martyrs of our shtetl; a tombstone for all those Jews who are no more, although the heart will not admit it to be so.

The heart is joined to every heartbeat of those people before they were murdered.

The heart sees the shape of its near and dear, of friend and acquaintance–they are with me everywhere, when I wake and when I dream.

I see those from my early childhood and my early years, in our common dreams and aspirations, among which the first spot was taken by our yearning for a free Jewish homeland.

This was in 1924, when, on my way home from school, I would cross Lifshitz's courtyard, which went between Wilenska Street on one side and Pshechodnia on the other. The Ser, Markovyetzki, Groysband, and other families lived there. On one side was the Polish Folkshule, which was in Anshel Jagoda's house. On the other side were the houses of Shtreich and Bendler.

In this courtyard, the members of Hashomer Hatza'ir used to assemble in their plaid shirts, and I loved to watch them and to hear the commands: attention, forward, and so on. Occasionally they would go out into the town, marching or walking in rows, and we children would be jealous and dream of marching in such a way.

Finally the day came when with great pomp they accepted us into the ranks of the smallest members. Our leader was Tuvia Ratbard, who was, to our eyes, tall and slender, and quite an authority figure.

The middle rank was led by Yosef Shapiro. The top rank, by Leibl Sheynboym. The oldest rank, who did not wear neckerchiefs, was led by Mendel Sheynboym.

We would meet twice a week, and we were so proud of our membership, with marching in straight lines. We also had our own bugler, Yidl Feinerman. On summer evenings he would play a call at Veynman's place. That was a signal for a meeting. It could be heard throughout the town, in the streets: Dluga, Leshne, Ogradave, Koshtshelne. After a while we were required to buy yellow neckerchiefs.

On Lag B'Omer we put on shirts and short pants and went to Radzimin, marching through the streets in four groups. In the first row were the oldest young men with Mendel Sheynboym at their head. He was the leader of the whole group.

Before my eyes, I see, as though they were still living, the members of the first group: Vinagora, Laskovski, Feynerman, Sheynboym, Zammer, and many others whose names I have forgotten.

In the village of Tcharne we stopped for breakfast. We came to Radzimin before noon, gathering at the Rabbi's spot, where the Jewish residents greets us. On the way back to Wolomin, we sang. It was already dark when we marched back into town with torches in our hands, parading down Dluga Street to the Shill–Place and back and back to our starting point in Sheynboym's house.

I remember those times, when Dina Felder managed Hashomer. She organized a celebration, brought a Jewish band from Warsaw, and we marched through the streets and to the woods with blue and white banners to the sound of the band.

Carefree childhood years, filled with study and play, but simultaneously with longing for redemption. As we played soccer, we thought about the future, when we would be pioneers in Eretz Yisroel.

More than once we broke windows and the shammos, Topol, would ask us kindly that we should play elsewhere, where there were no buildings with windows and where we would not disturb the beis–hamedrash students in their studies.

I remember how we once went to Mandelberg's place, where there were stacks of baking supplies that the bakers used. There we organized our games. Once, on a Friday, while we were playing, R. Nechemiah Mandelberg arrived and we fled out of fear, leaving behind the balls we had been playing with.

R. Nechemiah Mandelberg picked them up and called after us: "Children, why are you running? Come and play. No one will do you harm."

From that time on, that was our usual spot to play football, and R. Nechamiah Mandelberg was our guardian.

Several years passed. There had been an interruption in the activities of Hashomer Hatza'ir. With much effort, we decided to re–establish our organization with a new name: Mlodzi Stroj.

Again we conducted educational activities. After a while, Moyshe Flotkovski, Eliezer Bergazin, Moyshe Veynbrom, Golde Goldvasser, and Shloyme Tabakman, who had led the organization, went to pioneer training camp and younger members took over the leadership.

Several times we had to change our headquarters, going from Benders house near the depot to Tik's house on Agrodova and then to the Lastfogel's on Leshne Street.

We dreamed of making aliyah, but very few fulfilled that dream.

The great war destroyed Jewish life. The young people who survived the Nazi hell escaped to Soviet Siberia, or joined the partisans and are now with us in Israel.

[Pages 370-376]

My Last Day at Home

by Shmuel Zucker

Translated by Theodore Steinberg

It was a rainy day. There were dark clouds in the sky. There were thunder and lightning. It seemed as if nature was reflecting what went on in my mother's heart.

My mother was pale as she walked around the house. She could not stop her tears, which ran from her blue eyes down her sorrowful face. Our glances met silently, quiet glances that spoke more powerfully than words.

The sorrows of my mother's afflicted feelings screamed out from her face, the feelings of a mother at the moment that she loses her child.

I was also sorrowful, because it was difficult to part from my wonderful mother. At that moment I wished that I was once again a little boy falling asleep at the soft tune of my mother's lullabies.

My mother stood next to me, but her look seemed to focus on something far away. She stared into the unknown distances where her child would soon be going.

The house was still. The rain had ceased. Through the heavily laden clouds the sun shone, throwing out cold light, and then it again disappeared, as if it were playing with our emotions, a play of unknown fates. A little light and then darkness, twilight. Soon it would be completely dark. The day would be engulfed by darkest night.

That night, my mother could not sleep. She was searching, going through things and looking to be sure I had not forgotten anything, hoping to find something that I would need on my journey.

For a while she sat in a corner mending a sock or fixing an old garment. I felt my mother's stare, as if she wanted to bring me back and hold me close to her and to our home. She was silent, but I thought I could hear her whispering: "Who, my child, will protect you from stormy winds? Who will awaken at your footsteps? See, the chaos of night and danger–who will take you by the hand so that you do not fall?"

I went to her. I saw the unbounded sorrow in her eyes and the wrinkles on her forehead. For long minutes I stood in awful helplessness, with mixed feelings and a stormy heart. Poor Mama! My dear Mama! How much sorrow she had borne through her whole life. Now, too, I saw how she trembled at my light touch and from soft words:

"Mama, you are tired…Lie down for just a bit…"

The skin on my mother's noble, sorrowful face was as fine as silk. A thought arose in my mind, that I was being cruel by leaving her. I had tremendous pity for her. Oh, how happy I would be if I could take her with me.

Then I realized how senseless were such thoughts. I knew that I was going to Eretz Yisroel, which was not only far away but was not a land of milk and honey: that I would be going through cold and heat and that I was facing difficult days of hunger.

I felt an urge to embrace my mother, to grab onto and hold the waves of love. I was beset by fire, burning tortures–the suffering of my mother, who with great suffering brought me into the world, gave me life, raised me, and now I had to leave her, to go far, far away…

My mother heard me. She lay down on her sofa, with eyes looking at the ceiling. From time to time she cried. Then she sat there, bent over as if her heart would break into little pieces. She spoke haltingly because of her sobs:

"See, my son, I don't know how to hold on to luck…it is all tangled up…always such hardship…why does it desert us?…"

Her words inflicted more pain in my heart. The pain increased, and she could stop neither her words nor her tears.

Then my father awoke. Then my brother and sisters. They sat on their beds listening to my mother's imploring words. Their looks stopped me from responding.

I was so sad. I knew that anything I would say could not relieve my mother's sadness, but their glances tore these words out of me:

"My desire to make aliyah to Eretz Yisroel was not born yesterday. For years I have planned to make aliyah…The days and nights when I was not at home I was helping to prepare myself and others to make aliyah, to lead a new life in our own land, a healthy Jewish life…"

I saw how they all devoured my words, which encouraged me to tell them more about Eretz Yisroel, which for two thousand years lay forlorn and wasted. Jews around the world have not stopped longing for Zion, to rebuild and bring life to the wasted land. From everywhere aliyah was being undertaken, despite the interference of enemies of the Jews, and people were setting an example for how to overcome obstacles. I am one of those who has taught young people about the holiness of Eretz Yisroel. I have clarified for them the great pioneering work that needs to be done in Eretz Yisroel, and every Jew must help in this holy work.

Absorbed in my own enthusiasm, I assured them that when I had settled in I would not forget my dearest ones and I would bring them to Eretz Yisroel.

My mother's face, covered with tears, shone. My dear mother smiled a happy smile. My father got up from his bed, came to me, and hugged and kissed me. Then he turned to my mother and said,

"Rivkah, stop crying. You shouldn't cry. Our Shmuel isn't travelling to the ends of the world. He's going to Eretz Yisroel…You'll see that with God's help he will be a trailblazer, a leader for aliyah."

It seemed to me that my father had abandoned all his reservations that had earlier disturbed his rest. They were all gone. It was as if he would now assume all the responsibilities of a higher purpose. He soon murmured the prayer, "And our eyes will see your return to Zion…"

Through the cracks in the window shades the dawn began to show. I started to pack furiously and get ready for my trip. My mother had arisen from her bed and followed me with tiny steps, helping me to pack and close my suitcase.

I began to say my farewells to my brothers Moyshe, Yoel, Yisroelik and my sisters Leah and Freida. My father held my hand for a long time and pressed it, trying to give me his strength, his trust. My mother embraced me, kissed me, held me, and caressed me.

It was difficult for me to ask my mother not to accompany me. She understood. I took a last look at the house, at our things. In that moment, everything became dear to me and it was hard to leave.

As I started on my way, I could hardly see where I was going. My eyes were blinded by tears.

At the station, the other young people were waiting, those who were going to be pioneers, with whom I had spent so many years, so many musical evenings, learning with them to have love for Eretz Yisroel and to strive for the actualization of the Zionist ideals.

Soon a song broke out on the platform: "Who will build the Galilee? Who will build…" The song came from the deliriously happy group of young people, who lifted their heads in great ecstasy, danced the hora, and seemed to want to assure me that they would continue on the road that I had showed them.

Finally I boarded the train. On the steps I looked around once again at my friends, and I saw my mother as she stood in the crowd of travelers. She held her hands out to me. They shook in the air, like white birds who try to protect their fledglings from danger.

Years, many years later I write these lines, in moving remembrance of my nearest and dearest.

Where are they now, the souls of my dear parents, my brothers and sisters? Where are the sacred souls of the millions who were gassed and burned, the immortal Jewish martyrs.

The pages of this Yiskor Book accuse, and the accusation falls on all of Poland's bloody earth, on all of it, smeared with generations of Jewish blood and with a world drowned in tears.

[Page 375]

The Horrors of the Holocaust

Translated by Sara Mages

[Page 376]

> This is not a literary work, the authors of the articles, from the abyss of doom, have no ambitions in this field.
> They, the survivors of the Holocaust, yearn to describe their own history, and of all the loved ones and relatives who lived their last days in Wolomin Ghetto, and although they do not pretend to write history, we can easily, from the sequence of their events, imagine the events of the town's Jews.
> They are the people dear to us who were murdered in a world full of blood and oppression.
> Somewhere, on the border of the torments of the painful souls, we meet with them, past shadows and sounds, and our hearts will ache, will ache.
> And from the town of Wolomin, as in all the cities and towns in Poland, a quiet lamentation was heard:
> O how has the city that was once so populous remained lonely...
> She weeps, yea, she weeps in the night, and her tears are on her cheek; she has no comforter…
> For these things I weep; my eye, yea my eye, sheds tears…"
> Wolomin, our town, we will carry a lamentation for you, for your Jews because they are gone, we shall remember them forever and devote our memories to their sacred memory.
> There is no end to the pain and there is no limit to grief.

[Page 377]

The Holocaust in Wolomin

by Shimon Kantz

Translated by Sara Mages

The history of the Jewish nation is saturated with suffering, tears and blood, throughout its existence, from Pharaoh the king of Egypt, who turned the Jews into slaves, oppressed them and tortured them, and even ordered to throw their sons into the Nile; through Amalek, the evil Haman who plotted to kill and destroy them, the Spanish Inquisition who burned thousands at the stake, the Ukrainian rioters – Khmelnytsky and Petlura, and the Arabs who conducted pogroms, robbed property and murdered Jewish souls.

However, in all this bloody path of suffering, the persecution and murder did not reach, both in terms of their dimensions and in terms of the cruelty of the perpetrators, their methods and their actions, to such a criminal precedent, as the Nazi regime did.

There was nothing in the history of the martyrology of the Jewish people, and not in the history of all the nations of the world, that genocide of a nation would be planned, and carried out, in cold blood and sophisticated technical methods calculated to the minute details.

Only in our generation the regime of a big country arose over a peaceful defenseless population, on men, women, the elderly, children and infants – to exterminate them in all sorts of deaths: starvation, shooting, hanging, killing and suffocation, and all this in horrifying methods while the rest of the countries remained silent and stood on the blood.

The criminal precedent is also in the fact that this mass murder, which has no example in the history of the world, was not done because of a spontaneous flare–up, not according to individual plot, but with a criminal complicity in which thousands and tens of thousands took part, in uniform and without uniform, as well as organizations and units whose sole purpose was to fulfill the crime's tasks.

The heaviest blow was inflicted on the Polish Jewry which, before the war, numbered about 3.5 million. The terror and persecution against the Jews began immediately after the Nazi occupation of Poland.

[Page 378]

It was organized and managed by an organization established by the Germans specifically for this purpose and was headed by the oppressor, Adolf Eichmann, who planned and carried out the annihilation of the European Jewry. His emissaries were attached to all units of the German army and annexed to the regime in all areas of Nazi occupation across Europe.

Germans from all walks of life took an active part in planning the war against the Jews. Lawyers prepared the background, "the trial," to exclude the Jews from the protection of the law, turn them into defenseless people who can be humiliated, starve them, rob them of everything, enslave them and kill them.

Psychological warfare experts dealt with the exploitation of conflicting views of the local population in religious and cultural fields, and aroused anti–Jewish sentiment. Their economists planned how to dispossess the Jews of all their possessions, even the hair and the gold teeth of the dead. Intellectuals, artists, religious leaders, writers, journalists, and radio personnel, proved the righteousness of evil with great enthusiasm. The engineers designed gas chambers and incinerators, while medical professionals, "experts," trained on skeletons of human bodies.

The concentration camps became huge centers. Their millions of victims waited in line for death as they watched the smoke coming out of the crematoria's chimneys, symbolizing the end of suffering.

Chemists invent a special gas called "Zyklon." Several cans of "Zyklon" suffocated thousands at once. German manufacturers removed, with maximum efficiency, the last drop of perspiration from the Jewish slave, free, in hard labor, in starvation, during which the person turned, in a short time, to a – "*muselmann*" – a dying person.

The German army executed the orders faithfully. There is no mass murder without an army. No deportation without its support. They destroyed ghettos, and where resistance arose – everything turned into ashes. The ruins of Warsaw Ghetto were silent and faithful witnesses to this.

This mighty–force organization landed its blows on the European Jewry, and in order to mislead its victims used devious methods and various tricks to spread illusions until the last moment.

The Germans, in order to ease the task of extermination, established autonomous "Jewish councils" within the ghettos and camps. They were designed to perfect the processes of mass murder. These innocent people thought that cooperating with the oppressor would prevent the decrees, or weaken their power, and when they came to their bitter error – it was too late.

[Page 379]

The Jewish public did not accept the decrees imposed on it by the Germans and opposed them with its meager means in order to withstand the storm.

The resistance was expressed in all fields. In the economy, despite all the decrees and confiscation of Jewish property in industry and commerce, and despite the dispossession of Jews of all means of subsistence and livelihood and cramming them into ghettos, they fought for their existence and also took care of the needy. They fought a desperate war against epidemics, took care, with self–sacrifice and total devotion, sometimes at a high cost of human life, to bring food and medicine into the ghetto.

Despite the ban on schools, the youth studied in private lessons, in courses that were secretly organized. *Minyanim* were held despite the closure and the burning of the synagogues. Jews prayed in basements and attics. There were underground libraries. Organizations and political youth movements operated in secret and maintained contact with the Polish underground. Despite the terrible terror, and despite the severe prohibition of leaving the ghetto, when the only punishment was death, dozens and hundreds of young people left the ghetto in all sorts of ways and tricks, traveled throughout Poland and maintained a living relationship with the tortured Jews in the ghettos.

* * *

All this also took place in the Wolomin Ghetto, the same gradual liquidation of an entire community, the same epidemics and famine that quickly turned the members of the community into human skeletons, persecution and murder by shooting and hanging.

Panic–stricken, by what was going on, the Jews of Wolomin sought ways to escape. People gave babies to convents or built bunkers to hide until fury passed, and those who did not find shelter made sure to get a certificate from the Germans that they were effective professionals.

In the midst of all this, few found courage and dared to rebel against the horrific reality and joined the partisans.

As mentioned, these were few. As opposed to them, despair gripped and devoured. Helplessness dominated everything and illusions planted by others did not help. The murder machine was activated with all its cruelty and all the Jews of Wolomin, men, women and children, were sent to Treblinka.

Some fled from the cars and later found their death on the roads. A few managed to escape and now write in the book what they had gone through, and what is written is nothing more than a concentrated abbreviation that overlooks many cases and experiences.

Only a few rose from the pile of ruins and tried to draw light to the breath of existence.

[Page 380]

They took great pains, diligently and devotedly, to extract from the ruins of destruction all that is possible to perpetuate the memory of the martyrs, but the words that will express the magnitude of the destruction have not yet been created, that will describe the chambers of hell in which they were tormented, the thousands of different deaths in which our parents, brothers and sisters were extinct from the world.

The Yizkor Book for our community in Wolomin will join, without a doubt, the history book of the Polish Jewry and will serve as a spring to future historians and writers, and a warning to the entire world, not to forget what one nation can do, under the leadership of a murderer, to other nations, and a warning to the Jewish people not to forget "What Amalek did." A warning to the world Jewry to do everything to prevent the recurrence of mass murder, as it was carried out by the defiled Nazis before the eyes of humanity in the twentieth century.

What was written in the book is very little of what it was, a drop from the sea, a sea of trouble and torture from which our holy brothers and sisters suffered and in which they were tortured. With terrible cruelty they were tortured, and with great courage they bore their suffering, the suffering of a Jew for being a Jew, and with supreme self–sacrifice of *Kiddush HaShem* they took their last steps as the words "*Shema Yisrael*" were carried on their lips.

May HaShem avenge their blood!

[Page 381]

Wolomin Jews under Nazi occupation

by Yehiel-Yehoshua Eidelsohn, New-York

Translated by Sara Mages

With a heart filled with of feelings of grief and horror, I try to put on the paper a few things, and segments of things, about the days of the Holocaust in Wolomin, and what happened to the Jews in those days. I must tell, at least, part of everything that we have gone through during those terrible years in the ghetto.

At the beginning of my words I would like to point out that as one of the few who remained alive among those who went through the terrible path of suffering, that a person's imagination is unable to describe, I can proudly testify that we, the Jews of Wolomin, have not lost the image of God in this terrible period, we have not shamed the Jews' honor in general and the name of the community of Wolomin in particular.

All the members of Wolomin, wherever they may be, know that it is their honor to be counted among the family of this town.

Even when we were in a desperate and hopeless situation, not only did we stand up against reality, we also helped the local people and the masses that came from other cities and towns as refugees.

With the arrival of the Germans every day brought with it new decrees and the community committee was required to provide more and more people for forced labor. The Jews were employed in arduous work and were taken to work for whole weeks under poor nutrition conditions.

Life became harder from day to day. Food prices skyrocketed and those, who did not have valuables to exchange with the farmers in the area, suffered from starvation.

The first victims began to fall. Jews were murdered for no reason. There were gendarmes who killed Jews just for the pleasure of murder and without having to explain the reason. Only a notice was sent to the Judenrat about the place where the body of the murdered Jew was lying, and the committee was responsible for his burial.

Only a few fled. There were those who sought refuge with the Polish population but they were turned back. The Poles were, at best, indifferent to the fate of the Jews.

At the beginning there was contact with the Jews of Warsaw Ghetto. Over time the gentiles brought rumors about the liquidation of ghettos in the nearby towns.

[Page 382]

In Wolomin, the Jews deluded themselves that, by doing vital work for the Germans, they would not suffer from a similar fate. The Germans, on their part, encouraged this thought.

The Germans systematically continued their plans.

They declared a confiscation of valuables and furs. The sky of the Jews in Wolomin was covered with black clouds and sadness and without hope for a better future.

The ghetto in Sosnówka was surrounded by a barbed-wire fence and a local police guarded that no one would enter or leave.

In the imagination of every Jew were images of horror that he did not talk about. Everyone felt that the ground was burning underfoot. The pace of events and incidents was very fast. Every day, and every hour, brought new decrees and each was different and worse than the other. But, together with that, cruel acts were also committed like the burning of the synagogue and murders, abduction of Jews for forced labor, their humiliation during this work to the point of removing the image of God from them and the imposition of financial penalties in astronomical amounts.

It was a heartbreaking sight to see how gentle and spiritually intelligent Jews were led from place to place to clean the streets, and during their work they had to dance with the broom.

The discrimination, the insults and the curses of the animals in human form, were occasionally accompanied by blows until blood flowed, and only by miracle they withstood these attempts and returned home broken in their bodies and whole in their spirit.

I will never forget the night, the night of *Hoshana Rabbah*, when we saw flames breaking through the windows of Beit HaMidrash. The gentiles stood around Beit HaMidrash and watched, with expression of joy and satisfaction, the destruction of Judaism and its temple.

In the evening I entered the rabbi's home and saw him sitting on the floor without noticing me, and I heard a conversation between him and God. He pleaded: "*Ribono Shel Olam*, how can you watch what's happening here? This Beit Midrash, which absorbed the Torah and the prayers of God-fearing Jews, and just ordinary people, who poured their heart there with supreme devotion, a place in which the voice of Torah did not stop for even a moment, was destroyed in such a despicable and humiliated way by the defiled murderers without any response."

And as he spoke he banged his head on the wall, sat and cried like a little boy trying to get what he wanted with his tears.

When he noticed me he said in my direction, "See what happens to us ... What is our sin?"

I sat next to the rabbi and wept.

With a silent greeting I parted from the rabbi and in the darkness of the night I cautiously returned home, shocked and frightened by what my eyes had seen.

[Page 383]

I saw the skeletons of the smoky walls of Beit HaMidrash and they stood like tombstones on the grave of the Jews of Wolomin and its temple.

Over time, I saw the continuation of the process of destruction brought by the defiled hand of the oppressor of our community, destruction without revival and loss without compensation.

Rumors upon rumors arrived about deportations and the extermination of Jews from nearby towns and cities, faint news filtered about the establishment of death camps and gas chambers. We saw the transports to Treblinka, cars full of Jews being taken from their homes, some with suitcases and some nude and destitute.

I admit and confess: I do not give an account of the tragic events and write even a tiny bit of the terrible tribulations in the last darkest stage. Can a human heart understand, and can one's thoughts capture, even in the imagination, the feelings of people condemned to death as a sharp sword is placed on their neck?

When rumors grew that the turn of Sosnówka Ghetto for deportation and extermination is drawing near, it is impossible to describe the panic and the depression that have taken place. The sound of crying, prayers and pleading, came from every Jewish home. Everyone felt his end was coming. People were running around like in a trap searching for refuge in times of trouble, but all the roads were desolated and blocked.

The gendarmes caught Jews who tried to save their lives in a hiding place. The Jews were brutally tortured and beaten, and after the torture they were loaded onto trucks that disappeared to an unknown location…

If I were a writer, and devoted a thick book only for the deportation, even then I could not describe the tragic events in those terrible hours.

Small children were brutally removed from their mothers' lap and thrown into the cars or shot on the spot. Shocked, broken and devoid of any response, we stood watching the departing train. However, we have not been given time to observe our situation. With blows and shouts we were driven from place to place. The elderly and the weak fell without getting up. The shouts and the moans of the beaten continued for hours upon hours.

Beaten to the point of bleeding, with swollen callused feet, people stood in line to get a serving of soup. The noise, the shouts and the crying continued throughout the hours of the day and night.

Indeed I saved my life, but from here, until the end of torture and suffering, the road was still long. I will not elaborate on the additional wanderings with my family, in hiding, in a bunker and in a thick forest because I cannot put them in writing, even a tiny fraction of all the wanderings and the chambers of hell that we had gone through until we arrived there, and also the continuation of our struggle for our lives there and afterwards and, all the more so, the purpose of the memorial book is not to perpetuate the history of any individual or individuals.

I will not forget to mention the day when I returned with my brother, Shlomo, to Wolomin after the Germans retreated.

[Page 384]

As in a bad dream I saw the area in which Jewish life took place. All its tenants, its rich and poor, its "*heders*" and workshops, disappeared. The streets and the alleys are filled with gloom and despair. There are no houses of worship in our town without Jews. Those who walk here, the Poles - do they remember them? Mention them? Their lives, their deaths?

We peer into the houses where we knew each tenant. The houses are full, full. No empty space left for those who are gone. Those who do not know will not know what happened here.

The brain, apparently, cannot absorb the reality of terror. Our whole being is incapable of absorbing it. Here everyone continues with his normal life. The restaurant is full of diners who eat with appetite and their eyes sparkle with the satisfaction of the desire to eat, with these hands, with these many hands, that vigorously working with a spoon and a fork, and their faces rejoicing.

No, we cannot absorb the horrors of reality. Only in a dream at night it wears real and also strange forms.

We walk from street to street with a feeling of distress, the distress of a nightmare, a feeling of destruction.

The streets - their closeness is gone, they were taken at once from my love, my longing, my desire to tread in them. As in a horror dream that suddenly distances the family and relatives.

In a slow step saturated with anxiety, I approached the house that contained everything, our apartment, mornings and nights, longings and love, misunderstandings and reconciliations. With a burden of grief I stood still beside it, like next to a grave, and ashes strewn on the heart.

Here, next to this house, we cried openly, without shame and without disguising our feelings. Passers-by looked at us, some with an ironic smile and some in fear that we came to claim back the property they had stolen. And we did not want anything anymore, just to run away, to get out of a town inhabited by ghosts, ghosts of streets and alleys, ghosts of houses, ghosts of abandoned graves.

To save this town that is preserved in our soul, the beloved and the cherished. To save it as it had been preserved in the safest refuge from the devastating touch of time, life, history - in the depths of our hearts and in the depths of our memory.

[Page 385]

The News of the Liquidation

by Miriam Grodzitsky-Feignbaum

Translated by Sara Mages

Life in the town deteriorated daily and became hell on earth. The Germans conducted raids in public and private places, abducted Jews, both boys and old men, and employed them in hard physical labor. The abductees were forced to carry heavy sacks full of sand under the constant supervision of tyrants who abused their victims with great anger. They beat and kicked them with generous hand, not to mention the curses and hatred they constantly hurled at them.

In the town the food ran out in the shops and in the market, the overcrowding in the apartments was suffocating because several families of refugees found shelter in every Jewish home, they and their meager belongings.

In the ghetto, we, fourteen people, lived in an attic, in two rooms and a kitchen: my mother, my brother Yehiel with his wife and their three children, my brother Matityahu, my sister Chaya-Gitel with her husband and their two children, the two daughters of my brother Yakov and me.

It should be noted, in praise of the people of Wolomin, that they willingly volunteered to help the unfortunate refugees. In Sosnówka Ghetto they crowded together in a small place in order to house the refugees, divided their bread with them and encouraged their oppressed spirit.

That was how the people of Wolomin had always been, and they did not change their ways in times of anger and wrath.

I remember, from the days of my childhood, that my father devoted himself to helping others, and so did others. Wolomin had a reputation as a center of charity and love of Israel, until the enemies came and leveled it to the ground.

The night of *Shemini Atzeret* arrived.

The mood in the ghetto was tense and depressed. All the ghettos in the area had already been liquidated, only Wolomin and Radzimin remained. We waited for our tragic end. There were moments when we asked for the end to come quickly, because the expectation of death was terrible. We knew our end was approaching.

The Jews secretly organized to pray in a "*minyan*" at one of the neighbors. A sea of tears poured on the prayer books that were open before the men's faces. The prayers sought their way to the heavens, up to the Throne of God.

[Page 386]

There were those who tried to sing, but the mood was not festive. An overwhelming despair took over the holiday.

My mother said: "children, today is a holiday, it is forbidden to be sad."

But her eyes looked at us with a piercing grief, as if she felt that this was our last night together.

She began to set the table. Two small loaves of black bread constituted the holiday meal. Two small candles tried to drive out the darkness in the room and in the heart. My mother made the candles with her own hands.

My brother, Matityahu, returned from the prayer, washed his hands and got ready for the "*Kiddush,*" and as he was still standing with wet hands the door opened and Chancza, the daughter of our brother Mordecai, entered pale as chalk and stood without uttering a word.

The end that we had been waiting for in the last few weeks had come, yet, it hit us like a thunder.

Although we knew the bitter reality we waited, deep in our hearts, for a miracle.

The miracle did not come. Chancza's white face and her frightened eyes brought us the terrible news: Here's the end!

It's hard for me to say how long we stood paralyzed with fear, the words and the questions choked in the throat. Maybe it lasted only minutes, maybe an hour,

"Mother, what's happening, mother? Did the gendarmes come to kill us?"

The monstrous laugh

Here is the black reality with all its horror. Here came the enemies who seek our blood and the blood of everyone called a Jew, and we are in mortal danger. At that moment the gendarmes' laughter echoed in my ears. A short while ago, before we moved to the ghetto, we were in the shop: my mother, my sister Chaya-Gitel with her husband Pinchas and me. Two gendarmes passed by. We tried to hide deep in the shop so they would not see us, but they entered, took Pinchas out and ordered him to cross to the other side of the street and stand against the wall. My sister burst into tears and tore her hair. My mother pleaded before the gendarmes and asked them for mercy. But the murderers screamed and pushed her back.

Pinchas stood next to the wall with failing knees, pale as chalk and muttering: *"Shema Yisrael."*

The armed gendarmes took out a camera, took Pinchas' picture and burst out laughing, a hollow laughter, like the sound of tin, echoed over the houses for a long time.

[Page 387]

It was a terrible laugh, a monstrous laugh that resonates in my ears to this day.

And another terrible picture was engraved in my memory.

How they murdered Yoel

We lived in the ghetto not far from the barbed wire fence. Between our windows and the barbed wire fence was an empty lot. It was a beautiful day. I looked out the window and saw Yoel lying on the grass.

I do not know why Yoel lay down on the grass. Maybe he wanted to enjoy some fresh air since it was terribly crowded in the apartments.

I stood and watched how beautiful it was outside, how beautiful the world was for everyone - except for the Jews.

Suddenly I noticed that gendarmes were approaching the ghetto.

I left the window out of fear, because the arrival of gendarmes always ominous.

A few minutes later there was a terrible cry.

I approached the window and my eyes encountered a terrible sight. The gendarmes took Yoel out of the ghetto and ordered him to run. Two shots were heard, a terrible scream, and deathly silence.

Yoel fell dead.

The bloodthirsty Germans were satisfied. Their faces expressed satisfaction. They went to the Judenrat and ordered that the murdered man be brought into the ghetto.

In the spilled sea of blood

The clear recognition led us toward apathy, toward death.

We recovered despite the terror of death. It was a kind of religious experience that confronts the man and the absolute beyond the imagined reality of things.

And you don't have more intensive moments in life than the moments of standing in the face of the certainty of death, the fear, the sense of humiliation and the insult of terror, fall apart with the murderers' outburst.

My mother and sisters began pressuring me to escape and try to save my life. They, too, decided to hide. Only moments of extreme vitality that flare up in the presence of death remained, and I gave in to a glimmer of hope: maybe I could to help them.

That night I managed to get out of the ghetto into the darkness of the night and my ears caught the triumphant shouts of the Germans surrounding the ghetto. I trudged slowly to escape from the valley of slaughter to a hiding place.

When dawn came, the ghetto of the Jews of Wolomin was destroyed.

My family was among the few who tried to hide, but the day after the liquidation of the ghetto the Germans found their hiding place and murdered them all.

A terrible silence took over the ghetto.

[Page 388]

From the Depths of the Abyss

Tzipora Levita-Grodzitska

Translated by Sara Mages

I managed to finish six grades when we had to leave our home in Wolomin and move to Sosnówka Ghetto. The panic in the Jews' homes already broke out the day before. In the morning, when it began to clear, whole families, frightened and anxious, began to emerge from all the town's streets, from all the Jews' courtyards. They walked on the sidewalks, and in the middle of the road, laden with baskets, boxes and suitcases. Sacks bent the shoulders of the Jews until their faces were not visible. It was difficult to differentiate between one to the other.

The town emptied. Housewares and discarded old clothes were scattered along the road. Emptiness wandered from yard to yard, and from time to time the cry of a mother calling for her child, who had disappeared in the crowd, pierced this emptiness.

My father managed to escape from the ghetto. He wanted to sneak across the border, find refuge there, and later also get us out. We later learned that the Germans murdered him in Slonim.

In those days it was forbidden to leave the ghetto. My older sister risked her life and went outside the ghetto's border. She took me with her because we had to work in order to support the family.

We engaged in smuggling. We smuggled food, which we bought from the farmers, to Warsaw Ghetto, and brought back clothes, shoes and socks that we exchanged again with the farmers for food.

When we left the ghetto we never knew if we would be able to return. We put our trust in the Divine Providence.

We traveled by the train to the outskirts of the city, to Praga, and from there by tram that traveled to the Polish neighborhoods through the ghetto. Polish policemen made sure that no one got off the tram as it passed through the ghetto. The policemen, who accompanied the tram on its journey through the ghetto, usually performed their duty properly.

How did we manage? There were drivers who liked to take bribes and knew which of the policemen, who accompany the tram, also like to take bribes. They gave us signs by which we knew whether it was allowed, or forbidden, to get on the tram.

[Page 389]

When we received the permitting signal we got off in the turns where the driver slowed down, but also here we did not get off, we jumped. The policemen, or the drivers, did not constitute the main problem, but the civilians who were called "*Szmalcowniki*" [blackmailers].

They had a special talent for identifying Jews, even if they had Aryan facial features. They even knew how to explain how they succeeded in this, "your eyes betray you" - they said. No wonder, at that time the Jews' eyes expressed depression, sadness and fear.

The "*Szmalcownik*" knew how to exploit their talent. They attacked the Jewish traveler and stripped him of everything. In this manner they became rich from the terrible disaster of the unfortunate.

On my travels to Warsaw I had a chance to take care, without success, of a five, or six years old, Jewish boy - and the story is as follows.

In Sosnówka Ghetto lived the Shapira family, and this family had a married daughter in Warsaw. Once, Mrs. Shapira was informed that her daughter and son-in-law had died and their only son, who was five or six, was left unattended. Mrs. Shapira asked me to bring her grandson from an address she knew. My mother objected to that because she saw it as a terrible risk. Once, when I left the ghetto, I saw Mrs. Shapira standing and waiting for me. "Save my grandson"- she begged me - "thanks to this, God will save your father because he too needs mercy."

I agreed to bring the boy. I found him in a dismal state, hungry and dressed in rags. He was with his uncle who previously owned a clothing store and lived in the ghetto. I got him suitable clothes, dressed him and together we took the tram to Praga. On the tram, apart from us, were Germans and Poles. Suddenly, the boy began to speak in Yiddish and tell in a loud voice: "Here, in this house we lived … on this street…"

In an instant we were surrounded by policemen. They took us off the tram and brought us to the police station where we were beaten countless times. The policemen were convinced that I was a Christian who wanted to save a Jewish child for a decent payment.

Fortunately, a member of my family saw me walking with the policeman, understood what was going on, called my relatives and they rushed to bribe the police chief. With the last of my strength I dragged myself home.

The ghetto was liquidated on 2 October, 1942.

We felt that we could no longer suffer and, in spite of it, we deluded ourselves that our situation would change.

The day before the liquidation of the ghetto I left with my sister to visit the labor camp in Izabelin, a distance of about twelve kilometers from Wolomin, where they dug "turf," for heating furnaces. According to an agreement between the Judenrat and the Germans, eighty young people from Wolomin had to be employed in digging "turf."

Twice a week the gendarmes came to the ghetto and left laden with silver and gold, gifts from the parents of the young people in the hope that their children would survive.

[Page 390]

My sister and I left with the same gendarmes for Izabelin. We hoped to return home in the evening, but we did not find transportation to Sosnówka and spent the night in Izabelin.

At night we heard shots, but we did not know where they came from. Shortly before sunrise, at four o'clock, the teenager, Brodshtein, came and told us that the ghetto was liquidated at night. He jumped off the train to Treblinka.

It was clear that we should not return to Wolomin. After many hardships we, my sister and I, arrived in Milanówek. There, we managed to obtain documents with Aryan names and thanks to them we managed to get a job in Warsaw.

From time to time I visited the camp in Izabelin. A few weeks later, on my way to Izabelin I came across gendarmes on horseback and they were happy and cheerful. When I arrived in Izabelin a blood-curdling silence jumped over me. The Polish manager, Frank, sat on the hut's threshold and quietly played the accordion.

Shocked to the depths of my soul, I followed Frank to the hill where the bodies of the murdered were buried. One head protruded from the ground, it was the young son of Shabtai Dubner.

The Righteous Among the Nations

During that time I visited the teacher Zawadzki in Wolomin. He was a member of the Polish underground. He welcomed me nicely and said:

"My home is at your disposal. You can stay, but you must know that it is dangerous, the Germans are watching me."

He allowed me to take everything I needed from his home.

Zawadzki restored my faith in humanity and instilled in me a glimmer of hope.

Despite the certificate and my Aryan face, I aroused the suspicions of villains who denounced me and started to follow me, and I had to move to Warsaw.

The ghetto uprising

As I mentioned, my uncle, my mother's brother, lived in Warsaw Ghetto. After the liquidation of his store he was left with a certain amount of goods and from that he made a living. The Poles entered the ghetto in various ways and brought food in exchange for fabrics, socks, etc.

[Page 391]

Before Passover 1943, I had the opportunity to be with my uncle. He decided to conduct a "seder" and asked me to get raisins for him. I left the ghetto on April 18, and when I returned the next day with the raisins I managed to get to Nalewki Street and was not allowed to walk further.

The revolt broke out.

In the morning hours, announcements calling for an armed revolt appeared on the ghetto's walls. The slogans: "To die with dignity!" also appeared.

The first confrontation took place on Nalewki Street when the first German unit got closer to the triangle, Nalewki-Gesia-Francuskana. A hail of bullets, hand grenades and Molotov cocktails rained down on the Germans.

The battle on Nalewki Street ended in the rebels' victory. The Germans retreated leaving their wounded.

I returned to the "Aryan side"

The term, "Aryan side," was adopted after the establishment of the ghetto in Warsaw in November 1940. From then on, Warsaw was divided into two separate parts: the Aryan side and the Jewish side. With the closure of the Jewish population in the ghetto the contact with the Aryan side became quite difficult.

At the time of the establishment of the ghetto the number of Jews on the Aryan side was very small. Assimilated and converted Jews also lived in the ghetto for fear of punishment. Only a small handful of people of Jewish origin remained on the Aryan side. They had family ties with the Polish environment and could not summon the strength to wear the "Jewish ribbon."

It goes without saying, that the Hitlerites often caught these "criminals" and sent them to Pawiak Prison or to Auschwitz.

Only with the opening of the first "*aktzia*" to liquidate the ghetto on July 1942, only then, a considerable number of Jews began to move from the ghetto to the Aryan side. The first group to move there was part of the working Jewish intelligentsia who had friends and acquaintances among the Poles. A number of wealthy people also moved there.

This wave increased after the second "*aktzia*" on January 1943, when the hope of surviving in the ghetto was very slim. In those days this wave already flooded various social strata and also some of the public activists.

[Page 392]

Also during the ghetto uprising, and after its suppression, a certain number of Jews were saved by escaping to the Aryan side. There was also a fairly large group of people there, especially the young, who jumped off the trains on the way to Treblinka.

I was among those who had a "good" appearance, meaning that they did not have a typical Semitic appearance and spoke fluent Polish.

When I read in an ad the newspaper that a family was looking for a housemaid, I turned to them. I met twelve young women there who wanted to work, and only two of them were hired. I was among those who were allowed to stay in the house until they found work. There were also Jews among them, but no one knew their origin. Most were Polish women who came from small towns in the Russian occupied area.

I finally found a job and tried to be diligent. They were probably satisfied with me, but I did not work for long time because they asked for a residence registration certificate from a previous period.

The vast majority of Jews, who lived in the Aryan side, were forced to hide, to be "on the basis of knowledge," meaning, with the knowledge of the homeowners who brought in Jews. Most of them lived in hideouts built specifically for this purpose.

Of course, this arrangement involved large expenses. I only had the option of getting a job and living openly without revealing my Jewish origin.

There were many like me. These people did not hide. After obtaining forged certificates, first of all a birth certificate, an identity card and also a residence registration certificate, they registered as required by law.

It took a few days of searching until I found a job in a place that did not require a residence registration certificate, but it was precisely there that I had bad luck.

It was a family from the aristocratic stratum in Warsaw, wealthy and privileged. Once, after midnight, the men of the Gestapo broke into the apartment, ordered all the tenants to stand before them and announced: "A Jew is hiding among you, if he comes out on his own we would not conduct a search."

No one came out.

Then, the men of the Gestapo approached the homeowner, Sulima was his name, and said to him: "you are a Jew!" and took him to prison.

The event caused me great grief. I felt the family's pain and looked for ways to help them.

I knew that Zusia Lipman was active in the Polish underground, and her friend had an important position in the underground leadership. I turned to Zushia and days later I received an answer that it was possible to release Sulima at a price of 60,000 zloty.

[Page 393]

I hurried with the answer to Sulima's wife and she caused me trouble. The family suspected me of being a spy for the Germans, and that I had sneaked into their house to inflict disaster on them and win some of the ransom.

My explanations did not help and they fired me.

The wanderings from house to house began again and continued until the end of the war.

It is worth considering that also the Polish population, that Aryan side, lived under Hitler's whip of terror. Frequent searches, arrests, "street abductions," searches in the trains and the trams, deportation to work, the Pawiak Prison nightmare, the horrors of the concentration camps to which tens of thousands of Poles were sent - all these were the daily fate of the population of Warsaw. More than once, the blood of those executed in the middle of the street flowed through the streets of Warsaw.

Despite all this, many Poles helped the Hitlerites to spread anti-Semitic venom in all possible ways, and carried out incessant propaganda against the few Poles who helped the Jews.

In comparison to the ghetto, life on the Aryan side was like "paradise." The difference in those days was striking: on one side of the walls - death, torture and destruction, while on the other side - a relatively "normal" life - in the shadow of the terror of the Nazi beast.

On the ruins

With the liberation of Warsaw I returned to Wolomin out of hope of finding someone from my family.

My heart exploded inside me at the sight of the destruction.

Despair struck me and coolness pinched my heart and soul. Loneliness and apathy took hold of me with no way out.

The Jews of Wolomin were liquidated and their property was robbed.

Despite all these torments, people tried to draw hope and cling to life, wanted to build, rehabilitate, and re-grow felled branches.

Indeed, I met a few Jews who came with the same glimmer of hope in the heart, and were bitterly disappointed.

These moments were the worst in our lives. We could not believe, and could not accept the bitter truth that that slapped our faces.

During the short time we were in town we received threatening letters, in which the Poles informed us that if we did not leave Wolomin quickly, they would murder us and our fate would be similar to the fate of all the slaughtered Jews of Wolomin.

We knew that the Poles could carry out their threat and we left Wolomin, this time forever.

[Page 394]

On the train to Lodz a Pole entered my compartment. I immediately recognized him as the man that I worked in his house as a maid and the Germans arrested him as a Jew. He also recognized me, attacked me with insults, shouted that I worked as an informer for the Gestapo and spat in my face. Immediately people gathered around us, got me off the train and continued with insults and cursing. I burst into tears and tried to convince them that I was innocent, but to no avail.

All this took place in a small train station between Warsaw and Lodz. It seemed to me that my end was approaching and I was falling victim to a serious mistake. Suddenly we came across a Russian officer who was walking on the platform. He approached us and asked for an explanation for the commotion. I began to explain to him, but he did not understand Polish. I was surprised to hear from him that he was Jewish and he started to talk to me in Yiddish.

The Poles were astonished.

I saw how Sulima's face had changed. He understood his mistake, fell on my neck, kissed my hands, and his lips murmured words of forgiveness and apologies.

From darkness to light

In Lodz I met my husband and married him.

In 1950 we arrived in Israel.

With that, my memories of the period of horrors and the period of transition from darkness to light, came to an end.

Today I live with my family, and my people, in the independent and free State of Israel. I am excited and thrilled at the sublime wonders that take place every day in our country, both on the security level and in bringing Jewish immigrants from all over the world, the building of the country and the revival of the holy language.

I bow my head, with respect and admiration, to our brave and fearless sons and daughters, the soldiers of Israel Defense Forces, who stand on guard day and night and protect the borders of our country in the land, sea and air, and the security of the people living in Zion.

The great privilege that Divine Providence has given me to live and work in the State of Israel compensates me, to great extent, for the atrocities and tortures I experienced during the years of calamity and wrath.

The flourishing and prosperous State of Israel is a symbol of revenge for the massacre of six million martyrs, God's overwhelming response to the Holocaust that destroyed the best of the Jewish people, the glorious European Jewry.

I will never forget the noble figures of my parents, my brothers and sisters, my uncle and aunt, my relatives and the residents of my town, Wolomin, who were cut down, in various deaths, by despicable monsters.

I will never forget the destruction of my town.

[Pages 395-396]

In the Valley of Slaughter

by Tova Silberstein-Yagoda

Translated by Sara Mages

The Germans entered Wolomin on the eve of the holiday of Rosh Hashanah. The next day the Jews were ordered to open the shops, German soldiers arrived immediately, threw all the goods into the street and they were looted by the Polish mob.

Our anxiety is indescribable. Great terror enveloped us. But with all our might we restrained ourselves so that they would not recognize what was happening within us.

The Jews were afraid to go to the synagogue and organized "minyanim" in private homes. When the Germans discovered them, they expelled them dressed in tallitot and forced them to clean the toilets in Broszczynski's house. Among the deportees was also the slaughterer, R' Baruch Branzweig, who was forced, together with everyone, to clean the toilet with his own hands.

Life became more difficult day by day. The Germans caught Jews in the street and forced them to carry buckets full of water. Those who spilled a little water were brutally beaten.

The Jews began to look for ways to escape. We too were among the escapees to the Russian border. A Polish carter brought us to Bialystok. On the way the Germans stopped us, conducted searches and took all our meager property.

The women and children rode in carts. The men walked on side roads.

We stayed in Bialystok for about three months. We sold the few things we managed to hide from the Germans. My two sisters, who came with me, returned to Wolomin in order to bring our parents with them, but they did not return. The fate of all Polish Jews also befell them.

The men of the N.K.V.D in Bialystok began the deportation of the refugees. They came to us at night and loaded us on trucks that took us to the train station.

For six weeks we traveled under terrible conditions until we reached the Arkhangelsk Forests. There we were employed in logging. I brought the trees to the river and they arrived with the current to different cities.

We lived in wooden huts and when a typhus epidemic broke out I too became infected. I went through all the hardships until we were released in 1941 and traveled to Turkestan. There, the men were drafted into the Polish army and with it they left the Soviet Union and arrived in Eretz Yisrael.

We, the women and children, were left alone without means. We suffered deprivation and hunger. Many died. I got a job in a factory, but it was impossible to survive from the meager salary.

At the end of the war we began to wander west, from one train to another.

The members of the Yagoda family

According to legend, the hearts of parents and children are tied with a thin thread that can be stretched without limit. It stretches under the influence of geographical distances and expanses of age and time, but remains attached forever.

When we were children in our home in Wolomin, it seemed that the invisible thread was very sensitive and every slight movement in our souls, the soul of a family member, immediately took the whole family out of its serenity and it rushed to help. In this way the family was connected and felt, in all its essence, the feeling of supreme love that beat in the hearts of the parents and operated among the whole family.

[Page 397]

A Wedding in the Ghetto

by Pela Stalik

Translated by Sara Mages

In a whisper they talked about it in the ghetto. The Germans shouldn't have known what was going to happen. The preparations were made with sadness. Grief hovered on the parents' faces and the young couple looked at each other in trembling and fear. No one thought of music, singing and dancing.

A wedding in the ghetto - an almost tragic event.

The Germans forbade the Jews to marry, but the ban did not help. Life has its own laws, stronger than the orders of the Germans and the fear of death.

The blessings were sad, and the wishes of the parents and the relatives who congratulated their children and wished them a better life.

The ghetto in Wolomin was small and cramped. It was divided into two sections: the "blocks" and "Sosnówka." At the beginning of the ghetto the apartment blocks were at the edge of Sosnówka.

Only burnt ruins remained of them, and fear solidified in the eye sockets. We were surrounded by walls and policemen guarded the gates, S.S men disguised as human beings. They ambushed children like beasts of prey.

Jewish children died more easily, especially the infants, because they were not yet afraid, and if mother and child fell together, they were happy.

Not a day went by that the Germans did not prepare surprises for us. The moans of the tortured and the cries of the dying were music for the Germans, Beethoven's symphony.

If they had heard of a wedding in the ghetto, they would have given the couple and guests a death meal.

Therefore, a wedding in the ghetto became a secret act, and in place of music and singing, the participants in the meal recited verses of Tehillim that were familiar to them and soothed the fear in their hearts. Their lips moved in silent prayer so that their voice would not be heard and would draw death upon them.

The Stalik family

[Pages 398-399]

Days of great horror

It is a pure psychological phenomenon that after the bloodshed a strong desire for life arose in the ghetto, and from time to time the ghetto took on the image of a small town and adapted to the unusual conditions. Fear and anxiety were felt day and night, there were no schools, the youth were devastated, little children grew old prematurely, and everyone repeated the same words: What will happen? What to do? Escape? Where? How?

In those days it was customary to say: We will survive them.

Along with the fear many hopes for good days were also woven, and immediately the disappointment came and brought the recognition of the bitter reality. Horror and fear fell upon us and we realized that more bad and terrible days would come.

There was a force that held us all together in the ghetto, one comforted the other and the Jews of the ghetto became one miserable family.

It was forbidden to leave the ghetto, it was punishable by death. Still, people risked their lives to bring something to eat.

It is difficult to remember things that are very painful, but we must not forget them. I remember how the Germans captured a young girl who came out of the ghetto. The Germans murdered her.

The Germans burnt and murdered for only one reason: we were Jews.

I had an uncle, Yosef Zilbershtein, who was very devout. He obeyed all the Nazi's decrees, except for one decree. He refused to part with his tallit, the Germans murdered him together with his tallit.

On the day of the liquidation of the ghetto one called to the other: "escape," but it was already too late. The ghetto was surrounded by the men of the Gestapo. Where? Where to escape? A trap lay in wait for us in every place.

But, despite the fear we escaped at the last moment. There was no place to hide or turn for help. The Germans, as well as the Poles, ambushed us. We, the three of us, my husband, my brother-in-law and I lost each other. I remembered the address of a Polish family that my husband instructed me to turn to. I arrived at the Polish house and asked for permission to stay for only one night. They refused me, they were afraid, because the Germans searched the houses for Jews in hiding.

I finally found a Polish family, who agreed for a fee of five hundred zloty to let me sleep one night in the barn with the chickens under the condition that if the Germans found me there, I must say that I snuck into the barn without their knowledge.

There were many more difficult days of sufferings and tribulations, also in the road that I went through alone with Aryan papers.

The long-awaited day of liberation has come, but I was not happy that day. The day of liberation was imbued with sadness, accompanied by tears and deep pain for those who were no longer with us.

May their memory be blessed.

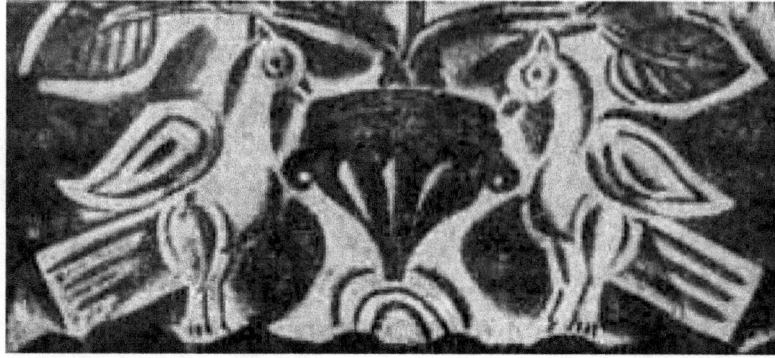

[Pages 400-404]

Rosh Hashanah, 1942

by Dvorah Grodzitzki–Schicht

Hard by the railroad tracks between Warsaw and Wolomin is the vacation village Sosnovka where the Jews of Wolomin were sent into the ghetto.

This was a large district with a small number of houses and cabins. The crowding, therefore, was terrible. On the average, ten people lived in each room.

In 1940, when the decree was promulgated, no one who lived in the ghetto would have thought that we would witness the funeral processions of hundreds of thousands, and even millions, of Jews on their death march that went from Warsaw and passed by Sosnovka on the way to Treblinka.

In those days, the eve of Rosh Hashanah, 1942, in the small ghetto of Sosnovka, things were astir. From the surrounding ghettos came horrifying reports of liquidation. The word "liquidation" hung in the air like a nightmare. People ran around like stampeding animals seeking a hiding place where they could save themselves, or a piece of advice, or a way out.

People escaped from one ghetto to another seeking a hint that would give them security or hope, assurance that surely the ghetto would be preserved. When that illusion came to an end, they tried to find another place, another ghetto, with the same hope, with the same accounting for the future, with the same false thoughts that there the Jews would be more fortunate…a guess that so far the Jews there had been left in peace. They hung on a promise, an assurance from a Nazi commander or policeman who gave them to understand that it would be different elsewhere.

People knew that the decree had been sealed. But everyone grasped at straws, went after the slightest bit of hope, of illusion, that everything was not lost. This was the illusion of life that comes at the most difficult times, when the heart stops beating because of the horror, because of the fear for little children who see death before their eyes and whose silent looks ask: Why?

At the same time, twice a day trains arrived with boxcars packed with Jews. These were transports on their way to Treblinka. They would stand there for a little while. One could see there different types of Jews: Greek, French, Belgian, Dutch, and others, in different types of clothing, with hats and umbrellas. Through the slats we could hear their questions: "Is it far from here to the colony of Treblinka?" Jews were afraid to approach the cars, but passing Poles relayed their questions. We could hear their voices in the ghetto, but we could not make out their words.

Not so naïve were the Jews from the Warsaw Ghetto, although in the earliest days of the campaign they did not believe that they were being led to their deaths. We recognized the Warsaw transports by the sound of their sorrow and suffering that emerged through the barred windows.

From one of the windows came a weak voice begging for water. From another car one could hear a child begging for a cup for a physiological necessity. Their voices went into a vast wilderness.

From many cars, pale, pained faces looked out, and their glances seemed as if they scorched the earth and in their last minutes sought among the passing Poles a familiar face. Perhaps they sought someone from their family who had escaped to the Aryan side, a husband or a wife. There were some who in their last minutes tested the strength of the bars but ended up powerless and despairing.

There were times when Jews jumped out of the train cars. They were seldom successful in escaping. Usually they were greeted by a bullet from a Ukrainian, German, or Polish murderer.

The Wolomin Jews in Sosnovka saw all this from afar. Twice a day the trains went by, one at dawn and the other in the afternoon. No one knew how many Jews were in each transport, but people said that each transport represented six thousand souls. The Jews in the Sosnovka ghetto calculated that each day, twelve thousand Jews went to an awful death.

Such was the atmosphere in Sosnovka. And with such thoughts, people approached the High Holidays. Even going to the Selichos service was a problem. It was forbidden to leave our houses from seven o'clock in the evening until five in the morning. The curfew was strictly enforced. Transgressors received capital punishment. Still, people came together in minyans and recited Selichos. People hid by the walls, took hidden paths, and in an apartment in a nearby neighborhood they gathered, wept, begged forgiveness and purification.

Oddly, at that time the Jews were particularly free of sin, but they were more fervent in begging forgiveness for their transgressions. Were their terrible sufferings, their inhuman pain that they felt day in and day out, not punishment for their sins? Was simple existence itself a sin?

So Selichos night passed and Rosh Hashanah arrived.

People gathered early to pray and they arranged to finish early so as not to be noticed by the murderers. Such prayers! Whoever prayed or heard such prayers could never get the sound of her ears.

Everyone was suffused with sacred trembling, the men wrapped in their taleisim and the women in their headscarves sobbed and cried. The two crowded rooms gave off an atmosphere of mournful sanctity. The men were pressed together in the bigger crowd, crying and pleading. The greatest request was for a year of life. The usual pleas for health and sustenance had disappeared. One desire, one request dominated everything: to live, to survive.

"Ribono shel olam, hear the prayer from our broken hearts," was heard from a corner, the lament of a young woman whose husband and child were far from home and from whom she had heard nothing for a long time.

I see them living in front of me, those who prayed in the secret prayer halls, men and women, broken, pained, and yet with so much belief in the justice of the Almighty. I see my mother before me, who laments over her sixteen–year–old son, who was the first sacrifice of Sosnovka, who was killed beside the ghetto. Everyone had someone to mourn. Each home had those who were killed who died a more natural death through an epidemic.

A great plea rose from everyone's heart, filled the air, floated up and penetrated the heavens: Let us live!

The children, too, who came to hear the shofar blown, were dominated by the communal fear, and with terror in their eyes they looked to their fathers and mothers, seeking answers to the many questions that disturbed their childish minds.

The children in the ghetto were not mischievous. In the ghetto, one did not hear childish laughter. It seemed that they completely lacked a childhood. All were old before their time. Little children felt and knew what was coming for them. They lived with fear, that engulfed them. It was especially strong and clear to those children who helped to support their families. They went thieving on the Aryan side. They begged and then smuggled food into the ghetto for their families. A number of them were killed by the murderers, by the German SS or by Poles.

All the children on that Rosh Hashanah experienced fear, just as the adults did, and were suffused with that one urgent prayer: to live!

Soon, silence fell. You could hear the deep sighs of the adults. People paid attention to the shofar blasts. The chazzan began with a trembling voice to sing "Lamnatzeyach," but suddenly a shot was heard..

Everyone's turned their faces in the direction whence the shot came. Everyone's thoughts were on the question of who had been shot. Everyone knew that the Germans didn't just shoot. The commotion lasted just a short while. The Jews had learned to be controlled and disciplined. They all waited for some information, and soon someone came in who told us that a policeman had shot an old Jewish woman who had tried to leave the ghetto.

Everyone felt the pressure in their hearts, but they could not dwell on it. It was a daily occurrence over which people gave a deep sigh or a sharp cry. Then they began their prayers again. As they said "Unethane tokef," a heart–rending cry filled the air of the tiny rooms. That was the prayer of the martyr Rabbi Amnon that people traditionally recited fervently and with great devotion, as they did then in the small congregation, in the crowded rooms of the ghetto in Sosnovka.

With their weary lips the Jews whispered: "Open the gates of heaven…" The gates of heaven had never for these Jews fallen on the Earth, but now, in the last days of their lives, they pleaded from deep in their hearts that their prayers should go to the Throne of Glory and their cries should be heard.

There were also some who desired in those moments that the gates of heaven should open and allow into the world all good, to establish eternal peace for their inhuman suffering and a bit of a reward for the hard travails that filled the days and nights of their lives on earth.

Hidden strengths, whose source no one knew, replaced their hard and bitter thoughts, and their souls were illuminated with sacred beliefs.

It seems that the Jews in the ghetto became more spiritual with God's holiness and were, at that moment, transformed into heroes, strengthened with the power of ancient holiness.

A great power infused the prayers on that Rosh Hashanah. Encouraged, the ghetto dwellers wished each other a year of life and left their secret synagogue, strengthened with trust and belief, that same trust that sustained the Jews in all the hard times of their existence.

On their way home, they encountered the train that had brought a fresh transport of Warsaw Jews on their last journey. It was as if the devil himself had played this trick. The Jews stood still and looked pityingly at the martyrs.

Then the train moved on.

[Pages 405-428]

My Experiences in the Ghetto

by Kopel Berman

In memory of my mother, who was killed in the ghetto at the age of 85.

I am responding to the assignment to inscribe the memories of experiences, my own and those of others, that took place among the general Jewish population of Wolomin–it is difficult and a heavy responsibility. Fate fell out that I am among the few survivors, hidden by a miracle and detained there for a certain time after the war, though I had to leave quickly because of the threats from the Poles.

It is clear to me that I do not have the power to convey the whole story. It is impossible to remember all the dates and names. Still, I write because I feel it is a sacred duty to record in the Yizkor Book the destruction of the Jewish community of Wolomin.

We came to Wolomin at the end of 1933. Before that we lived in the neighboring shtetl of Yodove. This was one of the scores of Jewish shtetls in Poland. In Yodove, ninety–five percent of the population was Jewish. Most of them were merchants and craftsmen. There were also quite a few who lived on air, or on miracles. Once a week, on Wednesdays, was a market day, when the peasants from the surrounding villages brought their products for sale and used the money to buy kerosene, salt, and other city goods that they needed.

Three kilometers from Yodove was the Arleh train station, where there was a large woods to which hundreds of visitors would come from the city in the summer, which contributed to the incomes of the Jewish residents. One could say that fifty percent of the population lived on the income from the summer season.

My financial standing in the shtetl as a watchmaker was no better than that of the others. My profession did not allow me to exist, so I had to seek a position with better prospects, which is what brought me to Wolomin.

Wolomin had that time had about twenty–five thousand inhabitants, of whom there were no more than three thousand Jews. The populace was closely bound up with Warsaw, where people worked as clerks or in other jobs, but because of the lack of apartments, they lived in Wolomin.

So it was among the Polish population and among the Jews.

Many of Wolomin's Jews worked in Warsaw as knitters, suitcase makers, and at other jobs. The economic position of the Jews in Wolomin was somewhat better than in other small shtetls. I was successful and did not do badly financially, and also socially I became acclimated.

Gradually I got to know the Wolomin Jews, those who took an active role in community life. People used to come to my home in the evenings, where we discussed various topics, political and societal, that were in the air.

Community life in Wolomin was colorful and intense. There were two libraries and supporters of all the parties, from the rightist Zionist organizations to Bundists and communists. There were many activities. There was also a Maccabee Sports Club. The leftist parties had members in the PPS Sports Club "Pramien." The Bundists also belonged there.

In 1933 there was a sharp rise in Poland of anti–Semitism, and Wolomin's Poles joined in that devilish dance, which seemed more pointed than in other small shtetls because the Jews were a small minority and the Poles were in close contact with the anti–Semitic centers in Warsaw.

People started to feel it in the economic realm. They also saw attacks on Jews in the streets. The members of the anti–Semitic organization NARA in Wolomin demonstrated their hooliganish acts, set up pickets by Jewish shops and businesses and did not allow entrance to Christian customers, and attacked the Jews, particularly those who appeared in Christian neighborhoods. In the evenings, people even feared to walk in Jewish neighborhoods.

On summer Shabbos days, when Dluge Street was filled with strolling Jews, one of them, Taybloom, was hit by a bullet from a revolver. A NARA criminal had shot him from behind. Naturally no one caught the criminal. No one would be a witness.

It became a habit to travel in groups, especially in the evening. It often happened that a Jew would arrive home from a trip with a split head. It also happened that Jews were thrown out of trains in the middle of a trip.

The Outbreak of the Second World War

With each day, the situation became worse, more dangerous.

A short time before the outbreak of the second world war, in hindsight it appears that the situation of Wolomin's Jews became a little better.

As the Germans were agitating against the Poles, many Poles recognized that they must do something, so a committee was formed in Wolomin, including Jews, for the purpose of raising funds for armaments.

This activity began with a huge loan, in which Jews played a large part. At the same time a committee was formed for the defense of Wolomin. This activity consisted of digging trenches around the town and preparing the populace for war in case the Germans threatened Wolomin. In those days, Jews and Christians sent outside the town to dig trenches.

On September 1, 1939, it was my turn to dig trenches. Early in the morning, as I stood at the worksite with my spade in my hand, two airplanes suddenly appeared in the sky. One plane was chasing the other and shooting at it. No one realized that it was a German plane chasing a Polish plane and shooting at it..

We did not know then that Germany had attacked Poland that morning. We were sure that these were the maneuvers of Polish flyers and we returned to our work digging trenches.

It was not long, however, before someone came from the town with the news that he had heard on the radio, that the Germans had attacked Poland at several spots on the border.

The first reports were that Poland was putting up a strong defense, but we threw up our hands, laid aside our work, and headed for home. A heavy depression fell on the shtetl, particularly on the Jewish residents. Chaos and horror seized the whole population. People saw how the police and the officials from the magistrate's office and other institutions prepared to flee, burning the archives and important documents.

The roads were full of people fleeing, in wagons, in cars, and on foot. People were heading east, in the direction of the Russian border. Among them were almost all the Jewish young people, intending to find safety on the other side of the Russian

The Town is Bombed

A week before the occupation, the town was bombed by German airplanes, which flew around above Wolomin for several hours and sowed destruction and obliteration. Nothing disturbed them. Their target was the train line, but at the same time they got Warshawski Street, Patschava, and others. The planes dropped incendiary bombs and shot their machine guns at the civilian population. People ran through the streets seeking shelter, but were killed.

On that day there were scores of dead in Wolomin as well as many wounded. For two days the buildings burned, but there was no one to put out the flames.

The next morning from the ruins appeared the shadows of those who had hidden, and they looked with horror toward the sky to be sure there were no planes. Normal life stopped. It was hard to buy anything to eat, and hunger was soon felt in the homes.

People lived on what they had stored and some traded whatever they had for bread. Food supply came to a halt. The shtetl became lawless. There was no one in control, neither the Poles nor the Germans.

This situation lasted for a whole week, until the Germans arrived.

On the second day of Rosh Hashanah, at seven in the morning, the town was bombarded by shells that landed in many houses but did little damage or hurt many people. In the afternoon came the first Panzer vehicles with German soldiers. No one dared show themselves in the streets.

From our hiding places we saw great streams of motorized troops. After several long hours, one military unit, led by an officer, stopped in the shtetl. The soldiers began to make their rounds in the shtetl. First they broke into Goldvasser's liquor store, which was quickly emptied. That was a signal for them to begin looting, along with the Polish mob. The Poles showed the Germans which shops belonged to Jews, and therefore the Germans left for them whatever was not worth taking.

On the third day, the situation quieted down a bit. A military command was established, and it ordered that stores be opened. The people were ordered to remain calm. A curfew was instituted from six in the evening until seven in the morning, though this did not stop the German soldiers and Polish hooligans from breaking into Jewish businesses both early in the day and late at night.

The First Decrees

Then the first decrees concerning the Jewish populace were issued. The Jewish slaughter of animals was prohibited; when a German soldier appeared, a Jew had to get off of the sidewalk; a Magen Dovid had to be shown in the windows of Jewish businesses; and on the front of Jewish businesses, the word "Jew" had to be written in large letters.

Transgressing these orders entailed strict punishments.

Right away there began a hunt for Jews to kidnap Jews for work details and assigning them to clean the streets or restore the rail lines. One man was beaten so badly while working on the rail lines that he died the next day.

Women were also seized for work, such as washing the floors in the dwellings that the Germans occupied. The women were forced to wash the floors with their own undergarments.

Leaving Wolomin

In those days began the second exodus from Wolomin. This time not only the young people left, but whole families. The Germans made no special difficulty. There were even times when the military commander provided lights to indicate the direction of the German–Russian border.

Two of my most trusted friends, Moyshe Vaynbroom and Moyshe Zucker, for the second time left Wolomin, intending to go to the border. I intended to go as a third party with them, and I made all my preparations. We planned to meet at five in the morning at my place and set out from there.

But in the meantime, I had to change plans. My wife and children broke into a pulsing cry, and at the last minute I gave up my resolution. When Vaynbroom and Zucker arrived at the appointed hour, I had to disappoint them. I had decided not to abandon my family. Sadly, my dear friends did not succeed in escaping. They were killed in Soviet Russia.

The bells started to ring to announce the German–Russian agreement, according to which the Russians could go as far as the Vistula, which would become the new border with the Germans. There were times when people approached the German commander for a document allowing them to cross the border, and he replied that it was not necessary because the Russians were coming. People said that already nearby the Germans were yielding. Thus the stream of immigrants ceased. Everyone waited with anticipation for the coming of the Russians, as if for the coming a new messiah.

The Shul in Flames

On Hoshanah Rabbah, at night, when religious Jews were in the shuls, waiting to celebrate at midnight, suddenly German soldiers appeared and began to jeer at the Jews. They ordered them to take the Torah scrolls out to the courtyard, forced them to strip off the covers, and set fire to them along with the shul.

This was a signal for the Poles that it was permissible to go wild, since the Jews were fair game. In a few hours, nothing remained of the shul but a memory.

Those who had expected that the Russians would come lost their last hope, as they learned that according to the Ribbentrop–Molotov agreement the border would be established between the Arva and Bug Rivers.

Again it became necessary to try to escape from the town in the direction of the Russian border, but now it was much more difficult. The border was closely guarded, and crossing it was very dangerous. The best possibility was that the Germans would seize whatever goods one had. In the late–winter months, scores of thousands of people filled the border passage awaiting the moment when they could make a break for Russia. Many died from the cold and from disease.

Several times the Germans rounded up all these people and sent them back to their homes, but this was not always the case. Many were shot along the road.

The German civilian administration took over power from the military. The criminal police, the Gestapo and the SS arrived. The Polish police immediately began to work with them.

Again they began to issue new decrees: every Jew, men and women twelve years and up, had to wear on their left sleeve a white band with a blue magen dovid; they must report to a work brigade and must do whatever work the Germans assigned them.

One decree followed another. Their purpose was to humiliate, depress, and poison the lives of the Jewish populace.

On one day they arrested the Jewish council members and held them for two days without food or water. Among them were: Mendel Vagenshteyn, Abba Fromm, Goldgrom, and others. During those two days, they were tortured. On the third day they were released with an order to organize a Jewish council with a Jewish head. The task of the Jewish council was to carry out the orders of the German authority, making them personally responsible for every order that was not carried out.

The First Tribute

The first order was to collect a tribute of a quarter of a million zlotys from the Jewish population of Wolomin. That sum had to be assembled within fifteen days.

This new decree prompted a new round of flights to the border. Young and old went by different roads and byways, best by terrible dangers

Wolomin looked as it had looked in the first days after the bombardment. The streets were deserted, empty. One saw almost no young people. At that time I also tried to escape from Wolomin. With great difficulty I managed to hire a cart, on which I loaded a few things and, with my wife and child, set out on the way.

When we got close to Jadova, it appeared that we would miss the train. Jadova lies on the way to Malkin, near the Russian border, and the town was therefore overrun with wanderers from every corner of Poland, fleeing Jews, who were stuck in Jadova and could not get across the border. They waited for news that the border guards were changing and a "good one" was on duty and would accept their bribes.

But such things seldom happened. Mostly those who tried to cross the border were beaten bloody and robbed of all they had with them.

In such circumstances, only the young could escape, for they had nothing to lose and were prepared to do anything to save themselves. It was harder for families, who could not decide whether to abandon their last possessions that they had brought with them in order to save the lives of their families.

The road from Jadova to Malkin was clogged with people, people in wagons and on foot. People went toward Malkin and back from Malkin. Those who returned from Malkin, who could not cross the border, remained in Jadova. Perhaps, they thought, better news would arrive and they would be able to escape from the German Gehenna.

I, too, decided to stay with my family in Jadova and await an opportunity that would allow us to cross the border. Eight days we stayed there with my wife's parents and waited for the longed–for news, but each day the situation worsened and the outlook was terrible. Living conditions in Jadova were unbearable. It became clear that we could not sustain this mode of living. Our final decision was to return to Wolomin, so that whatever befell the other Jews would happen to us as well.

Arriving back in Wolomin, we sought ways to accommodate ourselves to the new conditions. Like drunkards who grab at straws, we struggled for hope that the Germans would eventually settle down and retreat from their wild hatred for Jews and perhaps we could co–exist with them.

The Newly Formed Jewish Council

The newly formed Jewish council consisted of the old councilors and some new ones who had been forced into the position. At the head of the council was Blumberg. The council was responsible for collecting the tribute, and when they paid it, they were forced to agree to the Germans' demand that they account for the required number of laborers.

This seemed to be a simple accomplishment, because the wild hunt to capture Jews for work was always accompanied with blows and humiliation. No one was ever sure he would live through the end of the day.

Every day a messenger came from the Germans and brought to the council a list of things that they had to deliver, from furniture to foodstuffs. The council had to meet all their demands.

It was a lawless time.

A Jewish militia was formed. Life for the Jews was a bitter gehenna. Hunger dwelled in Jewish homes. Refugees continued to arrive, people who had escaped from their homes or who were expelled from other shtetls, from Vishkov, from Nashelski, from Poltusk.

A people's kitchen was established to provide lunches to those in need. This helped a little, but it did not solve the problem of hunger. The lunch consisted of a bit of miserable soup that could not satisfy the hungry Jews.

In charge of the people's kitchen was a young man named Toleshnik, a fine young man who devoted all his strength to easing the lives of the starving. He made superhuman efforts, but it was beyond his power.

Typhus

The first signs of typhus began to appear. Because of the lack of medication, many died. We had to conceal the cases of typhus from the Germans, because the Germans would isolate the houses of the afflicted, not allowing the inhabitants to go out or anyone to go in.

Outwardly things were growing worse. A Jew with a bead would not allow himself to be seen in the street. Many wrapped their beards in scarves, as if they had toothaches. They did this when they had to go outside, but it did not always work.

In the evenings, after six o'clock, people shut themselves in their homes, while outside the Polish hooligans, accompanied by German soldiers and the SS, robbed and destroyed businesses.

I was the only watchmaker remaining in Wolomin, so I had a lot of work, even from German soldiers, who often gave me bread and other kinds of food for my work. Materially, I was not badly off, so I could help others with foodstuffs and cigarettes that I received from German soldiers as though exchanged among acquaintances.

The problems began in the evening. German soldiers often would knock on the doors, when it would take me a little while to open up. The German soldier would force it open, with yells and curses, demanding that I would sell him a ring or some other bauble for his girlfriend. That girlfriend was usually a Polish girl who stood by his side, and he wanted to pay her for the love with which she had graced him.

Understand, I tried to explain that I dealt only with work, not with merchandise. Then he would hold a gun to my head. Helplessly I told him that he should look for himself, and if he found anything, he should take it.

Each soldier then conducted his own search, and when he was dissappointed he would leave, letting out his anger on everyone in the house.

Such visits were frequent, and they always had the same end.

Thus went this degrading life, hunger, humiliation, and oppression.

Lost Books

At Pesach, 1940, several Gestapo officers from Warsaw arrived and arrested more than twenty people, including Moyshe Teyblum. When they came to arrest him, he was, by chance, not at home. They took his wife and left a note that he should come to Gestapo headquarters and they would then release his wife. Early in the morning, he complied and was quickly arrested, but they did not free his wife. Neither of them ever returned home. The Christian families who were arrested at the same time were sent little boxes with the ashes of their husbands and a note that they had died of illness. The Teyblum family received no such boxes and no one knew how they had been killed.

During this whole time, there was practically no cultural life in the town. The few synagogues that were in Wolomin were burned down early on by the Germans. On Shabbos, neighbors would gather in a private dwelling where they could pray with a minyan. Observant Jews were afraid to be seen in the streets.

There were no newspapers to read. The few Polish papers that were published were bought up by the Poles. No one was interested in these papers, which were full of lies, of false reports. No one could listen to the radio. The Germans had confiscated all receivers. The Jews in Wolomin therefore conveyed news by word of mouth, always with optimism, with convincing hope for better times.

Before the war, there were two Jewish libraries in Wolomin, which were liquidated even before the Germans arrived. When the Jews were forced out to Sosnovke, people found most of the books from the Peretz Library in a stable where Yossel Berger had lived. No one could understand how the books got there. It was discovered by Shmuel Rozner, a Jewish policeman with whom we lived in the ghetto, just outside of Sosnovke, and we decided to sneak the books into our house, where we had a hiding place under the roof. The books were welcome there and were our only taste of intellectual life in the ghetto.

Life in the Ghetto

There are a lot of rumors as people get used to a ghetto. Rumors had begun to spread since people had started to build a wall in Warsaw around the Jewish streets. There were many people who reacted indifferently. They believed that with the separation of the Jews from the rest of the population, the Jews would be more secure and have no fear of going into the streets. They would have more secure lives. There were others who pretty much did not believe the rumors that the Jews would be shut up in a ghetto. "How would we live?" we asked each other.

At the end of the summer of 1940 came the order that the Jews of the whole district must by the fifteenth of October, 1940, separate themselves from the general population and live in separate places set aside for them. The German authority immediately began to carry out the orders. In Wolomin the ghetto was established in the summer resort of Sosnovke. The Jewish council tried to have this order negated, but they were unsuccessful. Nothing could change the order.

The ghetto began in the area of Shtutman's houses, a small quarter that was about a kilometer from the town. In normal times, that area could not accept even half of the Jewish population, because so many refugees who had escaped from other towns had fled to Wolomin.

The separation of the Jewish population by certain deadlines fell to the Jewish council, which had to be sure that not even a single Jew remained in Wolomin. The members of the council had to determine a spot for each person.

The well–to–do and those who had nice apartments in Wolomin could trade with a Christian inhabitant. Thus was established a wealthy quarter in the area of Shtutman's houses, according to the Jewish council's orders. The simply built summer homes of Sosnovke were taken over by the remaining Jews.

The deadline was very close and the Jews had to leave the town, and before the orders for their new dwellings could be completed, many people, with their poor belongings, lay in the streets. People were cramped together as if in a henhouse. On top of this, many of the poor from Rodzimin arrived and had to be accommodated in the ghetto.

According to the orders of the German authority, people could bring into the ghetto a single suitcase with their necessities, but regardless of the order, each person brought whatever he could. In particular they brought with them articles of food for the first days.

For several weeks the ghetto stood open and it was possible to obtain articles of food that people bought with their last groschen from the peasants, but that did not last long. Soon the Germans ordered the ghetto sealed for its nearly three kilometer circuit, surrounded with barbed wire, and on the entrance tower two Jewish watchmen had to be sure that no one could leave without permission and that no Aryan could enter the ghetto.

On the tower was a banner with the inscription: "Achtung, infectious disease. Entrance forbidden to Aryans!"

But that did not stop the Germans from coming every day into the ghetto with their orders for the Jewish council or to seize things, even people, whom they sent to work on local projects or to work camps.

With the closing of the ghetto, the Jewish council became a rule within a rule. The Jews were subject to the rulings of the Jewish council. The council could arrest people for disobeying their orders, and they had their own prison.

The head of the Jewish police was a member of the Jewish council, but he was subject to someone else.

Even a greater problem was the typhus epidemic, which took on catastrophic proportions. People lived in awful conditions, almost on top of one another. The plague spread with the speed of lightning, and the three doctors who were in the ghetto– Frank, Friedman, and Reznick–were helpless. There was no medicine. Dr. Friedman alone himself became ill and died.

In such circumstances, people had to be chosen for the two German work camps, in Wilianov and Isabelin, beyond Rodzimin. In the camps, people worked in unbearable conditions, and after a short time became quite ill. There were some who were sent back to the ghetto and who had to be replaced in order to satisfy Wolomin's quota.

The two work camps used up a great deal of youthful strength, so that older men had to be used for the local labor. No one was exempted from labor. The wealthy could pay others to work in their place. There was never a lack of people who would work in place of others for money.

From day to day, hunger grew sharper. Supplies that people had brought with them dwindled, and no fresh supplies were available. Children left the ghetto and bought a few products that they brought back to sell in the ghetto. These children were called "little merchants." There were also adults whose poverty forced them to leave the ghetto in search of something to eat.

In 1940, leaving the ghetto did not mean death. In the early times, before the German–Russian war, people managed to get a supply of flour to bake bread. There were still a few bakeries. The allocation was a hundred grams of bread per person, but it came neither regularly nor often. The rest people bought on the black market. For outrageous prices one could get enough bread. The bakeries also received flour from outside the ghetto, which peasants during the night brought to the barbed wire and from there was smuggled into the ghetto. There was a time when Christians came to the Jewish bakeries to buy bread which they sent to Warsaw for the black market. Such trade took place at night. There were also many primitive mills that in a variety of ways got corn to grind.

Finally, it was the same with heating. People obtained coal from the other side of the barbed wire. The Polish kids stole coal from the wagons and carried it to the wire where customers stood ready to buy the merchandise.

In Sosnovke, they also cut down the trees, which sufficed for burning during the first winter. In a short while, the famous summer resort stood without its woods. Hardly a single tree remained.

I remember a curious thing. I was at a wedding in Sosnovke, one of numerous weddings that took place in the ghetto. The groom was Konyakovski and the bride was Morgenshtern, Yisroel Morgenshtern's sister. The wedding was modest. In the middle of the wedding, the police came in, with Commandant Goldgram at their head.

They were on an inspection tour of the area of the woods, to be sure that no one cut down the last trees. As they passed by, they saw the wedding and came in.

It seemed that they were already a little tipsy from earlier. They took some refreshments and happily enjoyed themselves. Goldgram made a speech wishing the young couple a happy life together. Then he moved on to current topics, and he ended with humor: "People say that after the war I'll be hanged from a tree, but where will they find a hanging tree when the woods are no longer there?"

The defeats that the Germans suffered at the front had repercussions in the hinterlands. On the Jews in the ghetto fell the responsibility to provide warm clothing for the front. Jews had to give their fur coats. There was a deadline, and anyone who was found with a fur after the deadline would be shot.

The Jews in Wolomin turned in their furs precisely at the deadline.

Of course, there were a few who hid their furs in secure spots or with Christians. So it was with the Jews Fried, Pomerantz, and Loskovski, who hid their furs with a Christian. Someone told the Germans, and they arrested all of them and sent them to Rodzimin, where they were shot.

A short time later there was an alarm that every Jew who left the ghetto would be shot on the spot. The alarm came from Rodzimin, where a Jew had been shot for leaving the ghetto.

That same week, a young man named Novogradzki left the ghetto and wanted to take care of business in the town. By chance, some gendarmes approached and seized him. They tied him up with a rope to their sled and forced him to run after the sled, in which they were sitting. When his strength gave out and he fell, the sled did not stop and dragged him to Moranav Place, where they shot him.

Such scenes later became daily events. When the gendarmes came to Wolomin, they would grab anyone and play out such tragic scenes. Once when they had not found in Wolomin any victims, they called out a Jew who was standing near the barbed wire, and as he approached, they shot him. The gendarmes Shteyn, Schumacher, and Hoffa excelled in sadism. With them used to go a blond German beast who led them in their hunt for Jews. Having done their little work, the gendarmes came to the Jewish council and demanded that they should be paid two thousand zlotys for every bullet they shot. After receiving the money, they wrote out a receipt and left the empty cartridge cases. They casually said that the cartridge cases belonged to the Jewish council, because they had paid for them.

The End Approaches

In May of 1942 came the bitter news that the Jews of Tluszcz, Postelnik, and Varki had been driven out and taken to the Warsaw Ghetto. Many died on the way. In Tluszcz the Jews had been lined up in rows and ordered to hand over their money and valuables, with the threat, as later events would show, that anyone who held back would immediately be shot. There were some who tried to hide in secret places. Thorough searches were made, and if money or jewelry was found in anyone's home, that person was shot on the spot. In the square lay the bodies of scores of executed Jews. Many others were shot on the road when they could not maintain the tempo of the gendarmes, who were riding on horses.

The rabbi of Tluszcz was in those days in Jadova for the funeral of a prominent Jew, because there was no Jewish cemetery in Tluszcz. He therefore remained overnight in Jadova and was not in town for the liquidation. The Germans did not neglect to ask where the rabbi was and why he was not where he belonged. Someone told them that the rabbi was in Jadova. The next morning the Germans went to the Jadova Jewish council and demanded that they immediately produce the Tluszcz rabbi or they would shoot ten Jewish policemen. Turmoil erupted in the shtetl. People knew that they had no good choices. The agitation lasted a short time, but in the meantime the rabbi knew that the Germans were looking for him and had decided to make a martyr of him. With his head held high, he approached the murderers. The gendarmes fell on him with murderous rage, beat him horribly, and then shot him. They ordered him buried right there, in the courtyard of the Jewish council.

In 1948, we led the exhumation of the Jadova martyrs who were shot at the time of the liquidation of the ghetto and at other times, and we then buried them in other places. We also made every effort to find the grave of the rabbi and transfer his remains to the cemetery, but sadly we could not find them. The building that housed the Jewish council had been destroyed. Far and near was desolation, sown with potatoes. We negotiated with the Christians who had sown the potatoes, wanting to pay them for the damage, but they would not agree. It happened to be a market day, and at the cries of the Christians, a crowd of curious onlookers gathered. We saw that we could accomplish nothing and therefore turned to the Polish police, who approved our efforts at exhumation, but unfortunately we could not find the rabbi's remains.

Transports to Treblinka

Rumors flew that the Germans planned to create four large ghettos in which they would concentrate the Jewish population of all of Poland. We already had enough evidence of how the deportations from the smaller ghettos looked. The first victims were always the refugees from the destroyed shtetls. Those who could tried to send money to relatives or acquaintances in Warsaw. Some were also able to send clothing. The German tactics against the Jewish population was always a secret, and no one could know the method or the terms of transfer from one place to another. The officials always gave false information to calm the Jews down, saying that no harm would come to them. It did not occur to anyone that the Warsaw Ghetto would suffer first. We were the first to know the bitter truth about transport to Treblinka. The Germans told everyone that the transports were headed east, where work camps were set up and there would be better conditions. The Wolomin ghetto lay along the railroad tracks, so that we saw each transport that went once or twice a day to Treblinka. We heard the cries that emanated from the cars. It happened that a transport stopped at the station and we heard complaints and pleas for a little water; but by each car stood soldiers with rifles in their hands, ready to shoot anyone who tried to approach the cars. On the way back, Polish rail workers yelled at us and showed us in gestures what was done to the Jews. It would happen that a Wolomin train worker would enter the ghetto and tell us that when the trains arrived at Treblinka, German rail workers would take over and lead the train into the camp. On the way back, the cars were filled with clothing headed for Warsaw. The Germans who were in charge of the empty transports once told the Poles what had been done to the Jews.

At first people reacted to this news with disbelief. People did not want to believe in all these horrors. Even the most pessimistic could not bring themselves to believe that these things could happen. We took what the Polish rail worker said to be a nightmarish fantasy. There were some who held that he spoke with the intention of scaring us. There was even a case of a Wolomin shoemaker, who came from Vogrov and did not look like a Jew. He often went to the Aryan side. He himself spoke with a Jew who had managed to return from the camps by hiding in the clothing that was being taken to Warsaw. He related that the Jews who were being taken in the transports were told to take off their clothes and were then led to the gas chambers, where they were gassed, after which their bodies were burned. That Jew had been in a labor battalion, which had to sort the clothing of those who had been gassed. That gave him the opportunity to get into a train car and cover himself with clothes. When the transport had left the camp, he jumped out of the car. Most of the Jews in the ghetto held that his story was a false rumor.

When the awful truth finally became known, there was a terrible outcry in the ghetto. There were many who began to flee from the ghetto and who took things to hide. Some tried to obtain false documents with Aryan names. The young made for the Russian border. That journey was beset by grave dangers, and many from Wolomin paid with their lives. The goal of those fleeing was Zembrov, which was then at the German–Russian border, but seldom did people make it there. The danger began when exiting the ghetto. Polish gangs wandered on every road, and when they caught a Jew, they robbed him and left him naked. Those who went on a train were identified by the Poles, who either turned them over to the Germans or threw them from the moving train.

Those who remained in the Wolomin ghetto also had no peace and tried to find ways to leave the ghetto through the underground. There was an attempt to turn the ghetto into a work camp that would supply labor for the Wehrmacht. That would have to be done by those who ran Warsaw's trades and factories that worked for the Germans. Such attempts were also made in Minsk Mazowiecki, Lafyanka, and other shtetls. People began seeking protection from higher–ups, but without success. At one point there was an appeal to the railroad authority to set out a work plan for the Wolomin ghetto, saying that the train line required renovations because it was in bad shape thanks to the constant traffic of the transports that took war materiel to the Russian front. The rail authority should form Jewish work brigades in the Wolomin ghetto. The plan was approved. The Jewish council put out a notice that people should come and register for work. With mixed feelings, full of doubts and hesitations, people began to register. No one was sure if that would protect us from anything. It went on because of fear for men's wives, children, and parents.

Each day in the square near the Jewish council, a group of about a hundred fifty men gathered under the supervision of the Jewish police. They were led out of the ghetto to the train station, where they were divided into groups, which the rail officials assigned to their jobs.

The labor was difficult. They had to tear up the old ties to which the tracks were attached and lay down new ones. There were various other jobs, like, for example, gathering stones and putting them between the ties.

I was among those who registered for such work, not because I believed that I would be saving my life, which had little worth when there was no assurance that my family would be spared. I regarded this labor as a way to get out of the ghetto and into the fresh air. Understand, it was not a question of getting a little pleasure, just a way of changing places.

This was in the days of the transports that came from the Warsaw Ghetto, each day two or three transports of thirty or forty cars full of people. From a distance we heard their moans and pleas, saw the SS personnel, Lithuanian, Latvian, and Ukrainian bandits who guarded them, with their rifles pointed at us so that no one would try to approach the trains. One time a transport was made up of German luxury trains whose passengers, whom we could see through the windows, were dressed elegantly. We could see their beautiful suitcases. A few of them stood near the windows and, seeing us with our Mogen Dovids sewn on our shoulders, one of them made a joke. Showing a yellow Mogen Dovid that he had on his chest, he asked where they were being taken. They received no answer from us. The train cars went further, toward Treblinka. For us it was remarkable that their wagon was not guarded. Our consciences bothered us because we had not told them the truth. Perhaps some of them would have hidden themselves by jumping out of the moving train.

Meanwhile, more bad news arrived about the liquidations that were taken place across Poland. Even those places that had been turned into labor camps were being liquidated. Also in Warsaw they had stopped making exceptions for the workers, for those who had been designated as necessary Jews, who worked for the war industries and who in the beginning been spared. It was not long before they, too, just like the other Jews, were loaded onto the trains.

We no longer had any illusions that labor would save us. Many stopped showing up for work. And those who did show up no longer had any hope that it would save them. People walked around mechanically. Some believed that they would be in the ghetto for a while and they would stick with the work. Others went with the aim of getting food from outside the ghetto.

Every day people died from hunger and disease, and from being shot. They went around as if in the throes of death, sentenced to perish. And there were arrangements for entertainment. Even in this time of woe, of fear of death and peril, there was "Trouble Enough in its Time." It was founded by several bright young men and women who had a bit of acting talent, and they prepared a performance for every Shabbos afternoon. They performed pieces by Yaakov Gordin, by Sholem Aleichem. After the performances, people went to dig hiding places in secret places where they intended to hide themselves in case of a sudden raid. Strangely, no one believed it would be possible to survive this horrible time, but even so, each one sought a way to hide himself. These preparations lasted several weeks. We prepared food and water, some clothing, but no one needed it. On the night of Shemini Atzeres in 1942, the Polish police unit came to the Jewish council and delivered the news that during the night the SS, the gendarmes, and the Polish police would surround the Wolomin ghetto and the ghetto would be liquidated.

Understandably, this prompted a terrible outcry. People wanted to say that perhaps a miracle would happen, because similar rumors had been spread around earlier. In recent days rumors had spread, supposedly from official sources, that the shtetls of Wolomin, Rodzimin, and Jadova would not be liquidated, because they supplied food for the vital work camps. But that illusion was destroyed when people learned that Jadova had been liquidated ten days earlier.

Desiring to learn whether this news was false, I left my home together with my wife and child. I wanted to hear what was being said in the streets and if there was any news. This time the voice of the street was more intense that usual. Previously, the Jewish council had tamped down and given the lie to dispiriting rumors. This time, everyone was dispirited and acknowledged that the situation was desperate. People telephoned Rodzimin, where people reported that the situation was the same and urged that whoever could escape should. This time it appeared that the Wolomin ghetto was taking its last breath. We never returned to our home. Empty–handed, we fled in the dark along the train line.

Our hearts pounded from fear that we would encounter someone on the way. We left everything that we had prepared for our flight in the house. Before my eyes I saw my eighty–five–year old mother, who could not possibly have come with us. To this very day I am pained. I do not know how her last minutes seemed and how she died.

No one who did not experience all this can comprehend how it was possible that families that were so tightly bound together could suddenly be torn apart, as each person ran like a wild beast trying to avoid death.

After the war it appeared that only a few had escaped. Whole families who wanted to stay together were killed.

[Pages 429–432]

The Beginning of the Liquidation

by Miriam Feigenboim–Gradzitzka

Our home in the ghetto consisted of two little attic rooms and a kitchen. We called it a garret. It Is hard to grasp how we organized things there. Fourteen people lived there: our mother, my brother Yechiel with his wife and three children, my brother Matisyahu, my sister Chaya–Gitl with her husband and two children; my brother Yakov's two children, and myself. That which seems impossible was in that environment of abnormality simple and self–evident. At that time there were worse things. People survived harder situations that our clearer understanding today cannot grasp.

It was the last night of Succos. The situation in the ghetto was intense. Sadness and worry ruled over Jewish homes. On Yom Kippur, all the surrounding shtetls had been emptied of Jews. Remaining were only Wolomin and Radzimin, where the Jews lived in despair, awaiting their terrible end. There were moments when our nerves could not stand it. Some people hoped that the end would come quickly. Waiting for death was harder than death itself.

No one had any doubt that death was approaching.

No one who has not experienced and survived such dreadful days can dispute the horror of waiting for the end. The fear of death was horrible, but a thousand times worse was waiting for it and not knowing what further terrors the murderers would dream up for us.

The Jews in the Wolomin ghetto, religious and Godfearing people, wanted to observe the holiday with all its customs and did not want to darken it with sad thoughts. My brothers along with several other Jews organized a secret minyan and gathered in a neighboring apartment. They prayed, quietly sang the holiday prayers, but their hearts were like lead. The atmosphere was hardly that of a holiday, but my mother said, "Children, today is a holiday. Let's try to forget our sorrows and celebrate the holiday as God commanded." A deep sigh came from her heart. Her eyes quietly took each of us in, as if she wanted to satisfy herself with seeing us one last time. Perhaps she had a premonition that this was the last night that we would sit together.

Quietly she moved to the table and laid out two tiny pieces of brown bread. They had to be our holiday meal in the ghetto. She had set up two little homemade candles and went to light them. She covered her eyes, from which tears were running. These were bitter tears that did not lighten the burden on her heart.

My brothers returned from davening. Matisyahu washed his hands and prepared to say Kiddush, but at that moment, when he stood with wet hands, about to pick up the hand towel, suddenly the door opened and my brother Mordechai's daughter, Chanatshe, entered. Her face was deadly pale. She wanted to say something, but no words came from her. Without words, we all understood: the end has come, the end that we had expected for long weeks and that even so left us thunderstruck.

The truth is that as long as we did not know for a certainty that the end was inevitable, in our hearts we nurtured a tiny hope for a miracle. Everyone harbored in her heart a hope that at the last minute something would happen that would allow us to survive.

Everyone in the room remained standing, as if they had turned to stone. Misfortune was painted on our chalk–white faces, and no one tried to say a word. Nothing can erase from my eyes the picture of that moment when we grasped the bad news and Mordechai stood with two wet, dripping hands, as if petrified. I cannot even tell how long that moment lasted, perhaps a minute, perhaps an hour. The deathly silence was broken by a childish cry from Chaya–Gitl's little daughter, a four–year–old child: "Mama, what happened? The police are coming to kill us?…Why, Mama?"

The liquidation of the Wolomin ghetto would begin at dawn. My mother and my sisters begged me to try to escape and run away. They also decided to hide themselves, and their plan was that when I found myself outside the ghetto, I would find some way to save them.

That night, I managed to get out of the ghetto. I went with a heavy heart, but I trusted that I would be able somehow to help my mother, my sisters and my brothers, but in the morning, after the ghetto had been emptied, when the murderers searched for Jews in hiding places, they found them and shot them on the spot.

This was the end of the Wolomin ghetto, which had experienced all seven measures of Gehenna from the German killers. Every day there were new decrees, new persecutions and killings. From among the horrible images that are engraved in my memory, one that recurs is of Yoel, who had been shot. Our apartment in the ghetto was not far from the wire fence. Opposite our window was an empty lot. Once, as I looked through the window, I saw Yoel lying in the grass. Even now I have no idea why he was lying there.

Looking at the beautiful world outside the ghetto and thinking about how nice the world was, though not for Jews, I saw from a distance the approach of the police, who came into the ghetto. Fear drove me from the window. I knew that every approach of the police signified bad luck for the ghetto. Soon I heard a fearful shriek that pierced the air. I went right back to the window, and before my eyes I saw a terrible scene: the police dragged Yoel outside of the ghetto, told him to run, and with two shots killed him.

On the blood–smeared faces of the police appeared happy smiles. Then they went to the Jewish authorities and demanded that Yoel's corpse be brought back into the ghetto.

In the Valley of Pain

Alter Carmeli

No words, no comfort, no names for the killers. The murderers took our dearest that we had.

[Pages 433-439]

Days of Fear and Terror

by Noson Nungold

Our house burned down in the great bombardment of Wolomin at the beginning of September, 1939. I was sitting at the table that was set for lunch when suddenly I heard the screaming of the siren, the alarm, as German bombers approached. Not far from our home was the Wolomin electrical station, which was the German bombers' target.

Fragments of the bombs landed on the roof of our house and the whole house began to burn. The flames encircled the house on all sides. It was already too late to escape by the stairs, because the stairway was burning. My wife and I started to thrown all of our soft possessions outside–clothing, laundry, bedclothes–and then I took my two children and leapt out from the second floor.

Thus we escaped from the fire and took refuge in a neighbor's cellar until the bombardment ended.

My wife later stayed at our house to see whether she could salvage other things from the fire.

When I arrived at the cellar, there were already many people there, Jews and Christians. With every explosion, a whine arose. The Christians crossed themselves and murmured prayers. The small number of Jews who were with me in the cellar huddled by the walls and in the corners in an attempt to protect their eyes. I held my children close, trying to protect them and shield them from a falling bomb.

I don't remember how long it lasted. But as soon as the sirens announced that the planes were gone, I left the cellar and ran immediately to our burning house, of which only a pile of ashes remained. My wife had succeeded in sheltering herself from the flames. In the ashes I found the pot in which our last meal in the house had been cooking.

Thus was I left, even before the Germans arrived in Wolomin, without a roof over my head. Our older child, Rochele, was seven years old. The younger, Esterl, was two years and nine months.

When I went to the town magistrate, I was given part of a huge three–story house near the magistrate's office, a single room for my whole family.

My neighbor in this house was a well–known Wolomin big shot, Mattis Teiblum. His kind family gave us a lot of help as we started to organize our new home, which was totally empty.

So passed the days in fear and terror. We received terrible news from the front. The Polish army was totally crushed. Only in a few spots had the Polish military made a stand. The military showed great heroism in defending Warsaw.

On the second day of Rosh Hashanah, at six in the morning, a German military unit marched into Wolomin. The whole area was taken by a motorized battalion. Troubles and oppressive decrees began to rain down on the Jews. Jews were forbidden to stand in line for bread. They could not walk on the sidewalk. This was also the beginning of night raids on Jewish homes, which invariably ended in blows, arrests, and even death.

During the day, they used to seize Jews in the streets, shave off their beards or pull them out, along with chunks of flesh from their backs. Terror oppressed every Jew in the shtetl. Especially terrible was the nighttime fear. People didn't undress. They slept in their clothes. Some went to find sleep with their Christian neighbors.

In the beginning I convinced myself that my outward appearance–no beard, European clothing–would help me avoid the misfortune of being arrested by the Germans. Like so many reckonings, this assumption proved incorrect. The Germans made no distinction between a Jew with a beard or without a beard. They beat and murdered on all sides.

Jews began to consider escaping to the Soviet border, especially the young people.

The Last Night

One night my wife started to beg me to run away and try to find somewhere to hide.

"The Germans," my wife pleaded, "won't bother with women and children, won't do them any harm…The greatest danger is for the men."

She maintained that the war would not last long and the short time that I would be in Russia would give me a chance to survive and later return home to my wife and children. For a long time my wife pleaded with me and tried to convince me that there was no alternative but for me to escape.

One night a Jew from Vishkov stayed with us, a brother–in–law of my brother–in–law, a Chasidic Jew, with a big black beard. His name was R. Bunim. The Jews of Vishkov, whose houses had been completely destroyed by German bombs, scattered over the whole area. R. Bunim had divided his family among all their acquaintances–his wife in one spot, his children in another. He himself came to us.

He also advised me that I should flee to the Soviet border. He himself had decided to do so.

Our conversation lasted several hours and I still could not decide to abandon my wife and children and go by myself across the border, when suddenly I heard how near to our house the Gestapo's vehicles had come. Soon we heard the steps of their boots on the staircase. Then they came nearer to our home.

I was paralyzed with fear. My glance went from my wife to R. Bunim. By reading their faces, I would know what to do. We were all silent. Fear stilled our tongues.

The first sounds of the Germans knocking on the door could be heard. I hear their voices. I think to open the door, because otherwise they will tear it down, but I stand there in fear for the lives of my wife and children.

At that moment I could hear the words of the prayer "Al cheyt," which R. Bunim was reciting with trembling lips. I realized that he was saying his final confession, and I moved to open the door. However, at that very moment I heard that the Teiblum's Polish servant had opened the door of their apartment and told the Germans that Jews used to live there but that had moved away and the apartment now stood empty…

The Germans joked with the Polish young lady, who spoke German. She was actually from the area of Poznan. They went into the Teiblum's apartment with her, stayed there a little while, and then I heard them go down the stairs and away from our street.

This was a miracle. That night the Polish young lady had saved me from certain death.

After the Gestapo left, R. Bunim came to me and whispered: "Pardon me, R. Noson. Give me a little soap and water and a hand towel…I dirtied myself from fear…"

It was now clear to us that the only hope was to escape to the Soviet border. We figured that in the morning the Gestapo would either kill me or arrest me in the street.

That was my last night in Wolomin. I was careful not to awaken the children. With a pounding heart I stared at them, and then I left the house.

Truth and Dream

In my wanderings over Russia, I experienced all seven levels of Gehenna, in the Soviet camps of the Communist USSR. Over the Ural Mountains, until I finally arrived in Uzbekistan, in Tashkent, in Samarkand.

Through all these travels, I never forgot my home. Before my eyes floated the faces of my two little daughters, whom I had left with the Germans.

At the beginning of November, 1939, I crossed the border and arrived in Bialystokj. Because of my fear, I fell into a dark mood. When I heard a child cry, it seemed to me that I was hearing my daughters cry. With each day, my state grew worse. I was becoming a broken wreck. My terror increased.

One evening as I walked alone through Bialystok's streets, lost in sad thoughts about my children, crying voices reached me, and it suddenly seemed as if I heard the cries of my Rochele and Esterl. They were begging for mercy.

Like a lunatic I went around the square looking for the sources of those crying voices. It seemed that this was a synagogue, and between the afternoon and evening services some of the assembled Jews had gathered by the reader's stand and begun to recite Psalms. The Jews accompanied those recitations with a lachrymose chant.

Those Jews were like me, who had lost their children, and their mournful prayers seemed to me like the cries of my children.

Shortly thereafter, I was arrested in Bialystok and sent to a camp in the USSR. On the whole trip in the troop train, which traveled for long weeks, I had disturbing dreams that drained me physically and mentally. When I arrived at the camp, I was totally broken.

The pain and woe of my anxiety for my children gave me no rest in the camp.

At the end of August, 1941, I was released from the camp and I again wandered across Russia, Kirov, Molotov, Sverlovsk, Tchelebinsk, until I arrived in Tashkent.

I remember how once on a cold November night I was sitting on the steps of the train station in Tashkent. Thousands of refugees were there. I was so fatigued that I dozed off, but hunger and cold would not allow me to sleep, so I got up.

My nearby neighbor, an older man, heard my moaning and came near me, asking if I was ill. We started talking and I told him that I had been on the road for ten weeks with barely anything to eat.

I told him that more than hunger, I was tormented by the thoughts of my wife and our two small children whom I had left in Poland. I could not hold back my tears and started crying.

The stranger sat immersed in sad thought and was silent. Suddenly he pulled out a little bag of crackers and offered me some, saying, "I have no more…"

When I ate the few crackers, he handed me a blanket, saying, "Cover yourself. You'll feel better if you sleep…It will calm you down…"

I actually fell asleep. Better than the warmth of the blanket was the warmth of his words.

When I awoke, my neighbor was gone. I looked for him everywhere, but it seemed that while I slept, his train arrived and he left, leaving his blanket behind because he did not want to awaken me.

Jews of Wolomin in Samarkand

From Tashkent I wandered on without a goal or a trade. The whole way, in all my wanderings, I was beset with anxiety about my children, which disturbed my peace and my nightly sleep. Nightmares never stopped afflicting me.

On Erev Pesach in 1942 I arrived at Samarkand. After descending from the train, I went first to the bazaar, and I was thrilled to meet with Jews from Wolomin who had been freed from the camps. They already had places to live, somewhere in an Uzbeki lime house. They took me home with them and gave me something to eat.

After many long weeks, for the first time I was able to wash myself. The camp clothes that I wore I threw off and burned in the courtyard. The Wolominers gave me other clothing to wear.

After several days I found work in the electric station in the Samarkand train station. I lived together with other Polish Jews, who worked there and found a room in a collective workers dwelling.

I was given a bit of bread and a roof over my head, with which I was quite happy, like all the others who had no great aspirations and who were just happy at the opportunity to survive the war. Once again, however, thoughts of my children began to torment me.

One evening around Succos when I came home tired out from work and had lain down on the iron bed to rest a little, I experienced another nightmare: I saw myself go into a dense woods. It was so dark I could barely see where I was stepping. Soon I heard children's voices. In the pitch black I could not make out a face. I just heard lamenting voices, the steps of German soldiers, the barking of dogs. Struck with fear, I wanted to run, but my feet were like stone and I could not move a single step. I broke out in a cold sweat and I cried out, "Hide, hide..."

When I awoke, I saw my friends standing by my bed. They had shaken me, wiped the sweat off my face and asked, "What happened, Noson. Why were you yelling in your sleep?"

When in 1945 I returned to Poland, I returned to Wolomin in October. The surviving Jews whom I encountered told me about their existence in the ghetto, and they informed me that the liquidation of the Wolomin ghetto happened on Hoshana Raba, at the same time that I had that horrible dream...

[Pages 440-441]

We Were Ten Children

by Nisn Zilbershteyn

We were ten children in the house. Our father was a simple Jew who lived by his own labor. He worked hard to earn his bread. Nevertheless, our home displayed poverty and need. Our home was a miserable heap, and we often had to sleep under a roof full of holes, through which the rain came in during the summer and in winter the cold. There were times when we had nothing to cover ourselves with and so we lay in sacks of straw.

When the war broke out, I was in Bialystok, where I passed difficult months in the company of thousands of other refugees. With them, I was sent to Siberia by the military police.

Along with my torments, I suffered anxiety about my wife and children, who had remained in Wolomin, overwhelming worry about their fate.

It was hard to work even for a bit of bread in Siberia. We had nothing to do and had to work in the coldest cold. On my feet I wore pieces of rubber from tires, tied with strings, around which I wrapped rags so that I would not freeze. I do not know where I got the strength to bear everything. Fate decreed that I alone of my entire family should survive.

Later I was mobilized into the army, and I lived through many harsh battles until I was wounded outside of Berlin.

After I was demobilized, I wandered for days and nights around the deserted Jewish shtetls, looking for anyone I knew, until I found Malle Berman. I will never forget the warm friendship that she displayed. In their home I felt for the first time that I was with good, close people, and that gave me the courage to survive hard times and fight for my life.

With each passing year of my renewed life, I nourished the dream that such things would not happen again, because now the whole world came to know the horrors of the truth, of what Hitler's murderers had done. The memories would not be lost and everything would be done to erase suffering from the world.

So I restarted my life, remarried, left Poland and came to Austria, where our daughter Simele was born. From the camp in Austria we went to Eretz Yisroel.

We never lost the memories of the great destruction of our shtetl. Always before my eyes the lights of my home shine, the treasure of virtues, of excellence, and next to them so much wickedness and killing that destroyed our shtetl with all our nearest and dearest.

We will never forget them.

[Pages 442-453]

Blind Fate

by Chaya–Sarah Rubinshteyn–Scharfshteyn

Sixty years ago, my parents went from Tchizheve on the way to Wolomin, where they had decided to settle and build their new home.

My father had a leather business on Dluga Street in Wolomin. There were eight of us children and most of my brothers and sisters were married in Wolomin and continued to live there. My father loved his grandchildren and great–grandchildren. My mother, however, died at a young age.

In 1935, my father decided to go to Israel, where his son Ephraim already lived. He gave his business to his youngest daughter Miriam and her husband Abba Fromm, who came from Lomzhe.

My brother–in–law Abba Fromm was a fervent Zionist and dreamed for his whole life to settle with his wife and four sons in Eretz Yisroel, but the dreadful war nullified all his plans and he and his whole family were killed.

My father, after a short time in Eretz Yisroel, was seized by a great longing for his family, who had remained in Wolomin. It was hard for him to be so far from them, so he returned to Wolomin, where he shared the fate of his family and of the whole Jewish community. He was one of the resigned ones, who never tried to rebel and who accepted the situation as a decree from Heaven that human beings could not overturn and from which they could not escape. He was shot during the deportations from the Wolomin ghetto.

Together with my husband and part of my family, we were hidden by Christians, stuck in a hiding place in awful conditions. My husband could not bear such harsh conditions, and six months before the liberation he became ill. We could not bring a doctor to him. This hastened his death.

Wolomin was overrun twice, by the Germans and by the Russians, and then later again by the Germans. Those were hard times, when we floated between life and death. We were hidden in an old building lot near Wolomin, in Helenvuek. That was already our third hiding place. We had had to escape from the earlier ones because the neighbors learned about us and we did not want to endanger those who had saved us.

As the front drew closer, the Germans sent all the inhabitants of the area further from the front lines. We were desperate, not knowing whether we should go along with the evacuated Christian inhabitants, thinking for a moment that in the panic no one would recognize that we were Jews. Our Christian saviors dissuaded us. They said that the Germans would take the men away to work in Germany, and in the best of cases only the women would have a chance to escape. That was enough of a warning that people would recognize our Yakov as a Jew.

It was 1944. For two years we remained hidden in a pit that had been dug under the floor, in constant darkness. Above us we heard the sounds and movements of soldiers and of tanks that were headed to the front. The house was made of wood, and it was shot through by stray bullets.

From time to time our saviors would come to us, bringing us a bit of unspoiled apple, since bread was then so hard to come by. With each day we became weaker, broken both physically and mentally, and we thought we would never leave there alive.

The day came when our saviors told us the news that the Germans were gone and Russian tanks had already arrived. We were free. It sounded unbelievable. We could not grasp the great miracle. When we left our pit, we were so weak that we could barely lift our feet..

Among the first soldiers that we encountered there were Jews. When they saw us, they quickly ran to bring us food. The Christian inhabitants looked at us and shook their heads, saying, "Living corpses, they shouldn't be alive..." However, as if to spite all their bitter predictions, we slowly drew close to them. In Wolomin at that time there was a Christian doctor by the name of Izdevski, a respectable man, who showed us compassion and helped us regain our strength.

Several months after the liberation, we lived in Wolomin. A few surviving Jews came to us, until there were about seventy Jews who had escaped the horrors. Our Christian neighbors regarded us crookedly, evilly. They could not bear the returning Jews. They began to send us threatening letters, saying that if we did not leave Wolomin, they would put an end to us.

We figured that the murderers could make good on their threats, so we left for Lodz, because it was not possible to find a dwelling place in Warsaw. The city was in rubble.

In Lodz there were already a few Jews. This was in May of 1945, a few months after the liberation of Lodz..

For over five years we lived in Lodz, until in 1950 we made aliyah to Israel.

The nightmare of those horrible years is with us all the days and nights of our lives. We will never forget our near and dear ones who died such terrible deaths. They will always be engraved in our hearts.

Through Rivers of Blood

Our father used to tell us how he came with his family to Wolomin, when there wasn't even a minyan of Jews there, no cemetery. When a Jew died, they had to take the body to Radzimin or Ideva.

The reason my parents came to Wolomin was that they had heard of the new shtetl some eighteen kilometers beyond Warsaw. It seems that conditions for settling down were easier in Warsaw and in the vicinity of the big city, and they anticipated a quick expansion. People worked in Warsaw and lived in Wolomin. There was a train station in the town and every half hour there was a train. The trip to Warsaw took no more than twenty minutes.

My father came from Warsaw and consequently Wolomin appealed to him because it was close to whole family, who still lived in Warsaw.

The shtetl did indeed expand and had a reputation as a modern shtetl in the whole area around Warsaw. Clerks who held government posts in Warsaw began to settle in Wolomin. Conditions there were favorable. People started to parcel out the land around Wolomin and Polish government workers built small houses.

Little by little the population grew until, before the world war, Wolomin had thirty thousand inhabitants, among whom were three thousand Jews.

In September of 1939, the Germans arrived in Wolomin. As they had in other places, they undertook to eliminate the small number of Jews, to steal their possessions, exploit their labor, and then to liquidate them. After the unspeakable suffering and pain that the Jews in Wolomin were forced to experience, November of 1940 arrived, when the Germans nailed up posters in the streets, announcing that they were creating a ghetto for Wolomin's Jews, who were forced to leave their houses and go to the ghetto, which was located in Sosnovke, a resort three kilometers from Wolomin.

Thus began the difficult expulsion, the journey to Sosnovke. Some people traded with the Christians, taking their homes and giving away their own in Wolomin. They paid for a year in advance. Anyone who lacked funds was helped by the Jewish township so they would have a roof over their heads in the ghetto.

Mostly people lived in small apartments, single rooms. However difficult things were in the camp, no one could imagine that this was only a small part of the overall plan to exterminate all of the Jews, the whole Jewish people.

Many of the young people did not want to be satisfied with these humiliating conditions into which we had been thrown, and they planned to escape to Russia, stealing across the border to Bialystock or Galicia. At first the borders were not closely guarded, and many were able to get across and arrive on the Russian side and from there make their ways further into Russia.

There were seven of us children, five brothers and two sisters, all born in Wolomin. Of those, there remain only a brother who returned from Russia and a second brother who managed before the war to get to America. My husband, Yakov, and I, with our five children, remained in the ghetto with other family members.

After being in the ghetto for two years, we began to see the end, and we hid with Christians. We stayed with our two youngest children. Right after the war, our oldest son returned from Auschwitz. My daughter perished in Auschwitz. My son was in a camp in Wilanov, near Warsaw. This was a camp where the Germans sent Jews from the ghetto who were able to work. He never returned from there.

One of my brothers, who had gone to Russia was killed in Kavel when the Germans invaded Soviet Russia. Two other brothers tried to escape with their families. They escaped from the ghetto, but the murderers seized them and shot them. My sister was with her family in the Warsaw Ghetto. Her husband and brother–in–law were killed in the bombardment in 1939 as they were standing in a line for water.

My sister remained with four children, and my mother planned to go and live with them.

In 1941 I went by foot to the Warsaw Ghetto, looking for my mother and sister, to see what their camp was like. I wanted to see if I could help them. First I had to worry about getting a certificate that the Germans had given the township, giving me permission to go to the Warsaw Ghetto.

We were three women from Wolomin. When we arrived at the gates of the Warsaw Ghetto, they took our certificates. I looked for my mother and sister, wandering around for several days. I saw that I could not help them. I planned to return home to my husband and children.

My experiences during those few days in the Warsaw Ghetto rattled me. The images remain with me in their full horror. People lay in the streets like living skeletons, worn out, starving, begging for a piece of bread. Many had no place to live. Their end was near.

We went to the gates of the ghetto leading to the Aryan side. The guards, because of our Aryan appearance, did not take us for Jews and allowed us to leave without hindrance, but outside we were arrested by Polish police and led away to the prison on Danielovitzhevska, where they deposited us in the women's section.

After a while I was allowed to send a short letter to my family so they could know where I was. My husband undertook extraordinary efforts, which cost him a lot of money, but to this day I do not know whether those efforts had any effect and whether they were the cause of our being released. I sat in that prison for a whole month. In my cell there were other Jewish women, some of whom had converted. Some of them did not even know they were Jews, since they were third–generation Christians.

At the beginning of the second month, I and the two other Wolomin women were released. We were given papers that allowed us to return to the Wolomin ghetto.

There was great joy at our return to the ghetto. No one had expected to see us again. There had been many cases of people being shot in the prison.

It was truly a miracle, for a month later every Jew who had been seized outside the ghetto was shot.

Conditions in the ghetto became worse every day. A typhus epidemic raged, and there was no place to escape it. Whole families died from typhus, including my brother–in–law Chaim Rubinshteyn and his wife.

The Germans began to drive Jews from the surrounding shtetls to Warsaw. There were no apartments for them, so they had to live in barracks. We deduced that they would drive us out of Sosnovke. People spent sleepless nights lying on their packed bags waiting for them to come for us. Then we heard reports about death camps for Jews. Jews were kidnapped for work details. Those few who managed to get out brought back tragic news. From the Warsaw Ghetto, transports of Jews set out for Treblinka. These transports went through our ghetto. The whistles of the locomotives, which tore through the stillness of night, sent fear through us. Life became unbearable.

One night, a group of Jews jumped out of a train car and told us about the frightful actions in Warsaw, in Atvatzk, Falinitz, Rembertov, and other shtetls. It was clear that our days were numbered. The Jews in the ghetto began searching for ways to escape. Some forged Aryan documents, some constructed hiding places, some tried escaping to Zambrove, which had been incorporated into the Third Reich but which lacked a ghetto.

The confusion daily took on a more terrible character. In their panic, people took to dangerous ways of escaping. It was clear that Wolomin would suffer the same fate as the other shtetls.

The night of Succos arrived. Jews sat sadly by their tables, which held pitiful meals. People's thoughts were not on the holiday, but even so, everyone tried to hold on to just a bit of hope that they would survive these horrible times.

That night, a Polish police official came with the terrible news that he had received an order that the police should be ready that night to liquidate the ghetto.

That night will live forever in my memory. I went out to the street, which was shrouded in thick darkness. People–horrified and broken–were in turmoil, not knowing what to do, how to save their lives. There were some who left the ghetto. Some hid themselves in the ghetto itself. Many simply resigned themselves and remained sitting in their rooms awaiting their sad fate.

None of these methods offered any assurance. Each of them showed how feeble were the attempts to escape. Outside the ghetto, the Poles helped to seize the fleeing Jews who had tried to escape. The situation in the ghetto was no better, and there were only feeble attempts to avoid the end.

At first, they surrounded the ghetto with gendarmes and police, German and Polish. There was a command that all Jews should gather in the square and leave open the doors of their houses. Horrible scenes played out. Old people and the ill were shot on the spot by the police. In the community's home for children, a home for orphans, a sadistic gendarme walked around and struck each child on the head with an iron bar.

In the Wolomin ghetto there is a communal grave for all the tortured and killed.

The Jews who remained alive were led to Radzimin, and from there they were taken, along with the Jews of Legyonov, to Treblinka.

Thus was the end of the Jewish settlement in Wolomin.

A few Jews from Wolomin returned from Russia. A few returned also from the concentration camps, and a few even survived based on their Aryan documents or were hidden by Christians, in holes in the ground or in attics.

My husband, thanks to the harsh conditions, became ill and weak. Throughout the war he struggled to hide a portion of his family. When the war ended and we thought to begin a new life, we recalled all of our bitter experiences. The hard struggles and pain totally broke my husband. He died in Lodz.

The majority of surviving Wolomin Jews live in Israel. Some also made it to America and other countries, but like us, they feel bound to our shtetl in their memories, bound to the remnant of the Jewish community of Wolomin.

The Destruction of Wolomin

The Jewish people do not know about happy days. Each joy is mixed together with sadness. Each day is a memorial day for another Jewish settlement, another Jewish community that was extinguished by the Germans.

So, too, sorrows fell upon our Jewish community in Wolomin. Our shtetl is destroyed and empty.

The Yiddsh language has disappeared from Wolomin. No longer are our dear Jews there, no longer the great Jewish life in that small, beautiful shtetl that was all of eighteen kilometers from Warsaw.

Wolomin was a modern town with a population of 3500 souls, a town that was quickly being built and was becoming nicer from year to year. The shtetl was becoming more tightly bound to the greater Polish state. Every half hour, the train brought a mass of passengers from Warsaw and took back people from Wolomin. People did business in Warsaw and many Wolominers worked there. Little Wolomin had many Jewish businesses and workshops.

A beautiful Jewish life flourished there, with a school and a Talmud Torah, a school for Jewish children and a Bais–Yakov, with fine young people, many Zionist organizations and two sports clubs. Every year young people would come here for training, in order to learn how to work and prepared for a new life in Eretz Yisroel.

Jewish life pulsated grandly, until the coming of that dark year, 1939. When the German army marked in, little children marched after them in cadence, not knowing what awaited them. But we quickly felt the yoke of occupation. The first tragic days came soon, when the murderers burned down the school, with all its books.

Then began the ugly bacchanalia of robberies. People stole from Jewish businesses, kidnapped Jews at their work, snipped off beards and beat people to death. Jews had to get off the sidewalks if a German approached. Insults and humiliations had no limitations. Later–toward the end of 1940–came the order to establish a ghetto. We thought that they would send us to the Warsaw Ghetto, but they sent us to Sosnovke, a sanatorium three kilometers from Wolomin, where people from other towns were also brought. At first this was an open ghetto–people could come and go in order to work and earn a little bread or to sell things so they could sustain themselves. Most took to milling corn with hand mills. This was really hard work. So a year passed, and then the Soviet–German war broke out. The ghetto was shut up. Anyone who tried to get out was shot. The first victim was a sixteen–year–old young man, Chaim Gorbin's grandson. From that day on, no day passed without victims. The Jews wanted to preserve their lives, but outside, the murderers were always on the lookout. The murderers often visited the ghetto, each time demanding greats sums of money and threatening to shoot the leadership unless the money was forthcoming. Then came the typhus epidemic, which took many of us. Many of our young people were sent away to work in the concentration camps, from which they never returned.

The ghetto was located near the train tracks. Every day we would hear two trains passing with cars filled with people. We often heard desperate cries. We understood that these were transports of Jews being sent from Warsaw to Treblinka.

Many Jews who had escaped from surrounding communities that had been liquidated came to us. They thought that perhaps a miracle would happen and the destructions would cease. But every whistle of the trains filled us with the fear of death that was waiting for us there on the railroad tracks…

Sad were those days in the helpless ghetto, surrounded by enemies and violence.

Then came the tragic news. On the evening of Succos, a decent Pole came to tell us that early on the morning of Shemini Atzeres the "Action" would begin. Darkness fell over our Jewish hearts, a night of horrible anticipation. There was nowhere to escape. There were none of our former Christian friends who could hide us…

Before dawn on Shemini Atzeres we heard shooting, and the first victims fell–the Action had begun. Jews were herded into the square. They were told to leave their houses open. The Germans were helped by the Polish police and firemen. The Germans shot several Jews on the spot. One German murderer used an iron tool to beat to death most of the children from the children's home. The parents of these children had been killed earlier. A number of Jews hid themselves in the ghetto, but a cry from a child or information from a Pole gave them away and they were killed.

The Jews were led to Rodzimin and then, together with the community of Legyonov, to Treblinka. These were the last three communities left near Warsaw.

A few Jews were saved from the ghetto, but hardly any remained alive. Others managed to get to Zambrov (near Bialystok), where there were still some Jews. Many of those did not return. And those who got there shared the fate of the Zambrov Jews, who were sent to Auschwitz.

Such was the fate of Wolomin's Jews–just like the fate of Poland's Jewry. In the hearts of the remnant of Wolomin's Jews are deeply woven the golden threads of the spiritually rich Jewish life.

This description, that we are publishing in our Yizkor Book, is nothing more than a drop from the sea of agonies, horrible suffering, and bizarre deaths that we experienced and saw with our own eyes.

None of us could have imagined that such things were possible, that people could treat each other so badly, so coldly murder children and adults.

Each murdered Jew in the ghetto and in the camps was a martyr, and we should sanctify every memory, telling our children about their virtuous lives and their horrible deaths, telling them what our enemies did to us and what our current enemies are capable of.

Let us never forget what Amalek did to us!

[Pages 454-457]

A Wolomin Mother Becomes a Martyr

by Saul Rosenblum

The life of the Wolomin Jewish community flowed quietly. The shtetl had its schools, its beis–midrashes and Chasidic study houses, Zionist organizations, sports clubs, and professional organizations. The Jewish youth led an active community life.

The Loskovski family lived in the shtetl. He, Yoske, tall and thin, with a beautiful beard, was known as Yoske the Magistrate, because he had served as the magistrate of Wolomin under the czar. When he was at ease, he would tell about different episodes from those days, taking out a long golden key, which he had carried on his person as a magistrate and which had made him seem important.

His wife, Rochele, not too tall but a bit heavy, used to travel every year to Kuratzia in an effort to lose some weight. They were a well–to–do family, owned several houses, a dry goods store, and a field that was planted with potatoes, carrots, onions, and grain.

Of their six sons, only four were in the shtetl. The eldest, Avraham, was in America, while Shmuel was in Paris. They also had a single daughter. Aside from the ordinary worries of everyday Jewish life, they led a simple, peaceful life.

Yoske the Magistrate was known for his caring Jewish heart. People would come to him if they needed something, to help make a wedding for a poor bride or to do a good deed, to intervene in a problem with a Pole, and other such things.

When the Second World War erupted, the Germans came to Wolomin and the Gestapo became the rulers over life and death for the Jews. A decree was issued that within twenty–four hours, all Jewish women had to bring their fur coats to the Gestapo. Anyone who held on to a fur coat would be shot.

Loskovki's daughter–in–law, Moyshe's wife Chutshe, did not want to give up her fine fur coat, so she went to a Gentile who had worked his whole life for Yoske in the field. She gave him the coat to hold onto until the danger had passed…

This Gentile had received many benefits from Yoske and had, in peaceful times, shown his gratitude. He said that he would never forget what Yoske the Magistrate had done for him. He even referred to him as "my father."

Now the Gentile took the fur and ran right to the Gestapo, where he told them who had given him the coat for safekeeping.

The Gestapo immediately called for Mrs. Loskovski.

At home, they had a warning of the danger that hung over them. Wailing filled the house. Chutshe looked at everyone and passionately kissed her children, thinking that she was going on her final journey.

At the last minute, Rochele, her mother–in–law, could not stand the sorrow of the children and she called out, "Chutshe, you're not going…They demanded Mrs. Loskovki, so I will go. You have young children for whom you have to stay alive."

Chutshe struggled with this, but Rochele was insistent: "I've already lived three–quarters of my life….As God wills it, so will it be…Just pay attention to your father."

She spoke with a strong voice, with no crying. Yoske the Magistrate was silent. Suddenly he seemed older than his years. He was totally broken.

Rochele walked with bold steps to the corner, where her cane stood. Without the cane she had trouble walking. With her head held high, she set off for the Gestapo.

The news spread through the shtetl. The Jews in the street watched after her and marveled at her moral strength, the firmness of her character. Everyone knew that she had made a deal, that she was going on her final journey.

She walked proudly and quickly, as she used to when she went to shul to pray on the holidays. Thus she walked to the Gestapo building.

The Gestapo officer on duty was at first flummoxed by her proud bearing. He tried to demand that the younger Mrs. Loskovski should come, as he had been told that it was her fur coat, but Rochele argued firmly and said that was a mistake, because the coat was hers and she had wanted to hide it.

Finally the German let her prevail, called for her to be taken to Rodzimin, and in a few hours she was no longer alive.

People later recounted how the eyewitnesses saw the murderers tormented her with wild joy and watched her death agonies with sadistic pleasure.

After Rochele's death, Yoske could barely be recognized. Old, grey, and broken, he wandered alone through the ghetto, silent, not exchanging a single word with anyone until the liquidation came and he was herded with the other Jews into a train car; and those who stood near him heard him mumble to himself, "Now I am going to Rochele and we'll be together…"

Our shtetl produced many illustrious women. One of the most illustrious was Rochele Loskovksi.

When we think of and bewail the millions of dead, tortured and subjected to horrible deaths that are impossible for the human mind to comprehend, we plant an eternal flame, a yahrzeit light, for such illustrious figures who, in the last moments of their lives, demonstrated such proud humanity and dignity.

We are the greatest mourners in the world. The ashes of our martyrs are spread over wide areas, over field and woods, and forever their memory will recall their honor, their greatness, their beauty, which they bore from the beginning of their lives until the last minutes, without ever losing their dignity.

Rochele Loskovski carried the beauty of Mother Rachel, of Miriam and of Deborah the Prophet, and of all the sacred souls.

[Pages 458-460]

Our Martyrology

by Yankel Manketo

I know that there are many Jews who survived the horrifying Gehenna and who want to forget it, and so they flee the memories and descriptions of those fearful times. The circumstances in which we now live in America help in forgetting, in forgetting their own histories, the gruesome events that occurred only a few decades earlier. But for us it is clear that we must not forget. We must remember and think about them until the last days of our lives, and our recollections should remain for coming generations.

In my free time, therefore, I jot down not only what I experienced but also what I hear and read from others about the murders and suffering and the awful years of Hitler's reign.

We must not try to suppress the shudders caused by the Jewish martyrology. Our innocent, shed blood, the tears of the afflicted and the murdered must not sink into the depths of oblivion. Our people have always gathered and preserved in manuscripts and books everything that happened to us. Everything–we must collect everything, the endless horrible and sadistic beastliness; we must not rest, nor let others rest; we must not spare our nerves, not shrink back from weakness, not fear sleepless nights, only read and write, depicting everything that lies in our memories, what we lived through and what we read and heard from others.

Lying in front of me is the document collection *The Martyrology of the Children* which was compiled by Noach Gris and published by the Central Organization for Polish Jews in Argentina. Noach Gris writes:

"At first no one believed in the possibility of killing defenseless children, but the Germans went even further. In March of 1942, Himmler's order went out that people should stop shooting Jewish children but should bury them alive, thrown them to wild animals in the circus. It became a contest to excel in sadism. The murderers grabbed children with their hands and smashed their heads into walls, posts, and trees, chopped them up with axes, and threw them alive into the fire.

"On a street in Warsaw, a German officer seized two Jewish children and stopped several passers–by, ordering them to open the canal so he could throw the children in. With horror the children huddled together. The murderers took their time. They did not hurry opening the canal; they worked slowly in order to increase the fright of the children.

"Finally the canal was opened and the officer and the officer tore the young girl from her brother, raised her over his head, and with all his might threw her into the deep canal.

"The young boy fell to ground and cried out, 'Mama, Mama.'

The officer did his sadistic task cold bloodedly, slowly raising the boy and in the same manner throwing him into the canal…"

In Vilna, a German officer smeared the lips of a newborn Jewish child with poison.

In a letter written from Poligan, near Vilna, other stories are told:

"They tortured our children in a bestial fashion. Eight–year–old girls were raped. Lithuanians and Germans tied a twelve–year–old girl to a table and one after the other raped her. Her mother was forced to stand there and prevent her child from crying…

In Lublin, in the spring of 1942, the Germans forced people to dig graves in a field. A transport truck brought children there in their underwear, and a Gestapo troop undressed them and threw them into the graves.

In Ravne, they gathered together Jewish children in the barracks on Tarlova Street and kept them confined there for seven days. No one was allowed to see them. They were given no food and not a drop of water.

A few were able to hide from this Gehenna and later bore witness to the horrifying events.

Such deeds, and others, are conveyed in scores of books. Human understanding cannot grasp all of this, but should we therefore be silent?

No. A thousand times, no.

It should be written about, published, and distributed in all languages. Young and old should read, should remember what the world did when the murderers were in power.

It should also be proclaimed in our Wolomin Yizkor Book. In our shtetl, too, the nights were rent with the cries of children being forced out in hunger and fear.

The enemy spared neither old people nor children. They humiliated us and trampled us. Our fear became the patience of the martyrs.

[Pages 461-464]

Days of Sorrow

by Rachel Asch

I will never forget my shtetl of Wolomin, where I was born and raised, where I spent my childhood years, where I grew and led a family life, and where all the people were so dear and beloved. A thousand strings bound me to Jewish life in Wolomin, joining together sorrows and joys, with the happiness and the problems of every Jew in the shtetl.

Now it has become my fate to record in the Yizkor Book things about our dear shtetl, inscribing my own memories and thereby contributing to the monument for our devastated Jewish community, for our murdered martyrs, my own flesh and blood, my fellow citizens, whose interrupted lives will follow me like a shadow to the grave.

We led a colorful cultural life in our shtetl: a Peretz Library, a Tarbus school, a variety of Jewish youth organizations that cultivated a thirst for Jewish knowledge, for education. I have sorrowful recollections of every day in the year, of our childish summer evenings, of our joyful Shabbos and holiday celebrations, nostalgia for home, for the Jewish streets and alleys. I see before my eyes Koshtshelna Street, where my whole family lived. I see my uncle Yoske Loskovski with his whole family. My uncle Pioravitsch with his whole family, my aunt Beila Friedman. They were all family. Later on they were joined by my mother–in–law and father–in–law, Yitzchak and Malkah Asch with their extensive family.

Do not think that we lacked worries and problems, but it seems to me that we lived peacefully and happily until 1939, the beginning of the awful destruction, which did not skip over our shtetl.

On Chopin Street, where the Krieger family lived, the first bombs fell and several people were killed. Several days later the Germans set fire to the school on Leshne Street. My mind combines the awful picture of the burning school with the picture of the German murderers leading out the young men who learned there, ripping out the pages of the holy books and throwing them into the fire. Then they ordered the students to dance around the fire. That was a horrible image, and with unsteady legs I ran home. Even today I see before my eyes that gruesome infernal dance.

When I arrived home, my husband Hershel told me that the rabbi was in our house. People had told him that the Germans were seeking him so they could take him to the burning school. It was easy to get from the rabbi's dwelling through the courtyard to our house so the rabbi ran and was hiding with us. When things quieted down, he left.

Soon thereafter the Germans started to seize Jews at work. They bullied and jeered at the unfortunate Jews. They harnessed them to wagons instead of horses and ordered them to pull the wagons. Every day they issued new decrees and created new sorrows.

One day my husband arrived home and described how he had seen Yosef Krasiver harnessed to a wagon and pulling it with his last bit of strength. In Jewish homes the mood was a mixture of darkness and despondency.

We decided to leave Wolomin, and together with other Jews we came, after difficult experiences, to Bialystok, where we found thousands of people milling in the streets without a roof over their heads. People slept in the schools and the beis–medrashes. Somehow we learned of a dwelling where Jews from Wolomin went and were received with friendship and sympathy.

Problems were not lacking in Bialystok, and many Wolomin Jews returned home to their families that they had left in Wolomin.

In 1940 the NKVD sent us to Siberia, where we lived through dreadful times, but the whole time we lived with the hope of returning to our old home and seeing our dear friends and families whom we left in Wolomin. Until the very end, we did not know about the great devastation.

Only when the war ended and we returned to Polish soil could we determine the extent of the destruction. As soon as we crossed the Polish border, the Poles threw rocks at our wagon. When we came to Auschwitz, I went with several others to see the death camp, and for as long as I live I will never forget the horrible scenes that appeared before my eyes, the gas chambers, the crematoria, and the piles of children's shoes, taleisim, and a mass of letters that people had written before being murdered. The horror dulled our senses, but suddenly I began to tremble when someone found among the letters a letter signed with the name Eliezer Bergazin from Wolomin. I nearly screamed, â€œThat was our rabbi's son!â€ But the person who found the letter would not give it to me.

Eventually we came to Lodz, and I went further on to Wolomin, and that put an end to my hopes of finding someone I knew. Sadly, I met no one. I wandered the streets of Wolomin and my heart wept within me. There I was in my old home, where my parents had lived, and I didn't even know where their graves were. I imagined that I heard a stifled cry that hung in the air. The entire shtetl seemed like a desolate field, but the truth is that all the Jewish homes had been taken over by Poles.

I wanted to cry out loud, to bring up tears from the bottom of my heart, but the source of tears had dried up. Too great was the destruction. My tongue was dry. Every bit of the ground seemed like an open grave.

There was once a home that is no more; there was once a world that is no more

Broken and depressed, I returned to Lodz, and from there we began to wander again, and we wandered all over until finally in 1948 we came to our land.

Each year, at the memorial service for our shtetl, we meet other refugees from Wolomin and we are united by the memory of our martyrs.

[Page 465]

My Wanderings in Foreign Lands

by Tova Paskowitz-Taiblum

Translated by Sara Mages

The Taiblum family was a large, wealthy and respected family, among them were noble-minded and intellectuals. Several members of the Teiblum family left Wolomin at the outbreak of the Second World War, and I was among those who arrived in Bialystok.

In Bialystok we lived together as one family. We kept our personal belongings, our clothes, in shared suitcases and when the members of the secret police, the N.K.V.D, came to deport us to Russia, they did not allow me to take my clothes out of the suitcases. They expelled me from the house and I left only with the clothes on my body.

Miriam and Mordechai Teiblum and their children

[Page 466]

To those, who have gone through this journey, it seemed that the world was on fire. Many have already written, and more will be written, so that our sons after us will know all the hardships that have befallen us. Here I want to mention one detail:

Despite the harsh conditions, friendship and brotherhood was formed among the passengers. The shared destiny brings hearts together. I was very close to the Paskowitz family.
Have I ever hoped that one day I would be part of that family?

Our paths parted. I was sent to Komi Autonomous Soviet Socialist Republic, an area where the frost reaches up to over fifty degrees. It is told that the Cossacks, who rebelled against the Don, were deported there and they died after a few years.

Kulak families were also deported to the labor camp to which I was brought with another Jewish woman. The heads of the families were deported to another place and only the mothers and their children remained. They lived in wooden huts in the white frozen wilderness, and there we straightened our bones after the long freight train ride.

Everything was shabby and meager there. In the morning we were given soup in which potatoes were cooked with their peels. It rarely had a little salt in it. After this meal we went out to work in the forest.

We walked because they felt sorry for the horses. Where did we get the strength to work? We took out red berries from under the snow and ate them. We learned to pick berries in the summer and save them for the winter. In addition we made another discovery: some distance from us was a potato warehouse. Occasionally rotten potatoes were thrown out of the warehouse. In winter the rotten potatoes were covered in snow.

In the evening we received slices of bread. The size of the slice was proportional to the amount of work we did, but the size of the slice of bread depended largely on the wishes of the director, an ugly and bad woman in her forties.

The Kulak families had many belongings and valuables that they exchanged for a bucket of potatoes. They ate them uncooked and most of them got sick and died.

We, the only two Jews in the camp, tried to at least to cook our potatoes when we were able to get them, and because of them I also fell into a trap. Once, when I went out to look for them, and after I managed to hide several potatoes under my coat, I got caught. I was put on a trial and sentenced to one year imprisonment. In prison, I had the opportunity to come into contact with the members of the Russian intelligentsia, academics, people of education and culture.

[Page 467]

My condition was very poor. A doctor, Dr. Prywes, saw me and decided that I have to work in the kitchen. Under those conditions it was happiness. In the kitchen I was no longer hungry. At first, I I washed dishes in the yard and while doing this work my hands swelled and cracked. When the doctor saw my hands he ordered to move me to work in the kitchen. It was so good for me there that I was afraid to leave when the release order came.

At the end of the war all of us traveled west. I arrived in Kiev and worked there for a year until I received a letter from my sister Chana who was in Turkestan. She asked me to come to her and join her family. At that time, when everyone traveled west, I decided to travel east to my sister. I bought a train ticket and packed in a suitcase everything I collected during a year of work in Kiev. But, in Russia it was not enough to pay for a ticket. In every connecting station I had to get off the train to get a new stamp. It was necessary to wait two to three days for this stamp and several more days for the next train. In one of the train stations I was not able to enter any car. They were all locked up.

At that time there were masses of abandoned children in Russia, mostly orphans. These children were ready for any crime. Two of them stood on a small bridge between two cars. They called me and offered me a place next to them. I stood next to them. While traveling they snatched the suitcase from my hand and escaped. I shouted and the train stopped so I could look for the thieves. I did not find the thieves, but I stayed inside the car even though I heard some passengers say that I was a cunning Jew who shouted to win a ride in the car.

I got off in Kuybyshev [Samara] and had to continue on another train. And here I got lucky. An old woman came with her grandson and with a suitcase. She asked me to bring her grandson to Turkestan. In the suitcase, the grandmother said, there's food for both of you.

In this train a Jewish officer from the Russian army was revealed to us as an angel from heaven. He guarded us so that nothing bad would happen to us from the mob of savages that murder and robbery was like a game for them.

From then on he went with us at every station to the officers' canteen and there we received warm and delicious food.

That Jewish officer left a deep impression in my heart. Once he asked me to sing "*Mein Shtetle Belz*"... He smiled and tears glistened in his eyes.

In Turkestan I met again with the Paskowitz family. There, I also married my husband.

On the way back to Poland we traveled through burnt cities. Tens of thousands ruins stood in the cities of Russia and Poland, and tens of thousands of corpses were dumped on the fields of the world. The earth under our feet was wet with blood. I don't have the strength to write about those terrible events which are still engraved in the space of the world in letters of blood and fire.

In the darkness of the night I can still hear the cry of the tormented. When I meet our townspeople, who survived the massacre, I can read the horror story in their eyes.

[Page 468]

The Righteous Among the Nations

I will always remember those days as a long winter, murky and cruel. As I reflect on them, I see frost-strewn fields and dead trees that black ravens nest in their dead branches.

We left Russia exhausted mentally and physically. The cry of crisis and disaster of our slaughtered people accompanied us on our way. But, in the darkness of the night there was a soft ray of light, human light and human love.

A Catholic priest, who had returned from his exile, traveled with us in the same car. At each stop, when Polish hooligans wanted to enter and abuse Jews, the priest stood in the car's doorway and did not allow them to enter. He scolded them: "you have nothing to do here. Get out of here."

The Poles harassed the Jews when they saw them getting off the train. My husband and brother-in-law had to go off to get milk for the babies, but returned broken and sad. When the priest saw this, he did not let them go out, and in every station he brought milk and also food for us.

The Righteous Among the Nations.

Like glowing lights they are planted in the world to illuminate the darkness of human loneliness. God did not make wings for human beings and therefore gave them radiant lights, which would serve as their wings, so that they could rise and pass over all the abysses and darkness lurking for them in the world.

The Righteous Among the Nations.

On the verge of extinction we found them and we will remember them forever. They appeared as a glowing light when there was darkness around us. Darkness. Darkness.

[Pages 469]

In Blood and Fire

by H. Rubin

Translated by Sara Mages

Dedicated to the memory of my father Pesach, my brothers Yitzchak and Eliezer Rubin z" l

In the months of October-November 1939, a considerable portion of the Jewish population in Wolomin was preparing to head east to reach the demarcation line in the city of Malkinia on the Bug River. At that time the other side of the bug belonged to Soviet Russia after the division of territories between the Soviet Union and Germany.

At the same time everyone wanted to get rid of their household items, like furniture and some personal belongings, because it was difficult to move them to the other side, and the monetary income was also needed.

Since there were many sellers the Christian buyers, who saw the Germans' abuse of the Jews, bought at half a price or even took without paying.

My father invited a farmer named Zich from the village of Lipiny to sell him furniture and other items.

Of course, my father told him a price that was ten percent of the real value of that time.

The farmer said: "one way or another, you will travel and leave everything, so why should I buy?"

My father took an ax and broke all the furniture in the house and said to the farmer, "Now I will transfer the wood to a Jewish baker," and so it was - Garbine the baker received the wood.

My father managed to cross to the Soviet Union and stayed with us in Siberia. There, he fell ill and in 1946 we returned with him to Poland. A month after our arrival he passed away. We buried him in the Jewish cemetery in the city of Swidnica in Lower Silesia. The tombstone was destroyed by anti-Semitic Poles.

My brother Yitzchak worked in a tank factory in the city of Chelyabinsk where we lived together. He was an engraver by trade and one of the outstanding workers in his department. He studied this profession in Wolomin with the Letkes brothers.

In early 1942, the evacuation of the engine factory in the city of Kharkov began because the Germans were approaching the city. In Chelyabinsk there was a shortage of apartments and the houses commanders began to check the Jews' passports, especially Jews who had come from Poland.

[Pages 470]

Yitzchak Rubin fell in the
Second World War near Leningrad

Here lies an honest man….. R' Pesach son of R'
Eliezer Rubin Katz, born in 1883, died in 1946, May his
soul be bound in the bond of everlasting life.

At the time we were given Soviet passports with Section 38. Since we did not know the Soviet passport law, we thought our passports were like those given to every Soviet citizen.

My father, and the rest of my family, received a 24 hours deportation notice (my family and I survived because we lived in a different area that had not yet been checked).

My family left to live in a state farm far from the city of Chelyabinsk, and as soon as they left the city my brother Yitzhak was drafted into the Red Army.

For two years he fought on all fronts, and on 15.1.1944 he fell in the village of Il'ino in the District of Leningrad. According to the notification of the Soviet Ministry of Defense he was buried there in a mass grave.

My brother Eliezer was not with us. At first he lived in the city of Mogilev on the Dnieper River. He was drafted during the war and in 1941 returned with his unit to the city of Baku [Azerbaijan].

At the beginning of 1942, he was sent to the front in Smolensk. The last news from him was that he was fighting in the Smolensk area and his unit is trying to stop the advance of Hitler's army on Moscow. We did not receive more information from him, and to our questions to the Ministry of Defense about his fate, we received an answer that he was lost and his whereabouts are unknown.

[Page 471]

My years of wandering from Wolomin to Hanover

by H. Kryger

Translated by Sara Mages

I was born in Wolomin in 1923. My parents were Peretz and Elka Kryger. In Wolomin we lived in a Christian neighborhood. The house where we lived was hit at the beginning of the war, my mother, my two aunts and fourteen neighbors were killed. I was wounded in my head. I had a ten year old sister and a four and a four and a half year old brother, and together with our father we lived with my uncle whose wife was also killed. My ten-year-old sister ran the household.

When the Germans entered the town they started to abduct us to all kinds of hard work. I worked in loading lumber in very difficult conditions. I started to hide and later decided to escape to Russia.

About ten thousand Poles and Jews wandered around the no man's land in the Malkinia area. We slept on the ground, in the cold, rain and the snow of the month of November until the Russians transferred us by train to Bialystok. There, I got job unloading cement. It was a hard work and I earned ten rubles a day. The foreman was a Jew.

I corresponded with my aunt in Moscow and she offered me to come to her. I informed my father about it in a letter that was delivered by Sedovnik. My father did not agree to my trip to Moscow and strongly demanded that I return to Wolomin.

I returned to Wolomin in the company of the same Sedovnik, who traveled all the time between Bialystok and Wolomin and specialized in crossing the border, but this time he was unlucky. The Germans captured us, twenty five people, Christians and Jews.

It was in January 1940 and the border was already closed. We have been told that the Germans would execute the Jews, but the Germans sent us to Malkinia. In Malkinia, the Poles attacked us and took all the money and valuables we had in our possession.

In Wolomin the Jews wore a yellow patch with a Star of David on their sleeves.

[Pages 472]

In Wolomin the Poles beat me and threw snowballs at me. When I returned home, my little brother did not recognize me. I was dirty, swollen, and my hands were frozen. The "home" this time was my uncle's apartment. My uncle and I were kept in the back room. The door that led to the room was hidden by a cupboard so that the Germans would not find us when they were searching for people for forced labor. For the most part the "cupboard" method proved itself.

In the spring, I started to show up for work on my own free will because I somehow managed to bring home a little food and a little wood. It was possible to get along with the regular German soldiers. The worst were the men of the SS and those who wore black uniform. They pushed us with their rifles and beat us with very cruel blows.

In October, all the Jews moved to the ghetto in Sosnówka and in the Shtutman buildings (next to Sosnówka). At first we worked in processing skins and in baking bread which was smuggled to Warsaw. People smuggled grain into the ghetto, we secretly ground it and sold the flour to the bakeries. We also knew how to produce saccharin balls.

The situation worsened in 1941. The Jews were not allowed to leave the ghetto's boundary. The Germans had a special method of punishing those who were outside the "boundary." They tied their legs, tied them to a sled and dragged them around the town until the victim died from the torture. The body was thrown into the main entrance of the ghetto.

In the fall of 1941 it was dangerous to leave the ghetto even with a permit from the Gestapo. The Germans used every opportunity to murder Jews.

At the same time a typhus epidemic broke out in the ghetto. There was absolutely no way of getting out of the ghetto. The Jewish doctors, who were in the ghetto together with us, were helpless. Medicines could not be obtained. Every day 5-15 people died. There were not enough horses to take out the bodies of the dead to the cemetery, and then the bodies were loaded on a human-drawn cart.

Once, on a dark and gloomy night, some friends and I snuck out of the ghetto and approached the railway tracks. As the trains passed we heard the voices of children begging for bread and water. Then we realized that our end was approaching.

From the beginning of 1942 trains traveled day and night with Ukrainians on the roofs of the cars. From Warsaw the trains were full of Jews. To Warsaw the cars returned empty.

Every day a hundred Jews left the ghetto for work along the railroad tracks. When they returned two or three were always missing, they were shot by the Germans.

On the holiday of Simchat Torah, after the *hakafot* at the Margolis Shtiebel, Polish policemen came secretly to the ghetto and told us that busses with men of the Gestapo, gendarmes and the SS arrived in Wolomin. It was a sign that the ghetto would be liquidated that night.

[Pages 473]

The manager of the Wolomin train station was a good friend of my father and had connections with a Polish anti-Nazi organization. He obtained an identity card for me and a Catholic priest from a church on Stelowa Street in Praga gave me a birth certificate under the name of Henryk Wozniak. Both certificates cost 700 zloty.

On the eve of Simchat Torah, at nine in the evening, I left the ghetto together with Frum and Rubinstein and we hid in Zielonka the third station from Wolomin. On the way the Poles attacked us and took everything from us and even the shoes were taken off our feet. This was the occupation of many Poles: to search and find Jews, rob them of all their possessions and hand them over to the SS for a kilo of sugar and a liter of vodka. For some reason they did not have the time to turn us over to the Germans. It was probably better for them to chase and search for more Jews. They were convinced that the Germans would find and kill us.

I had the face of a gentile and since I grew up around Polish children my Polish was natural. Therefore, my friends decided that I had to go to the station and buy three tickets to Malkinia. In Zielonka station a Pole approached me, started a conversation with me and asked about my occupation. I told him that I was smuggling goods to Austrolanka. "Don't be stupid" - the Pole said to me - "come with me and we will catch a number of Jews. In any case, they will fall into the hands of the Germans and they would send them to Treblinka."

After the war I learned that the Jews of Wolomin were deported on foot to Radzymin, a distance of ten kilometers. The weak were shot by the Germans and the road was strewn with bodies and blood.

On the train from Zielonka to Malkinia we witnessed atrocities. The Germans rounded up Jews, ordered them to kneel and shot them in the head. We got off the train in Malkinia. We handed our tickets in the presence of a Polish student whose duty was to help the Gestapo determine which of the passengers was Jewish.

In Malkinia, the Germans rounded up about twenty Jews and tied them with barbed wire the way logs are tied. I learned that the situation in Malkinia was dangerous. We headed northeast. There was a Jewish camp there and the Jews lived in more or less acceptable conditions. They did not believe us when we told them what was happening in our town.

In the morning they gathered the people for work, each one was called by his first and last name and what he had to do… In addition, a German approached us and told us that he knew who we are, that we tell all kinds of horror stories. Very soon the Gestapo will come and take us back to where we came from.

We fled from the place. We walked to Zambrów and there we found acquaintances who gave us food. A rumor circulated that at four, or five in the morning, the Germans would come to abduct people for the camps, therefore we left Zambrów and headed for Lomza. On the way I parted from my friends. They walked to the big ghetto in Lomza because they had relatives there. I remained in Czerwony Bór and worked in the quarry for four weeks. The employee was the Judenrat.

[Pages 474]

Four weeks later we learned that the men of the SS had arrived. My friends to work tried to calm me down and told me: "don't be afraid, the Germans would not do anything to us." But I was already educated and knew what to think about all this. I took a loaf of bread and escaped to the forest.

At four in the morning I heard shoots. Sometime later the same people, who tried to reassure me that the Germans would not hurt them because they were doing productive work, arrived.

In the morning I parted from them and walked to the unknown.

I had a birth certificate and a little luck. I thought of joining the partisans. I wandered from village to village and the Poles gave me advice: come with us, we will search for Jews, catch them, hand them over to the Germans for a fee and divide the Jews' money and diamonds.

In the village of Poczta I stayed to work for a farm owner who later discovered that I was a Jew and insisted that I should leave the place. He was afraid that the Germans would confiscate the farm.

The farmer's son felt sorry for me and hid me in the storeroom for a week.

I tried my luck in another village and managed to find work. However, after three weeks came an order that everyone must obtain a "*Kennkarte*" [identity] document. Otherwise, he would be considered a Jew or a partisan and sentenced to death.

I turned to the head of the village and he gave me a document that I am a good worker, I worked in the village for over six months.

My homeowner harnessed two horses to a cart and we traveled to the city to obtain a passport, but the clerk was very busy and had no time for me. He told me to come after Christmas.

After Christmas I traveled again to the city and managed to get the passport.

My intention was to get to Germany. I found a family whose son, a sergeant in the Polish army worked for a German farmer in the vicinity of Hanover, fell ill. The farmer agreed to let him go as long as another worker would be sent in his place, and I was chosen to work for him.

It was a complicated process. I needed a doctor's certificate. We turned to the doctor's assistant, gave him sausage, eggs and lard, and in exchange he gave me a document that I was healthy and able to work.

In Lomza we tried to get a ticket to Germany not through Warsaw, but through East Prussia. My contention was that in Warsaw I might be abducted for work.

In Hannover I turned to a policeman, showed him my documents and he put me on a train that took me to the village where I worked until the end of the war.

[Page 475]

The End of Days

by Shmuel Zuker

Ah, my father!

Ah, my only father, full of
blood and tears is our cup.
I am told much
about your tortured being.

You fell with your face to the earth.
Your skin and bones remain
when your life has departed,
quiet in the empty field.

Snow and rain have washed away
the evidence of murder,
But the bloody drops cry out:
The earth will never cover up that
sin;
my grave lacks a monument.

I see your sacred image
wrapped wholly in strength.
My heart holds silent tears
over your terrifying murder.

The fervent desire
watches always in me.
Today and forever
my tears overflow.

I owe you a monument,
not of bronze nor of stone,
But yet more powerful–
of tears and lament.

[Page 476]

Moyshe Zuker

Moyshe, my fine brother!

Far way on the road to Russia
you left in blood.
Wind and snow
covered your tracks.

With nothing etched in a stone
nor written on a board,
no memory of you
yet remains.

In a terrifying storm
frost, like a sharp sword,
hunger cramps, agony,
Drew you to the ground.

On your frozen fingers
you counted the days,
believing things would be better
on your terrible journey.

Wearing only torn shreds,
you stumbled in terror.
Every day seemed
like a year.

When you considered the wounds
on your tortured body,
It was like a voice crying in the

wilderness–
such was your cry.

We must assume
that you wept like a child,
and the bitter winds
knew what you meant.

Your strength gave out
and you fell face forward into the
snow
and thus you died
with a final groan.

Mother, father, brother–
you are remembered in all my
laments;
In all my prayers from the Siddur
I proclaim you with tears.

[Page 477]

My Shtetl

Shmuel Vinagara

My shtetl off Wolomin,
the sound of your labor
and your Talmudic study
in the beis-medresh
mark your eternal
existence. Your light
shines for all time.

Over the dark abyss
you stand as a high tower.
you surmount the dead
with terrible suffering.
You are a ruin, Wolomin,
but your light
will forever endure.

The quiver of your holiness
will never be interrupted.
I carry your whole
heritage in my heart.

Your children are scattered
over continents and countries,
though Israel has the best of them,
people of culture, founders of
kibbutzim.

Rescued from death,
saved from conflagration–
I see them on the streets
of Tel Aviv and Haifa.

Wolomin, my sacred town,
though turned into ruins,
you remain
a fearful monument.

[Page 478]

My road in a period of suffering and anguish

by Menachem-Mendel Teiblum

Translated by Sara Mages

I was nineteen at the outbreak of the Second World War. I attended a vocational school in Warsaw and in my spare time I helped my father in his business. The work in the shops, and in the lumber warehouses, was difficult and my father was already old then.

On the seventh day of the outbreak of the war, Radio Poland announced that all young men should leave their place of residence and head east.

Chaim Rubin, Lestvogel, Mendel-Lipa Teiblum and Zagoshtinsky and I left the town and headed east. During the day German planes bombed the roads and shot at pedestrians and we had to hide in the forest and in the field. We walked in the darkness of the night until sunrise and again we looked for some shelter, until we learned that the Russians had invaded Poland we decided to go towards them.

We were among the first refugees to arrive in Bialystok.

Our legs were swollen and injured and wrapped in rags, and when we got to the first aid station our appearance was so miserable that the people of Bialystok thought we were beggars and wanted to give us alms. We explained to them that we did not need money, only a home where we could rest.

A Jewish woman took pity on us and took us to her house. She fed us, prepared hot water for bathing, until we managed to find an apartment in a baker's house. We lay there for ten days. We could not get up and were served food in bed.

We stayed in Bialystok until the first snowfall. When it started to get cold we had nothing to wear so we decided to go back to Wolomin, once again on foot, to pick up our winter clothes.

When we arrived to my parents' home they already lived with my uncle, Yitzchak Teiblum, on Koshchelene Street, and refugees who escaped from Warsaw, lived in our home.

[Pages 479]

In Wolomin the Germans imposed a curfew from seven in the evening until the morning hours. The town was in the jaws of the predatory Nazi beast and depression and despair prevailed in it. The noise and joy, the bustle of commercial life and the voices of youth, fell silent. Many left the town and never returned.

Silence in the streets, worry at home. The Germans are robbing and there is no security in life. Every now and then - a Jew is murdered in broad daylight.

Therefore, we sit at home, but even here there is a bitter feeling of melancholy and despair. The life of the Jews is worthless. Outside - abuse, beatings and forced labor, at home - fear. At any moment, they are likely to evict you from the apartment and rob your property.

Not a trace remained from the public life that Wolomin was blessed with before the war. Nothing survived from the youth organizations, the activities, youthful joy and hopes.

Under these conditions I decided to return to Bialystok. I tried to convince my parents to leave with us, but to no avail. My father remembered how bitter was the fate of those who left their home in the First World War. Could he have imagined the horrible plots that the Germans had plotted against us?!

In Bialystok the Russians demanded us to declare: who is interested in Soviet citizenship, and who wants to return home. We all stated that we intend to return, and that sealed our fate.

In the middle of the night we were taken out of the house and led to an abandoned factory where all those, who had stated that they wanted to return, were concentrated. The overcrowding was terrible, people fainted and there were also deaths.

A few days later we were loaded on a train, in freight cars, without windows, in the cold and hunger, until we arrived, two weeks later to a dense forest near Arkhangelsk. We lived there in barracks and worked in logging.

I, along with Beni and Noah Brisker, belonged to a group of excellent workers, stahanovichim. We worked in unloading cargo from ships, a hard and tiring work. Sometimes I got tangled up in logs and found myself in the water. The situation worsened with the arrival of winter. The logs were immersed in ice at a depth of a meter or more, and I had to blow the ice with dynamite.

I worked in this job for over a year, until the outbreak of the war between Germany and Russia, and then we were given the opportunity to arrive in Samarkand. There, I met Beni Brisker and from him I learned that my sister Chana and her husband were in Turkestan. I decided to join them.

When Polish citizens began to be drafted into the Polish army I was one of the few Jews accepted and sent to Persia.

[Pages 480]

The conditions were harsh and I contracted typhoid fever. I was hospitalized in Tehran for about two weeks and after I recovered I was taken to a secluded camp where there were only Jews. The Polish army was not interested in us, did not take care of us and did not provide us with food.

The shocking news that came to us about the Nazi atrocities made us want to fight, we wanted to defend the Jewish honor.

Having no choice, we decided to leave the camp and demonstrate our desire to fight. We lined up as a regular army, left the camp and marched toward the British headquarters to present our problems to them.

We marched through the streets of Tehran and suddenly a Polish colonel stopped us and asked for the reason of t the march.

We told him the truth and he ordered us to return to the camp and promised to take care of things.

He kept his word. The next day we received food and equipment. Sometime later, we left on a train to which special cars were attached for the Jewish soldiers.

We arrived in Eretz Yisrael and underwent intensive training for six months. Then, we were transferred to Iraq to teach the soldiers in the Polish army camp the new methods of warfare that we learned with the help of the British equipment in Eretz Yisrael.

From Iraq we returned to Eretz Yisrael and held various positions until the order came to leave for the front in Italy.

I passed a long way by car and on foot, I saw flowers of Jewish life that were trampled and burned. To this day I hear their death's whispers and I cannot describe all that we have suffered. I have told very little of my journey, from the day I have left Wolomin and until my arrival in Eretz Yisrael in the uniform of a Polish soldier.

Life taught me how to overcome my suffering. Oh! How painful it was, and the wound had not yet healed.

Yet, despite all our torments and injuries, we, the survivors of the terrible Holocaust, continue to build our lives and before of our eyes the greatness of our holy ancestors, the greatness created day by day, and hour by hour, even in the smallest Jewish community.

Wolomin, my hometown, you remain real and alive for me to this day. I still remember most of the day and night events in your alleys and your extensive market, and they fill my heart with both horror and happiness from passed worlds. My childhood atmosphere in your alleys, from the joy of life to the horror scenes I saw in you, and the horror news that came when I was away from you.

Despite all the tears our ancestors shed on your land, there was also joy in their lives, joy of work and creation.

[Pages 481]

Under your sky generation after generation forged a chain of customs and lifestyles, of holidays and Sabbaths.

My ears pick up the voices of my brothers and sisters, and I see before me the delicate faces of my parents, uncles and aunts.

Almost all members of the Teiblum family engaged in the lumber trade. Their economic situation was good, and they had a good reputation because many of the townspeople made a living from them. They also had a generous hand, gained the trust of the town's residents and enjoyed the respect they received from Jews and Christians alike.

The chapter of my parents' life in the town hovers before my eyes. All their days a good word shone on their lips, and a warm and endearing smile was kept within them for each person.

My father's mind absorbed every detail in the lives of the residents of Wolomin, and it was a real pleasure to listen to his opinion in various fields.

I knew my mother's love in all its deep clarity and she gave me moments of glamour and happiness.

Wolomin is empty of its Jews.

They are gone. They were annihilated, executed, massacred, and burned.

The Teiblum family

[Page 482]

For these things I weep

by Sara Baum

Translated by Sara Mages

In this book we seclude ourselves with the memory of our martyrs and loved ones who perished in the terrible Holocaust. We all carry in our hearts the town of our childhood and youth. Sometimes, we wake up at night from insomnia, turning over from side to side, our eyes heavy and our thoughts leading us in different stations of our lives towards the distant past. Before our eyes pass the events whose impressions have left their mark on us and we live them again.

In these moments stand before me the Baum family and I see the noble figures of R' Yehudah-Leib with his wife Shprinze, and their daughters: Friedeleh and Scheindele. Here, Friedeleh is about to get married and Scheindele, on her way from Eretz Yisrael to America, stopped in Poland. Her husband was waiting for her in America and Scheindele wanted to meet with her family in Wolomin.

The war broke out and prevented her and her little daughter from leaving Poland, and their fate was sealed. They all perished in the cruelest way.

[Pages 483]

As if from a dream I bring up in my memory these good people from my husband's family. I remember the Sabbaths and the holidays when I was invited to their table. I am trying to recreate what my eyes see and bring up from the abyss of oblivion our beloved figures that are no longer with us…

Friday, 1933.

Here, we arrived from Warsaw to Wolomin, Friedeleh, my future sister-in-law, and me. We got off the train and turned to Dluga Street. The store was already half closed. At the door stood my future mother-in-law and welcomed us with a bright face. I hear her soft voice:

"Sara'le, how glad we are that you came. Come, get into the house!"

The sun of the Holy Sabbath eve has not yet gathered its last golden rays into the endless heavens. By this time the house was already clean and dignified and all the secular tasks in honor of *Shabbat HaMalka* had been completed.

On the table, covered with a white tablecloth, clean of any stain, were laid, in holiness and purity, two braided challot, a reminder of *Lehem Mishneh*. The challot were pointed at both ends and smeared with egg yolk. Poppy seeds were scattered on their surface, as is the custom of the seven species that our country was blessed with. Next to the challot, which were covered with a tablecloth embroidered with gold threads, was the knife, and the words "*Sabbath Kodesh*" were engraved on its handle.

In the middle of the table stood a beautiful polished bottle, shiny as crystal, inside it shone spectacular clear wine, and colorful small glasses for Kiddush stood around it like guards. The silver goblet for Kiddush was decorated with flowers, made by an artist.

R' Yehudah-Leib, and the rest of the family, had already bathed and were dressed in Shabbat clothes. The mother, in her Sabbath clothes, was standing by the silver candlesticks that stood on the table. She stuck the candles in them, put a white scarf on her head, tucked her hair inside it, tied the ends of the scarf under her chin, and with shudder of holiness, which surrounded the family members, lit the Shabbat candles.

[Pages 484]

And it seemed to us then that lights were turned on in her eyes as well.

She spread her hands three times until she covered her face with her palms, and the blessing was heard from her mouth in a clear distinct voice: "...*lehadlik ner shel Shabbat*."

And her lips whispered: "…like the light of these candles my son's eyes will shine in the light of the Holy Torah."

Her face glowed from her spread fingers in a supreme glow and a tear dropped from her eyes.

After lighting the candles her eyelids trembled in the glow of *Sabbath HaMalka*.

In a quiver of holiness, and in her soft feminine voice, she greeted us with "Good Shabbat."

These two words, in which a melody of melancholy was hidden, still resonate in my ears to this day and will not be erased from my memory forever.

The men, R' Yehudah-Leib and his son Shamai, my future husband - went to the synagogue and I stayed with the women. We chatted. Scheindele's friends immediately arrived, the Sabbath's expression was spread over their faces and time passed pleasantly.

The meal, the Friday evening meal, was held in good taste and knowledge and excelled in the abundance of her special dishes, and how wonderful and glorious were the Shabbat songs that the father and son sang and excited everyone with sacred feelings.

The house was illuminated in a pleasant light and the mighty singing burst through the windows and resounded in the city streets. Is it possible that these voices are no more, and with the disappearance of the city these voices were also silenced and disappeared?

In these moments I hear the voices that filled the space of the town, its streets and its houses, the voices of the residents of Wolomin as they greeted *Sabbath HaMalka*.

The voices remained within me. They did not leave me or let go of me.

[Pages 485-549]

A Saga of Pain and Heroism

by Tzvi Shedletzki

I Am Mobilized for the Army

On August 24, 1939, I was working in Warsaw, where I had a job as a carpenter. It was before noon when I received a phone call that I should come home because I had received a mobilization notice ordering me to appear on that very day in Rembertov for the third battalion.

This was one week before the war. I said farewell to everyone at work and I went home to Wolomin. On that same day, many of my friends were mobilized, and after noon we all went to Rembertov. When we got to the regiment, there were many mobilized men in the square. We were led to the doctor and from there to the quartermaster to receive our equipment. There we encountered our first instance of disorder.

There were no uniforms and no rucksacks, and most other things were missing. I got a rucksack that was torn up and the mess kit had a hole in it. Later the mess kit was taken from me. Uniforms were brought from the soldiers who would be staying at the regimental headquarters. They took them off and we got their clothes.

That same day we received rifles, spades, bayonets, and the other things for taking care of the arms. This was exactly a week before the war. We slept that night and at dawn we were awakened. Soon after breakfast we were led to Vover. There we were loaded on a truck and taken to Tchiekonov and from there we went by foot to the area of Mlovo, where we were quartered in the villages.

The local population was hostile toward us, because many of them were German. We stayed there until September 1, 1939, until the outbreak of the war.

The War Begins

September 1, 1939

We awoke early and heard the sound of artillery firing. Immediately an officer came running. He gathered us together and announced that the war had begun and that the Germans had bombed various sites in Poland.

They gave us ammunition–ninety bullets each and grenades for some. A staff officer arrived and talked about the significance of the war. They told us to eat quickly, because they would take us immediately after eating to a second regimental headquarters.

As we sat down to eat, we heard a shot nearby. When we got the square, we discovered that one of our soldiers had committed suicide. He left a note for his parents. The soldier was a Christian.

After breakfast, we were led out of the village. We had traveled only a short time when we were led into a little woods, not large, but with big trees.

In the woods we cleaned our gear until the cooks came and brought lunch. When the cooks appeared, so did an airplane, which passed over the woods at a high altitude two or three times. The last time, he trailed a white streak. The officer who was with us told us that this was an English airplane, so that the soldiers stood up openly and did not try to hide.

We did not have time to eat, because artillery began to fire at the woods, and the dead and wounded began to fall. They shot at us until evening.

At the time that they were shooting at us, there was a young officer who had just left officer school. He did not know what to do. In the evening, when the barrage was a little lighter, another officer appeared who had us assemble and who led us to Shassay. But Shassay was under heavy fire, so we quickly passed through.

Thus we put a distance between ourselves from the shooting. The officer was quite pleased that he seemed so military, that he had experienced his first attack. A little later more military men appeared and we were all led away to the front lines.

As we arrived at the front, we were immediately ordered to turn back, because the whole line was moving back. After a little while, we came to a river, and on the bridge were soldiers–laying mines. They told us that we were fortunate, because they had received an order to destroy the bridge, but they had seen us and waited for us. When we told them that the army was coming behind us, they gave a wave of the hand and said that the army could swim across, because they had to destroy the bridge.

After moving on another short while, they divided our group and we dug in. There we remained with our young officer, who was barely oriented in matters of war. We came to realize that we were in the middle, the center, and other divisions were on both sides of us.

The night was awfully dark, so that nothing could be seen. At about two in the morning, the officer sent out a patrol of five men. I was in that patrol.

After sufficient time, we returned and we sat in the trench until morning. Then artillery fire broke out again, and when the artillery quieted down, we saw light armored cars and many soldiers, who took us to the attack, but after strong fire from our side, they started to retreat.

When no more Germans were seen in the field, we sent a patrol, which ran into a small patrol of Germans that was absorbed in looking at a map. After a brief exchange of fire, our side captured one German, who was sent back to headquarters. Then heavy artillery fire opened up again and lasted until that night.

That day we had many wounded. We had for a whole day–since yesterday's lunch–had nothing to eat, only what we found in the fields near us–carrots and cabbages. We were like that until eleven or twelve at night, without uniting with other groups.

The officer sent groups of soldiers to both sides of us to inquire what they had heard. The soldiers returned and told us that the trenches were empty and they encountered no one. Then the officer, on his own, ordered us to move back.

I Am Wounded

We went through a village where we encountered several soldiers who told us in what direction the army had gone. We went back toward Shassay, and we were nearby. Suddenly I heard an explosion and I fell near other men. I did not lose consciousness. I checked to see how I was. My right leg was torn up under my knee. My right arm was damaged above the elbow. My left hand was also bloodied. And blood was running from my left leg, from the knee. My shoulders and back were wet. I realized that the wetness was blood.

A few minutes later the officer returned with several soldiers. They examined me and said I should be quiet so that the Germans would not hear. Later, when it was possible, they would send somebody for me. They left and I never saw them again.

A Captive of the Germans

I was lying near a cart, and on the other side of the cart I saw in a field a small house, and I figured that I might get help there. I began to crawl a little. I crawled over Shassay. I stopped to rest a bit, and I lost consciousness.

Early in the morning I heard screaming. I raised my head a little and then saw coming toward me two Germans with the symbol of the Red Cross. I begged for water. They gave me some kind of spicy drink as well as water. They brought a greatcoat and laid me on it, then covered me with a second one. They told me that they would come back for me. So it was. They soon returned and carried me in a stretcher to the cart, where an ambulance wagon waited and took me, along with other wounded men, to an assembly point in the field.

They quickly took me to a tent, a field hospital, and after examining me they amputated my right leg above the knee. The other wounds they bandaged.

When I regained consciousness, I was lying in a bed. The doctor came with a nurse. He asked if I felt all right. He gave me a small glass and said that I should drink, that it was rum. Then they asked my name, my city, my religion, and other details. I gave them my real name.

After all this, they took me to another place in the field where there were many wounded Poles and hospital cars to transport them. They took us all to a hospital in a German border town.

We remained for three days in the hospital. The first two days I do not remember because I was unconscious. On the third day I did not feel too bad. During the night they took us to the train station. They loaded us in a hospital car and took us to Konigsberg.

For the seven weeks that I was in Konigsberg, conditions in the hospital were not bad. Specifically, I suffered no ills because of my background. After several days in the hospital I was taken to the operating room because my wound, which had been closed up, opened, so after putting me to sleep, they closed it up with a brace.

I do not remember the dates of each operation, but during those seven weeks I had the brace on my leg after the amputation, an operation on my hand so that the hand was in a cast. Then I had a hemorrhage in my hand and they amputated the hand.

A couple days after the first operation on my hand, there was an inspection in the hospital by a high–ranking doctor. When they came to me and the nurse had removed the bandage and cleaned out the wound, the doctor was thoughtful and they went into the next room. The nurse said that they would return soon and she would rebandage the hand.

After a few minutes I felt wetness. I noticed blood coming from my hand. I started to call for help. The nurse came, as did the doctor. They immediately took me to the operating room, and after sedating me, they stopped the bleeding.

Three days later, my hand turned black. I could not move my fingers. The doctor said that they would have to amputate my hand because it was septic, and thus I lost my hand.

When they brought me back to my bed, it was the first time that I really complained. I had also hurt my right ear. Because of the explosions of the bombs, I still do not hear well.

Immediately my right side became fiery red, and for a long time I had to use compresses.

I had to lie on a rubber hoop, because my back was wounded. I lay in a small room with another wounded man. The medic who was responsible for our room was an old German man who was not a follower of Hitlerism, so his care was good. He would bring cigarettes from home, apples, candies, and he was the first one who would lift me from the bed when the nurse came to change the linens.

When he was not there, a second medic, a young man, who also lifted me from the bed when the nurse came for the linens. He did it specially.

One day the nurse came with two young men from the Hitler Youth, and they took me into a large hall where there were ten or twelve beds. As they pushed the cart, they shook it especially hard so that I was in great pain.

The chief doctor in this section was a young German who often came into the hall and asked questions of the ailing. As a Jew, I used to translate, so he would always sit near my bed. After a while he learned to speak fluent Polish. He said that he knew Polish well because he was from nearby, but he hated speaking Polish.

I did not receive bad treatment from him, though he was very anti–Semitic. One day he said that if he were at the front, he would not take Jewish soldiers as prisoners but he would should them right there in the field.

There were times when SS officers would shoot wounded people at the front regardless of who they were. I had the courage to ask him: since he knew who I was, why did he treat me so well, contradicting his own speech. He answered that he was a doctor and I was a wounded person and it was his duty as a doctor to help.

There was no point in speaking further about it. This was in 1939. It is possible that a few years later, if I fell into his hands, I would not have asked and he would not have answered.

After being in the hospital for seven weeks, the nurse came with the doctor and they indicated that I would be transferred to a second hospital. I had no fever. That same day, around noon, I was taken into the courtyard, where trucks were waiting, and we were taken as a large group to the station, where a train was waiting.

In the car, straw was spread on the floor. Those who could walk entered the car and sat on the straw, while the seriously injured were carried in on stretchers and were put, in their stretchers, on the floor.

It was already cold and frosty, and we were not far from the sea. I was covered only with a blanket.

When it grew dark, we came to a small train station called Stabloch. There we were transferred to trucks and taken nine kilometers to the camp hospital, which was called Stalag A1.

The road was rough. The trucks went fast and rattled our insides. It was so cold that we arrived at the camp half dead. When we got the camp, we saw a great number of little huts. I was put with a group of wounded, among whom only one could walk a little, in hut number 9. My bed was near the door. It was freezing, and I had only one blanket, but we were told that in the morning we would receive another blanket.

The cold was not the worst thing. Worse was trying to sleep that first night. The "mattresses" were filled with fresh–cut straw, and through the material I could feel the knots in the ropes that bound the straw. When they laid me in my bed, I could feel that knot right in my back, and all night it aggravated my wound.

There was no one to speak to. We saw no orderlies the whole night, so I moaned all night.

That lasted all night. At six in the morning, the orderly brought coffee. Each person received a cup of coffee and no bread. That was our breakfast. When we asked for bread, the medic announced that at noon we would receive lunch and at five or six we would get bread and coffee, but breakfast was only coffee.

I said to the orderly about the know in the mattress and that I was in pain. He could not help me until he received permission. Then he and another orderly undid the knot.

It seemed that the orderlies lacked the barest knowledge of their jobs. The Germans used captured soldiers as orderlies. Their work was to bring food for the ill, remove waste in the morning. When someone needed rebandaging, they took him to the operating room. They also had to take our temperatures.

For most this was an easy job. The orderly went to each patient and asked if he had a fever. Whatever the patient answered, the orderly wrote down, whether it was high or low.

No one worried about washing himself. Thus, I lay there for a couple of weeks without water ever touching my face. The bandages were made out of paper, so after a short time they were soaked with pus and falling apart, but still we had to wait two days to get a new dressing.

At noon or one o'clock they brought lunch for all ten of us in one container. There were different lunches. Often there was a container of water with a little head of cabbage. With great ceremony the cabbage was divided into ten portions, and that was lunch.

There was also a lunch of kasha, which brought great solemnity to the barracks, because however hungry we were, the tins of food sat on the table while we waited for them to cool off, because that made the food thicken.

After two weeks, the less severely wounded began to leave their beds, and they began to have bad experiences, but with bread it became worse. The orderlies brought in the bread and put it on the table. The ill, who were mobile, cut it. The result was that they had double portions.

This is how it was: twenty portions of bread were cut and laid on the table, and when the cutting was done, they gave a yell and those who sat at the table took a large portion of bread and those who were lying in their beds received a smaller portion.

The bread was old, and during the cutting it crumbled. Those who sat at the table knew enough to gather the crumbs, so that added to their portions. The same thing happened at lunch.

We tried a variety of experiments with the bread. Some tried to save their bread for breakfast, but at night, when hunger was overwhelming (the whole piece of bread was only about 200 grams), people would take an occasional bite, so that by morning nothing was left.

We drank our coffee with a special ritual. Each person held his cup, and one called out, "Ready! One, two three!" By "three" we had each finished our coffee and began the wait for lunch, for the little bit of water that they called soup.

From one meal to the next, we talked about how we used to eat at home, all the good things, and we waited for the day when we could cut our own bread.

One day, after about three weeks, they changed my sheet because it was covered with pus and lice, but they did not wash me nor change my garments, so I was as filthy as ever.

When they changed my clothes, they did not change the sheets, and the sleeping bag and the straw remained filthy and lice–ridden.

After several weeks , several German came with the orderlies, and they told the orderlies that some officers were coming for inspection and the hut had to be washed and the soldiers had to be washed and shaved.

When the orderlies responded that they had no razors, because it was not permitted to have them, they sought out a hairdresser. He had a razor and he did the shaving.

By bed was right by the door, so I was the first to be shaved. My beard had grown well. When he began to shave me, I started to yell, because the razor was dull and he cut my face. He left my beard half–grown. They washed me a little, and that refreshed me a little bit.

The Inspection

Several higher officers arrived, one of them a doctor. There was a briefing on each wounded man, and when they came to me, he told them to remove my bandage. He examined my wound and then spoke with the other Germans. Then he asked if I had any requests. I said that it was difficult for me to lie on the straw sack and that I was hungry.

I was lucky. He ordered them to give me a soft cushion, a rubber tube, and *extra rations*, supplemental food for a month. But until the extra rations arrived, I lost half my weight.

The supplement that I received consisted of two potatoes and twenty grams of meat.

The secular new year arrived. We received 600 grams of sugar and a larger portion of bread, and lunch was a bit better. We were also visited by a clergyman who spoke Polish.

We also received coal, briquettes, like bricks, and everyone who was mobile went out to bring in the coal. One day they brought in so much that the space under all the beds was full.

One Sunday we were visited by a German civilian. He held a carton, and in the carton was dry bread, hard as iron. He gave each man a piece of bread. I also got a piece. There was no way to take a bite, but I was very happy with it because I could not eat it quickly. I gnawed and gnawed at it for a half day until I had consumed it.

By then I could get out of bed and hop to the table, and others also could do so. We sought a way to prevent anyone from being cheated of bread. We made a primitive scale and weighed the bread.

After weighing it, we laid the bread out in a row. One man stood with his back to the table and someone held a piece of bread behind him. They asked him whose piece it was and whoever's name he called, that piece was his.

I Receive a Foot

In February, two orthopedists came from Konigsberg and began to make prosthetics for all those whose wounds had healed. They made plaster of Paris models. In March they took us to Konigsberg to try out the prosthetics.

That was a good day. The workers gave us sandwiches. We devoured them. After fitting the prosthetics, we returned to the camp hospital.

In April they brought us the prosthetics. Each individual was called into the operating room. We were the first group of over twenty men. An orderly carried me on his shoulder, because I could not walk with a cane, as others did. I had to hop, but the operating room was too far away. Each person was called in, and I was the last, because my name began with the letter "shin."

Lacking the patience to wait, I hopped to my prosthesis. Each one had its owner's name on it. I put it on, with the orderly's help. I grabbed a cane and immediately began to walk. When they called my name, I was already walking on my prosthesis.

My prosthesis was made of leather to the knee, and below the knee was a cane–like piece. For all the invalids who had lost only a foot, the prosthesis was made of plaster of Paris above and the cane–like piece below. Men who had lost both feet received a normal prosthesis.

Back in the barracks, I could already walk by myself, though I had trouble with stairs for the first couple of days, and the entrance to the barracks had stairs.

I Make a "Life"

On that same day I went to the hut of the carpenter so that he could shorten my cane, which was too long. After he fixed the cane, he gave me two pieces of bread with schmaltz. When I returned to the barracks and began to eat the bread, I heard someone say, "He's got quite a life!"

It was permitted for people at home to send packages, but not more than 250 grams per package. One time I saw my name listed among those for whom packages had arrived, and when I went to get them, there were five packages from five different people. The packages had taken a long while to arrive at camp. In normal times, I might have discarded them, but there they were very good.

A Letter

I wrote my first letter from the hospital in Konigsberg, but I received no answer. I wrote my second letter from the camp hospital, not to my parents but to my uncle in Warsaw, because I had received no answer from home. I guessed that my parents had gone to my uncle in Warsaw.

I received an answer to my second letter after a few months. Then we were allowed to write two letters a month, but only on special paper that we had to pay for in the canteen. Anyone who had no money sold a piece of bread, and for the money he could buy two cigarettes without writing paper. One time I sold my whole portion of bread so I could buy shaving equipment.

The Life of the Invalids

The invalids would go into the kitchen to bring out their lunch, and when the German was not in the kitchen, we would get the food from those who worked there.

Once it happened that the German was hiding under the counter where we stored water in case of fire, and when a number of the invalids had gathered by the window, he opened the water and began to shoot it at us in a strong stream. We quickly got away, but the water drenched us, so we were fifteen soaked invalids on the ground, and he continued to pour water on us so that we were even wetter.

There were times then when packages of good would arrive for the prisoners and the Germans did not give them to us. They took the good stuff, like sausage and schmaltz, and then they repacked the packages arbitrarily.

These packages of miscellaneous goods they brought to the camp hospital. Sausage, schmaltz, butter and other things were all mixed together. As the things appeared, we would lay them out and spread them on bread. This happened once a month.

The truck that brought these things also brought dry bread from the packages. Each time a different barrack received the bread.

One time I was by chance near the kitchen when the truck carrying the bread was standing by the open window. I put down my cane and went quickly to the window, where I snatched a piece of cake, but at the same moment a half of a bread fell out of the sack. When I grabbed at the bread, the cake fell from my hands and someone else seized it. I was left with the bread, about three kilograms of fresh bread.

At least when I left that scene I was not so hungry.

The other invalids complained that their prostheses were not so good. An expert came from the factory and he was ordered to exchange the prostheses. My prosthesis was also somewhat tight because when I received it I was so thin that my bones could be seen, but when I started to eat, I put some meat on my bones and the prosthesis became tight. Still, when I was asked if it was okay, I said that it was fine. I did not want them to take it from me so that I would again be confined to my bed.

Among the Jews

There was in the camp hospital a small group of the severely wounded. All the others who had recovered were sent to the camp at Gerken

I was still in the camp hospital at the end of May when a group of French prisoners were brought in. There was not enough room, so a group of us were transferred to a prisoner of war camp, Stalag 1, in Gerken. At that camp I was assigned to a Jewish barracks.

In that camp there were about seventy thousand prisoners. After they took down all our information in the recording station, I was told which barracks to go to. when I arrived at the barracks, the Jewish commander showed me where I would sleep.

I looked around to see where in the world I was.

It was a huge camp surrounded by two rows of fencing, and between the rows was barbed wire. There were also guard towers with machine guns.

Each collection of four barracks was surrounded by barbed wire. That was called a battalion.

In the middle of the camp was the canteen. In the canteen we could get paper to write letters, shaving supplies, and other little things. We could also get soda water, but there were few takers. There were also times when we could buy onions–all for money. But no bread.

At the entrance to the camp was the recording station, and near that was the infirmary. They had brought a Jewish doctor into the infirmary. I went to him and said that I could not walk on the platforms of several of the floors, so he admitted me to the infirmary.

A little further on was the worksite entrance, and near that was a post office. In the square was the illegal bazaar, which the Germans did not interfere with.

The bazaar was called Kerzelak. There we could buy anything, even serious stuff, for a quarter, a half, or a whole portion of bread. A whole portion of bread consisted of 200 grams.

We could also get a teaspoon of salt, tobacco, cigarettes and also a half a cigarette–all for money, or people bartered.

A packet of tobacco cost between three and four hard marks. There was real money and camp money. A Reichsmark, which we called "hard," was worth four or five camp marks. The difference was so large because that was the will of the guards, who smuggled in the tobacco. For a packet of tobacco that cost fifty pfennig, they wanted two or three marks. I don't remember the price of cigarettes, but it was approximately the price of a packet of tobacco.

It often happened that the guards came to the bazaar and whoever they seized there selling his portion of bread, they took the bread away and gave it to an invalid..

When the guard left, the invalid would return the bread for a cigarette or two, but the guards saw what was going on, so they would stand next to the invalid while he ate the bread.

Outside of the bazaar there was also a business in soup. A mess tin of soup cost about three marks, or a full mess tin with thick coffee cost two marks, if it was sweet, and one mark if it was bitter.

Invalid Eke Out a Living

In the camp I asked if the invalids were exempt from the food lines, and they answered that they go into the kitchen and when a course of watery soup was ended, they gave what remained in the pot to the invalids.

I tried going into the kitchen from the other side and I stood there inside the door. The head of the kitchen, an older German, noticed me and called me to him. He asked what I wanted and I told him a meal. He called out to everyone to give me something.

The same thing happened then in many of the kitchens, though not all, because some kitchens were staffed by young Germans who chased the invalids away. There was no meat in the meals. They made the lunches with big fish that were stored for a long while in salt. They were not nearly fresh. At least they were filling.

The food was heavily salted and the fish were old, but even so the men ate with big appetites and sucked on the fish bones.

There were also days when the food was prepared with horse bones. After cooking, they removed the bones from the pot because they were so big. They put the bones in a crate outside of the kitchen. No one dared go there, but no one paid attention to the invalids, so that invalids were always there tearing little bits of meat off the bones.

Invalids also benefited from the stores and storehouses for bread. Several times every day a truck brought bread. The bread was thrown in through a window, and while being thrown, it often broke into smaller pieces. The Germans gave the pieces to the invalids who stood around the storehouse.

The allotment with the bread consisted of a teaspoon of marmalade and a tiny bit of margarine or a similar amount of ground fish. When the storehouse keeper finished a tub of margarine, he gave it to an invalid who stood by the window and who, with a spoon, scratched out whatever was left. And when the keeper opened a new margarine, he ripped off the paper covering and gave it to an invalid. On the paper there were always little bits of margarine.

Our regular meals were like those of non–invalids: 200 grams of bread for lunch and coffee in the morning.

When I was taken from the camp hospital into the camp, life in the camp had become routine. But earlier, the Jewish prisoners had suffered–they had been beaten and tortured. Even after I arrived in the camp the Germans would for no reason beat the Jewish prisoners. There was a Polish officer in the camp of German ancestry who always wore a beret on his head. All the Jewish prisoners trembled before him.

Every evening there was a roll call, not in the barracks but outside. After everyone was accounted for, the invalids were let go and everyone else was made to stay out in the dark doing calisthenics over and over or just being made to lie in the mud and crawl in the mud while being beaten.

There was one sergeant who sought any opportunity to persecute the Jewish prisoners.

French Prisoners of War

One day they locked up all the battalions and stopped all activity. A little later they began to lead in French prisoners, many of them. I was then in the infirmary, which was next to the registration office. It took a half day to register all of them.

The Frenchmen had many good things, like English cigarettes, chocolate, good clothes, and wool socks, but they had no razors, so that every time that I made a trade, I had to quickly sell cigarettes so that I could get money to buy razors in the canteen.

In the battalion where they were led, there were guards who did not allow in any older prisoners, but we conducted business through the wires when the guards were not attentive. People bought socks, underwear, shirts, all for cigarettes or tobacco, and in the early days–and also later–for bread.

Among the prisoners were also aristocrats from Vilna and nearby. Russia and Germany were getting along then and it was permissible to send products from both sides, and they received large packages full of good things, like sausage, bacon, and other things. But each of them cared only for himself, with no interest in anyone else.

The barracks was divided in two parts, with a small washroom in the middle. There was also a big pot for boiling laundry, but it was used more often to cook food.

The cooking was done on a contrived oven. Everyone combined their potatoes in a rag and tied them together. This was put into the pot. The pot was filled with water and thus we cooked. When the potatoes were done, we emptied the water and each man took his rag with the potato. The outhouse was a hundred meters from the barracks. Between the barracks and the toilet, a guard marched.

We had to salute every guard, but some guards, when men saluted them, struck them and yelled, "Jew, why are you saluting?" But if men did not salute them, they were beaten for not saluting.

One day a young soldier appeared at the post. He appeared fresh and very military. He had no experience. He did what he had been taught, that is, when someone saluted him, he saluted back. When one of us went by him and saluted as required, the German responded, so the prisoner came back to the barracks and recounted the miracle. In the next few minutes, many went to the toilet and the poor German stood the whole time at his post holding a salute.

One day the Jewish barracks was closed and several men were taken away for an investigation into a serious matter–espionage.

This was the case: The paper that we got in the canteen for writing letters was manufactured with defects, with red dots. No one paid attention to them, but when the letters arrived at the censor, he noticed the dots and alerted the commandant, and from there they came to arrest the letter writers. After an investigation and after controlling the paper for letters in the canteen, the arrested men were released.

The Germans Shoot Jewish Prisoners

Before I was taken to the camp, when I did not yet have a prosthesis, that was in March of 1940, there was a transport of wounded men, including Jews who were fit for transport. They were freed and sent back to Poland. I was not suitable because I did not yet have a prosthesis.

All of the Christian prisoners in the transport were freed, but only the Jews from the Gubernia General were freed.

The Jews from other areas that belonged to Russia and to the areas outside of the Gubernia General , which the Germans considered German territory, were sent to Byala Podolsk, and we in the camp got news that they were all shot there.

This was all confirmed later. How people in the camp found out about it I do not know.

Later on there was a transport from Cracow, but it was only Christians, no Jews. I wrote a letter to my parents asking them to go to the command center and ask for me to be freed, so they wrote to the commander and asked for my freedom.

They received an answer–that they should send a note saying that they would take responsibility for me and a certificate from the city council that I was a Volks–German and then I would be freed.

Understandably, I could not obtain such documents, so I remained imprisoned.

There were also many Ukrainians in the camp. Once I was walking around and I saw all the Ukrainians gathered in front of the block with several German officers. One officer read to them a document in Ukrainian about an independent Ukraine, after which they sang songs and then each one went up to the officer and signed a declaration.

One day all the Jews were assembled and led to a nearby second camp. This was a separate section of the same camp. It was called Camp L.

The Germans said that the Jews were conducting too much dishonest business.

In Camp L there were also Africans and Arabs from the French front and a small number of Englishmen. We thought there that we would starve to death, because there was no way for us to organize ourselves. We had only what we were given in the kitchen. But after a few days, the camp plumbers arrived. They were German civilians who worked in the camp and smuggled in different goods.

For these goods they accepted money, sweaters, and socks, which we would buy from the Africans and the Arabs in the usual way.

Also in Camp L I got a place in the infirmary. When I arrived at the infirmary and they showed me my bed, I sat down and looked around. It was a large room with twenty beds. In the middle of the room was a stove which burned nicely because the Africans and the Arabs were freezing, even though it was summer and the Europeans were sweating.

Also the French prisoners were permitted to wear their greatcoats because it was cold.

Also there was no work outside the camp for the Jewish prisoners.

We were in the camp for several weeks and then we were taken back to the first camp, where we were placed under arrest. A guard was stationed by the entrance to prevent anyone from leaving, but when the invalids went out, he pretended not to notice.

Everyone else was allowed in the evening to register for the doctor, and on the way they conducted business.

There were rumors in the camp that a transport was going to set the sick prisoners free. I went to the registration hall to ask if I was on the list, and when I was told I was not, I asked to be able to see the commandant, if that was possible.

They wrote it down, and early in the morning I went with a group to the commandant. Because of me, the departure was delayed for a whole day.

At the command post I asked that I should be freed and put on the list for the next transport. The commandant spoke nicely to me, saying that he would not answer my request. He said that he would telephone the registration hall of the camp and there I would receive a precise answer.

That night I was back in the camp, and early in the morning I went to the registration hall, where I was told that they would not list me for the next transport because that transport was only for Christians. Then I was told that in a short time, all the Jews would be sent from the camp to Poland.

Rumors started to fly–that only men from the Guvernia General would be freed, or that men from the Russian territories would as well. The Jewish prisoners discussed whether they should list themselves as Polish or Russian.

There were also prisoners who were listed as Christians, but when they heard that the Jews would be released in Poland, they announced that they were Jews. Among these "new" Jews was a doctor.

One day about 800 Jewish prisoners were brought into the camp. From their first day as prisoners they were put to work, even while all the Jews were being processed.

Yom Kippur in the Camp

After several requests, the commandant gave permission that no Jewish prisoners should be required to work on Yom Kippur and that they should be allowed to davn. Among the religious Jews there was one whose name, I think, was Cotton, and that group arranged things.

Early on Yom Kippur, when everyone gathered to davn, there was a group of anti–religious men who called for an anti–religious lecture in the same place where men were davning. While the speaker was carried away, a group of Germans came into the hall, and everyone who was not occupied in davning undertook various activities.

The day came when they announced that we should be ready. The Germans made sure to take early in the morning and at night to the station, which was several kilometers away. Snow and frost were on the ground.

I remember it was mid–October. We were put into train cars. We were given a little bread and food for the way and we started. A military transport was either in front of us or behind us. I don't remember how long we traveled, because we often stood still. We were not allowed out of the cars.

Finally we came to another prisoner of war camp in Hammerstein. There was Stalag 2B. We were there for several days. A group of us invalids went to the commandant and asked for warm clothing because it was so cold. And a miracle happened–he gave us invalids warm clothes and even winter coats.

We were loaded back into the trains and traveled even further until we came to a border town which before the war belonged to Poland. The train stopped not at the station but a little beyond. We were told to leave the cars.

In the town were Poles and remarkable Polish uniforms. They brought bread and threw it through the fence to us. But we did not collect the bread because the Germans kept us in the cars, and later that same day we arrived at Byala Podlosk.

Under Jewish Leadership

We were led from the station through the empty streets, where we occasionally saw a Christian who was out late. We arrived at a civilian work camp.

It was as though we had slept through the night. In the Byala Podlosk work camp the local Jews were the leaders, though understandably with German oversight. I remember one who was called Black Janek, but other names I do not remember.

There was also a Jewish doctor, but the doctor and the local Jewish commanders did not live in the camp. They just spent the day there.

They were there to berate the Jews in the ghetto. It was permitted at lunchtime for the Jewish women of the town to bring meals for the men in the camp.

There was a rumor in the town that Jewish prisoners of war would be brought to the camp, so the Jewish women began to bring pieces of bread or whole loaves. They stood by the fence and waited for the gates to be opened so they could enter.

We were all quite hungry, so when the women entered, each man tried to be the first to grab a piece of bread, and we all ran to the women with the baskets. The Jewish commanders also played a role. They fell upon us with whips and sticks and began to beat us murderously. At first we did not react, but soon we took a stand and returned the blows.

In the kitchen we received lunches that were worse than when we were in prison, but those who had money to pay the cook received better food.

Those who worked in the kitchen were among those who had been required to work, but they had paid off the Jewish camp leaders and got to work in the kitchen and do whatever they wanted.

The same was true in the bathhouse. Anyone who wanted to go and wash had to pay off the bathhouse workers.

Medical Treatment

In the morning, everyone who was ill gathered in the square for roll call. The orderly had to determine whether a person could go to work or not.

We, a group of invalids, stood around trying to see how the examinations went. One fellow came out from among those who worked in the camp. He had been appointed orderly, not because he was an orderly but only because he could pay to hold the post.

A group of twenty to thirty men stood there. The orderly went and asked what bothered each one and quickly said he could go to work. There were some among the ill who had severe wounds on their feet, running with pus, and the orderly said that they could go to work. At the prison, such men had received medical help.

We invalids who were standing and watching how the orderly handled himself took to cursing him. He left the sick men and went away.

The prisoners of war were set to work building an airfield, and while working they told the officer in charge about conditions in the camp, so he came to see for himself.

The next morning a military truck arrived at the camp bringing sleeping bags, wooden slats, and bowls for food.

Prisoners of war were also assigned to the kitchen and to the baths, so that the conditions ended up being a little better.

We invalids demanded that we should be exempt from work, according to cards we received as prisoners. The cards said that we should be exempt. The local Jews, the leaders, said that the cards did not apply to us and we had to go before a Jewish doctor who worked in the camp and was also one of the camp leaders.

Immediately a rumor spread that if we gave them our cards, they would free us, but none of us wanted to relinquish our cards because they were our only evidence that we were invalids from the war.

The commission met on Shabbos, or on Sunday.

We stood and waited. There were 180 of us. The first one who went before the commission was from Warsaw. I remember that his name was Soshikin. He had a below the knee amputation on one leg and an injury on the other foot. The doctor told him that he would not be exempted: because he could write, he would work in the office as a writer.

When he returned from the doctor and told us what the doctor had said, we all left.

I Am Released

We asked the group leader of the prisoners of war who were working on the airfield that they should tell the German officers about the invalids' predicament. Early the next day, when they were away at work, they told the Germans about the invalids and also about the doctor who would not exempt them.

At noon, a truck arrived with a high–ranking officer and one of the prisoners. He assembled all the invalids and sent for the doctor and the camp leader. When the doctor arrived, the officer raised a fuss and cursed him, then asked the doctor what right to cancel the orders of the German high command.

The officer immediately ordered that he did not want to see an invalid in the camp after 10 the next morning, and he went away.

The next day, the camp commanders summoned all the invalids. They demanded from us that we should promise that we would travel on our own money. They would no longer give us money. We had no money, but not wanting to make further difficulties, we promised.

Next they demanded that we should return the military coats that were totally new. There they ran into opposition, but luckily for the invalids at that moment the German doctor from the airfield arrived and prevented the seizure.

This was before lunch. We were taken to the Jewish committee, where we demanded money for train–cards, and they gave us cards worth several zlotys.

That night we were a group of twenty–some men on our way to the station. I went to the ticket office and asked if there were inexpensive tickets to Warsaw for invalids. He replied that there were no cheap tickets, not even for Christian invalids. But he also said there was a midnight train to Warsaw and the conductors were friends of his, so he could arrange for us to travel to Warsaw without tickets. He told us to wait in the waiting room until he would notify us.

We sat down in the waiting room and waited. After a half an hour, the cashier came with two men from the Red Cross who brought a big pot of tea with bread and shmaltz and a few zlotys for each man.

A little later they again brought bread and shmaltz. When the train came, the cashier sent for us and said that we should get into the first two cars. Thus we made it to Warsaw.

Home Again

I didn't want to go home immediately because I didn't want to enter the shtetl in daylight for my first meeting with my parents. I got onto a tram and went to my uncle who lived in Warsaw and I stayed there until evening, when I went to the train station. I arrived at the last minute. All of the cars were overfilled. I went to the stationmaster and begged for a spot. He opened a military car and asked them to make room and then invited me in. When I was seated in the car, I noticed a Pole from our town who was known before the war as a confirmed anti–Semite. In his lapel he wore the badge of Volks–Deutsch. He was reading a German newspaper. When we got under way, he stopped reading and started telling the Germans how he had fought to prevent the Wolomin ghetto from being created in the town, but rather outside the town. He had gotten his way. Surely he did not recognize me, since he gave everyone cigarettes, including me. After twenty–five minutes we got to Wolomin. It was really dark. No Jews could be seen in the streets, since Jews were only allowed out after six in the morning.

It Was 11/7/40

I cannot describe how my father first received me, but it was the first time I had seen him cry. My mother and brother were not in our home because they, with a group of other Jews, were in the ghetto. It was a week before everyone had to be in the ghetto.

I also cannot describe my meeting with my mother. I don't have the words. I will simply say that there were two of us brothers, and I was my mother's son. So, too, the meeting with my brother. I have begun many times to describe it, but each time I have put aside my writing, because it is too hard to recreate the whole scene on those days when I was reunited with my parents and my brother.

The Wolomin Ghetto

On November 15, 1940, all the Jews had to be located in the ghetto. The ghetto was not yet fenced in and lay near the train tracks. The name of the area was Sosnovke. There were two divisions–one section near the tracks was made of big blocks where the Jewish Council and the well–off lived. The larger section was in the woods. It contained little wooden houses. The crowding in this section was terrible. Altogether there were two thousand Jews. I, my parents, and my brother lived in a room that was nine square meters. In our home was a lathe workshop (my father was by trade a woodworker), a kitchen, a bed, and at night we set up another bed. When the second bed was set up, we could not open the door.

The Jews lived off goods that they would buy from Christian smugglers or from Jews who got goods from the wealthy and smuggled them into the village. They brought them in by back roads. Another kind of livelihood involved smuggling leather and other materials, which were worked by Jewish craftsmen. People also smuggled in corn and milled it with hand mills. With the flour, Jewish bakers made bread, which was bought by Christian smugglers.

As I recall, the ghetto was not at first fenced in. There were no guards and people could move about freely. In the beginning people would work for the Germans according to lists compiled by the Jewish Council.

A little while later, the ghetto was fenced in on the side where the train lines were. People could no longer move about freely, and they could only go into the town with a permit from the commissar or in secret. If a Jew was seized in the town without a permit, he was brought before the Jewish Council, which had to fine him up to 2000 zlotys. The Jewish Council formed a militia to prevent people from leaving the ghetto.

I should also note that most of the people were hungry. The community provided lunch and distributed bread. Some Jews served by stealing wood from the forest or digging up wooden fences and selling the wood to the bakers.

In the town there was an organization of Christian war invalids. I went to its chairman and showed him my certificate that I was a prisoner of war and asked his advice for how to get help. He told me that he could not help any Jew but that I should go to Warsaw for a hearing in the military hospital. After the hearing, I should write to the Crisis Bureau for Invalids to get a pension. I wrote a letter to the hospital in Warsaw and asked for a hearing. The hearing was scheduled for the beginning of 1941. I got a pass from the commissar to go to Warsaw and permission to enter the Warsaw Ghetto. At the hearing, I was awarded 98 or 100 per cent by the German doctors. I received a certificate to that effect, and I went to the Warsaw Invalid Organization, where I was told that I should write a request, but there was little hope that I would get help. I wrote the request, but I never received a response.

The Problems Get Worse

The end of 1941 was very trying. If Jews were caught in the town, they were punished not only by a fine from the Jewish Council, but were often shot. The German police chief often announced in the Jewish Council that he had shot a Jew, or several Jews, and for every Jew he shot, he demanded two or three thousand zlotys. In the span of several minutes they had to come up with the money. If they failed, he threatened to shoot them. Members of the militia in the nearby rooms physically seized whatever money they wanted.

Among the Jewish militia there were sadists who enjoyed inflicting punishment: they assaulted and robbed and so on.

At the same time, a typhus epidemic spread. At first the doctors could not diagnose the illness. The afflicted died within two days. The epidemic especially afflicted the wealthy and healthy. There were no medicines in the ghetto, and no one wanted to risk his life by smuggling from the town. I, having no alternative, used to go in the evening into the town and bring back what was needed. For my efforts I received a half kilo of bread.

During my time in the ghetto, I never tasted meat. My friend, who was a butcher, gave me a gift of 200 kilos of meat On Shabbos, when he gave me the meat, I felt that I could not eat it and that I was feverish. I left the house and went to Dr. Resnick. The doctor decided that I was ill with typhus. He asked me if I would rather be at home or in the hospital. I said the hospital. The next morning I went to the hospital.

The hospital was in a house with broken windows that were covered with boards. Each sick person had to bring his own bedclothes and food from home, because there were no orderlies. The rooms were cold and dark. I was in the hospital for fifteen days. When I left the hospital, worn out and starving, I was given a little bit of bread that served as breakfast, lunch, and dinner.

There was an orphan home in the ghetto with about seventy–two children. The Jewish Council had commissioned wooden shoes for the children from my brother. My brother pointed out which trees he wanted to cut down in the forest. The Jewish Council had to promise his pay for the work, since he had to pay with bread.

In the neighborhood of Warsaw (Wolomin was about eighteen kilometers from Warsaw) was the Volnov labor camp. The camp was under the supervision of the Germans and in the camp was a Jewish militia. The commander of the Jewish militia was Alexander, a Jew from Otvotsk. The Jewish Council received an order that they should send a certain number of workers to the camp, so the Council summoned all the able–bodied and chose a number of names. All whose names were chosen were allowed to go home, while the rest had to answer the call. Among those who had to go to the camp was my brother. I made way to the chairman of the Jewish Council and made clear to him that my brother was the only one in our home who could work and I begged that he be released. He answered that he had to send men to the work and he had no alternatives.

It is worth mentioning that at first people took account of my situation. Thus, for instance, when my brother was sent to work in the town, I went in his place. When they called out the names and my brother's was called, I called my own. The chairman and the commander of the militia looked at me and said, "We called your brother," and I answered, "If my brother goes to the labor, there won't be anyone who can take care of our household." So they told me to go home.

Out of the Ghetto

The transports from the Warsaw Ghetto to Treblinka passed near our ghetto. Every day transports went by, each one taking about twenty minutes. It was the time of the High Holidays. In the ghetto we knew where those people were being taken and what awaited them. I remember that on Yom Kippur I was standing in the ghetto while Jews davened in their taleisim. On one side I heard Jews crying and pleading with God and on the other side the transports carrying Jews to Treblinka. I could hear the Jews screaming from the train cars.

We learned the fate of those being taken to Treblinka from the train workers. It also happened that someone from our shtetl had been in the Warsaw Ghetto and was sent to Treblinka but had managed to escape. In Treblinka he had worked at loading wagons with the possessions of those who were murdered. He hid among those possessions and thus got out of the camp. On the road, not far from Wolomin, he jumped out of the wagon and made his way to our ghetto.

We called his father the Baal Shem. He lives today in Poland.

The small ghettoes in our area were liquidated. Some of the Jews were shot along the roads, while the rest were taken to the Warsaw Ghetto.

Only the ghettoes in Jadow, Radzymin, and Wolomin remained. On the first day of Succos in 1942 one of our village smugglers came (he looked like a Christian), and told us that the Jadow ghetto was liquidated. Only Radzymina and Wolomin remained. People felt that the liquidation of those two was nearing.

I resolved to leave the ghetto, and I was encouraged at home. As in invalid, I would certainly have no hope during the liquidation, so I had nothing to lose. I looked good, so it was worth a try. Again, I had nothing to lose. I thought that if I was caught, at least I would have tried. I had a good new overcoat that I put on. I went to the nearest village, "Kubolka," where I bought a train ticket to "Ostrov Mazavietzk." My plan was to go to Zambrow, on the other side of the Bug. Each region obeyed the Third Reich, and there were still ghettoes that were unguarded.

I traveled by train to Malkin, where I had to transfer to another train. At the crossing from one platform to the other, Germans were watching out to prevent Jews from sneaking by. But they paid me no attention. I boarded the train for Ostrow and arrived safely late at night. In the Ostrow station I ran into several young men from my shtetl, smugglers. When they noticed me, they tried to get away from the station before I could notice them. They were afraid that I would go with them, which would draw attention to them. I saw how they left the station and began to go on their way. I went through a fence, though even today I cannot tell how I got through it. Because they had to move carefully (since no one was supposed to go that way), they went slowly and I was able to follow them. On the way we met several Christian women (one with a child), who were going in the same direction. At dawn we arrived at the border (meaning the Russian–German border of 1939). Before we arrived at the border, the Christians said that if we heard shooting, we must stand still. As we got to about ten meters from the border, we heard shooting. We stood still. After a couple of minutes, a German soldier came from the border guards with a dog and led us to his commander. When we came to the commander, it was light outside. Outside of the commander's headquarters, the German told the Christian with the child and myself to wait outside while all the others were led inside. The Christian woman told me that we would not suffer any large penalty.. We would have to wash the floor or chop wood and do other heavy labor, after which we would be released. I should say that the Jewish young men looked like Christians, and that I had also been taken for a Christian.

Weary from the journey, I lay down on the grass. Fifteen minutes later, when the guard emerged from the commander's and saw me lying on the grass, he came over and asked me why I wanted to cross the border. I responded that I was a war invalid who could not work, that I had relatives across the border who I believed would help me. He took me aside and said that at noon, the watch on the border changed, so that there would be few guards for a time. He also told me that not far from the border was a tower and that if I proceeded immediately to the tower I would encounter no guards and would be able to cross the border at noon.

I should note that the region I came from (Wolomin) belonged to the Gubernia General. The other side of the Bug belonged to the Third Reich. One dared not cross the border from the Gubernia General to the Third Reich.

I did not know the way to the border. I told the woman with the child what the German had told me. Before noon, the Christian and I went to the border according to the advice of the German soldier, and, in fact, we ran into no one. Arriving at the fence, the Christian woman went over it and crossed the border. I could not get over the fence because of my disability. I crossed the lower wire, but I got hung up on the upper one. I lay stretched out on the ground and squirmed over to the other side of the border.

I quickly put distance between the border and myself and came to a village. I went to the first house and encountered a peasant woman who had lost her son in the war. She gave me food, and I rested there. No one asked who I was.

The Zambrow Ghetto

As I made my way to Zambrow, I was given a ride in a passing wagon.

I had to enter the Zambrow ghetto by a side way. The Jewish police did not allow strangers into the ghetto. I met some friends who advised me to go to the Jewish Council and ask for help. The leader yelled at me, saying that refugees brought danger on the Zambrow ghetto and would receive no help.

Life in the ghetto when I was there (at the end of 1942) was like the Garden of Eden compared to Wolomin. The Jews worked at different occupations for the Germans, both in and outside of the town. The Jews went to their work without an escort. Food was also available.

Knowing that in the Gubernia General they had liquidated one ghetto after another, and believing that the same would happen here, I did not sleep in the ghetto. In the evening I went to a nearby village where the village magistrate gave me permission to lodge with a peasant. At the peasant's I was able to get supper and breakfast. I could lie all day in the field. I used to spend the night in different villages. I received permission from the magistrate to spend the night with no questions. I went into the ghetto once or twice a week so I could get the news. Thus I lived for a month.

The day of the liquidation of the Zambow ghetto, Shabbos or Sunday night, I was not in the ghetto at all. In the ghetto, life went on as usual, with no feeling that they were on the verge of liquidation. As usual, I was spending the night in the village. When I got up in the morning and wanted to go to another village, I noticed from a far a fellow resident. He did not go on the roads but through the fields, very carefully. When he saw me, he came towards me. His first question was whether I knew what happened in the Zambow ghetto. When I answered him that I did not, he told me that last night the ghetto had been liquidated. He managed to escape. He also told me that he would flee to Warsaw. We parted and I headed toward the east, desiring to reach the neighborhood of Slonim. I knew that area from my military service and I remembered that the Jews in Slonim had been rapidly killed. I hoped that they had been forgotten. I hoped to be closer to the unoccupied Russian territories. After the liquidation of the Zambow ghetto, or at the same time, the ghetto of Bialystok had also been liquidated. I was afraid to move around freely or to enter a village. At night I slept in a shed for potatoes. During the day I traveled in the direction of the sunrise. I went through woods. One day I walked the day and ended up back where I had started.

My Life in Danger

One evening, feeling worn out and terribly hungry, I came to a hamlet. I approached a house, hoping to beg for a piece of bread. There I was seized by a twenty–year–old Christian., who cried out that he had caught a Jew. As much as I tried to argue that I was not a Jew, it did not help. He held that a Christian invalid would not go around dressed as I was (I had a new coat). He led me to the village magistrate.

At the magistrate's, two peasants searched to see if I had weapons. The Christian kid said that I had only to live until morning and I would see what they did with "Zhids." The magistrate was not at home. When he arrived, he spoke with the kid and said I should be released because I was a Polish invalid, but this speech did not work.

In the morning I was put into a wagon and taken to the shtetl of Lapy. With me went the magistrate's representative, an older Gentile of about seventy. The young Gentile was not with us. On the way, I told the magistrate's representative that I was prepared to give away–my coat, a gold watch, and 100 Deutschmarks, if he would let me go. The representative told me that for his part, he would free me without taking anything, but he showed me that behind us were many other wagons and he therefore was afraid to let me go.

Travelling further, we encountered a coach with German police. I begged the representative that he should not call attention to ourselves and he should take me to the town. Our concentration made the time go slowly. Not far from the town, I told the representative that I would give him everything I had on the condition that he would not reveal to the commander that I was a Jew but only that he had brought a vagrant. He responded that he did not want me to give him my things. I told him that everyone would see that he was taking me to the commander and he was not responsible for anything else.

We arrived at the police station (the police spoke Polish), and there the representative declared that he had brought in a vagrant, but he did not know who the vagrant was.

To the policeman's question of who I was, I answered that I was from Warsaw, but because I had nowhere to live, I wandered from village to village. I had my discharge papers from the German captivity and I showed them to him. The family name was Christian, and the given name, Hersh, he read as Hershitz, so he took me for Polish. He ordered that I go back to Warsaw.

The magistrate's representative had left, and the police took me to the commandant. The commandant read my papers the same way. He yelled that I was from the Gubernia General and that I should not be found in the Third Reich. If he caught me again, I would get a bullet in the head. He ordered me to go to the local commissar where I would be given a valid pass to

Warsaw. The warning about getting a bullet in my head, which would normally have caused me to break out in a cold sweat, struck me as good news, because I could still live.

I arrived at the local commisar's at 9 a.m., but he was not there yet. When he came in, the police gave him my papers, saying that I was to be given papers to get to Warsaw. My papers were given to the secretary, who was told to write out travel papers.

As the secretary began to write the travel papers, I took my papers back. It was the case that although my name was Polish, my given name of Hersh showed my Jewish roots. The Germans had not grasped this, and the paper from the prison camp with its swastika made a good impression. The secretary, however, was Polish and she would have known who I was. At that moment they would have become aware, so I decided to create my own luck. My trick saved me from death. My luck held out. The secretary looked for my papers, so I told her that I had them. She did not ask for them. Instead she asked my name. I said "Henrik," and that is what she wrote down.

I soon had a valid document to travel to Warsaw. At the station I had no trouble getting a ticket to Warsaw. Seeing that my beard had grown, I was afraid that that my raise suspicions. I took a chance and went to the barber for a shave. Leaving the barber and heading toward the station, I was stopped by a policeman. He was in charge of inspecting documents, and everything went well. But at the train checkpoint, the conductor asked why one document named me "Henrik" and the other "Hersh." On the spot I responded that "Hersh" is a short form for "Henrik." That answer sufficed.

The trip went well. The checkpoint at Malkin, at the border between the Third Reich and the Gubernia General, presented no problems. There was a brief stop at my shtetl of Wolomin. I was afraid that Gentiles from the town might recognize me. I wrapped myself up in my coat, and since it was cold, that created no suspicions.

Warsaw

When I got to Warsaw, it was dark. I had nowhere to sleep. At a stop on the tramway I met a Polish invalid who lacked a foot. He told me that he lived in Grochow. I told him that I had come from the Third Reich (Zombrow) and I had nowhere to sleep. He invited me to go with him. Arriving in Grochow, my acquaintance said that because he had only one small room, I should go to the magistrate and ask for a place for the night. He offered that if I could not get a pass from the magistrate, I could come to him. He promised to wait. The magistrate told me to go to Warwur where there was an inexpensive lodging house. The Polish invalid did not wait for me.

I arrived at the lodging house (the Notzlegawi) and said, "Good evening." I forgot that I should have said, "You should be well." The overseer of the house was drunk and immediately said, "This is a Jew." His wife said, "You can see that he is no Jew," and I said the same thing, but the goy insisted. Finally he said that he didn't care and I could stay over night. He took me to a large room where many people were sleeping (without mattresses), and said that I could sleep there. He also told me that he would leave the door open and in case anything untoward happened, I could get out. In the morning, the goy had totally forgotten his suspicion that I was a Jew and he gave me breakfast.

On the Aryan Side

While I was in the camp, I was in the sick room. Near my bed lay a sick Polish soldier. Since the war had begun, he became a motorman on the tramway.

As an invalid, I ate in the kitchen, outside of the normal routine. I used to give my neighbor some of my food. He would always say that if I were ever in Warsaw and I needed anything, I should make my way to him and he would do whatever he could to help. Having come to Warsaw, I began to search for him. I did not have his address. I asked for him among the tramway workers, and they immediately asked if he owed me money, stressing that he had underworld connections. This did not frighten me at all, because this type of person was involved in business. I learned his address in Praga [a district of Warsaw]. He lived in an attic room. Arriving there, I found the room locked. I came another time, after a fifteen–minute trip. The door was again locked. Near the door was a small niche. I went in and decided to wait for him. I was somewhat hidden.

After about two hours, I heard his voice. He was singing drunkenly. I also heard a woman's voice. I was afraid to show myself, so I stayed in that niche. After a short time the woman left. I left my niche and knocked on the door. He opened the door and recognized me immediately. His first words were, "Do you know what awaits me?" and he took me into his room.

That night, lying in bed with him, I explained that if he could procure for me a birth certificate for someone of my years who had disappeared, I would be able to use it to get an identification card. He responded that his brother had disappeared in 1939. He was my age, and his birth certificate was at his mother's. He would bring it and help me get an identification card. Until the matter was settled, I should stay with him, but he warned me not to leave the house. In the morning he took my coat, and that night he arrived back without the coat, drunk, and he told me that he had pawned the coat so that he could get food for me. During the next four or five days, he took my watch, a gold chain, and a suit of clothes. He himself was short, and he gave me his pants, which went to under my knee.

On the fifth day, when I had nothing left, he told me that I could no longer stay with him, because the home was not his and he was subletting. The owner of the dwelling was a prostitute, and it would be bad if she found me. He also told me that he would go with me to Grochow to another tram worker and tell him that I was his brother and we would take a room for both of us. We came to Grochow, to the tram worker. He did not want to rent to us, saying that his wife, who was travelling, would not agree; but when my "protector" took out a flask of brandy, he said no more and allowed us to spend the night. The next day I walked the streets. In the evening, I returned to the house, but it was locked. I waited until midnight. The janitor said that he could not let me into the house and he made me leave. He advised me to go straight to Grochowski Street, where there were open courtyards and I could spend the night on a staircase. After passing thirty or forty houses, I found an open courtyard. The stairways were locked up. But I noticed steps that led to a cellar. I went into the cellar and sat on the lowest step. I did not notice that in the neighboring courtyard, which was divided by a fence, there were German military vehicles and soldiers. After a few minutes, they shone a light on me and yelled in German that I should come out. They asked me what I was doing in the cellar. I explained to them that my friend was not at home and I had nowhere to sleep. At first they did not believe me, alleging that I was up to something. When I showed them that I lacked a foot and a hand, they said that I could still do more than others. They argued over whether I should be taken to their officer or released. One said that possibly I was telling the truth and should be released. They told me to get going. As I went back towards Praga, I noticed a broken down kiosk without doors, windows, or a floor. I stayed there until dawn.

In the morning, while it was still dark, I heard the sounds of the first tram. This was the signal that people could go out into the streets. I boarded the tram and went to the last station in Warsaw, Narotawicz Place. There I wound a waiting room for the tram workers, and it was warm.

I sat in the waiting room and warmed up. My situation was desperate–without money, without food, hungry, not knowing my next move. Across the street was an inn and I noticed that by the building were sitting beggars, both men and women. I decided that the only profession for me was to be a beggar.

I went to the door of the inn and stood there, not having the heart or power to go further. As I stood there for a while, passersby gave me donations. I took in twenty zlotys. I left there and went to Narotawitcza Place, where there was a bazaar. I bought a kilo of bread and I spent the rest of the day eating in the tram workers' hall.

I knew the location of the bar where my "protector" did his drinking. That evening I went to the bar and found him. He told me that he had no place for me to live. He advised me to go to Praga, Jagalonski Street. There I would find an inn called "The Brothers Albertinov." He said that no one asked questions there. For ten groschen, one could get a place to sleep.

My First Evening in Fshitolek [?]

My "chaperone" led me to 19 Jaglonski in Praga, where the lodging house was. I paid ten groschen at the window and they showed me to a bed, the closest to the entrance. It was a bunk bed. There was no mattress, only boards. . In that room where I found myself, there were forty such beds. A small blue electric lamp cast a weak light in the room. All of the sleeping places were occupied. Outside of my room there were bigger rooms. I climbed into bed and took out a large roll. As soon as I did so, one fellow, who had been talking with two others, approached me and invited me to join their company. They had brandy and they proposed that I should share my roll. My voice was low, weak, and I thought that a drink of brandy would not hurt. I went over to their bed. They poured some brandy into a cup so that it looked like lighter fluid, but because of the darkness I thought it was brandy. I drank it down in one shot, and only then could I make out its real taste. I was embarrassed to show that I was not accustomed to such drinks, but after this "meal" I retained that taste in my mouth.

I stayed in that place until the Polish revolution in Warsaw, in August of 1944. In the beginning I practiced my profession as beggar in the same spot by the inn in Narotawitcza Place. Before noon I would earn forty or fifty zlotys. This was enough to sustain me–it bought bread and something to go with the bread. There was a little left over. When my "overseer" knew that

I had a couple of zlotys, he would come and take the money. I had to give it to him because I was afraid of blackmail. In order to prevent him from taking my money, I converted it to larger denominations (paper money) and concealed it. The "overseer" instituted an overall search and took whatever he found.

As I mentioned, my "overseer" said that he would give me his brother's birth certificate. When I still had not received it, I told him that if I did not get it soon, I would give him no more money. It was all one to me, because without the document I could not exist. He grasped that I was serious and told me to wait in the spot where we had met and he would bring me the birth certificate, which he had found at his mother's. Not trusting him, I sought a hidden spot where I could observe whether he came alone or with someone else. I saw him alight from the tram, and he was alone. I emerged, and he gave me the birth certificate. The birth certificate was in the name of Edward Kempkowitsch, born in Warsaw in 1913, my birth year. I had then about a hundred zlotys, which I gave to him. I did not see him again for several weeks.

I wanted to get an identification card. I was told that if I had a profession and slept in the same place for six months, I could get an identification card. I went to the secretary and asked for a certificate. He told me that he could not give me a card because I had not lived in the same place for six months. After I gave him money, he immediately gave me a certificate. I gave the birth certificate to the city council along with the certificate and two pictures in order to get an identification card. They told me to come back in a few minutes.

I remembered that I had converted my money into larger denominations. I hid the money in different places. One day I came to a grocery store to convert the money. By the counter stood a tall, pockmarked goy. His appearance did not make a good impression. When I gave him my change, we talked a bit. My instincts alerted me and led me to pay more attention to our business. In the course of a couple of weeks, I converted my money with him. He ran the business with his brother–in–law. His name was Robert Barutzki, and his brother–in–law was Henjek Grabowski.

During those couple of weeks, I became friendly with Barutzki's wife.

Yes, I Am a Jew

One day when I came as usual to convert money, Mrs. Barutzki's wife was alone in the store. She called me in, looked around to be sure that no one could here or see us, and said, "Edward! I believe that you're a Jew…"

It was all one to me. Begging had become hateful to me. In the place where I slept there were beggars, thieves, drunks, swindlers, and me.

I answered her curtly, "Yes I'm a Jew." I answered in an agitated voice, and then I continued: "I shed blood and was wounded on your Polish soil." Then I asked, "Don't I have a right to live with you in Poland?

She turned pale and then began to explain that she meant no harm. On the contrary, she was my friend and would help me. At these words, I left and went to the tram workers' hall. At four in the afternoon she came and called me to the store. When I got there, her husband was eating lunch. The same lunch was set out for me.

"Edward! Don't worry. Better times will come." He invited me to their home on the following Sunday.

The next month I arrived at the town council to get my identity card. I went to and from the window several times. I feared that the owner of the birth certificate was still alive, and then all would be known. From a distance I could see the papers they were preparing for me. Seeing my papers near the secretary, and no police, I approached the window. She said to me that there was no identification card for me and that I should go to the central town council office on Theater Place in Warsaw, but for what purpose I did not know. They told me that I absolutely must to the central town council office or I would be taken there. I was afraid to go there. The flunkies in the office told me that they understood from the notice that I only had to go there to register. This news relieved me a bit, because I was still worried about the birth certificate.

Early the next morning I headed to the central town council office, to the window to which I had been directed. I left with the news that instead of giving me an identification card, I had just been invited there. The commissioner had taken out my file and said that I could not obtain an identification card because I was not registered in Warsaw. I carefully explained that I had attached a document showing that I had lived at my residence for six months (which was required to get an identity card). I explained that there was no official record there, only a registry for those who slept there and that must suffice. A nearby commissioner said that as far as he knew, that was enough. He stapled the papers together and told me to go back to the first address in a month. So it was. When I came to the town council, I got my identity card. My picture was on the card, and it said that I was Roman Catholic. After I got the card, I went to my acquaintances on Narotowitsch Place. They were very happy.

With an official document identifying me as Edward Kempkowitsch I felt more secure. A little earlier I had bought a Catholic prayer book and I learned the prayers, the names of the saints just like a born and baptized Pole.

I Change My Profession

I mentioned that Barutzki and his wife were my friends. Therefore I was bold enough to ask them to look out for a job for me, legal or illegal. As natives of Warsaw, they knew a lot of people. Barutzki told me he would be interested in helping.

Barutzki dealt in black market meat. A butcher who made sausage would come to him from Bielen. The butcher would buy at the market and also from Barutzki. The boy who used to transport the meat had found other work (the butcher himself did not transport the meat), and there was no one to replace him. Barutzki proposed that I would transport the meat. He declared that he would stand behind me. The butcher was cautious. I had to get twenty–five kilograms of meat and take it on the tram to Bielen and then from the station carry it several kilometers. For me, in my condition, that was pretty difficult, especially the first time., when I had no rucksack. For each package of meat that I transported I earned twenty zlotys. An lunch with the butcher and then thirty or forty individual sausages. I made this journey four or five times a day. I also brought the sausages back from the butcher, for which I was also paid. I should add that Barutzki's guarantee was that I would not steal, but if the Germans interfered, no one would be held responsible.

It was cold and I had no warm clothing. I had about 700 zlotys. I asked Barutzki to go with me to the old–clothes market on Kazhimirizhe Place. He went with me. I was looking for a jacket in accord with the money I had, but my friend had a fur in mind. I said to him, "Robert! I don't have such money…" He responded, "That's not your worry. What you need, I will give you."

He bought me a fur coat that cost twice the money that I had.

Before I began working for the butcher, Henyek Grabowski, Barutzki's brother–in–law, had a friendly conversation with me. He also knew that I was a Jew. He asked what organizations I had belonged to before the war. When I said that he would never have heard about them, he responded that he knew them all. I told him that I had belonged to "He–chalutz ha–tzair." He then declared that if I wanted to be a communist, he would not help me. He told me to come to the store the next morning at 3 or 4 in the morning. He would be at the store then. I should look in and if I saw a tall young man with a mustache, I should come in, stay for two minutes, say nothing, and then leave. He also told me to write my name in Yiddish on a piece of cigarette paper. He said that I would get support from him.

I did as I was told. I went to the shop, saw the tall young man with the mustache, stood there for two minutes, and went away. When the young man left, I went into the shop and asked who he was. He told me, "It's enough for you to know that he is from your people and his name is Antek." About two weeks later, Grabowski gave me 500 zlotys. He asked if I knew where the money came from. I replied that it was from Antek, and he said to me, "You know nothing!" I said, "I know nothing!!!" At the same time, Grabowski introduced me to Mrs. Irena Adamovitch.

In the Polish Underground AK

Near the shop of my friend Barutzki was a kiosk where they sold drinks and desserts. The kiosk belonged to Barutzki's brother. I used to patronize the kiosk often. I noticed several times that some unknown men would come, and the owner of the kiosk (Barutzki's brother) would eat with them before closing the kiosk and going away with them. It seemed mysterious. One day, in the evening, during the winter of 1943, the owner of the kiosk, Jan Barutzki, sent two of his friends outside and then approached me. "We know that you are aware that we have a chapter of the AK. Do you want to join?" I immediately answered, "Yes." Then one of the unknown men took out a paper and read to me, in a quiet voice, the oath and I repeated it after him. He also explained that anyone who revealed secrets would be executed. One asked me what pseudonym I chose, and I immediately said "Kulov" , but then I realized that there were people in the area who might know that name and I might be unmasked to the German police. I proposed a second pseudonym, "Tzenti," and this was accepted.

Soon after my first days as a member of the AK, I was sent to perform various duties. On Zvawitshela Place, near the barracks, lived a teacher, a Christian, who worked with the Gestapo. The AK knew which house she lived in, but they did not know which room. I had to adopt my old "profession" of begging. I went to the highest floor. The house had six or seven stories, and I had to go begging from door to door. As they expected, I recognized her dwelling. A little while later I read in the daily news that she had been sentenced to death.

Another time I was assigned to investigate the approach to a place where military equipment as stored. The place was bordered by a courtyard, and I had to spring whatever fence divided the place from the courtyard. There was a German club in the courtyard. I went into the courtyard and when I was by the end, a German approached and asked what I was looking for. I answered that I was looking for a toilet. He threw me out of the courtyard. A couple of hours later I re–entered the courtyard and came to the fence, which was made of barbed wire.

The post office and telegraph office were on Fiyus Street. I was given the assignment of determining how many people worked there, whether there was a kitchen, when the shifts changed, and making a diagram of the approaches from neighboring buildings. Opposite the post office is where the German embassy was before the war, and in front of that building was a high brick wall. I had to determine if there was a military guard there. It was already the summer of 1944, not long before the Polish rebellion. I had to carry out my task on a Sunday. At 3 o'clock I took up my post as a beggar about 50 meters from the post office. In front of the building's tower stood a Pole in the uniform of a post office official, unarmed. After I had watched for a while and saw that there were no Germans, I started to approach the Pole. I acted like a peasant and asked if the telegraph is what one pushed with one's finger. He took me for an ignoramus. While I was begging, I had a little conversation with him and stole glances into the courtyard. There I saw an armed German guard. After a couple of hours, I had become friendly with the Pole, and he told me how many people worked there and even invited me into the kitchen for a bite. I also noticed when the shift changed. Just when he wanted to take me into the kitchen, a German civilian approached, one of the post office directors. He yelled at the Pole and drove me off.

A little later I entered a neighboring courtyard so that I could make an accurate diagram. While I was doing so, I noticed three couples going by me, taking turns. I was later assured that they were also from the AK and were keeping an eye on me.

After finishing the diagram, I had to confirm if there were any military people in the house across the street. As I recall, there was a high brick wall there. I sat by the entrance and considered how to carry out my task. At the moment the door opened and the housemaid came out. She warned me to leave that spot right away, because if a German came out, he would beat me, since it was forbidden to sit there. I replied, "What are you carrying on about? This house is empty and there aren't any Germans there." To this she responded, " What are you saying? The house is full of military men." So I knew everything. I left that place and resumed my begging. I did not dare leave my post without permission. A little later a couple walked by, and between them was someone who had been sent to me. He came over to me and gave me alms and then whispered that if I had finished my work, I could leave. I stayed there a little while, counted the money I had collected, and left. After I had gone a little way, I suddenly noticed that two policemen across the road were going in my direction. I was, understandably, petrified, but I did not panic. I took a cigarette out of my pocket and went up to them, asking for a light. They yelled at me, but they gave me a light. I went to my assigned spot and gave all the information that I had gathered.

Another time I was sent with an accomplice to determine what was happening at a certain villa, not far from Narotawitch Place. The street was called Filtrova. Many villas were there, occupied by SS men. In one of the villas were offices. We sat on a bench in the square and tried to figure out how people got in. At that moment a car arrived, equipped with weapons, and SS men got out, looking for workers. My accomplice was taken. I had nothing to do but wait until he returned. He got all the information.

I also used to distribute underground bulletins. Mostly I used to put the bulletins in the tool kits of the tram workers and city workers and so on. One time in the evening I was late for the last tram before curfew. I got into the tram that was still in service. This was at the corner of Marshalovski and Krulewski. This tram was headed for Praga. As we approached the Cambridge Bridge I noticed people shooting at a tram that was going from Praga to Warsaw. I was standing next to the motorman. It was already dark. In my pocket I had a stack of bulletins. I quickly hid the bulletins under the engine. After we crossed the bridge, the police stopped the tram and demanded our passes. They looked me over and asked what I was doing. I told them that I was late for the last tram and now I was going home. One of them thought about it, looked at my wooden leg and gave a contemptuous wave of his hand, as though to say I was not worth bothering with. I did not mind his contempt…

Miracles

When I think today about my experiences during the war, I do not know how to account for the fact that I am still alive. As one who lost a hand and a leg in the war and then was saved from the ghetto, from the camps, and then lived for two years in Warsaw, it was not only luck. It was a miracle! Luck alone would not be enough. I do not believe in miracles. And for many of those who will read my writings, many facts will seem unbelievable. But they happened. The best evidence that these miracles happened is that I am still alive. Anyone who had been there would know that without miracles my fate would have been the same as that of millions of other Jews. I did not escape because I had money. The couple hundred zlotys that I gave do not count as money. It could be that my weak appearance, my being such an invalid, saved me. In any case, it is beyond my ability to understand. The facts have to stand for themselves. I can go no further.

In Pshitulek, in Praga, where I resided for two years, Polish agents often came dressed in civilian clothing. They sought out new residents, particularly Jews. Each room had its leader, who had to point out the new boarders. A few weeks after my arrival in Pshitulek, the agents arrived and the leader pointed me out. I was sitting on the bed, putting on my pants. The agents asked if I was missing a hand. I answered that I also lacked a leg. They gave a wave of their hands and went away.

During my time in Pshitulek, three agents came looking especially for Jews. On the floor where I lived, the agents came in 1944. A fellow boarder told me that they were coming. I was completely flustered, but my neighbor did not notice and went away. Suddenly a messenger came and called the agents back to their headquarters. They did not return.

Once a week we had to go to the baths. In the baths there were enclosed showers. What frightened me about the baths–I cannot write down. But I found a solution. Everyone took along his few valuables. I put my things in a military sack. I carried the sack in front of me and it hid my "Jewishness." Later on I learned that for half a zloty, the bathkeeper would give a note saying that I had washed.

Generally I got along well with my fellow residents. Later on, when I had real work and could buy drinks and snacks with them, we became friendly. In Pshitulek there were different types of people. There was a colonel from the Czarist army, a big drinker. When he got hold of a bottle and drank it down, he began to give commands. Then he would hold the bottle before his face and talk to it for an hour or more.

One fellow who was a mute told me I should buy some holy pictures. I should not ask the price. Whatever you thought you should pay, he told me in sign language, you should give more. Right away I went and bought holy pictures.

A son of a Petersburg bank director in Czarist times, an outspoken anti–Semite, lived with me and awaited the moment that the Germans would take Leningrad, so that he could claim his inheritance. He had letters of recommendation from a variety of people, and thanks to those letters he became involved in a number of undertakings. He gave me several addresses, saying that the people there would surely help me. I used them with varying degrees of success. I will say that most of the residents had no interest at all in Jews, either for good or for bad. They were interested in stealing a little and having some schnapps.

My bed stood in a corner, which was some advantage, because on the one side I had no fear of thieves. On the other side I kept a number of reflectors on the bed. One evening I got home and found another fellow lying on my bed. I asked him to get out of my bed and he began to fight with me. (This was at a time when I already had good friends, thanks to my "tributes.") When my friends heard the fighting and saw what was going on, they threw him off my bed and said that if he bothered me, they would smash his bones. When my friends left, he said to me, "Remember, I have suspicions about you. If you don't give me your bed, you're in for trouble." I acted like I did not know what he was talking about, and I did not give him my bed. The next day, when I got home, I found him lying paralyzed in his whole body. Nor could he speak. The brothers (monks) took him to the hospital and he died a week later.

Encounters

During the time of the ghetto, they used to lead Jews out of the city for different kinds of work. I used to follow them and watch the Jews from afar. I just wanted to see Jews.

On the streets were loudspeakers which delivered news four times a day. My usual spot for hearing news was on Narotawitsch Place. One day the loudspeaker was out of order. The nearest one was at the corner of Marshalkovska and

Yerezalimska (not far from the main train station). I went there to get the news. Afterwards, as people drifted away, I remained there. Suddenly I felt an impulse to turn my head. I did so and saw a young woman named Grodzitzka. I did not want to go towards her. People were afraid of each other and I did not know if she wanted me to "recognize" her. After two or three minutes, she noticed me. She approached me and we spoke for about five minutes. As were separating, I put my hand in my pocket with the intention of giving her money. Simultaneously she put her hand in her pocket with the same intention. We both smiled and parted. (She is still alive.)

It was my custom after hearing the news that the Germans were retreating that I would go to my friend Jan Barutzki and have some brandy in honor of the free state. They knew how many places the Germans had given up. After drinking I used to name those places. After my encounter with the young woman from my town, I ordered a big glass of brandy. After I drank it, I was asked the purpose of the big glass. I answered that I had met someone from my town. He understood…

Once, at night, as I went home, I noticed a German settler named Chwapek from my town. I did not know if he recognized me. I went further and then turned my head. The German was standing there looking at me. I understood that he had no mind to chase me. I went over to him. He gave me his hand and said that he was also in hiding. He had done something for which the Germans were after him. When he left, I watched him for a long time, and then I turned. I wanted to be sure he could not know where I lived.

Typhus

It was announced in the streets that there would be an exhibit about typhus. I went to the exhibit. Under glass there were different kinds of lice, with diagrams showing how the lice fed. In another room was a film. The film showed a path, and it a Jew was walking. Then the Jew was replaced by a louse. Behind the Jew a Christian woman was walking with her child. The film showed how the louse seized on the child. Arriving at home, the child developed a high fever. The doctor diagnosed typhus. The end of the film consisted of writing stating that Jews brought typhus, so do not hide Jews because they bring illness.

My friends the Barutzkis chastised me for going to such places. Why should I pay attention to such nonsense?

Once I worked as a translator. This was when a German soldier wanted to trade a Christian a box of matches for eggs. I was their translator. After concluding the transaction, I asked the German for an egg. He said to me, "You're a Jew!" I said to him—"Just because I ask for an egg I'm a Jew. And if I hadn't asked, that would have been all right." Then he gave it to me.

Frequently the Germans would enter trams and search the passengers. The meat that I carried for the butcher, I carried on the tram. I was never caught. Either the car I rode in was not searched or the whole tram was ignored. On those occasions when I was searched, I was not carrying meat.

I used to take the tram from Bielany, but I would get on at the station before Bielany and then go to Warsaw. At the last station I used to stand and watch the soldiers who were exercising. One time one of them came up to me and said, "Your rucksack smells like sausage–Ha? You're not saying anything." I responded, "Which is better, to smuggle or to beg." He gave a wave of his hand and dismissed me.

In Warsaw, Hungarian Jews were working for the Germans. They were dressed in half–military and half–Hungarian garb. They traveled on the trams without guards. One time when I was on the tram and saw no Germans, before I got off I asked one of them if he knew German. (I was afraid to speak to him in Yiddish. He said that he did. I took out a pack of a hundred cigarettes and gave them to him, letting him know that we were similar. (Don't think about the expression I used to say this.) Then I quickly got off the tram.

The Warsaw Ghetto Uprising

Since I lived on the Aryan side, I did not, understandably, dare to show any intimate relations with Jews. Aside from a few select people, like Barutzki and his wife and the one who got my documents, no one knew that I was a Jew. I mingled quite freely among the Germans, as I have shown.

I learned about the uprising in the Warsaw Ghetto from a tram worker. It was on Narotovitsch Place, the place where I often spent free time. When a tram came from Bialany and it had been shot through by a bullet. Then the tram man told me that it was shot from the ghetto. Other Poles said that they had seen in the ghetto blue–and–white and red–and–white banners. I heard a variety of reports from Poles, although, for obvious reasons, I could not ask questions. Some of them spoke scornfully. They laughed, not believing that the uprising was a serious matter. On the other hand, others believed that the Jewish uprising would bring with a general uprising. That was at the beginning. A few days later, when people saw had the Germans had sent reinforcements of soldiers and tanks, everyone developed respect for the uprising.

One day I came to Kraszinski Place, not far from the ghetto. There, not far from Miadava Street, was a unit that was firing on the ghetto. At the same time on Kraszinski Place there was a carousel which operated on Sunday as never before. Among the Poles rumors were spreading about many German dead and heroic deeds of the Jewish rebels.

The tram system in the direction of the ghetto broke down. From the sounds of the shooting and the from the flames and smoke of the burning ghetto we knew that the battle was continuing. I once saw a group of rebels, young men and women, being led, covered with soot and dirt, in the direction of the east station.

After the liquidation of the ghetto, the Germans brought Greek Jews from Auschwitz, so people said, to clean up the ghetto from the destruction. The bricks, iron, and other building materials the Germans sold to the Poles. Other materials they took for themselves. They took loads of stuff to the Vistula. The tramline was back in operation and I saw the ghetto in ruins.

After the uprising I would encounter groups of Jews that the Germans had captured. This was in Szalibasz and other spots in the neighborhood. Once on Narotowitsch Place I saw a Polish policeman leading a thirteen–year–old girl. a janitor sent a German gendarme after a young man who was about to board the tram, saying that he was a Jew. The German examined his documents, which were in order. He wanted to let him go, but the janitor insisted that he was a Jew. He was taken to police headquarters and I never saw him again.

Such things I saw often. I could only look but never do anything.

The Polish Uprising in Warsaw

A week before the uprising I left the Pshitulik in Praga. My friend Barutzki knew about the uprising, but he did not tell me when it would occur. He advised me to come to his place because of the possibility that Praga would be cut off from Warsaw and I would suffer from hunger.

There was a sense in the air that something was about to happen. Many divisions of the German army were coming back from the eastern front, marching through Warsaw on their way west. Not many soldiers were left in Warsaw. The bridges over the Vistula were mined by the Germans.

On the day of the uprising in August of 1944, I was on Grayetzka Place. We heard shooting and I and others hid in shelters. We were in the bunker for a whole night. At dawn a German came into the bunker and announced that anyone who lived in the neighborhood could go home, but with our hands in the air. Others could stay in the shelter. My friend Barutzki lived at the second corner of Grabska, so I went home with my hand in the air. At home, everyone was in the cellar. The area was held by the rebels. Through our courtyard marched groups of rebels with weapons, some in uniforms and some in civilian clothes. Passageways were made in the walls of the houses so that they could go from one courtyard to another.

Soviet airplanes dropped leaflets signed by the high command of the Polish army in Russia, General Berling. They said that the Soviet army was now near the Rodzimin Woods, near Praga, and called on the rebels to persevere. The tone was dignified.

On the next day we learned that the Soviet army had gone back to Sedlce. On that day or the next we heard the sound of tanks. Looking out through the holes, we saw on the streets German tanks and many Ukrainians. They knocked on the doors, and when the doors were opened they called the people from the cellars. A group of Ukrainians shot people on the spot. Others occupied themselves with looting. They sent the men to a gathering spot in Zeleniek Place. I got away with a watch, which they took from me. After we left the houses, they were burned down.

About twenty thousand men were assembled in Zeleniek Place. The place was surrounded, and all the walls were Ukrainians with machine guns. The next day a German general named Zelenen arrived with a group of officers and announced through loudspeakers that because many German officers had been killed, he had sent an inquiry to Berlin about what to do with us–to kill us there or to send us out of Warsaw.

We had no water. From a broken pipe dripped a little water, and at that spot there were dreadful scenes. We received no food. Barutzki's wife had, as she was leaving the courtyard, grabbed a bread and bacon. This food was shared by Barutzki, his wife, his child, his in–laws and me. Fear showed on everyone's faces. People pleaded, cried, and trembled about the future. At night the Ukrainians would rape the women and then shoot them. There were no toilet facilities, so people had to relieve themselves in public.

A day later they announced that an order had come from Berlin to take us out of Warsaw. They took us to the west train station. On the way the Ukrainians shot into the marchers and many were killed. Among the thousands on the march were women, children, the elderly, as well as many young men. We arrived at Pruszkow and were put into the waiting rooms. There we were guarded by Germans and Vlasovtsy (Russian deserters from the Red Army who fought on the German side). In Pruszkow we "overnighted." In the morning the Germans announced that those capable of labor would be sent to Germany to work and those not capable would go to Lowitz and then be scattered among the peasantry.

We were put into transport wagons. On the way, the train stopped. A young Pole, a bit lame, tried to escape. The train was full of police. They shot at him. Not far from the spot where the train stood there were German police, who also shot at him and killed him. The people in the cars said this was a sign that we would all be killed, because if not, why had they shot him? But now it seemed that fear was useless. At the station in Lowitz there was no military presence. Instead there were nurses from the Red Cross. They opened the doors of the train cars and called us out.

The nurses told us to follow them, and we left the town. There were barracks just like those in the ghetto, as the Poles had told us. I stood still, fearful to enter the barracks. I wanted to see whether people only entered or whether they also came out. When I saw that they went in and out, I went into the courtyard. They registered us and told us not to wander off, because soon wagons would come from the villages among which we would be divided.

It was getting late and the peasants had not arrived. I heard people speaking among themselves that it was dangerous to spend the night there and it would be better to spend the night in the nearby village. I went with them–there were about ten of us–and we spent the night with a peasant in a stable. When we returned to the barracks, most of the people were not there. During the night the wagons had come and took them to the villages. We were told that more wagons would arrive soon. When the peasants came, I inquired how far the village was from the town. I was going to a village nine kilometers from the town. I should add that the dividing up was voluntary. Each person got into a wagon, and when it was full, it left.

With The Peasants Until the End of the War

I and an older Christian were quartered with a peasant. We were treated well. We were given a big bowl with potatoes and milk. I was really hungry after not eating for a couple of days, so I got right to eating. Before the elderly Christian got to her bowl, I had eaten half. When she put her spoon into the bowl, I could eat no more. The peasant noticed and said that he understood that as a city person I was not used to eating out of a bowl. He promised to give me special food.

In the village I lasted only one day. The reason is that according to tradition, what would suffice for a peasant for ten days will suffice for someone from Warsaw for one day–and what will last twenty days for a peasant will suffice for three from Warsaw. The village mayor said that the village met up to that saying. I was sent to another village, but the mayor said that my new landlord was a carpenter and new about city life, so I would be comfortable with him.

The peasant treated me well. People ate together. The landlord was young. They had a small child, and his father also lived with them. Obviously when they asked me who I was and so on I did not want to give them too much information. Therefore I asked if I could go with an old peasant to look after the animals. Later on I took care of them by myself. I wanted to be useful, so I used to saw and chop wood, cut the fodder, clear manure out of the stalls, all this with one hand and a wooden leg.

As long as it was warm, I slept in the stable. When it got cooler I slept in a room on straw. After that I put together a bed and slept in the stall with the animals.

I was with this peasant for five months. People never spoke about politics there. Instead they told stories. A rumor went around that someone from the underground was in the area and was planning an uprising that would free them. From time to time I would throw in a word or two. That made me seem important, and they took me for an officer.

Life went on quietly. But there were moments of terror. The animals used to pasture in the field that was not far from the road. Once a truck passed with German police. They asked who I was and examined my documents. That ended peacefully.

A Jewish Woman in the Village

Every week there was a meeting of the peasants in the village. They talked over the village's affairs. In these meetings they considered various matters of village life like, for instance, the appropriations for the Germans, the plowing, the sowing, and the like.

Once my peasant asked me when he got back from a meeting, if I might know an older woman who lived in the village and who said that she was from Warsaw and lived on Groyetzka Street, the street that I lived on in Warsaw. I replied that in Warsaw many people lived in a single house, more people than in the whole village, so surely I did not know all the residents of that street.

The peasant told me that at the meeting, the peasant with whom the woman lived had raised the suspicion that the woman was Jewish. The meeting created a commission of three peasants, among whom was mine, to look into the question of whether she was Jewish or not. The next day they spoke with her, but her Polish was better than theirs. After this conversation, she disappeared from the village. She said that she was going to look for her husband. I believe–that she was Jewish.

Liberation

Halfway through January of 1945, when the offensive against Warsaw began, we in the village heard the sounds of artillery bombardments. The next day a peasant woman from nearby who had escaped from the front and arrived at our village reported that she had seen how German tanks had tried to cross the water at Sochochov (the water was frozen) but remained stuck because the ice had broken. That same evening, at 10 o'clock, a German military vehicle was all lit up. On the road, another vehicle went toward the village (about 100 meters).

The peasants were afraid the whole time that they would not be evacuated as the front drew closer. Everyone had packed a bag with necessities. When they saw the lit up vehicle, they believed that they were about to be evacuated. The vehicle stood for a half hour and then, after asking the way, it left. We were overcome with terror.

This was in the early morning hours. Day dawned. Suddenly I heard banging in the stall where I was sleeping. When I opened the door, my peasant surprisingly let me know that the Bolsheviks were there. You can imagine what I felt at that moment. I cannot describe it. I did not even notice how the news affected my peasants. From sheer joy I ran outside, nearly naked and barefoot, even though there was a heavy frost (I do not remember the exact day, but I think it was the eighteenth of January). Finding myself outside, I asked where they were. The peasant answered that they were in Lowitz. I have to admit that at first I did not believe the good news. When I looked at the road, I saw how a peasant was driving a wagon and pulling a small German car. That was the best sign that the news was true.

I waited impatiently to see the Soviet military, but by the end of the day they still had not arrived at our village. They only came the next day.

I stayed in the village for another week. At my request, the peasant took me to Lowitz. There was no way to get to Warsaw. The Red Cross put me up in a school with refugees from Warsaw. That did not last long, and a column of empty military vehicles was going to Warsaw. They took a number of refugees, including myself. That very day, in the evening, I arrived at Praga.

Back Among Jews

Arriving at Praga, I asked a militiaman to recommend a place where I could sleep. He examined my document. The main job of the examiners was to stop the smuggling of Volksdeutsch. They gave me a place to sleep in the commissariat. In the morning I found a Red Cross office where returning refugees had stayed. But they gave out no food.

Near that office were cars on their way to Lublin. Near one car I noticed an officer who had a Jewish face. I watched him, which he noticed and immediately asked, "Amcha? [Are you a Jew?}" When I responded, "Amcha," he asked what I was doing there. I told him my situation, that I had nowhere to go. He asked why I did not go to the Jewish Committee in Warsaw. This was the first time that I ever heard of such a group.

Arriving at the Committee in Praga, 34 Torogowa, I registered and was given the number 293 or 294. First I received a quarter kilo of bread and a quarter kilo of sugar. There was a crowd in front of one door. This was the entrance to the chairman's office. Next to the door was a doorman who recognized me. His name was Kazak and he was with me in the prison camp. (He now lives in Israel.) The chairman gave me 500 zlotys.

In the office I recognized a young woman from our shtetl who had served with the partisans. She told me that there were some Jews in Wolomin.

I Come Home...

The road to Wolomin was not easy. The train tracks had been torn up. You had to go by way of Radzymin, but even to Radzymin you could not go by train. I small train went about half the distance. I met a peasant who took me to Radzymin. Arriving there, it was already dark. I went to the police station and asked for a place to sleep. The police commander said that it was cold in the commissariat. He advised that I go to a rich Jewish family where I would certainly be given a place to sleep.

A militiaman took me to the Jew. The militiaman explained what was going on and left. They showed me into a room and I sat by the stove to warm up. In the next room, music was playing. There were guests there. After I sat there for two hours, they brought me a glass of tea and a piece of bread. I was told that I could not sleep there because the place was too small. I asked if I could sit near the stove because I had no strength to go on. He did not agree, stressing, "What's the problem. Not far from here lives another Jewish family and there you'll sleep like a prince." He offered to go with me, and I had to agree.

When the door of the second dwelling opened and when the inhabitants saw who it was, they greeted him with curses and then invited me into the room. It was a small room for three young men. There were three beds made of boards. They were just cooking dinner (kasha). They honored me with a plate of kasha and one offered me his bed. They told me that the Jew who would not let me sleep at his place was quite rich, lived like a count, but would not allow a Jew to sleep over.

I still had nine kilometers to go to get to Wolomin. There was no rail line, so I went on foot. The road I took was the same as the one the police used to take to the ghetto. It filled me with terror. Each snap of a twig made me tremble.

Arriving at the center of town, I asked a Christian about several Jewish families. The Christian looked at me and then yelled, "You're still alive?" That was my reception in the shtetl. I got the address of the Rubenstein family. There I first encountered a Jewish home, a Jewish heart. The churban had created woe, but there was also a bit of consolation. Of my family–my father, my mother and brothers–nothing remained. I went to the ghetto, hoping to find a picture or another keepsake, but nothing remained.

After I had rested a little, I headed toward Warsaw in search of my friend Barutzki. I found them at their old address. Our joy was tremendous. They made a special dinner, and when I was in Warsaw I stayed with them.

I also saw my old employer, the butcher. He also rejoiced to see me. After several glasses of brandy, we spoke about Jews. He proclaimed, "Yes, whoever had money survived." I responded, "I had no money, but I survived." He said, "What did you say?" and I repeated my words. Then he said, "Are you a Jew?" Then we began to drink again. By chance he told me the story of a Jew who had been hidden with his brother–in–law.

The butcher's brother–in–law lived in the next house. He worked at the Warsaw gas works. A Jew and his wife hid with him, obviously for money. When the Warsaw Uprising broke out, the whole family, including the Jews, came to the butcher's house. During the uprising, everything was very expensive, if you could get things at all. The Jew took out much gold and dollars and wanted to give them so that he could continue to stay there. According to the butcher, he said, "I'm no speculator and I won't take anything from you. When the war ends, you can pay me back for everything. The family stayed with him until the liberation.

The butcher asked me to go to the Jewish family, They had established a factory in their house, and he wanted me to ask them for money, because he was in a bad way. I asked what he needed and he said 1500 zlotys.

I went to the Jew. A serving–girl answered the door and asked me in. When I told the wife that I had come from Benju (that was the butcher's name), she was so happy and confirmed his story that he had told me (which I had earlier doubted). She simply called him an angel.

I conveyed the request of her "angel" and she said that her husband was not at home but she would take care of it. A month later I accidentally ran into her at the Jewish Committee. She came up to me and asked if I was going to Benju. She said that 1500 zlotys was too much, but she could give 500. I was embarrassed and walked away from her. I didn't go back to Benju out of shame. It makes me sad to have to write such a thing. It's a sad fact.

On the Way to Israel

I began to think about going to Israel. It was not such an easy thing. I could not go with every transport of the "B'richah." After the pogrom in Kielce, a transport of German Jews was organized to Germany. The organizers were the POR (the Bureau for Repatriation). I went to West Germany. For ten months I was in Bad Reichenhall as an active member of the PKhH (Partisans, Soldiers, Pioneers). Then I received a certificate.

In July of 1947 I arrived in Israel.

[Pages 550-553]

My Eyes, Tears Fall From My Eyes

by A. Feldberger

In deep sorrow, with broken hearts, we recall for you and mourn your gruesome death, dear parents, brothers and sisters, relatives, friends–Jews from the town of Wolomin.

Old people, weak and innocent children, whose only sin was carrying the name of Jew, their membership in the holy Jewish people.

Surrounded by bloody–minded enemies, there was no one to help you, to protect you in the last days of your lives.

Your pure souls will remain consecrated in our hearts, engraved in our memories.

Dear and holy remains the figure of R. Yechezkel Feldberger, a great Torah scholar and fearer of Heaven who also enjoyed his work. He had a little factory for making brooms, plus a shop, from which he made a living and supported his family.

Gifted with virtues and good qualities, he radiated the quality of trust, and in his soul shone a genteel joy that always illuminated his face like a newly dawned day and brightened those who came near him.

A quiet bliss shone from him even in bad times. He believed that the Creator's mercies were spread over all the Jews.

On weekdays, sitting at his work table, he composed songs and rhymes that he would sing on joyous occasions.

On Shabbos he would sing out deeply felt melodies touched with nostalgic joy that would elevate his listeners' souls, calling forth a sea of love, love of God and love for Israel.

R. Yechezkel translated the Shabbos and Shabbos–ending songs into Yiddish, in rhyme. So he also translated numerous piyyutim.

Even today people sing those Yiddish translations of songs and piyyutim in different cities of the world, where Jews from Wolomin have settled.

Industrious, and beset with the problems of earning a living, still there always dwelt within him a religiously inspired hope for a better time, for a time when all would be good. Those who knew him well felt that an ever–present joy vibrated through his veins, like the strings on a violin. The movement of a finger would bring forth music that traveled from heart to heart.

Modest and respected was R. Yechezkel's wife, Zipporah–Reizel, the daughter of R. Reuben Rozenzweig of Rika, one of the finest people produced by the Jewish communities in all of Poland. He was a giant in Torah and Chasidism. His son, Rabbi Yakov–Yehuda Rozenzweig was the Yezherner rabbi.

The Feldberger's oldest daughter, Bracha, was a Goldnodl after her marriage. She lived in Lublin. At a young age, before the war, she became a widow. She and her three children were killed by Hitler's killers..

Their second daughter, Maleh–Freida, married Rabbi Yerucham–Yisroel–Mayer Skurnik, from Shedletz, who became a rabbinical judge in Prague, with Rabbi Yakov Zilbershteyn. Later he was in Vahin, near Rodzin.

They had four children, who were killed with them.

The son, Rabbi Yakov–Yitzchak Feldberger, was one of the best students in the Lubavitch yeshiva in Warsaw. He was a very virtuous person and received rabbinic ordination in the Warsaw and Lublin rabbinates. He married Feige, the daughter of R. Yakov Rachman of Warsaw. They were killed together with their five children.

A son, Ezriel, who in 1934 made aliyah to Israel together with his wife Shifra from Nashelsk and they live today in Petach–Tikvah.

The son Eliezer, a student in the Lubavitch yeshiva, thanks to his excellent insights and proficiency in the Talmud and the commentators, was accepted as a student in the Lublin yeshiva. He managed to live through the hard times of the Second World War and lives today in America, where he is a rabbi in Cleveland.

Just a few survivors of a large, meritorious family, large–souled, always prepared to do mitzvos and good deeds. R. Yechezkel was one of the community leaders before the war's outbreak. In 1942, on the sixth of Nisan, he died in the Warsaw Ghetto. His wife, two daughters, his son, and their families were killed in that horrifying time that came upon the Jewish people.

May God avenge their blood and may their memories be blessed.

[He appends some of R. Feldberger's Yiddish translations of zmirot.]

[Page 554]

Woe for the loss!

by Dr. Sara Mandelberg

Translated by Sara Mages

In the landscape of Wolomin was a picturesque family, the Goldstein family. Many factors, intellectual and spiritual, shaped this life that perished in the terrible Holocaust. The family of David and Sima Goldstein belonged to the town's dignitaries. They made a living from a housewares and kitchen store. Not only Jews, but also peasants from the area, were among their admirers. They shopped at their store because of their honest attitude towards the buyers, their devotion to each person, and their warm heart that never disappointed their friends.

The sense of inner nobility has left its mark on their whole being. In the most difficult moments the smile did not leave their pleasant faces.

David Goldstein (left) at a Wolomin Merchants' Association party

David and Sima established a beautiful generation. They had three sons: Avraham, Yakov and Chaim, and two daughters: Miriam and Zipora.

They were all blond, handsome and clean, and served as an educational role model for others.

The fate of the family: The parents David and Sima, the children Avraham and Miriam, were murdered by the Nazis.

Survived: the youngest son, Haim, is now in America. The youngest daughter Zipora, now Feigelman, lives in Haifa.

After the Holocaust, which passed in such a bitter cruelty over our heads, fathers and sons were separated from each other. Brothers and sisters were uprooted from each other. The connection of thousands of families was torn to pieces, and their roots were uprooted and destroyed - in these lines we will deepen their memory in our hearts.

[Page 555]

"How Does the City Sit Solitary" Wolomin

by S. Vinagara

How did this happen, my shtetl?
For so many generations you lived in Poland
until Hitler made it free of Jews,
annihilated it, destroyed it with fire and blaze.

Wolomin, my Jewish town,
you lived by struggle, with trust and courage,
Shabbos you celebrated in. Holy light,
as home, street, market all rested.

Every day, fathers and grandfathers
hurried on their way
in the early morning to the beis-medresh
to pour out their hearts in prayer to God.

Until the that terrible September arrived,
Elul, when even the fish in the water trembled
on those fearful days, shattered with shofar sounds
and with the sound of bombs.

The German hordes filled the streets
and every heart felt confused.
then Jews headed toward the shul.
Fear made everything seem dark.

[Page 556]

Quickly came that dark day
when Jewish homes were closed and destroyed.
Flames leapt from the shul
as the fire burned and crackled.

In the flames of agony, Wolomin's Jews
in their last rush
cried out that woe like heroes,
their fiery prayers rising toward heaven.

Laden down with woe
but keeping their Jewish pride,
true to their faith, like heroes,
murdered as holy martyrs.

[Page 557]

Upon the Ruins

[Page 558]

On the ruins I will walk

K. Shimonovich

Translated by Sara Mages

On the ruins I will walk, on the deserts of the world,
and all the martyrs of my town will chase me.
They will uproot every paving stone,
and tears will flow down every stream and river.
On the night the holiday was sanctified on foreign, gentile, land,
bells are ringing with joy and domes of mosques are cheering.
Echoes from afar will answer, from wide snowy fields,
the lights are lit in their direction, greedy eyes are flocking.
They are in quiet houses. The green tree sparkles…
Cheerful windows are laughing, laughing in the shadow of the light,
only the Jews' windows are sealed, only the shutters of their houses are closed
and a strange silence is seen in them as from the eyes of the blind.
Bells are ringing and answering and crosses dancing on domed roofs,
and a wind carries into space the ringing of enthusiastic joy - - -

Only closed shutters are shaking, shutters of sealed windows
and an anxious Jewish mother presses her child to her heart.
On the ruins I will stand and cut, cut.
Until a spring in the desert will herald redemption,
until darkness will turn into a powerful light,
until my town will ascends to the heaven of heavens.

[Page 559]

On the Ruins of Our Shtetl

by Moyshe Burshteyn

It was in 1944. I was in Lukov when the news came to me that Wolomin had been freed by the Russians. Immediately, without thinking about the difficulties, I decided to go there.

With the first steps that I succeeded in taking, I arrived at Rembertov. From there I managed to get an illegal ride on a transport train that was going to Zielanke, where I arrived at midnight.

I felt anxiety about knowing more about Wolomin. In the Zielanke train station I tried to speak with the Poles, trying to learn something about my shtetl. I knew that Wolomin had been taken by the Russian army two days earlier, but no trains were going in that direction because the tracks had been destroyed.

At that time it was forbidden to appear in the street until five in the morning, so I decided to stay at the station, which was filling up with people from all over the country. Among them were some who were involved in business and some who sought family members or who wanted to be further from the front lines. Unhappily, I sought among the thick crowd a Jewish face, but sadly there was not a single Jew among them. Finally dawn arrived, 5 a.m. The sky was full of heavy clouds. A fine rain fell, and my spirit was restless as I went on my way, trying to follow the rail lines.

The way was muddy, and I was thoroughly soaked from the rain. This encouraged me to go even faster. I was under the illusion that I would meet someone I knew. That gave me the courage to continue on this difficult journey.

In this way I continued on to Kabilka. The rain stopped and the sun came out. My steps became lighter. I was already only a half kilometer from Wolomin when I saw someone approaching.

When he got close, I asked him for a match to light a cigarette, and then I asked about Wolomin, if any Jews were still there…

I noticed that the man began to tremble, shaking his head no. He did not want to speak further with me. He hurried away, leaving me standing there.

His demeanor sobered me up and removed all the illusions that had earlier given me strength to make the long journey on foot.

*

Broken and discouraged, I could hardly manage the last hundred meters to Wolomin. For the whole trip I had tried to believe that perhaps someone had survived. I said to myself, "Moyshe, you have been through so much. Don't fail now. Be strong. Maybe someone close to you survived, but the survivors are afraid to show themselves openly…"

I knew that Wolomin was twice taken, by the Germans and the Russians, and then back again, and I had forced myself to believe that perhaps in these circumstances the Jews had remained in their hiding places, afraid to show themselves in the streets.

Many conflicting thoughts raced through my mind, good and bad. There would be a promising thought, raising my spirits and giving hope, but soon there would come a darker thought, filling my heart with despair and disappointment, taking my last bit of strength. My feet were giving up, could go no further because of their weakness, so I had to restrengthen myself, remake myself and go on with hope that perhaps…

In this way I made it to the Wolomin train station, in the shtetl, walking the long streets until I arrived at Leshne Street, where there used to be the center of Jewish life, the beis–hamedrash, the Torah Foundation. It used to be alive with Jewish tumult, with Jewish life.

I stood in an empty place and looked for the beis–hamedrash that had always stood there. But the spot was bare and empty. An abandoned field, full of garbage. On the side was a deserted building of old wood and tin, a primitive bathhouse for the Germans, for Hitler's murderers.

On the other side, where the Torah Foundation used to be, was a ruin that looked like a leftover from a thousand years ago. It reeked of horror, desolation, and ruin.

*

I stood there for a long time, rooted to the spot as if turned to stone, looking for something that remained, a trace of the former Jewish life, but everything was empty and ruined, like a cemetery, and in the wasteland hung the memories [?] of those who were never mourned and who were so cruelly killed.

In my ears I heard the sounds of the melodies sung by those who were praying and studying, of the fine, beautiful Jews who lived there, who studied, who prayed, warm, quiet, and joyful, blessed with the strength of their belief that the evil would pass away and the evil ones would disappear. They had the greatest trust in a merciful and forgiving God...

I saw how in the long winter nights there would be discussions among the fine young men over a verse, over a difficult passage in the Gemara.

Ah, beautiful, strong Jews from our shtetl, who with their fine qualities and customs were masters of a higher morality and therefore were etched in the memories of the surviving Wolomin Jews and would never be forgotten.

Standing in that empty field, grown over with wild grass and sharp thorns, with discarded papers and horse droppings, everything, that whole former life, seemed like a long–vanished story.

The soul of the shtetl was gone. It had been extinguished, as if it had been killed. It appeared as if it had been thrown back hundreds of years, before the Jews had arrived and it was only a small peasant settlement.

Now I remember the sticky filth from the horrible crimes that took place there and will never be forgotten.

Soon I felt my whole body bathed in a cold sweat and my teeth chattering. I felt even more strongly the destruction that had come upon us.

Once again I recall how it used to look. Not far away had dwelt Fishele the teacher, and nearby–Aryeh the grave digger, Tzolke the cereal maker, Froike the baron, Sholem yud–vavnik in his business where his horse would pull the wagon. A little further on lived the shochet Dovid Edelson and scores of other fine, good Jews, blessed with good deeds, fine and sincere, with good smiles on their faces, with the quiet glow of scholars.

I could not hold back the tears that ran from my eyes, and I let out a bitter cry. My lips murmured this plea to heaven:

"Riboyno shel oylam, why did this have to happen? Did your people sin so badly that such horrible woes should afflict them?"

*

Suddenly I felt as if something moved on my shoulder. I was so deeply sunk in my thoughts and my pleas to heaven that it seemed to me at first like a touch from another world. When I turned around, I saw before me an old woman, apparently somewhat over sixty. She looked at me sympathetically and asked if she could help me.

In despair I answered her: "It's too late."

It was hard for me to speak. The words stuck in my throat.

She understood me, looked silently at me, as if she could read my great sorrows on my face, and I saw tears in her eyes. She crossed herself and walked quietly away.

Again I stood alone in that deserted place. In my mind the question continued to echo: "How could this have been possible?" How could it have been possible to exterminate this beautiful Jewish settlement?

*

In despair I allowed myself to head for the marketplace, and again I relived my memories of how the preoccupied and weary Jews and Jewesses used to come and trade with the peasants; how the Jewish women would blow between the feathers of the fowl to see how fat the bird was. Before my eyes I seemed to see the street stalls with various goods, and Jews everywhere, Jewish shops and stores around the marketplace. No hint remained of all this.

Everything had disappeared.

I encountered not a single Jew.

Coming to Kashtchelne Street, I stood before house number 19, where we had lived.

I forced myself to go up the stairs to the door of our home, where we had lived for so long.

I stood there for several minutes gathering my courage until I decided to knock on the door. At first I knocked weakly, as though in shame, as one does at the door of a stranger when one does not know who might open the door.

My knocking gained strength, and finally the door opened and a fifty–year–old man appeared. His wife stood behind him. They asked who I was looking for.

I stood there as though paralyzed, absorbed in another world, and I could not answer, could not find the words to explain why I knocked on a stranger's door.

I wanted to tell them, to answer them, to let them know of my experiences, my troubles. But my answer stuck in my throat. I could not speak.

It seems, however, that my mournful expression, my despair, my eyes, red from lack of sleep, answered for me.

After a few minutes the wife asked whom I sought, and when I did not answer, standing and peering at them with a despairing look, she spoke again: "Excuse me, sir, but perhaps you have the wrong address?"

At that moment, I came to myself and realized that there was nothing there for me. I stammered, "Perhaps...Excuse me..."

I quickly ran away from the stoop, trying to get away from my house, from the past, from the horrible misfortune.

*

Across from our house had been a butcher shop. It was open. I went into the shop, and there stood the Christian Mrs. Janitzka, whom I had known for a long time. I greeted her, and she recognized me, called me by name, and excused herself, ashamed, saying that she had given money to my parents when they were in the ghetto.

I stood there as if on hot coals, as if the earth were burning under my feet. I thanked her for her goodness...I hurried out and went into another shop, inquiring whether they knew about any Jews who had been in hiding.

They immediately looked at the house across the street. Back in his former home was living Fried. He had had a shop for cobbler's supplies. I went across to them immediately and they invited me in. I learned that Yakov Rubinshteyn and his family had hidden with them.

I went to them immediately and found the Rubinshteyns in their home. They all shared our experiences, the difficulties we had encountered, and we mourned those who had been killed.

With each new day we learned more about the awful disaster. Gradually a few more hidden Jews appeared, women who had survived thanks to their Aryan papers and appearances; others who had survived in other ways, by other methods, who had been miraculously rescued.

Sadly, there were not many such cases.

All was forlorn. The same houses stood there, orphaned, like nests from which the birds had flown away and black crows had taken their place. But what remained in them were the cries that were left behind by their residents who had left on their final journey.

Alone I wandered through Wolomin's streets and I felt that every stone dripped with blood. I heard the screams that came from every wall. Instinctively I stood by the familiar, well–known doors, wanting to knock...Their handles slipped in my fingers.

It quickly became clear to me that there was no one there for me to seek, nothing more for me to do.

There had been a Jewish Wolomin, but it existed no longer.

[Pages 566-568]

After the Catastrophe

by Shloyme Blumboym

Broken from bitter experiences, with eyes drowned in tears, I cannot cease mourning for my murdered children and for all the good and sincere Jews of Wolomin.

I feel tied by a thousand threads to the shtetl where I established my tannery, where scores of Jewish families earned a living. We led an intense and dynamic life, but now it all seems like a nightmare. All of our beautiful hopes were nothing more than an illusion that lasted until the outbreak of the Second World War.

Who could have foreseen that there would come a time when people could without punishment rob and kill innocent people simply because they were Jews.

As soon as the Germans entered Wolomin, they stole everything from the factories: leather, material, chemicals, and even the wood for the fires. To move out all this stuff, they seized twenty–five Jews, whom they urged on with terrible beatings.

The Germans rushed, wanting to have the whole job done in a single day, taking all the materials out of their spots, out of their barrels, and taking them all to a special train to Germany.

My younger brother Littman was staying with a Christian family outside of Wolomin. Although he had paid them well, they robbed him, taking all his money and jewelry and handing him over, along with his entire family, to the Germans.

When the Germans came to arrest him, they pretended that they were prepared to give him his life in return for gold and gems. My brother believed them and led them to a hiding place in the factory, dug up all his possessions, and gave them to them.

The Germans took everything and then shot my brother and his family on the spot.

My brother Littman was then forty years old. His wife was thirty–eight, and their son was ten.

After the war, I found their remains and gave them a Jewish burial in the Jewish cemetery in Wolomin.

In those evil days I brought my father from Warsaw so that he could be with us in the Wolomin ghetto. My father was quite ill and needed an operation, but there was no possibility of having one in the ghetto. It broke my heart to see how he suffered such terrible pains and no one could help him.

After many torments my father died in the ghetto and was buried in the Jewish cemetery in Wolomin. Near the grave of my father, R. Yosef Blimboym, lie my brother Littman and his wife and son.

Foreseeing the end, I thought about how I could get away from the ghetto. I succeeded in escaping to Bialystok. Again a ghetto with all its hardships and decrees. From there I reached the woods and then went back to Warsaw, where I lived for a time with Aryan documents as Jan Saviski.

When the rebellion broke out, I fell into the hands of the Germans, but because of my Aryan documents, they sent me to Germany, where I stayed until the end of the war, doing a variety of jobs.

After the war, I took my earliest opportunity to get back to Wolomin. In my heart there was a slight spark of hope that I would meet someone I knew, but the actuality of what I found in post–war Wolomin extinguished that spark.

With a broken heart I wandered through Wolomin's streets, leaned against the walls of the houses that once belonged to Jews.

I asked everyone I met about my children, my daughter Feyge and my son Ephraim, but the answer was bitter and dark: my children were murdered along with all of Wolomin's martyrs, and no one knows where they are buried.

Everything that was destroyed, all who were so brutally killed–they live in our hearts and memories. May the pages of Yizkor Book serve in the place of stone or marble monuments–Do Not Forget!

[Pages 559-571]

Wolomin–Today
(The Traces of a Forgotten Jewish Life)

by A. Bercovitch

With a heavy heart I wander around the shtetl where once pulsated a warm Jewish life. Taken away is the spirit of the shtetl. It was blotted out, withered away. Today it is hard to fathom that a whole community life pulsated there. But it appears to me that the surviving death horrors left deep traces in the shtetl. None of the Poles whom I meet fail to note that I am a Jew, and it is hard to have a conversation with them about matters of Jewish interest.

It is already many years since they have seen a Jew, and so the Pole Nazhitzki tells me about his illnesses whose origins the doctors cannot explain, and people think that they are God's retribution for their sins against the Jews. He calls out names: Vishenik, Rolenko, Smolnik, who stole much Jewish property. All of them have children who were paralyzed, lingered for years, and then died.

The tradition of robbery, which today is done in form of hoaxes, forgeries, and other kinds of abuses, still continues in the shtetl.

A short time ago there was a trial. The militia had arrested someone named Jan Sklodkovski, who had fifteen metal seals with which he worked a variety of scams. He had stolen the seals from different offices, from the presidium in the Voyovodish National Council in Raisha [?], then in Crakow. In Wolomin he stole from the magistrate's office, and there he was caught red–handed and confessed that he had worked with accomplices. Wolomin goyim.

At the trial, one of the witnesses, a woman named Borokovska, recalled that Sklodkovski had stolen a great deal of Jewish property at the time of the ghetto. But the judge finally laid no new charges against him on this account.

In response, Sklodkovski refused to accept these accusations and began to make accusations against the witnesses, among whom were some who occupied high offices in the magistrate's office. One of them had built for himself a luxurious villa in the shtetl, and Sklodovski showed that he had exchanged gold and jewelry that he had stolen from the Jews…

*

Later on I went to one of the houses on Leshne Street, knocked on the best door, asked for someone with a fictional name, and began a conversation.

Although before the war I had never been in the city, I was still certain that Jews had lived there earlier. I felt a need to sit in such a house and to absorb the lament of the walls and to see how the Pole, the current occupant, who had built his house on such tragic, horribly unfortunate murdered victims, would react.

When I suggested this, the Poles did not stir a hair, felt no embarrassment. They responded that before them, five Polish families had lived there, but one after the other they had moved away because the house brought them bad luck. One had mutilated his hand on a piece of glass that was a remnant of the Jews' dishes, and the hand had to be amputated. For a second, his ox had gone mad and stomped a five–year–old child to death; for a third, his daughter went out in the middle of the night and in the darkness an unknown figure raised up a white hand and from fear she became a mute…

The Poles showed me the horseshoes they had put on the thresholds and frames of the doors, but they did not help. They lived in terror that each day something bad might happen. In the shtetl there were vengeful spirits. The souls of the robbed and murdered Jews wandered around seeking vengeance.

The houses were run down. I felt that people lived there out of necessity, because nowhere else could they find shelter, but they sought to escape as quickly as possible, trying to escape the horror that pursued them.

*

Walking around the shtetl, I was tormented by disgust for the whole area, and for myself. I had the feeling that I was walking around among the related filth of crimes and dejection that could not be redeemed for any price, not even for the horror and fear that afflicted the robbers and murderers.

The Skrabatsch family, the owners of the mill, were well known for their excellent qualities both among the Jews of the shtetl and among the peasants in the surrounding villages. Like many other Jewish families in Wolomin, they excelled in their work. The property of the destroyed Jews was stolen, but their souls float over the ruins of Jewish life in the shtetl, where the robbers, who helped the Nazi murderers in their bloody work, walk around freely and openly. But from time to time there resounds over the shtetl an echo of those who were so terribly destroyed, as if from a world that has disappeared.

[Pages 572-580]

My Little Shtetl of Wolomin

by Yosef Eizenberg

It is already thirty years since the Nazi murder machine began the gruesome extermination of hundreds of Jewish towns and shtetls in Poland. Each town and shtetl, each Jewish dwelling, had its own particular merit. We, too, the remnant of the Wolomin Jewish community, are proud of our past, with its warm, multi–colored Jewish life that we led in our little shtetl.

Each of us must keep in his heart, as a special obligation, an accounting of our martyrs whose lives were cut short, for we are responsible for their memory. The beauty and moral grandeur of our parents and relatives must always enlighten us and the coming generations. Day and night we must repeat the vow: Never forget! We will never forget their holy lives nor their awful deaths as martyrs for God and for their people.

Wolomin remains empty and devoid of its Jewish inhabitants, their bones and ashes scattered over the fields and woods. We cannot visit their graves, because they received no Jewish burial.

Even the Jewish cemetery, where those lie who died natural deaths, is desecrated and defaced. On their sacred resting places now tread the pigs of the Poles who took over Jewish property and goods.

In my memory will always remain the images of Jewish life in Wolomin, community and cultural affairs, the religious and simple Jews and the enthusiastic Chasidim.

All this I left behind forty–five years ago.

In my ears I can hear the singing of the young people in the Peretz Library, the poems of great yearning for Zion by Yehuda Halevi and Ibn Gabirol, of Chaim Nahman Bialik and Tchernikovsky, the Yiddish poems of Peretz and Avraham Reizin, of Dovid Einhorn and other folk poems.

Beautiful and energetic sounded the various melodies of Wolomin's Chasidic prayer houses, from the Ger and Kotzk Chasidim, the Vurk and Modzhitz Chasidim. Sincerely and with haunting longing the Yeshiva students chanted their Gemara melodies and fervently conducted their arguments over difficult passages, over the arguments between Beis Hillel and Beis Shammai.

Jewish Wolomin was engulfed by music on Friday evenings, when you could hear Shabbos evening songs from every dwelling.

Full of joy and the desire for life were the High Holidays in the shtetl, especially Simchas Torah, when the Jews would go hand–in–hand, shoulder–to–shoulder, and lose themselves in a fiery dance, singing with great spirit, throwing off the everyday, forgetting all their worries and troubles, giving themselves wholly over to the joy of the holiday. Who has ever known rejoicing like that?

It's all gone now, all gruesomely cut off.

The Destruction of Wolomin

Many painful years have passed since the Nazi murder machine began its brutal extermination, whose chief victims were the Jews.

Hundreds of Jewish communities, towns and shtetls in Poland, were destroyed in the bloody slaughter carried out by Hitler's bands, may their names be wiped out. So we who came from Wolomin must keep alive in our imaginations that Jewish life that was so cruelly destroyed. Our old home has been emptied of its Jewish residents–our dearly beloved, who never received even a Jewish burial. Their bones are scattered and spread out across foreign fields and woods. The murderers could not even allow the dead to have rest, as they demolished their graves and monuments. Thus the peasants allow their animals to walk freely over the sacred ground of the cemeteries.

When I left my home town of Wolomin on August 12, 1924, there was a Jewish life, with Chasidic tunes from Ger, Rodzimin, Amshinov, Kotzk, vurke and others, and Jewish houses crowded the streets. There was an exchange of songs about war and freedom from a large portion of the local youth, along with a symphony of music and Torah from the yeshiva students and of Yiddish folksongs and more recent songs in Yiddish and Hebrew.

Who can forget the images of our Shabboses and holidays, filled with song and lively dancing?

For a hundred years the Wolomin Jews built their shtetl, constructed their houses and institutions. How was all that so quickly destroyed?

We must recount the story so that the memory of the Jewish community of Wolomin will stand from generation to generation.

[Pages 581-582]

Volomin Remembered

Riva Kopyto Pfeffer

Typed up by Genia Hollander

This is the year 1970. Twenty-eight years have passed since the Nazis put the Jews of Volomin to death. When I was asked to write my impressions of the town of my birth, I, at first, refused for I knew how painful it would be to recall the people and the experiences that left an indelible impression on my memory.

I see before me the faces of my dear parents, my beloved grandfather, my sister Chava, my brother Shlomo and so many friends and neighbours. I recall my school friends – so young then – so alive and now dead.

How fine were the people of Volomin? I remember many poor families, so proud that they endured their poverty without complaining. Later, in the ghetto, they were the ones who suffered most because they had nothing of value to sell in order to buy the food that was so exorbitantly priced. They were the ones a person saw in the streets, swollen from hunger. Their eyes betrayed their desperation. They were the first to die.

*

The typhoid epidemic of 1941 killed hundreds in Volomin. Among those who died were many devout people and many prominent people. It was as if God had chosen them to die this way to spare them from more suffering and more hunger, and to spare them the horror of death in the gas chambers.

As time went on, food became more and more difficult to get. Mothers risked death by going outside the Ghetto to try to get food for their families. I remember seeing one woman, pregnant and the mother of several children, shot before my eyes. Incidents like this occurred daily throughout the time we were in the Ghetto.

Because there were so many orphans, an orphanage was hastily established. People contributed whatever they could but there too was hunger, cold and suffering. Each day it seemed that we had reached the limits of our endurance. Life was an agony from which the only escape would finally be death.

I remember the trains. Day and night, they rolled from Warsaw on the way to Treblinka. I could see faces pressed against the small openings of the cattle cars. I could hear the cries of women and children. Often, notes were found thrown to the ground by someone in the transport warning: "Save yourselves": "Do something; we are on our way to destruction". But of course, there was nothing we could do. It was too late. We were exhausted, starved, diseased, beaten.

Often the guards watching the trains were not even Germans. They were Hungarians, Lithuanians or Ukrainians. The Nazis found willing help in their horrible endeavours.

*

In the years since the Holocaust, I have often thought about my own survival. How is it possible that I am alive? How is it possible that all the others are dead? Thoughts of this kind bring back the pain, the deep sorrow, and the question "Why?" Of course, there is no answer. But one thing is certain: the world will never understand what it is like to have lived through the Holocaust and to have to live with the memory of those times.

And forever, we will mourn our parents, our brothers and sisters. And of all the six million.

[Pages 585-595]

Wolomin List of Martyrs

Transliterated by Judy Petersen

Family name(s)	First name(s)	Gender	Marital status	Father's name	Mother's name	Name of spouse	Remarks	Page
א Alef								
ASCH	Yitzchak	M	married			Malka		585
ASCH	Malka	F	married			Yitzchak		585
ASCH	Chaya	F		Yitzchak	Malka			585
	Nasha	F	married	Yitzchak	Malka		maiden name ASCH	585
		M	married			Nasha	wife's maiden name ASCH	585
ASCH	Aharon	M		Yitzchak	Malka			585
ASCH	Perl	F		Yitzchak	Malka			585
ASCH	Efraim	M		Yitzchak	Malka			585
OSTEROVSKY	Gershon	M						585
OSTEROVSKY	Golda	F						585
OSTEROVSKY	Chava	F						585
OPFEL	Melech	M						585
OPFEL	Rivka	F						585
OSTEROVSKY	Pinya	M	married					585
OSTEROVSKY		F	married			Pinya		585
OSTEROVSKY	Sarah	F		Pinya				585
OPFEVER		M					his family	585
ACKERMAN		M	married				had children--girls and boys	585
ACKERMAN		F	married				had children--girls and boys	585
ב Bet								
BERMAN	Devora	F						586
BRISKER	David	M	married			Osna		586
BRISKER	Osna	F	married			David		586

BRISKER	Luba						586
BRISKER	Mordechai	M					586
BORKOVSKY	Gedalyahu	M					586
BORKOVSKY	Chava	F					586
BERGZIN	Rabbi Zev	M	married				586
BERGZIN		F	married			Zev	586
BERGZIN	Ita	F		Zev			586
BERGZIN	Sarah	F		Zev			586
BERGZIN	Perl	F		Zev			586
BERGZIN	Mendele Eliezer	M		Zev			586
BERGZIN	Yankele	M		Zev			586
BAUM	Meir	M					586
BAUM	Menucha	F					586
BAUM	Leah	F					586
BAUM	Rachel	F					586
BAUM	Esther	F					586
BAUM	Feivel	M					586
BAUM	Chava	F					586
BAUM	Moshe	M					586
BAUM	Yakov	M					586
BAUM	Yehuda Arieh	M	married			Sprintze	586
BAUM	Sprintze	F	married			Yehuda Arieh	586
BAUM	Scheindele	F		Yehuda Arieh	Sprintze		586
BAUM	Friedeleh	F		Yehuda Arieh	Sprintze		586
BROMBERG	Yakov	M	married				586
BROMBERG		F	married			Yakov	586
BROMBERG	Yisrael Yitzchak	M		Yakov			586
BUDNY	David	M	married			Rivka	586
BUDNY	Rivka	F	married			David	586
	Duba	F	married	David	Rivka	Yishayahu	maiden name BUDNY	586
	Yishayahu	M	married			Duba	586

	Esther	F		Yishayahu	Duba			586
	Leahleh	F		Yishayahu	Duba			586
GRIZSHAK	Channa Priva	F						586
BURSTEIN	Avraham Yosef	M						586
BURSTEIN	Reizel	F						586
BURSTEIN	Velvel	M						586
BURSTEIN	Leah	F						586
BURSTEIN	Shlomo	M						586
BURSTEIN	Eli	M						586
BURSTEIN	Yankel	M						586
BURSTEIN	Freida	F						586
BURSTEIN	Rachel Mindel	F						586
BURSTEIN	Sarah	F						586
BURSTEIN	Rivka	F						586
BRATSTEIN	Moshe	M	married				2 children	586
BRATSTEIN		F	married			Moshe	2 children	586
BRATSTEIN	Mirel	F						586
BURSTEIN	Ziskind	M	married			Itka		586
BURSTEIN	Itka	F	married			Ziskind		586
BURSTEIN	Channah Gitel	F					her family	586
BRANZWEIG	Baruch	M					Chazan/Shochet for the Beit Hamidrash in Wolomin	586
BRODA							whole family	586
BURSTEIN	Chanoch	M	married			Miriam		586
BURSTEIN	Miriam	F	married			Chanoch		586
BURSTEIN	Rivka	F		Chanoch	Miriam			586
BURSTEIN	Ita	F		Chanoch	Miriam			586
BARAN		M	married				children	586
BARAN		F	married				children	586
BORNSTEIN	Moshe	M	married				children	586
BORNSTEIN		F	married			Moshe	children	586
BERMAN	Leib	M					family	586

BERMAN	Itke	F					family	586
BURSTEIN	Leibel	M						586
BURSTEIN		M		Leib				586
BURSTEIN		F		Leib				586

ג Gimmel

GLICKMAN	Reuven	M	married					586
GLICKMAN		F	married			Reuven	children	586
GRIZAK	David	M					children	586
GRIZAK	Brayna	F						586
GRIZAK	Feiga	F						586
GRIZAK	Gitel	F						586
GRIZAK	Freida	F						586
GROSKOPF	Feiga	F	married			Yosef	maiden name GRIZAK.	586
GROSKOPF	Yosef	M	married			Feiga		586
GROSKOPF	Beila	F		Yosef	Feiga			586
GROSKOPF	Gite	F		Yosef	Feiga			586
GOLDSTEIN	Shia	M	married			Chaya		586
GOLDSTEIN	Chaya	F	married			Shia		586
GOLDSTEIN	Devora	F						586
GOLDSTEIN	Nechama	F						586
GOLDWASSER	Avraham	M	married			Pessa	grandmother	586
GOLDWASSER	Pessa	F	married			Avraham		586
GOLDWASSER	Nechama	F						586
GOLDWASSER	Golda	F						586
GOLDWASSER	Reizel	F						586
GOLDWASSER	Leitsche	F						586
GOLDWASSER	Yisrael	M	married			Rivka		587
GOLDWASSER	Rivka	F	married			Yisrael		587
GOLDWASSER	Shimon	M						587
GOLDWASSER	Hanoch	M	married			Leah		587
GOLDWASSER	Leah	F	married			Hanoch		587
GOLDWASSER	Tzvi	M						587
GOLDWASSER	Feigele	F						587

GOLDWASSER	Gitel	F						587
GOLDWASSER	Frumet	F						587
GOLDWASSER	Scheindele	F						587
GOLDWASSER	Meir	M						587
GOLDWASSER	Leib	M						587
GOLDWASSER	Avraham Yitzchak	M	married					587
GOLDWASSER	Eidel	F	married					587
GOLDWASSER	Sima	F						587
GOLDWASSER	Shimon Natan	M						587
GOLDWASSER	Mordechai	M						587
GOLDWASSER	Frumet	F						587
GRINSTEIN	Shakhne	M					on the list it's written: and their daughters	587
GRINSTEIN		M	married			Leah		587
GRINSTEIN	Leah	F	married				on the list it's written: Aunt	587
GOLDBERG	Meir	M	married			Yenta		587
GOLDBERG	Yenta	F	married			Meir		587
GOTLIEB	Yisrael	M	married			Gitel		587
GOTLIEB	Gitel	F	married			Yisrael		587
GOLDWASSER							unclear if the surname refers to an individual or to a family	587
GURA	Baruch Meir	M	married			Tova Rivka	children	587
GURA	Tova Rivka	F	married			Baruch Meir	children	587
GRABINA	Mirka	F						587
GRABINA	Baruch	M						587
GRABINA	Shlomo	M						587
GRABINA	Yitzchak	M	married			Channah Gitel		587
GRABINA	Channah Gitel	F	married			Yitzchak		587
GRABINA	Avraham	M		Yitzchak	Channah Gitel			587
GRABINA	Henya	F		Yitzchak	Channah Gitel			587

GRABINA	Yidel	M	married			Henya	587
GRABINA	Henya	F	married			Yidel	587
GRABINA	Yakov	M		Yidel	Henya		587
GRABINA	Avraham	M		Yidel	Henya		587
GRABINA	Shmuel	M	married			Freidel	587
GRABINA	Freidel	F	married			Shmuel	587
GRABINA	Elias	M		Shmuel	Freidel		587
GRABINA	Moshe	M		Shmuel	Freidel		587
GRABINA	Yosel	M	married				587
GRABINA		F	married			Yosel	587
GRODZITSKY	Moshe	M	married			Shifra	587
GRODZITSKY	Shifra	F	married			Moshe	587
GRODZITSKY	Yeshayahu	M	married			Freida	587
GRODZITSKY	Freida	F	married			Yeshayahu	587
GRODZITSKY	Miriam	F		Yishayahu	Freida		587
GRODZITSKY	Toveh	F		Yishayahu	Freida		587
GRODZITSKY	Mordechai	M	married			Rachel	587
GRODZITSKY	Rachel	F	married			Mordechai	587
GRODZITSKY	Nesha	F		Mordechai	Rachel		587
GRODZITSKY	Channah	F		Mordechai	Rachel		587
GRODZITSKY	Leah	F		Mordechai	Rachel		587
GRODZITSKY	Miriam	F		Mordechai	Rachel		587
GRODZITSKY	Moshe	M		Mordechai	Rachel		587
GRODZITSKY	Feiga	F					587
GRODZITSKY	Perele	F					587
GRODZITSKY	Yechiel	M	married			Libeh	587
GRODZITSKY	Libeh	F	married			Yechiel	587
GRODZITSKY	Shmuel	M		Yechiel	Libeh		587
GRODZITSKY	Aharon	M		Yechiel	Libeh		587
GRODZITSKY	Moshe	M		Yechiel	Libeh		587
GRODZITSKY	Avraham	M	married			Chaya Male	587
GRODZITSKY	Chaya Male	F	married			Avraham	587
GRODZITSKY	Channah	F		Avraham	Chaya Male		587

GRODZITSKY	Aharon	M		Avraham	Chaya Male			587
GRODZITSKY	Shmuel	M		Avraham	Chaya Male			587
GRODZITSKY	Henya	F		Avraham	Chaya Male			587
GRODZITSKY	Matityahu	M	married			Channah		587
GRODZITSKY	Channah	F	married			Matityahu		587
GRODZITSKY	Freida	F		Matityahu	Channah			587
GUTBERG	Shmuel	M	married			Channah		587
GUTBERG	Channah	F	married			Shmuel		587
GUTBERG	Mali	F		Shmuel	Channah			587
GOLDSTEIN	David	M	married			Sima	brother of Miriam GOLDSTEIN	587
GOLDSTEIN	Sima	F	married			David		587
GOLDSTEIN	Miriam	F					sister of David GOLDSTEIN	587
GOLDSTEIN	Avraham	M		David	Sima			587
GOLDSTEIN	Yakov	M		David	Sima			587
GOLDSTEIN	Leah	F		David	Sima			587
GORDON		M	married				husband and father; given name not written.	587
GORDON		F	married				wife and mother; given name not written.	587
GORDON		M					son; given name not written.	587
GOLDWASSER	Efraim	M					his family	587
GRINSPAN	David	M	married			Feiga		587
GRINSPAN	Feiga	F	married			David		587
GRINSPAN	Freida	F		David	Feiga			587
GRINSPAN	Sarah	F		David	Feiga			587
GRINSPAN	Gitel	F		David	Feiga			587
GRINSPAN	Channah	F		David	Feiga			587
GRINSPAN	Yehuda Leib	M		David	Feiga			587
GRINSPAN	Alta	F		David	Feiga			587
GRINSPAN	Chava	F		David	Feiga			587
GRINSPAN	Henya	F		David	Feiga			587

ד Dalet

DONDA	Shimon	M	married			Fania	587
DONDA	Fania	F	married			Shimon	587
DONDA	Ursula	F		Shimon			587
DONDA	Lutek	M					587
DUBNER	Shepsel	M	married			Duba	587
DUBNER	Duba	F	married			Shepsel	587
DUBNER	Moshe	M		Shepsel			587
DUBNER	Yitzchak	M		Shepsel			587
DUBNER		F		Shepsel			587
DANCZIGER	Yitzchak	M	married			Gitel	588
DANCZIGER	Gitel	F	married			Yitzchak	588
DANCZIGER	Esther	F		Yitzchak	Gitel		588
DANCZIGER	Nathan	M		Yitzchak	Gitel		588
DANCZIGER	Hinda	F		Yitzchak	Gitel		588
DANCZIGER	Yakov	M		Yitzchak	Gitel		588
DANCZIGER	Dache	F		Yitzchak	Gitel		588
DANCZIGER	Channah	F		Yitzchak	Gitel		588
DANCZIGER	Naftali	M		Yitzchak	Gitel		588
DANCZIGER	Rachel	F		Yitzchak	Gitel		588

ה Hey

HAZENMUS		M				his family	588
HOLTZKANER	Shloima	M					588
HOLTZKANER	Moshe	M					588
HOLTZKANER	Yosef	M					588
HOLTZKANER	Simcha	M					588

ו Vav

WEINREB	Etka	F					588
WEINREB	Yosef Meir	M					588
WEINREB	Chava	F					588
WEINREB	Baruch	M	married			Baruch	588
WEINREB	Freida	F	married			Freida	588
WEINREB	Roza	F		Baruch	Freida		588

WEINREB	Feiga	F		Baruch	Freida			588
WEINREB	Yeshayahu	M		Baruch	Freida			588
WEINREB	Rivka	F						588
WEINREB	David	M						588
WEINREB	Hinda	F						588
WEINREB	Nechama	F						588
WILENSKI	Rivka	F	married			Leizer Lukas		588
WILENSKI	Leizer Lukas	M	married			Rivka		588
WILENSKI	Roza	F	married			Zvi Koppel		588
WILENSKI	Zvi Koppel	M	married			Roza		588
WILENSKI	Fishel	M	married			Chava Scheindel		588
WILENSKI	Chava Scheindel	F	married			Fishel	maiden name KOPPEL	588
WEINBRUM	Avraham Yosef	M	married			Rivka Leah		588
WEINBRUM	Rivka Leah	F	married			Avraham Yosef		588
WEINBRUM	Sarah	F		Avraham Yosef	Leah			588
WEINBRUM	Moshe	M		Avraham Yosef	Leah			588
WEINBRUM	Leib	M		Avraham Yosef	Leah			588
WEINBRUM	Shmuel	M		Avraham Yosef	Leah			588
WEINBRUM	Mordechai	M		Avraham Yosef	Leah			588
WEINBRUM	Isser	M		Avraham Yosef	Leah			588
VIERZSHABINSKY	Shmuel	M					on the list the surname is written VIERZSHABIMSKY, possibly in error.	588
VIERZSHABINSKY	Paye	F					on the list the surname is written VIERZSHABIMSKY, possibly in error.	588
VIERZSHABINSKY	Hinda	F					on the list the surname is written VIERZSHABIMSKY, possibly in error.	588

VIERZSHABINSKY	Yisrael	M				on the list the surname is written VIERZSHABIMSKY, possibly in error.	588
VIERZSHABINSKY	Beila	F				on the list the surname is written VIERZSHABIMSKY, possibly in error.	588
WEINMAN	Yehuda	M				his family	588
WEINSTEIN		M	married			children	588
WEINSTEIN		F	married			children	588
WERTSHAUSER	David	M	married		Devora Leah Feiga		588
WERTSHAUSER	Devora Leah Feiga	F	married		David		588
WERTSHAUSER	Yitzchak Binem	M					588
WERTSHAUSER	Asher Zeilik	M					588
WINOGURA	Noach	M	married		Peshe		588
WINOGURA	Peshe	F	married		Noach		588
WINOGURA	Nachman	M	married				588
WINOGURA		F	married		Nachman		588
WINOGURA	Henya	F		Nachman			588
WINOGURA	Noach	M		Nachman			588
WINOGURA	Meir	M	married			child	588
WINOGURA		F	married		Meir	child	588
WINOGURA	Avraham	M	married		Beshe		588
WINOGURA	Beshe	F	married		Avraham		588
WINOGURA	Chayale	F		Avraham	Beshe		588
WINOGURA	Golda	F	married			Her surname is probably different. Husband & children	588
WINOGURA	Gitel	F	married			children	588
WINOGURA	Dovele	M					588
WAGMAN	Nisan	M					588
WAGMAN	Peretz	M	married				588
WAGMAN		F	married		Peretz		588
WAGMAN	Chava	F					588

WAGMAN	Pesse	F					3 children	588
WALITZA	Velvel	M					his family	588
WEISBORT		M	married				children	588
WEISBORT		F	married				children	588
WISNEVSKI	Moshe Aharon	M					on the list "father" is written: he is probably the husband of Chaya Sarah WISNEVSKI	589
WISNEVSKI	Chaya Sarah	F					on the list "mother" is written: she is probably the wife of Moshe Aaron WISNEVSKI.	589
WISNEVSKI	Eidel	F					children	589
WISNEVSKI	Sheva	F					children	589
WISNEVSKI	Tova	F						589
WISNEVSKI	Bluma	F						589
VIEZBA		M					his family	589
WOLFOWICZ	Heniek	M	married			Manya		589
WOLFOWICZ	Manya	F	married			Heniek		589

ז Zayin

SILBERSTEIN	Efraim	M	married			Sima Leah		589
SILBERSTEIN	Sima Leah	F	married			Efraim		589
SILBERSTEIN	Yitzchak	M		Efraim	Sima Leah			589
SILBERSTEIN	Chaim	M		Efraim	Sima Leah			589
SILBERSTEIN	Yankel	M		Efraim	Sima Leah			589
SILBERSTEIN	Shlomo	M		Efraim	Sima Leah			589
SILBERSTEIN	Velvel	M		Efraim	Sima Leah			589
SILBERSTEIN	Baruch	M		Efraim	Sima Leah			589
SILBERSTEIN	Motel	M		Efraim	Sima Leah			589
SILBERSTEIN	Malka	F		Efraim	Sima Leah			589
ZABERTZOK	Yechiel	M	married					589
ZABERTZOK		F	married			Yechiel		589

SILBERSTEIN	Yosef	M						589
SILBERSTEIN	Freida	F		Yosef				589
SILBERSTEIN	Chaim	M	married	Yosef				589
SILBERSTEIN		F	married			Chaim		589
SILBERSTEIN		F		Chaim				589
SILBERSTEIN	Chaim	M	married				children	589
SILBERSTEIN		F	married			Chaim	children	589
SILBERSTEIN	Yisrael Yitzchak	M	married			Feiga		589
SILBERSTEIN	Feiga	F	married			Yisrael Yitzchak		589
SILBERSTEIN	Sarah	F		Yisrael Yitzchak	Feiga			589
SILBERSTEIN	Dina	F		Yisrael Yitzchak	Feiga			589
SILBERSTEIN	Shlomo	F		Yisrael Yitzchak	Feiga			589
SILBERSTEIN	Moshe	M		Yisrael Yitzchak	Feiga			589
SILBERSTEIN	Mendel	M		Yisrael Yitzchak	Feiga			589
SILBERSTEIN	David	M		Yisrael Yitzchak	Feiga			589
SILBERSTEIN	Yentsche	M					his family	589
SILBERSTEIN	Binyamin	M	married			Perl	sons	589
SILBERSTEIN	Perl	F	married			Binyamin	sons	589
PASTOLSKY	Moshe	M	married			Rachel		589
PASTOLSKY	Rachel	F	married	Binyamin	Perl	Moshe	maiden name SILBERSTEIN	589
ZAGOSHTINSKY	Arieh	M					his family	589
ZOMER		M	married					589
ZOMER		F	married					589
ZOMER	Hershel	M						589
CHECHANOVSKY	Tshesha	F	married				maiden name ZOMER	589
CHECHANOVSKY		M	married			Tshesha		589
ZONABENT		M	married				husband and father of three daughters whose given names are not listed.	589

ZONABENT		F	married				wife and mother of three daughters whose given names are not listed.	589
ZONABENT		F					eldest of three daughters whose given names are not listed.	589
ZONABENT		F					middle of three daughters whose given names are not listed	589
ZONABENT		F					youngest of three daughters whose given names are not listed	589
ZELVIANSKY		M	married					589
ZELVIANSKY		F	married					589
ZELVIANSKY	Alexander	M						589
ZOLBERBERG	Shepsel	M					daughters	589
ZOLBERBERG		M		Shepsel				589

ח Chet

CHONOVITZ	Yisrael	M	married				sons	589
CHONOVITZ		F	married				sons	589
CHONOVITZ	Yosef	M	married				sons	589
CHONOVITZ		F	married				sons	589

ט Tet

TEPPER	Godel	M	married			Chaya Beila		589
TEPPER	Chaya Beila	F	married			Godel		589
TEPPER	Mordechai	M						589
TEPPER	Gitel	F						589
TEPPER	Avraham	M						589
TEPPER	Mendele	M						589
TEIBLUM	Matityahu	M	married			Perl		589
TEIBLUM	Perl	F	married			Matityahu		589
TEIBLUM	Yosef	M						589
TEIBLUM	Yisrael	M						589
TEIBLUM	Chava	F						589

TEIBLUM	Rachel	F						589
TEIBLUM	Itka	F						589
TEIBLUM	Meir	M						589
CHECHANOVETZKY	Shimon	M						590
CHECHANOVETZKY	Esther	F						590
CHECHANOVETZKY	Gitel	F						590
CHECHANOVETZKY	Miriam	F						590
CHECHANOVETZKY	Mordechai	M						590
CHECHANOVETZKY	Leib	M						590
TENCZA	Yisrael Mordechai	M	married			Leah		590
TENCZA	Leah	F	married			Yisrael Mordechai		590
TENCZA	Gedalyahu	M		Yisrael Mordechai	Leah			590
TENCZA	Yehuda	M		Yisrael Mordechai	Leah			590
TENCZA	Chaim	M		Yisrael Mordechai	Leah			590
TENCZA	Yosef David	M		Yisrael Mordechai	Leah			590
TENCZA	Moshe	M		Yisrael Mordechai	Leah			590
TENCZA	Tzirl	F		Yisrael Mordechai	Leah			590
TENCZA	Yehudit	F		Yisrael Mordechai	Leah			590
TENCZA	Freida Rachel	F		Yisrael Mordechai	Leah			590
TOPOL	Chaim	M	married			Gisha	from Kosov	590
TOPOL	Gisha	F	married			Chaim	her husband was from Kosov	590
TOPOL	Yehuda Leib	M		Chaim	Gisha		his father was from Kosov	590
TENNENBAUM	Rozala	F					family	590
CHECHANOVITZ	Yisrael	M	married				children	590
CHECHANOVITZ		F	married			Yisrael	children	590
CHECHANOVITZ	Temme	F						590
CHECHANOVITZ	Bentzion	M	married				children	590
CHECHANOVITZ		F	married			Ben Tzion	children	590

CHECHANOVITZ	Moshe	M					his family	590
TROSTERMAN	Leibish	M					his family	590
TABAKMAN		M					his family	590
TAUB	Tzalkeh	M	married				children	590
TAUB		F	married			Tzalkeh	children	590
CHECHANOVEITZKY		M					Community Head of Wolomin	590
TSHEVOTSKY							it's not clear whether the surname refers to an individual or to a family	590
SHUTTMAN		M	married				husband and father of a son. Given names not recorded.	590
SHUTTMAN		F	married				wife and mother of a son. Given names not recorded.	590
SHUTTMAN		M					son. Given name not recorded.	590
TEIBLUM	Mordechai	M	married			Mariem		590
TEIBLUM	Mariem	F	married			Mordechai		590
TEIBLUM	Egiah	F		Mordechai	Mariem			590
TEIBLUM	Yitzchak	M	married			Itka		590
TEIBLUM	Itka	F	married			Yitzchak		590
TEIBLUM	Cava	F		Yitzchak	Itka			590
TEIBLUM	Zissel	F		Yitzchak	Itka			590
TEIBLUM	Yitzchak	M	married			Mariem		590
TEIBLUM	Mariem	F	married			Yitzchak		590
TEIBLUM	Lanya	F		Yitzchak	Mariem			590
TEIBLUM	Chaniek	M		Yitzchak	Mariem			590
TEIBLUM	Moshe	M					family	590
TEIBLUM	Yisrael	M						590
TEIBLUM	Leah	F						590
YELLIN	Mordechai Motel	M	married			Sheva Scheindel		590
YELLIN	Sheva Scheindel	F	married			Mordechai Motel		590
ROSENBERG	Peshe	F	married			Nechemia	maiden name YELLIN	590
ROSENBERG	Nechemia	M	married			Peshe		590

ROSENBERG	Asher	M		Nechemia	Peshe			590
ROSENBERG	Sarah	F		Nechemia	Peshe			590
ROSENBERG	Esther	F		Nechemia	Peshe			590
ROSENBERG	Moshe	M		Nechemia	Peshe			590
ROSENBERG	Yidel	M		Nechemia	Peshe			590
ZISMAN	Rochtze	F	married			Reuven	maiden name YELLIN	590
ZISMAN	Reuven	M	married			Rochtze		590
ZISMAN	Sarah	F		Reuven	Rochtze			590
ZISMAN	Chaya	F		Reuven	Rochtze			590
ZISMAN	Ayzik	M		Reuven	Rochtze			590
KLEINMAN	Baltze	F	married			Yosef	maiden name YELLIN. 2 children	590
KLEINMAN	Yosef	M	married			Baltze	2 children	590
ROSENHEIM	Channah	F	married			Reuven	maiden name YELLIN	590
ROSENHEIM	Reuven	M	married			Channah		590
KUTZOLEK	Hadassah	F	married			Nachum	maiden name YELLIN	590
KUTZOLEK	Nachum	M	married			Hadassah		590

י Yod

YELLIN	Yente	F						590
YELLIN	Sarah Scheindel	F						590
YELLIN	Ita	F						590
YELLIN	Devora	F						590
YELLIN	Asher	M						590
YELLIN	Yisrael Alter	M						590
YARZEMSKY	Moshe	M						590
YARZEMSKY	Chava	F						590
YARZEMSKY	Leah	F						590
YARZEMSKY	Itka	F						590
YAGODEH	Antschel	M	married			Ita		590
YAGODEH	Ita	F	married			Antschel		590
YAGODEH	Peshke	F		Antschel	Ita			590
YAGODEH	Baruch Ele	M		Antschel	Ita			590

YAGODEH	Channah	F				family	590
YELLEN	Idel	M	married				590
YELLEN		F	married		Idel		590
YELLEN	Naomi	F		Idel			590
YELLEN		M		Idel			590
JEDWABNIK	Leah	F	married		Froika	children	590
JEDWABNIK	Froika	M	married		Leah	children	590
JEDWABNIK		M				his family	590
JEDWABNIK	Mendil	M	married			children	590
JEDWABNIK		F	married		Mendil	children	590

כ Kaf

KATZ	Efraim	M					591
KATZ	Mates	M					591
KATZ	Moshe	M					591
KATZ	Yitzchak	M					591
KATZ	Shalom	M	married		Irka		591
KATZ	Irka	F	married		Shalom	maiden name KIRSCH	591
CZUKKER	Zashe	F	married		Yekhiel	maiden name KATZ	591
CZUKKER	Yekhiel	M	married		Zashe		591
FORER	Kalya	F				it states next to her name "daughter of her sister"	591
KANTOV	Avraham	M					591
KANTOV	Sima	F					591
KANTOV	Channah	F					591
KANAN	Eylya	M	married		Lala	child	591
KANAN	Lala	F	married		Eylya	child	591
CARMELI	Yosef	M					591
CARMELI	Channah	F					591
CARMELI	Cheshe	F					591
CARMELI	Hinda	F					591

ל Lamed

LASKOVSKI	Chaim Yosef / Yoske	M	married		Rachel		591

LASKOVSKI	Rachel	F	married			Chaim Yosef / Yoske		591
LASKOVSKI	Avraham	M						591
LASKOVSKI	Shmuel	M						591
LASKOVSKI	Moshe	M	married			Channah		591
LASKOVSKI	Chava	F	married			Moshe		591
LASKOVSKI	Avraham	M		Moshe	Chava			591
LASKOVSKI	Shmuel	M		Moshe	Chava			591
LASKOVSKI	Nachum Ayzik	M	married			Bracha	children	591
LASKOVSKI	Bracha	F	married			Nachum Ayzik	children	591
LASKOVSKI	Shmuel	M	married			Sarah		591
LASKOVSKI	Sarah	F	married			Shmuel		591
LASKOVSKI	Yakov	M		Shmuel	Sarah			591
LASTFOGEL	Arnold	M	married			Chava	children	591
LASTFOGEL	Chava	F	married			Arnold	children	591
LUSTIGMAN	Yakov	M	married				children	591
LUSTIGMAN		F	married			Yakov	children	591
LIEBERANT		M	married				children	591
LIEBERANT		F	married				children	591
LICHTMAN	Shlomo Zalman	M					his family	591
LICHTMAN	Yekutiel	M					his family	591
LICHTMAN		M	married				3 children	591
LICHTMAN		F	married				3 children	591
LICHTMAN	Herschel Akiva	M						591
LICHTMAN	Tzesha	F						591
LIPA		M					his family	591
LEVITA	Elimelech	M	married			Estherel	Meilich the watchmaker	591
LEVITA	Estherel	F	married			Elimelech		591
YADOVNIK	Feiga	F	married			Eliezer	maiden name LEVITA. 5 children	591
YADOVNIK	Eliezer	M	married			Feiga	5 children	591
SCHWARTZ	Yehudit	F	married			Yechezkel	maiden name LEVITA. 4 children	591

SCHWARTZ	Yechezkel	M	married			Yehudit	4 children	591
ROSENWEIN	Leah	F	married			Simcha	maiden name LEVITA. 2 children	591
ROSENWEIN	Simcha	M	married			Leah	2 children	591
KNOBLICH	Perl	F	married			Moshe	maiden name LEVITA. One child	591
KNOBLICH	Moshe	M	married			Perl	child	591
LEVITA	Chaim	M	married				scribe	591
LEVITA		F	married			Chaim		591
LERMAN	Avraham Zindel	M					his family	591

מ Mem

MAKUTOVITZ	Moshe	M						591
MAKUTOVITZ	Leah	F						591
MARKREICH		M	married				medical orderly	591
MARKREICH		F	married		Regina Czilla			591
MARGOLES	Yakov	M	married			Sarah Leah		591
MARGOLES	Sarah Leah	F	married			Yakov		591
MARGOLES	Feiga Roizel	F						591
MINTZ	Herman	M	married					591
MINTZ		F	married		Genia	Herman		591
MINTZ	Stashek	M	married			Pola		591
MINTZ	Pola	F	married			Stashek		591
MOGERMAN		M	married				children	592
MOGERMAN		F	married				children	592
MENDELBERG	Nechemia	M	married			Channah		592
MENDELBERG	Channah	F	married			Nechemia		592
MENDELBERG	Miriam	F		Nechemia	Channah			592
MENDELBERG	Henya	F		Nechemia	Channah			592
MENDELBERG	Yehuda Leib	M	married					592
MENDELBERG	Yehudit	F	married					592
MENDBERG	Baruch	M					the surname is probably	592

						MENDELBERG. His family	
MOROCCO? /MAMARAKO?						it's not clear whether the surname refers to an individual or to a family	592
MANNA	Chaim Noach	M	married			Chaya Rachel	592
MANNA	Chaya Rachel	F	married			Chaim Noach	592
MANNA	Moshe	M		Chaim Noach	Chaya Rachel		592
MANNA	Yechezkel	M		Chaim Noach	Chaya Rachel		592
MANNA	Melech	M		Chaim Noach	Chaya Rachel		592
MANNA	Freida	F		Chaim Noach	Chaya Rachel		592
MANNA	Devora Maraka	F		Chaim Noach	Chaya Rachel		592
MANNA	Ida	F	married	Yosel			592
MANNA	Mendel	M					592
MARKOEFELD						whole family	592

נ Nun

NUNGOLD	Yehudit	F					592
NUNGOLD	Rachel	F			Yehudit		592
NUNGOLD	Esther	F			Yehudit		592
NOVOGRODSKY	Shia	M	married			Freidel	592
NOVOGRODSKY	Fraidel	F	married			Shia	592
NOVOGRODSKY	Esther	F		Shia	Freidel		592
NOVOGRODSKY	Chaim	M		Shia	Freidel		592
NOVOGRODSKY	Temeleh	F		Shia	Freidel		592
NOVOGRODSKY	Saraleh	F		Shia	Freidel		592
NAGOR		M				his family	592
NADVORNY	Chaim Yankel	M	married			Ita	592
NADVORNY	Ita	F	married			Chaim	592
NADVORNY	Moshe Yehoshua	M		Chaim	Ita		592
NADVORNY	Leib	M		Chaim	Ita		592

NISENKEREN	David	M	married			Chava Golda		592
NISENKEREN	Chaya Golda	F	married			David		592
NISENKEREN	Yitzchak	M		David	Chava Golda			592
NISENKEREN	Mashaleh	M		David	Chava Golda			592
NISENKEREN	Chonotze	F		David	Chava Golda			592
NISENKEREN	Gitaleh	F		David	Chava Golda			592

ס Samech

SKORKE	Shyeh	M					his family	592
SAPIRSTEIN							it's unclear whether the surname refers to an individual or to a family	592
SKRAVATSCH	Yitzchak Meir	M						592
SKRAVATSCH	Elke	F						592
SKRAVATSCH	Sarah	F						592
SKRAVATSCH	Chaya Enya	F						592
SKRAVATSCH	Bluma	F						592
SREBNIK		M					his family	592

ע Ayin

EVRO	Efraim	M	married			Channah Leah		592
EVRO	Channah Leah	F	married			Efraim		592
EVRO	Moshe	M						592
EVRO	Yisrael Azriel	M						592
EVRO	Sarah Golda	F						592
EVRO	Scheindel	F						592
EHRLICH		M					family	592

פ Peh

PUTTERMAN	Moshe	M					his family	592
FELDBERGER	Yechezkel	M	married			Zipora Reizel		592
FELDBERGER	Tzipora Reizel	F	married			Yechezkel		592
GOLDNADEL	Bracha	F	married			David	maiden name FELDBERGER	592
GOLDNADEL	David	M	married			Bracha		592
LAKORNIK	Mala Freida	F	married			Meir Yitzchak	maiden name FELDBERGER.	592
LAKORNIK	Meir Yitzchak	M	married			Mala Freida		592
FELDBERGER	Yakov Yitzchak	M						592
FROMM	Abba	M						593
FROMM	Miriam	F						593
FROMM	Zvi Yakov	M						593
FROMM	Yitzchak	M						593
FROMM	David	M						593
FROMM	Shalom	M						593
FRANK	Zvi	M						593
FRIEDMAN	Zvi	M					his family	593
PLATKOVSKI	Shmuel Eizik	M	married			Zlata		593
PLATKOVSKI	Zlata	F	married			Shmuel Eizik		593
PLATKOVSKI	Moshe Aharon	M		Shmuel Eizik	Zlata			593
PLATKOVSKI	Avraham	M		Shmuel Eizik	Zlata			593
PLATKOVSKI	Channah	F		Shmuel Eizik	Zlata			593
PLATKOVSKI	Chaya	F		Shmuel Eizik	Zlata			593
PLATKOVSKI	Golda	F		Shmuel Eizik	Zlata			593
FRENKEL		M					his family	593
PALKOVITZ		M	married				children	593
PALKOVITZ		F	married				children	593
FEIGENBAUM	Chaim Shlomo	M	married			Channah		593

FEIGENBAUM	Channah	F	married			Chaim Shlomo		593
FEIGENBAUM	Esther	F		Chaim Shlomo	Channah			593
FEIGENBAUM	Nachman	M		Chaim Shlomo	Channah			593
FEIGENBAUM	Feiga	F		Chaim Shlomo	Channah			593
PAVSTOLSKY	Esther	F						593
FINKELSTEIN	Yakov Arieh	M	married			Channah Beila		593
FINKELSTEIN	Channah Beila	F	married			Yakov Arieh		593
FINKELSTEIN	Rivka	F		Yakov Arieh	Channah Beila			593
FINKELSTEIN	Miriam	F		Yakov Arieh	Channah Beila			593
FINKELSTEIN	Breina	F		Yakov Arieh	Channah Beila			593
FINKELSTEIN	Freida	F		Yakov Arieh	Channah Beila			593
FRIEDMAN	Yitzchak	M	married			Chaya		593
FRIEDMAN	Chaya	F	married			Yitzchak		593
FRIEDMAN	Velvel	M		Yitzchak	Chaya			593
FRIEDMAN	Leah	F		Yitzchak	Chaya			593
FRIEDMAN	Zelik	M		Yitzchak	Chaya			593
FRIEDMAN	Natan	M		Yitzchak	Chaya			593
FULSTEIN		M					his family	593
POLITZMAN	David	M	married				children	593
POLITZMAN		F	married			David	children	593
PUTTERMACHER	Mania	F					on the list "mother" is written	593
FIOROVITZ	Shia	M	married			Reizel		593
FIOROVITZ	Reizel	F	married			Shia		593
	Rivka Esther	F	married	Shia	Reizel		maiden name FIORVITZ	593
		M	married			Rivka Esther	wife's maiden name FIORVITZ	593
FRIEDMAN	Beila	F						593
FRIEDMAN	Velvel	M						593

FRIEDMAN	Zelig	M						593
FRIEDMAN	Menucha	F						593
FRIEDMAN	Eli	M	married				daughters	593
FRIEDMAN		F	married			Eli	daughters	593
FRIEDMAN	Baruch	M		Eli				593
PIERNIK		M	married				husband and father of a son. Given names not recorded.	593
PIERNIK		F	married				wife and mother of a son. Given names not recorded.	593
PIERNIK		M					son. Given name not recorded.	593
FIEKAZSH		M					his family	593
FIEKALIEK		M					his family	593
FORER	Berl	M	married				sons	593
FORER		F	married			Berl	sons	593
PLATKOVSKI	Shlomo	M	married					593
PLATKOVSKI		F	married			Shlomo		593
PLATKOVSKI	Yankel	M	married			Sarah Chaya		593
PLATKOVSKI	Sarah Chaya	F	married			Yankel		593
PLATKOVSKI	Yosef	M		Yankel	Sarah Chaya			593
PLATKOVSKI	Avraham	M		Yankel	Sarah Chaya			593
PLATKOVSKI	Zlata	F		Yankel	Sarah Chaya			593
PLATKOVSKI	Chasya	F		Yankel	Sarah Chaya			593

צ Tzadik

CZUKKER	Henoch	M	married			Rivka		593
CZUKKER	Rivka	F	married			Henoch		593
CZUKKER	Leah	F		Henoch	Rivka			593
CZUKKER	Moshe	M		Henoch	Rivka			593
CZUKKER	Yoel	M		Henoch	Rivka			593
CZUKKER	Freida	F		Henoch	Rivka			593
CZUKKER	Yisraelik	M		Henoch	Rivka			593

CZUKERT	Rivka	F						593
CZUKERT	Yakov	M						593
TZURTEK	Shmuel	M				Esther		593
TZURTEK	Esther	F		David		Shmuel		593
TZIECHANSVIETZKY	Khiel Meir	M					family	593

ק Kof

KAVER	Mordechai Matel	M						594
KAVER	Feiga Zissel	F						594
KAVER	Ella	F						594
KAVER	Moshe	M						594
KAVER	David	M						594
KAVER	Channah	F						594
KAVER	Golda	F						594
KAVER	Scheindele	F						594
KAVER	Rachela	F						594
KAVER	Mosheleh	F						594
KAVER	Chaya	F						594
KAVER	Scheindele	F			Chaya			594
KAVER	David	M			Chaya			594
KANARICH	Mordechai	M						594
KREUZMAN	Chaim	M						594
KREUZMAN	Rachel	F						594
KAMINKOVSKI	Moshe	M						594
KAMINKOVSKI	Mareide Miriam	F						594
KAMINKOVSKI	Eta	F						594
KAMINKOVSKI	Elazar	M						594
KRIEGER	Peretz	M	married			Elka		594
KRIEGER	Elka	F	married			Peretz		594
KRIEGER	Luba	F		Peretz	Elka			594
KRIEGER	Avraham	M	married			Zissel		594
KRIEGER	Zissel	F	married			Avraham		594
KAPITO	Peretz	M	married			Chentsche	children	594

KAPITO	Chentsche	F	married			Peretz	children	594
KITSCHKOVSKI	Pinchas	M	married			Chaya Gitel		594
KITSCHKOVSKI	Chaya Gitel	F	married			Pinchas		594
KITSCHKOVSKI	Rivka	F		Pinchas	Chaya Gitel			594
KITSCHKOVSKI	Freida	F		Pinchas	Chaya Gitel			594
KAPELUSHNIK		M					his family	594
KAPELUSHNIK	Pesach	M	married					594
KAPELUSHNIK		F	married			Pesach		594
KAPELUSHNIK	Esther	M		Pesach				594
KAPELUSHNIK	Avraham	M		Pesach				594
KAPLAN		M	married				children	594
KAPLAN		F	married				children	594
KUSHNIER		M	married					594
KUSHNIER		F	married	Kuba				594
KUSHNIER	Yechiel	M						594
KRASOTZKI	Avraham	M	married			Shayna		594
KRASOTZKI	Shayna	F	married			Avraham		594
KRASOTZKI	Aharon	M		Avraham	Shayna			594
KUVATZ	Yehudit	F					mother	594
KUVATZ	Leah	F						594
KUVATZ	Moshe	M						594
KUVATZ	Yosef	M						594
KUVATZ	Simcha	M						594
KUVATZ	Chaya Sarah	F						594
KUVATZ	Mordechai	M	married			Etka		594
KUVATZ	Etka	F	married			Mordechai		594
KUVATZ	Freida	F						594
KUVATZ	Shmuel	M						594
KUVATZ	Feiga	F						594

ר **Resh**

ROSNER	Yakov	M	married			Channah Luba		594

ROSNER	Channah Luba	F	married			Yakov		594
ROSNER	Shmuel	M						594
ROSNER	Perl	F						594
RUBINSTEIN	Menachem	M	married			Esther		594
RUBINSTEIN	Esther	F	married			Menachem		594
RUBINSTEIN	Chaim	M		Menachem	Esther			594
RUBINSTEIN	Tova	F		Menachem	Esther			594
RUBINSTEIN	Rivka Mala	F		Menachem	Esther			594
RUBINSTEIN	Chava	F		Menachem	Esther			594
RUBINSTEIN	Yehoshua	M		Menachem	Esther			594
RUBINSTEIN	Yosef	M		Menachem	Esther			594
RUBINSTEIN	Rachel	F		Menachem	Esther			594
RUBINSTEIN	Roiza	F		Menachem	Esther			594
RUBINSTEIN	Yitzchak	M						594
RUBINSTEIN	Ita	F						594
RUBINSTEIN	Avraham	M						594
RUBINSTEIN	Nachum	M						594
RUBINSTEIN	Zvi	M						594
RUBIN	Chuna	M						594
RUBIN	Beila	F						594
RUBIN	Nachum	M						594
RUBIN	Shimon	M						594
RUBIN	Schmerel	M						594
RUBIN	Pesach	M						594
RUBIN	Rivka	F						594
RUBIN	Elazar	M					.	594
RUBIN	Yitzchak	M						594
ROZSA	Meir	M	married				daughters	594
ROZSA		F	married			Meir	daughters	594
ROZSA		M		Meir				594
RUBIN	Yitzchak Meir	M						595
RUBIN	Chaya	F						595
RUBIN	Sima	F						595

RADZMINSKI	Hirsch Mordechai	M					595
RADZMINSKI	Avraham	M					595
RADZMINSKI	Eizik	M					595
RADZMINSKI	Aharon Yakov	M					595
RADZMINSKI	Channah	F					595
RADZMINSKI	Yosef	M					595
RADZMINSKI	Malka Gitel	F					595
RETIK	Zvi	M					595
RETIK	Malka	F					595
RETIK	Blumtsche	F					595
RETIK	David	M					595
RETIK	Aharon	M					595
ROSENBLICH		M	married				595
ROSENBLICH		F	married				595
ROSENBLICH	Henia	F					595
ROSENBLICH	Yakov	M					595
ROSENBLICH	Heniek	M					595
ROSENBERG	Naomi	F					595
ROSENBERG	Miriam	F					595
RUSTEIN	Yonah	M					595
RUSTEIN	Chava	F				family	595
REICHMAN	Ziskind	M	married		Etel		595
REICHMAN	Etel	F	married		Ziskind		595
REICHMAN	Dabe	F					595
REICHMAN	Sarah	F					595
REICHMAN	Avraham	M					595
REICHMAN	David	M					595
REICHMAN	Yitzchak	M					595
RECHTMAN		M				family	595
RUBINSTEIN	Yehoshua Yechezkel	M					595

ש Shin

SHULMAN	Aharon	M	married		Leah		595

SHULMAN	Leah	F	married			Aharon		595
SHULMAN	Levi Yitzchak	M		Aharon	Leah			595
SHULMAN	Baruch	M	married			Chava		595
SHULMAN	Chava	F	married			Baruch		595
SHULMAN	Scheindele	F		Baruch	Chava			595
SCHARFSTEIN	Chaim David	M						595
SHEDLETZKY	Yudel	M	married				children	595
SHEDLETZKY		F	married			Yudel	children	595
SHEDLETZKY	Etsche Meir	M					his family	595
SCHULTZ	Aharon Binem	M	married			Tova Leah	children	595
SCHULTZ	Tova Leah	F	married			Aharon Binem	children	595
SCHULTZ	Shlomo	M	married			Esther Malka		595
SCHULTZ	Esther Malka	F	married			Shlomo		595
SCHULTZ	Dina	F		Shlomo	Esther Malka			595
SCHULTZ	Etel	F						595
SCHULTZ	David	M			Etel			595
SCHULTZ	Chaim	M	married				6 children	595
SCHULTZ		F	married			Chaim	6 children	595
SHMIETANKA	Noah	M	married					595
SHMIETANKA		F	married			Noach		595
SHMIETANKA	Chuna	M		Noach				595
SHMIETANKA	Hershel	M		Noach				595
SHULMAN	Peshe	F						595
SHULMAN	Leibel	M			Peshe			595
SHULMAN	Yossel David	M	married					595
SHULMAN		F	married			Yossel David		595
SHULMAN	Avraham Yitzchak	M		Yossel David				595
SHULMAN	Esther	F		Yossel David				595

SHEDLETZKY	Matis	M	married			Tovah		595
SHEDLETZKY	Tovah	F	married			Matis		595
SHEDLETZKY	Moshe	M		Matis	Tova			595
SHTUTMAN	Chaim	M	married			Feiga		595
SHTUTMAN	Feiga	F	married			Chaim		595
SHTUTMAN		M		Chaim	Feiga			595
SHTULMAN	Yitzchak	M	married					595
SHTULMAN		F	married			Yitzchak		595
SHTULMAN	Moshe Feivel	M		Yitzchak				595
SHTULMAN	Sarah Leah	F		Yitzchak				595
SCHEINBAUM	David	M						595
SCHEINBAUM	Channah	F						595
SCHEINBAUM	Chava	F						595
SCHEINBAUM	Chaya	F						595
SCHEINBAUM	Leizer	M						595

NAME INDEX

www.ingramcontent.com/pod-product-compliance
Lightning Source LLC
Chambersburg PA
CBHW050409110426

42812CB00006BA/1836